CANADA'S RELIGIONS

RELIGIONS AND BELIEFS SERIES

The Religions and Beliefs series includes books bearing on religions in North America. The series welcomes manuscripts written in either English or French.

Editorial Committee
Robert Choquette, Series Director, University of Ottawa
Peter Beyer, University of Ottawa

In the Same Series
Pauline Côté, *Les Transactions politiques des croyants: Charismatiques et Témoins de Jéhovah dans le Québec des années 1970 et 1980*, 1983

Adolf Ens, *Subjects or Citizens? The Mennonite Experience in Canada, 1870–1925*, 1994

Robert Choquette, *The Oblate Assault on Canada's Northwest*, 1995

Jennifer Reid, *Myth, Symbol, and Colonial Encounter: British and Mi'kmaq in Acadia, 1770–1867*, 1995

M. D. Faber, *New Age Thinking: A Psychoanalytic Critique*, 1996

André Guindon, *L'Habillé et le Nu: Pour une éthique du vêtir et du dénuder*, 1997

Vicki Bennett, *Sacred Space and Structural Style: The Embodiment of Socio-religious Ideology*, 1997

Colin Grant, *Myths We Live By*, 1998

Louis Rousseau et Frank W. Remiggi (sous la direction de) *Atlas historique des pratiques religieuses: le Sud-Ouest du Québec au XIXᵉ siècle*, 1998

Anne Marie Dalton, *A Theology for the Earth: The Contributions of Thomas Berry and Bernard Lonergan*, 1999

Daniel J. Elazar, Michael Brown and Ira Robinson, *Not Written in Stone: Jews, Constitutions, and Constitutionalism in Canada*, 2003

RELIGIONS AND BELIEFS SERIES NO. 12

Canada's Religions:
An Historical Introduction

ROBERT CHOQUETTE

University of Ottawa Press

University of Ottawa Press gratefully acknowledges the support extended
to its publishing programme by the Canada Council and the University of
Ottawa.

We acknowledge the financial support of the Government of Canada through
the Book Publishing Industry Development Program for this project.

National Library of Canada Cataloguing in Publication

Choquette, Robert, 1938–
    Canada's religions: an historical introduction / Robert Choquette.

    (Religions and beliefs series; no. 12)
    Includes bibliographic references and index.
    ISBN 0-7766-3027-X (bound).   ISBN 0-7766-0557-7 (pbk.)

    1. Canada – Religion—History.   2. Canada – Church history.   3. Religion
    and sociology – Canada.   I. Title.   II. Series.

    BL2530.C3C56 2004   200'.971   C2003-903831-9

Copy edited by Stephanie VanderMeulen
Cover design by Laura Brady

ISBN 0-7766-0557-7 (paperback)
0-7766-3027-X (cloth)
ISSN 1480-4700

© University of Ottawa Press, 2004
542, King Edward, Ottawa, Ontario Canada K1N 6N5
press@uottawa.ca   http://www.uopress.uottawa.ca

Printed and bound in Canada

To Nancy and Geneviève

Contents

Chapter 4: The Encounter between Amerindians and Europeans

Chapter 5: Missions of Many Kinds

Chapter 11: The Churches and the State

Chapter 12: The Evangelical Crusade

Chapter 17: Secularization and Church Reform

Chapter 18: Immigration and Religions

List of Illustrations

1. Ameridian Funeral Procession. Bernard Picart. National Archives of Canada, c-005342.
2. Piegan Medicine Pipe. National Archives of Canada, c-019970.
3. Medicine Bundles. National Archives of Canada. Department of Mines and Technical Surveys collection, c-024482.
4. Martin Luther. Engraving by C.E. Wagstaff from the painting by Hans Holbein. National Archives of Canada, c-008907.
5. Jesuits welcomed by the *Récollets*. Charles William Jefferys. National Archives of Canada, c-028332.
6. Hôtel-Dieu Hospital of Québec in 1850. Drawing by Charles William Jefferys. National Archives of Canada, c-069810.
7. François de Laval. Engraving based on a painting by Claude Duflos. National Archives of Canada, c-005183.
8. Capuchin friar in Acadia, 1633. Henri Beau. National Archives of Canada, c-011979.
9. Church at the shrine of Saint Anne de Beaupré in 1876. National Archives of Canada, PA-148905.
10. A wayside cross on the Lachine Road in 1866. Francis Ann Hopkins. National Archives of Canada, c-002737.
11. View of the bishop's house and the ruins looking from Upper to Lower Town Québec in 1761. Richard Short based on engraving by J. Fougeron. National Archives of Canada, c-000352.
12. Hutterite settlers near Winnipeg. National Archives of Canada, c-036153.
13. Riel and his councillors during the Red River rebellion in 1869–70. National Archives of Canada, PA-012854.
14. The Reverend Egerton Ryerson. National Archives of Canada, c-014235.

CHAPTER 1

Introduction

The book advocates no particular ideology in the understanding of religions. I have started from the fact that the vast majority of people in the world, past or present, have been and are religious. That is to say that they acknowledge a spiritual or transcendent dimension to reality. This I take as given. It appears in their stories about their origins as a people and about the origins of the world; in their beliefs and explanations about natural phenomena, morality, society, dreams, and human relations. Most of these people acknowledge distinct spirits, gods, or often one God. In sum, God or spirits are part of reality.

Religion is the organized way in which people conceptualize, express, worship, communicate with, or obey God; religion is the articulation of the relationship people have with God. Religions may include sacred texts, rituals, beliefs, institutions, clergy, doctrines, revelations, visions, or rules of behaviour. Given the many ways and forms of the above, religions are numerous. Moreover, each religion contains its own wide range of forms of expression and behaviour that vary widely over time and place. In this book, I will tell the story of the most practised religions found in Canada from the sixteenth to the twentieth centuries. I will do so by focusing on their role in Canadian society rather than on their doctrine, ritual, or polity. I will not judge which religion is better or worse; indeed, I avoid any faith stance or attempt at proselytism, that being the domain of the religions themselves. I intend to present the history of Canada's faith communities as accurately as possible on the basis of the historical record. My goal is to inform, not convert.

For the past forty years, I have studied religions in Canada. My teaching, research, and publications have focused primarily on the history of Christianity – the religion of the vast majority of Canadians, but it has also included the history of other religions. This book undertakes to tell the story of the leading religions in the country; that is to say not only the religions of the Catholic and Protestant Christians who still comprise more than 75% of Canadians (2001), but also those of the Jews, the Muslims, the Hindus, the Buddhists, and of the many alternative religions and new religious movements that have appeared, particularly during the last hundred years. Given the overwhelming importance of Christianity in the story of Canada, however, Catholics and Protestants occupy centre stage in the book.

Such a story is even more necessary at a time when education about religion has been removed from all levels of our public education. Coupled with the dramatic drop in church attendance since the 1960s, this has resulted in a generation of Canadians who have little if any knowledge or understanding of their religious heritage or of religion.

This growing ignorance about religion produces, at best, perplexity and, at worst, injustice and dangerous behaviour when Canadians are confronted, as they are more and more frequently in their lives, with issues relating to religion. In addition to the usual spiritual and moral questions that arise on a regular basis, these issues have included the birth of new religious cults that are considered strange by mainstream society; crimes, suicides, or other aberrations in which some of these cults indulge; allegations of physical and sexual abuse in church-run schools; the resurgence of fundamentalist beliefs in several religions; the Islamist terror campaign, especially the attack on the World Trade Center in New York in September, 2001; and political controversies both over the religious beliefs of some political leaders and over the legitimacy of confessional public schools in Canada. Public schools do not educate us as to how Canada's religious leaders and faithful have dealt with the basic human questions of life, suffering, death, and love. We debate ethics, but refuse to consider morality. While debates rage in the media over these issues, among others, all too often Canadians find themselves incapable of understanding them, our multicultural society, and various international issues because the study of religion has not been part of their educational curriculum.

The history of religions in Canada is a necessary and fundamental element in the story of the country and in our understanding of it. Canada's Amerindian people have always understood the world as created, animated, and led by spirits; the Canadians, be they French, British, or other have belonged with few exceptions to the Christian church, Catholic or Protestant; other immigrants from the U.S.A., Asia, Africa, or Latin America also have, with few exceptions, professed a religious faith. Indeed, it was only during the last quarter of the twentieth century that secularist voices managed to hold sway and succeed in shunting religions aside in Canada's public square, despite the fact that nearly 90% of Canadians still hold religious beliefs. We need to understand these religions in order to understand our country.

My purpose is to provide an historical introduction to Canada's religions. Why? Because such is not available at present, and it is needed. Indeed, there exists a growing number of publications on various aspects of the religious history of Canada, including some that tell the story of religious groups and institutions from their beginning. None, however, tells the story of all the leading religions in Canada from the time Europeans first arrived in the sixteenth century to the present.

Given the vast scope of this book, I am much in debt to many scholars on whose publications and research I have relied. This is true throughout the book, but even more so for subjects that are far removed from my own scholarship – Eastern religions and alternative religions for example. The work of these scholars has been listed in the bibliography at the end of each chapter.

This book does not claim any new discoveries or methodologies in the study of religions in Canada. Its more modest ambition is to provide a solid, well-informed, balanced, and inclusive introduction to the history of religions in Canada, from the sixteenth to the twentieth century. The book is a synthesis of the contributions of many scholars as understood and interpreted by the author. What is lost here in the variety of interpretations, is gained in the unity of perspective.

Given the need to explain and make sense of broad segments of our history, the book necessarily includes some sweeping interpretations, the kinds that make many scholars nervous. Nevertheless, I believe that such risks are necessary and warranted if one is to tell the story of Canada's religions. I use the name Canada throughout to designate a country that has experienced numerous territorial and name changes over the years. The Amerindians and French settlers of New France, the British and American immigrants of the days of British colonial rule, and the expanding variety of nationalities represented among Canada's more recent immigrants, all proudly identify as Canadians. This is the story of their encounter with God as reflected in Canadian society.

Over the years, conversations with students, colleagues, and educated Canadians of many walks of life have consistently shown me the need for such a book. Canadians seek basic knowledge and understanding of the subject of religions in the Canadian context, whether in relation to doctrine, morality, schools, churches, cults, government or personal belief. They do so, as do all students of history, in order to better understand themselves and the present, in order to act more effectively in the future. If this book serves that purpose, I will be gratified.

Suggested Readings

Albanese, Catherine L. *Nature Religion in America. From the Algonkian Amerindians to the New Age*. Chicago: The University of Chicago Press, 1990.

Bowker, John, Ed. *The Oxford Dictionary of World Religions*. Oxford and New York: Oxford University Press, 1997.

Brunet, Michel, G. Frégault, and M. Trudel. Eds. *Histoire du Canada par les textes*. Montréal: Fides, 1952.

Cross, F. L. and E.A. Livingstone. Ed. *The Oxford Dictionary of the Christian Church*. Oxford: Oxford University Press. Third edition, 1997.

Davies, Norman. *Europe. A History*. Oxford: Oxford University Press, 1996.

Diamond, Jared. *Guns, Germs, and Steel. The Fates of Human Societies*. New York: W.W. Norton & Company, 1999.

Fay, Terence J. *A History of Canadian Catholics*. Montréal & Kingston: McGill-Queen's University Press, 2002.

Halpenny, Francess G. Ed. *Dictionary of Canadian Biography/ Dictionnaire biographique du Canada*. 14 vols. Toronto and Québec: University of Toronto Press and Les Presses de l'Université Laval, 1966-present, ongoing.

Hobsbawm, Eric and Terence Ranger. Eds. *The Invention of Tradition*. Cambridge: Cambridge University Press, 1983.

Lippy, Charles H. and Peter W. Williams. Eds. *Encyclopedia of the American Religious Experience*. New York: Charles Scribner's Sons, 1988.

McBrien, Richard P. *Lives of the Popes*. San Francisco: Harper, 2000.

Murphy, Terrence and Roberto Perin. Eds. *A Concise History of Christianity in Canada*. Oxford: Oxford University Press, 1996.

Quinn, D.B. *North America from Earliest Discovery to First Settlements: The Norse Voyages to 1612*. New York: Harper and Row, 1977.

Quinn, D.B. Ed. *New American World: A Documentary History of North America to 1612*. 5 vols. New York: Arno and Bye, 1979.

Rogers, Edward S. and Donald B. Smith. Eds. *Aboriginal Ontario. Historical*

Perspectives on the First Nations. Toronto: Dundurn Press, Ontario Historical Studies Series, 1994.

Southern, R.W. *Western Society and the Church in the Middle Ages*. London:
 Penguin Books, 1970.

Thwaites, R.G. Ed. *The Jesuit Relations and Allied Documents, 1610–1791*. 73
 vols. Cleveland: Burrows, 1896–1901.

Voisine, Nive. Ed. *Histoire du catholicisme québécois*. vols. 2 & 3. Montréal:
 Boréal Express, 1984, 1991.

Winks, Robin W. *The Blacks in Canada. A History*. Second edition. Montréal &
 Kingston: McGill-Queen's University Press, 1997.

CHAPTER 2

The Religious World of Canada's Amerindians

The origins of Canada's Amerindian people

Most historians explain the origins of the people of North America by referring to a series of migrations that would have occurred from Asia, across Beringia, the land currently flooded by the sea at the Bering Straits, and into Alaska. From there the earliest human occupants of North America would have migrated south toward the southern portion of the United States and Central America. These migrations by land were possible because of the Ice Age that prevailed some 40,000 years ago, resulting in the lowering of the sea level, and the emergence of the land of Beringia. When global warming ended this Ice Age 35,000 years ago, the migrations were interrupted for some 10,000 years as the sea reclaimed Beringia. Then another Ice Age, the last, occurred between 25,000 B.C.E. and 15,000 B.C.E. allowing further migrations from Asia to America.

The subsequent melting of the glaciers, after 15,000 B.C.E., not only closed the land bridge between Siberia and Alaska, but also allowed descendants of the people inhabiting the central portion of North America to migrate northwards in the wake of the retreat of the glaciers. This would explain the earliest settlement of the St Lawrence lowlands, that vast valley drained by Lakes Erie and Ontario, and the St Lawrence River. This occupation of the northeastern woodlands of the continent is believed to have occurred around 8,000 B.C.E. Subsequently, around 4,000 B.C.E., the Inuit, a group of later migrants from Asia to Alaska, migrated eastwards across the Arctic to occupy much of Canada's northernmost coasts.

So it was that the ancestors of Canada's Iroquoian and Algonkian linguistic families of Amerindians arrived in their ancestral lands of eastern Canada some ten thousand years ago. Over time, the Iroquoian nations evolved from exclusively hunting and gathering cultures into ones that engaged more and more in horticultural pursuits, a change that became apparent after 500 C.E.

While the Algonkian people continued to live much as they always had, in the fourteenth century C.E. a major cultural change swept through the Iroquoian societies that lived north and south of Lake Ontario. They lived in larger communities and larger houses, developed more elaborate fortifications around their villages, and depended more and more upon horticulture for their sustenance, although fishing and some hunting continued as important activities. As villages and clans grew in size and complexity, more elaborate social organization developed, new group rituals and symbolism developed, and previously autonomous settlements associated to form tribes, which in turn necessitated different political arrangements. Community councils developed into tribal councils. Then some tribes banded together into confederations such as that of the Wenda (Huron) or of the Five Nations. The latter became Six Nations when the Tuscarora joined them in the eighteenth century. Medicine or curing societies appeared, engaged in healing people while weaving together the threads of tribal solidarity.

By the time the Europeans arrived in the sixteenth century, there were some 500,000 Amerindian people in Canada, divided into some twelve linguistic families numbering more than fifty distinct languages. The majority inhabited the Northwest coast where six of the twelve language families were found. Of the other six linguistic families, the most prominent in our story will be the Algonkian, the Iroquoian and the Athapaskan; linguistic families that included just about all the Amerindians of Canada east of the Rockies. The Algonkian group spread from the Rockies to the Atlantic, the Athapaskan occupied the unglaciated portion of northwestern Canada east of the Rockies, and the Iroquoian centred in the Iroquois and Huron confederacies of central Canada. Given the early residency of Europeans among the Algonkian and Iroquoian people, their way of life is better known from the accounts of the missionaries and traders. Athapaskans were to become better known during the nineteenth century, while the Inuit people would not become the subjects of extensive reporting until the twentieth.

As will be seen in Chapter 3, Canada's Amerindians had some

contact with Europeans from the beginning of the sixteenth century, but Europeans became resident in Canada only from the early seventeenth century. During these two centuries of initial contact, Amerindian societies in eastern Canada changed extensively. The first European explorers, Cartier and Roberval for example, had noted the presence of Iroquoian Amerindians in the St Lawrence valley from Gaspé, through Québec (Stadacona) to Montréal (Hochelaga) in the 1530s and 1540s. By the end of the century, those communities had vanished, leaving the St Lawrence River valley devoid of Amerindian inhabitants. Historians are still trying to explain this retreat of the Iroquoians.

When the French founded their first permanent colony on Canadian soil in 1608 (Québec), the Amerindian peoples of eastern and central Canada were divided into two major linguistic families – the Algonkian and the Iroquoian – the former being hunters and gatherers, and the latter heavily engaging in agriculture. The Iroquoian group included the Confederacy of the Five Nations south of Lake Ontario and west of Lake Champlain, the Wenda (Huron) confederacy of four nations inhabiting the Lake Simcoe region of central Ontario, and the related Petun (Tobacco) and Neutral nations whose lands were on Ontario's Bruce peninsula and the eastern shore of Lake Erie respectively. The Algonkian linguistic family included most other Amerindian nations such as the Mi'kmaq of New Brunswick and Nova Scotia, the Montagnais of Québec, the Algonquin of Québec and the Ottawa valley, the Nipissing of north-central Ontario, the Ojibwa and Ottawas of northwestern Ontario, and the Cree of northern Québec and Ontario.

The numbers of Amerindians at the time of contact with Europeans has been and still is the subject of much speculation, given that scholars have at their disposal very little reliable data upon which to base their calculations. While earlier anthropologists estimated the total number of Amerindians north of the U.S./Mexican border at around one million, recent scholarship estimates the numbers to have ranged between three and ten million people at the time of European contact. While scholars also agree that the epidemics that swept through the Amerindian nations in the wake of European contact were devastating, the precise effect on the numbers of Amerindians is unknown.

It is not any easier to determine the population numbers of the particular Amerindian nations most directly involved in the Canadian story. It would seem that the Huron people numbered some 30,000 before the epidemics of the 1630s, and one third of that after 1640; these were the numbers reported by various European witnesses at the time.

The numbers of Five Nations Iroquois were similar. Data remains even more unreliable for the Mi'kmaq and the various other nations.

Amerindian realignments during the seventeenth century

The fur trade was the driving force in the relations between Europeans and Amerindians in the seventeenth century. The French competed with the Dutch and the English for the control of the trade. The Amerindians were forced to take sides in the developing commercial war, while simultaneously endeavouring to ensure the hegemony of their particular nation over the trade networks that appeared among the Amerindian nations themselves. So it was that the Hurons established their central role as middlemen in the trade between the French and the Amerindian nations inhabiting lands further to the north and west of their traditional territory, just as the Iroquois confederacy, allied with the Dutch and the English, made war on most Amerindian nations to the north and west of their homeland in an effort to either reduce them to subservience, or to destroy them altogether. Moreover, among the Five Nations, the Mohawk bent every effort to ensure that it was their nation that controlled the trade, and not the Oneidas, Onondagas, Cayugas, and Senecas.

Throughout the seventeenth century, while allied with the neighbouring Dutch and English at Fort Orange (Albany) on the Hudson River, the Iroquois were at war with the French and their allies who included just about all the Amerindian nations living north and west of the St Lawrence and Great Lakes. Armed with guns provided by their European allies, beginning in the 1640s the Iroquois undertook a war of extermination against their Amerindian rivals in the fur trade. The first to fall was the Huron nation which was annihilated by 1649–50, shortly before a similar fate befell the neighbouring Petun. Other nations like the Nipissing and Algonquin of north-central Ontario fled west before the Iroquois juggernaut. Then it was the turn of the Neutrals who disappeared from history as their hunting lands were seized in the early 1650s. Barely pausing to regroup, the Iroquois war machine turned west and swept away the Erie nation in 1654–57, thereby opening up the Ohio valley to their hunting parties. In later years, they would range as far west as the Mississippi, making war on the Illinois nation, always with the objective of eliminating their rivals in the fur trade.

During this century of warfare, the aggressive Iroquois suffered some serious setbacks that would ultimately signal the end of their hegemony. Because of their constantly threatening presence and raiding, in 1666–67 the French sent the 1,000-man Carignan-Salières regiment on search-and-destroy missions into the land of the Iroquois. This resulted in a peace agreement in 1667, one that was followed by nearly twenty years of peace for the settlers, although the aggressive Five Nations were busy raiding other Amerindian nations further west. When hostilities broke out anew between the French and the Iroquois after 1686, which continued until the end of the century, the Iroquois suffered serious setbacks, which led to a permanent peace agreement in 1701 between the French, the Iroquois, and thirteen other nations. Moreover, while the Iroquois were being subjected to punishing raids by the French during the 1690s, their Ojibwa rivals jumped at the opportunity to invade and eject them from their hunting grounds of southern Ontario. Thereafter, the region was occupied by the Mississauga, an Ojibwa nation. So it was that by 1701, the configuration of Amerindian nations in east-central Canada had changed dramatically.

The religions of Canada's Amerindians

When compared to the study of Christianity, the study of the religions of Canada's Amerindian people implies two special difficulties. The first is the fact that Amerindian spirituality was so much a part of everyday life, so enmeshed in personal, communal, political, economic and military activities, that it oftentimes became difficult to recognize the specifically religious factors in Amerindian life. Indeed, as some of the first missionaries observed, the Amerindians had no clergy, no churches, no supreme god, etc. Some concluded that they had no religion. The second difficulty is that Amerindians had no written records. Therefore, the only empirical evidence of their past lives is found in the artifacts dug up by archeologists (pottery, arrow-heads, skeletons, etc.), and in the secondary reports of European explorers, particularly missionaries. Of course, the latter necessarily observed Amerindian life through the lens of their own cultural values, which frequently led to them distorting or misunderstanding what they witnessed.

In studying the Amerindian societies of the sixteenth and seventeenth centuries, the data obtained from artifacts and the written records of European observers is then supplemented by the oral traditions, the stories, legends, and myths passed down from one generation to the next among Amerindians. This is the task of ethnohistory, a new discipline that exploits the traditional written sources of historians, the artifacts of archaeologists, and the oral traditions of ethnologists.

Finally, in order to better understand the religions of Canada's Amerindian people, one must also invoke the methods of the history of religions since that discipline's focus is specifically the religious dimension of human societies, it can bring significant insights into the analysis of Amerindian myths, beliefs, spiritualities, and religious practices.

While some of the basic beliefs, practices, and themes common to many of the religions of Canada's Amerindians will be studied below, it is important to underline at the outset the great diversity and variety that characterized the lives and religions of Canada's many Amerindian societies, communities that spanned the entire landmass of the Americas. Pre-contact religions in Canada reflected the diversity of nations, tribes, languages, cultures, lifestyles, mythologies, and world views that were in place. The many tribes spoke more than fifty languages, several of which were as different from each other as Greek is from Chinese or Spanish or Russian.

Over the course of thousands of years, each of the Amerindian nations developed expressions of their sense of the spiritual and of their experience of life in myths and stories that told of their origins, of their destiny, and of their relationship with the spirits. Each developed religious practices that served to appeal to the spirits, to satisfy their requirements, to appease them, and to communicate with them.

Some French observers such as Jean-François Lafitau and Baron de Lahontan had many good things to say about the Amerindians they encountered, and many French authors lauded their egalitarian values. Similarly, Chrestien Levesque saw no devil-connection with the shamans whom he called *jongleurs*, while Father Jean de Brébeuf praised the civil virtues of the Amerindians whom he found wiser and more gifted than rural Frenchmen. Nevertheless, most Euro-Canadians were inclined to view the cultures and religions of the Amerindians as an undifferentiated amalgam of savagery and sorcery, although over time, some came to acknowledge the depth and the power of at least some elements in their religions. However, it was only in the latter part of the twentieth century that the religions of Canada's Amerindians were belatedly acknowledged as authentic and legitimate expressions of the spiritual experience of aboriginal Canadians.

Some basic themes in Canadian Amerindian religions

The prevailing theology of European Christianity in the seventeenth century, in its simplest expression, explained the world as a vale of tears which one sought to escape through the portals of death into another world, hopefully of heavenly bliss, but all too often of eternal damnation. Human beings were but temporary visitors on this planet, no longer Paradise, an abode tainted to its core by human sin. Long-term goodness, perfection and happiness were only to be found in another world.

In contrast, the world the Amerindian lived in, the only world he or she knew, was not to be escaped, but was to be held in equilibrium by ensuring that the forces that disturbed that equilibrium were countered. This world was considered to be fundamentally sound and good, provided it remained in balance. This balanced world was simultaneously both material and spiritual. This meant that rocks, trees, rivers, waterfalls, animals, and every other part of the material world were fundamentally both good, and permanent. It also meant that the spirits that were just as much part of this world could be encountered anywhere, for there were animal spirits, rock spirits, indeed spirits of all kinds, because all of reality was spiritual. While the thrust of Christian spirituality was to escape this vale of tears, the thrust of Amerindian spirituality was to keep the world they knew in equilibrium. After death, the Amerindian believed he went to a spiritual world where he would be reunited with his loved ones, a world where his accustomed lifestyle would continue in perfect form.

While the Christian theology of the seventeenth century divided the world into distinct material and spiritual compartments, the natural and the supernatural, the secular and the transcendent, the profane and the sacred, the first tainted and the other unsullied, Amerindian spirituality tended to see the world as one undivided reality. This 'whole' world was both spiritual and material. Such contrasting understandings led to very different attitudes and behaviour. For example, the Christian who understood himself, as per biblical teaching, as being created in the image of God and as having been given the mandate to subdue the world and rule over it, never hesitated to kill animals whenever he so desired, and did so without any qualms. In contrast, the Amerindian only killed animals when necessary for subsistence, and even then was careful to appease the spirits of the animals lest they be offended. European Christians were less respectful of nature because they considered that it was there for their use, while Amerindians were more respectful of nature because they understood themselves as part and parcel of it, on a continuum with it, not rulers ordained to subjugate it.

The world of the Amerindian was animated with very real and powerful spirits. While minor spirits were found everywhere such as in special rocks, waterfalls, thunder or animals, Amerindians also believed in some major spirits, those of the heavens for example, because these latter controlled the wind, the seasons, and the tides. In some cases there appeared to be a supreme spirit. Thus the Algonkians had a Great Spirit, one that the Christians sometimes understood as akin to their own God.

Whatever the particular constellation of spirits present in one tribe or another, some were good and others were evil. Therefore, one had to avoid offending them, and they sometimes needed to be placated. For example, one did not feed the bones of certain animals to the dogs, for fear of offending the spirits of these animals. For similar reasons, offerings of tobacco were left at waterfalls or rapids in order to placate the spirit of the place so that disaster would not be visited upon the traveler. This legion of spirits represented the supernatural power that underlay and permeated the world of the Amerindian.

One communicated with these spirits and tapped this power through dreams, which were therefore to be obeyed because they were the voices of the spirits. The Jesuit missionary Jean de Brébeuf wrote about the Huron in 1636:

> They have a belief in dreams that surpasses all belief ... They take their dreams for orders and irrevocable decrees whose execution must not be deferred ... The dream is the oracle that all these people consult and obey, the prophet that predicts the future, the Cassandra that warns them of the dangers that threaten them, the ordinary physician in their illnesses ... It is the most absolute taskmaster that they have. If a captain advises one course of action and a dream another ... the dream is the first obeyed ... The dream often dominates their councils: trade, fishing, and hunting are usually undertaken under its guidance, and only to satisfy it; nothing is so precious that it will not be given up to satisfy a dream; if they have had a bad hunt, if their fishing has been a spectacular success, it is because of a dream. A dream will sometimes cause them to give up their food supplies for an entire year. It prescribes feasts, dances, songs, and games. In a word, here the dream is all powerful, and is truly the leading god of the Hurons ... My experi-

ence of five years in studying the customs and ways of our Amerindians compels me to speak thus.[1]

Much like traditional Catholics who each had their own guardian angel, teen-aged Amerindian boys and girls were encouraged to seek their own personal encounter and vision with a spirit, usually the spirit of an animal. The young men and women were prepared for this rite of puberty and went off into a remote part of the forest on their vision quest. There they fasted and meditated for several days awaiting the visitation of the spirit. Upon appearing, the latter would give the seeker a symbol of the encounter along with a special personal identity that would give its bearer power and meaning for the rest of his or her life.

In Amerindian society there was no special class of people who had a monopoly of access to the spiritual world. Everyone could communicate with the spirits. Nevertheless, there existed specialists in communicating with spirits. They were known as shamans. Shamans had a dual role: communicating with spirits and curing people of illnesses. This is why they were also known as medicine men. Given that the primary means of communicating with spirits was through dreams, shamans were primarily concerned with interpreting dreams, telling people what they meant.

Like their societies, Amerindian religions were democratic and egalitarian. Just as each clan's chiefs of peace and war were elected by their clans because of their personal qualifications for the office, shamans were acknowledged because of their personal expertise in communicating with the spirits. They had proven especially adept because of their direct visions of the spirit world. In trances they travelled to the land of the spirits, returning with messages and advice. Frequently, the shaman was one who had suffered from psychic illness and had experienced noteworthy healing through his commerce with the spirits. The shaman was therefore more skilled than others in healing the sick, whose illnesses were understood as resulting from the presence of evil spirits.

Equality was maintained and ensured in Amerindian societies by the pervasive practice of gift-giving, the key to the social universe. Amerindians felt compelled to share, to give gifts, to receive gifts, and to return gifts in kind. The gift received was necessarily returned. Gift-giving was the foundational rule of social intercourse and bore great symbolic and religious meaning. The recipient owed a debt to the spirit of the donor, a debt that had to be paid back in one form or another.

Upon repayment, the debt shifted back to the original donor who was bound in turn, a social custom that ensured the permanent circulation of goods and wealth. When someone defaulted on this obligation, the donor acquired over him or her powers related to sorcery, becoming empowered to cast a spell over the defaulter.

This culture of gift-giving meant that when a hunter returned from a very successful hunt, he shared everything he had, by holding a feast. Indeed, in Amerindian societies, social prestige was primarily acquired by the giving of gifts. The most highly respected members of the tribe were those who gave away the most. Peace chiefs were usually chosen from them. One also acquired social prestige by showing courage in war, the usual criterion for choosing war chiefs.

Just as gift-giving was weighted with social, symbolic, and religious meaning, so was trade with outside tribes and strangers. Trade was both material and symbolic. Trade only occurred with people who were at peace with one's tribe. Alliances were a condition for trade; they had to be ritually re-affirmed before trade occurred. This meant that presents, speeches, and dances preceded any commercial exchange of goods. The other's good intentions were demonstrated by a reciprocal generosity. To give generously was to demonstrate one's friendly intentions, which in turn imposed an obligation on the recipient who could give even more generously at the next opportunity. Conversely, to be miserly in exchange demonstrated unfriendly disposition. And the spirits were always intimately associated with these exchanges.

For Amerindians, anything in this world can be carriers of the entire cosmos. Anything can symbolize all of reality, or be a meaningful, religious figure. Since Amerindian societies had no churches, clergy, or written doctrines, the common understanding of their origins, history, and destiny was transmitted in the format of stories handed down from one generation to another. These stories were myths in that they explained the origins of all that existed; the land, the sky, the seasons, the people, the tribe, the spirits; they served to found the institutions of their respective cultures, and the moral code that was in place. The stories were told around the campfires where the families and clans gathered.

The beliefs of Amerindians, although frequently not apparent and implicit, permeated all aspects of their lives. Each Amerindian tribe had its creation story, much as Christians, Jews, or Hindus have theirs. A myth of origins that was common among Amerindians throughout North America was one that told of a primordial perfect world that had preceded our present world into which the advent of good and evil was ascribed to a pair of creator twins. An example of a typical creation myth is contained in the Seneca version. This initial perfect world in the sky originated in a giant tree in the centre of the world, a world where there was no death and food was plentiful. A band of brothers uprooted this tree of life in order to save the life of their brother and to generate life in a new world that was created below the first one. Since the wife of this man was to become the mother of the new world, he pushed her into the hole in the sky that was created by the uprooted tree. She was then impregnated by the wind as she fell towards the new watery world below. A flock of birds then broke the woman's fall, deposited her on the back of a big turtle, the only creature capable of carrying her in the new world of water. As she rode the turtle, other creatures busied themselves diving into the water, and returning from the bottom with portions of earth which they built up around the turtle. This was the building of their land. The pregnant woman then gave birth to a daughter who played in the water which impregnated her with twins. These two were soon fighting one another, even in their mother's womb. When birthing time came, one brother was born in the normal way, but the other burst forth through the side of his mother's womb, thereby killing her. Her buried body then became the source of corn and other food plants for humans. The names of the brothers were Good Spirit and Bad Spirit.

As adults, Good Spirit and Bad Spirit each became creators of different things. Good Spirit made human beings, rivers and lakes, and the useful plants and animals of the world. Bad Spirit was the creator of monsters, pests, disease, plant blight, and death. Although Good Spirit was unable to undo all the evil things done by his brother, he was able to force the latter to help people in return for not being killed by his good brother. This is the reason that the Seneca, along with other Iroquoian people, have 'Societies of Faces.' There, members prepare masks representing the many forms of Bad Spirit, who ritually is engaged in helping to cure disease and other good deeds, in accordance with the promise he made to Good Spirit.[2]

The myth is rich in its teaching. Among other things, it tells of a primordial perfect world, of a tree of life being at the centre of that world and of our world; it explains the origin, and frequent ambivalence of both good and evil, and of the ultimate domination of good over evil; it teaches that all the earth's foodstuffs are a gift from the body of the dying mother of the twins, just as the people, the good animals, and all the good things of this world were created by the Good Spirit. Finally, it explains the purpose of the Society of Faces in Iroquoian society.

Trickster stories were another type of myth widespread in Amerindian tribes and very popular around the campfires, especially among children. This mythic figure represented the human desire to be free of rules and regulations, to be unbound by time, space, and society. Frequently humorous, the stories also served to remind people that cultural and moral codes were to be observed, and that there was a price to be paid if one disregarded the tribe's rules.

The trickster figure defied definition. Frequently, it was represented by a coyote, but a coyote that could take on a variety of forms and appearances. While one story among the Cheyenne told of a Trickster who could project his eyes out of his head, and then recall them at will, another among the Winnebago focused on the unbounded sexual urges of a Trickster whose penis was so extraordinarily long that he had to carry it in a box on his back. The story can be summarized as follows.

One day the Trickster spotted a group of girls swimming across the lake from where he watched. Deciding to take advantage of his extraordinarily long penis, Trickster sent it floating across the lake and penetrated the chief's daughter. Since the girls in their panic didn't know how to respond to this invasion by an unknown creature, a wily old woman came to the rescue. She knew and recognized the ways of Trickster. Riding his penis with an awl, she gouged it such that he withdrew it suddenly, throwing the woman a great distance away. But the chief's daughter was rescued from her aggressor.[3]

Myths such as these were the glue that held Amerindian tribes together, that explained their origins, history, and destiny, and explained and justified the moral and cultural norms that prevailed. In sum, myths gave meaning to their world.

As Sam Gill[4] explains, myths were reinforced by the rich symbolism that ran through Amerindian cultures, in social structure, mythic geography, and architecture. Landscapes, villages, ceremonial grounds, ceremonial lodges, and common homes replicated the form and process of the cosmos. Among the Delaware, for example, the religion of the Big House symbolized the origin of the world. The floor of the lodge represented the earth, the four walls the four quarters of the world, and the roof the vault of the sky. The centre post of the lodge bore the carved image of the creator, while faces carved on the support pillars of the walls represented the spirits of the cosmic regions. Doors

Fig. 1.   *Amerindian Funeral Procession.*[5] Bernard Picart. National Archives of Canada, c-005342.

on the east and west were associated with the rising sun which symbolized the beginnings of the world, and the setting sun a symbol of the end.

Many other elements such as costumes, face painting, and rituals continued the rich symbolism of daily life. Artwork on utensils, masks, drums, ritual objects, and sacred pipes symbolized the various elements of the world and its spirits. The carvings of the Inuit were the expression of the process whereby the carver revealed and released the form that was buried within the raw material. Similarly, Amerindian craftsmen of the Northwest Coast who carved totem poles liberated the forms pre-existent in the wood. The carving process is not merely one of imposing one's imagined representative designs on soapstone or wood, but rather one of freeing forms of reality that are already present in all things.

Finally, it must be emphasized that these religions were not closed upon themselves, not frozen in some primordial time, not static, but dynamic. They included, even identified as sacred, some of the disturbing and disruptive elements with which Amerindian history is replete.

Fig. 2.   *Piegan Medicine Pipe.*[6] National Archives of Canada, c-019970.

Fig. 3.   *Medicine Bundles.*[7] National Archives of Canada. Department of Mines and Technical Surveys collection, c-024482.

Their world views and spiritualities were constantly changing and adjusting to incorporate their new experiences. Like other persistent and successful religions, Amerindian world views integrated new experiences and the foundational defining elements of their traditions.

Illness and healing

In the modern Western world, the meaning of health has all too often been restricted to physical health and/or avoidance of illness. When health fails, our culture teaches us to heal by taking drugs or adopting other interventions to restore physical wellness. In Amerindian cultures, the physiological would only be one aspect of health, a term designating a much more encompassing state: the individual as integrated within the family, tribe, and world, a world which was primarily spiritual.

Amerindians ascribed numerous and varied explanations for the causes of disease. The Huron, for example, like many other Amerindians, recognized three kinds of illnesses: the physical, the psychological, and the spiritual. Natural, physical illnesses were cured by medicinal plants, dieting, sweating, and incisions. Psychological illnesses resulted from unfulfilled desires. The cure was to have a shaman identify the unfulfilled desire, and then assist the patient in obtaining satisfaction. Spiritual illnesses resulted from a spell being cast against the afflicted person. A witch or other antagonist would have caused some specially prepared charm to enter the patient's body. A cure could be obtained from a shaman who succeeded in extracting the unwelcome charm.

Shamans, either individually or as members of tribal curing societies, were usually called upon to diagnose the illness and to prescribe appropriate remedies, be they medicinal, psychological, or spiritual. They knew of a wide range of herbs and techniques to cure physical ailments, as Jacques Cartier's people discovered in the winter of 1535–1536 when the Amerindians around Stadacona (Québec) showed them how a drink made from Vitamin C-rich white cedar cured scurvy. The 'medicine men' (shamans) were also skilled at setting broken limbs, and extracting projectiles from the body. When dealing with spiritual ailments, they would individually or collectively fast, dream, enter trances, and perform rituals intended to cure the patient.

Psychological ailments were believed to result from unsatisfied sexual or other desires, and the remedy was either to satisfy that desire or, if that proved impossible, to offer appropriate presents or ritual performances in lieu of that. For the Huron, dreams carried desires and the messages of the soul. Consequently, if one did not respond to them, illness or even death could ensue. For example, if they considered it necessary, Huron shamans could prescribe a collective ritual called *andacouandet* whereby the unmarried maidens of the village were gathered by a patient's bedside as a result of the patient's expressed wish or of the decision of a shaman who had diagnosed the illness. The young women would each choose the young man with whom they wanted to spend the following night. These youths of the village were then convened by the master of ceremonies to spend the night in the patient's domicile to indulge in group sexual intercourse, while two captains stood guard at each end of the longhouse chanting the night away. This ritual performance was enacted to comfort the patient and satisfy an expressed desire of his or hers.

Spiritual illnesses, which resulted from unfriendly charms that had entered one's body as a result of a spell cast by an opponent, were treated by a shaman who identified and then extracted these charms. Hurons believed that the prime motivation for witchcraft was jealousy. Therefore, in order to avoid arousing such jealousy, they took great care to share whatever they had with their neighbours, reinforcing again the practice of gift-giving. Jealousy, however, and the consequent possibility of being the target of evil charms and illness could not always be prevented, since they sometimes resulted from the malice of members of distant tribes, or from the irrational hatred of someone or other.

Throughout the Americas during the sixteenth and seventeenth centuries, a series of devastating epidemics decimated most Amerindian tribes. Although specific statistics are unavailable, some observers estimate that perhaps as many as 95% of Amerindians died as a result of these pandemics. In Canada, the best known of these epidemics are those that swept through Huronia during the seven years after 1634 when the Jesuit missionaries were present, diseases that reduced the population of Huronia by two thirds. The result of the deadly onslaught was that the Hurons associated the Jesuits with the tragedy. Some wanted to put the latter to death.

As the epidemics spread, Huron ritualism developed apace, demonstrating the resilience of Huron beliefs. When particular rituals failed to cure the sick, rather than discrediting the religion, it led shamans to intensify their efforts to communicate with the spirits in order to discover more effective rituals. When the epidemics eventually subsided, as they invariably did, the rituals were credited with having obtained the cure, thereby reinforcing the religious beliefs that underlay them. Indeed, a surge in the number of healing cults in Huronia during the winter of 1639–1640 is telling.

In fact, the very presence of Christianity in Huronia during the 1630s and 1640s served to confirm some Huron in their traditional beliefs. So many Hurons died in the epidemics that occurred on the heels of the arrival of the missionaries in the country, many held the Jesuits responsible for the deaths. From the Jesuit point of view, a vicious cycle seemed to be in place. The Huron only accepted baptism when on their death bed, in the hope of trying another ritual after the traditional ones had failed them. This meant that the missionaries were only baptizing the dying. When most of these in fact died, the Hurons concluded that it was the ritual of baptism that had killed them. Their conclusion was confirmed by the fact that the Jesuits themselves did not die from the epidemics, proving that they held the secret cure that they refused to share with the Amerindians – an ungenerous behaviour totally foreign to their practice and expectations.

In the late 1630s, the missionaries came very close to being totally exterminated by their hosts. Nevertheless, they managed to remain in the country because the Hurons needed the favour of the French colonial officials, their sole source of European goods which they had come to feel they could not do without. Moreover, the officials at Québec had warned the Huron on several occasions that all trade would cease if the Jesuits were harmed. In their eyes, Christianization went hand-in-hand with civilization.

Although Huron religious practices emerged from the epidemics unscathed, the large number of deaths, particularly among the more vulnerable elderly, dealt a severe blow to traditional religious knowledge. There would henceforth be far fewer elders to tell stories around the campfires at night; the glue that held the Huron nation together was weakened, as it was in most tribes that were stricken by epidemics.

Like all Amerindian religions, the traditional religion of the Huron was inextricably tied to the fate of the culture and society as a whole, of which it was part and parcel. When the nation's culture and society were destroyed in war, the religion necessarily followed suit. In the case of the Huron, growing numbers of them turned to Christianity when they saw that their traditional ways simply did not work anymore after their Iroquois enemy undertook to exterminate them in the late 1640s. In the case of other linguistic families, the Athapaskan and Algonkian for example, a similar pattern emerged in later years, although they were not faced with a war of extermination like the Huron were. Instead, their cultures were gradually submerged under the spreading juggernaut of North American society in the nineteenth and twentieth centuries.

Conclusion

Amerindian religions were integral to Amerindian society and culture because Amerindian people were immersed in a world that was spiritual through and through. Their origins were spiritual, their history unfolded under the tutelage and guidance of the spirits, their behaviour was regulated by them, and their destiny likewise. When they encountered European Christianity, the misunderstandings and consequent conflicts were pervasive. Although Amerindian world views continually adjusted and changed to incorporate new experiences, experiences that were necessarily spiritual, nevertheless the foundational insights and understanding of both parties were so dissimilar that neither was able to achieve sufficient *rapprochement* to facilitate mutual understanding. The growing majority of non-aboriginal Canadians, one that would in time become overwhelming, would make the preservation of aboriginal traditions, rites, and rituals difficult at best.

Suggested readings

Dickason, Olive Patricia. *Canada's First Nations. A History of Founding Peoples from Earliest Times*, Toronto: McClelland & Stewart, 1992.

Gill, Sam D. *Native American Religions. An Introduction*. Belmont, California: Wadsworth Publishing Company, 1982.

Jenness, Diamond. *The Amerindians of Canada*. Ottawa: National Museum of Canada, 1960.

Lafitau, Jean-François. *Moeurs des Sauvages Amériquains* (1724). Translation by William N. Fenton and Elizabeth Moore. 2 vols. Toronto: The Champlain Society, 1974, 1977.

Lane, Belden C. *Landscapes of the Sacred: Geography and Narrative in American Spirituality*. New York: Paulist Press, 1988.

Trigger, Bruce G. Ed. *The Handbook of North American Amerindians*. Vol. 15. *Northeast*. Washington: Smithsonian Institution Press, 1978.

Trigger, Bruce G. *The Children of Aataentsic: A History of the Huron People to 1660*. 2 vols. Montréal: McGill-Queen's University Press, 1976.

Wallace, Anthony F.C. *The Death and Rebirth of the Seneca*. New York: Vintage, 1969.

CHAPTER 3

European Religions on the Eve of Encounter

The religions of Europe before the seventeenth century

With few exceptions, the Europeans who came to Canada were Christians who carried with their religious faith a cultural baggage going back hundreds of years. It included elements of the religion of the Hebrews, the culture of classical Greece, the political and administrative legacy of the Roman Empire, and the civilization of the Middle Ages, and in addition, many elements of pagan European tradition.

The early Christian heritage

The Bible of the Christians was their foundational document, their sacred scripture the primary vehicle through which was transmitted God's self revelation. This was a collection of books in two parts, designated by Christians as the Old Testament and the New Testament. The Old Testament, which was in fact the sacred writings of the Jews, included the five books of the Jewish Law (Genesis, Exodus, Leviticus, Numbers and Deuteronomy) in addition to a series of historical, poetical, and prophetical books. They had been written before the birth of Jesus of Nazareth, over the course of several centuries. They reflected ancient Hebrew concepts and images. This ancient Jewish understanding was thus constantly before the minds of Christians in subsequent centuries, since Christians regularly read the Bible in their quest for greater understanding and communion with God. The New Testament, written at intervals between the years 50 and 100 C.E. following the death of Jesus Christ, the son of this God, comprised the books of the four Evangelists called the

Gospels, and the works of sundry other Christians, especially Paul of Tarsus.

Since Christians believed that this key figure – Jesus of Nazareth – was the messiah promised by the Old Testament Jewish prophets, and that he was the Son of God, the Nazarene's life and teachings became of utmost importance for them. So it was that various writings produced by followers of Jesus were soon considered the sequel to the revealed Word of God found in the Old Testament. These new writings included historical, poetical, prophetic, and apologetic literature written by various Christians during the century following the death of Jesus. After some three centuries of consideration, the Christian Church declared twenty-seven of these texts to be inspired by God. This was the New Testament, the second part of the Bible, privileged source of God's Revelation.

The New Testament reflected the cultures of its time, including the Jewish culture, but also that of classical Greece that had become dominant in the Mediterranean world, and that of imperial Rome, the area's dominant world power at the time. This meant that as subsequent Christians meditated and reflected on the New Testament, they were pondering and weighing words, ideas, and images drawn from the cultural crossroads that informed Palestine during the first century C.E.

The early Christian church grew in spite of constant resistance to its existence from various Roman imperial governments, and the coterminous Jewish religious traditions from which it had emerged, then flourished with the full support of the Holy Roman Empire after Emperor Constantine brought Christianity under his protection in 313 C.E. By the mid-fourth century, the church had rapidly expanded to become the majority religion in the Roman Empire. In the process, it moved further and further away from its Jewish roots, taking on more and more of the cultural forms, customs, and images of Græco-Roman civilization as it established itself in Europe and in the East on the opposite shores of the Mediterranean. It was during these first four centuries of its history that the church defined its faith in more conceptual and rational forms, while gradually distancing itself from the more personalist and holistic understanding that had been dominant in Jewish culture, as it distanced itself from the geographic centre of that culture.

From the outset, Christians came together in official meetings to determine questions of faith, morals, worship, and discipline. This culminated in the first ecumenical Council of Nicaea in 325 C.E. where

Christian leaders promulgated the doctrine of the Trinity, whereby God was declared to be Triune: three distinct persons in one God – Father, Son, and Holy Spirit. It was at the Council of Chalcedon in 451 C.E. that Jesus the Christ (the anointed one) was proclaimed to be the Son of God, one person living with both a fully human nature and a fully divine nature. In sum, many Christians who used to be content with having encountered Jesus in their lives and having decided to follow him together with their Christian brothers and sisters, now felt the necessity of defining in more rational or conceptual terms the nature of both their faith and their God. Christianity was adjusting to a new cultural climate. This was the preoccupying motif in the realm of theology – or 'God talk' – the term used for the enterprise which seeks to explain faith using contemporary ways of thinking. The committed apologetic theology of the first century's Paul of Tarsus became more mystical, spiritual, and rationalist in tone in the writings of Greek-speaking Fathers of the church such as Athanasius, Origen and Gregory Nazianzus. Later, as the military conquests of the so-called 'barbarian hordes' from the East and North swept away Roman civilization in the West after the fourth century, new generations of theologians such as Jerome and Augustine, writing in Latin, interpreted anew Christian faith for a society in turmoil by the violence, the suffering, the sin, and the unreliability of a world that was threatening to come to an end.

Medieval Christendom

Eventually, after what has been characterized as more than four centuries of a wasteland for civilization, society was rebuilt in the West. One of the foundational pillars of the Middle Ages was the Christian church. Though favouring monasticism, a way of life chosen by those Christian men and women who sought to escape from the society of their day, the self-described 'One, Holy, Catholic, and Apostolic' church of the Middle Ages was closely integrated into the society of its day. Sometimes creating and sometimes copying the social, economic, political, and class divisions of its day, the church of the Middle Ages taught the faithful to attend Mass regularly, to receive the Eucharist and to confess their sins to a priest at least once a year, to avoid damnation, and to work to be admitted into heaven at the end of their all-too-brief days on earth. The world was a vale of tears to be endured while awaiting the Kingdom of God promised to Christ's followers. In the meantime, the church had been entrusted with the responsibility of guiding Christ's flock, with the assistance of the Holy Spirit.

There was only one truth, the one revealed and entrusted to the care of the church. Erroneous doctrines (heresies) were to be repressed, by force if necessary. Bishops ruled the church under the pope in Rome as successors of the apostles with divinely given authority, care, and responsibility; the numerous clergymen were assistants to the bishops. The role of the faithful was to pray to God, obey the church leaders, and financially support their church. The latter worked hand-in-glove with the State; they were the two pillars upon which rested this Western Christendom.

A major renewal of Western Christianity occurred after the end of the first millennium of Christian history. This Gregorian Reformation which began in the eleventh century included revitalized and renewed monastic orders such as the Benedictines, the creation of several new religious orders of men and women such as the Franciscan and Dominican Friars and the Cistercian Fathers, a reformed papacy, the creation of universities such as those at Oxford, Paris, Cambridge, and Bologna, and a new theology created by men such as Thomas Aquinas, and Duns Scotus. It also included the crusades, the wars of religion whereby Christians of the West unsuccessfully sought to wrest control of the Holy Land of Palestine from its Muslim rulers. This high-water mark of medieval Christendom achieved during the twelfth and thirteenth centuries remained the model for Christian theology and church organization until the discovery and evangelization of the New World.

During the fourteenth and fifteenth centuries, however, this golden age waned as Christendom and Western society slid into disorganized confusion and social chaos. Schism and discord led to popes no longer residing in Rome during most of the fourteenth century (1309–1377), much to the confusion of many Christians. Then the pope's return to the Eternal City in 1377 was followed by the simultaneous election of first two popes, and then three popes. The leadership of the Christian church was in disarray, seemingly unable to solve its own problems of internal government. Simultaneously, internal dissent grew progressively worse as more and more critics of the church emerged following the repression of the Cathar heresy during the thirteenth and fourteenth centuries, Catharism being a major dissenting movement that seriously threatened the unity of the church. Thereafter during the fourteenth and fifteenth centuries, reforming priests such as John Wycliffe (1330–1384) in England, John Huss (1372–1415) in Bavaria, Pierre D'Ailly (1350–1420) in France, and Girolamo Savonarola (1452–1498) in Italy demanded reforms in the doctrines and practices of the church. This all occurred in the context of the Hundred Years War between England and France (1337–1453) and the Black Death, a strain of bubonic plague that killed some twenty-five million Europeans after 1347, decimating entire towns and regions.

For many Christians of these late Middle Ages, God seemed to have turned his back on his children. Their society, their church, indeed their lives were constantly threatened. This led a goodly number to seek assurances of salvation by alternate and unusual means. Pilgrimages to holy places that sheltered the relics or the remains of martyrs and saints became more and more popular, thousands of pilgrims travelling to shrines like the tombs of the Apostles Peter and Paul in Rome and to Santiago de Compostela in northwestern Spain, supposedly the burial place of St James the Apostle. Despairing of a church riddled with divided leadership, deficient clergy, and confusing theology, Christians sought their salvation by turning their backs on the world. So it was that during the fifteenth century emerged and blossomed a movement of 'Modern Devotion' whose classic expression is the little book *The Imitation of Christ* by Thomas à Kempis, a book still sold in bookstores more than five hundred years after its publication. The movement stressed the inner spiritual life of the individual and methodical meditation on the life and Passion of Christ. Many joined together in new groups of piety known as 'Brethren of the Common Life.'

In an irrational and cruel world, uncertainty, apprehension, and an adherence to extreme behaviours emerged as chronic disenchantment with this world set in. While some endeavoured to earn tickets to heaven by performing passion plays, earning indulgences, and practicing excessive forms of asceticism such as self-flagellation and refusal to eat, a deepened and sometimes morbid sense of sin developed, most Christians believing that salvation was reserved for the few while damnation was to be the lot of most. A heightened sense of guilt and sin became characteristic of Christians for whom God was more a harsh judge than a forgiving father. Theologians interpreted the world as the devil's playground, and the flesh was synonymous with corruption and damnation. It therefore followed that the holiest state of life was that of the monk and nun, the life that was farthest removed from this corrupt world. Jean-Jacques Olier (1608–1657), the founder of the Sulpician Fathers who played an important role in Canada wrote: "Lord, what is the flesh? It is the effect of sin; it is the principle of sin... All the hatred, all the malediction, the persecution that fall upon the devil must fall upon the flesh ... Men, angels and even God should therefore persecute us without cease."[1]

Medieval society became suspicious and fearful of women, a bias that would leave a profound imprint on Christianity down to our own day. Odo (879–942), the Benedictine abbot of Cluny, opined that feminine beauty was only skin-deep and wondered how men could embrace such 'bags of dung.' Francesco Petrarch (1304–1374), the Italian poet and humanist, loved his imaginary and angelic Laura while warning that real women were devils. One of the first Jesuits, Francis Xavier (1506–1552), wrote of the irresponsibility of women who were said to be inferior to their husbands. His rhetoric was surpassed by Jean Eudes (1601–1680), the founder of another religious congregation active in Canada, who "spoke of women as 'devil's Amazons' bent on making war on chastity, armed with their curly hair, bare arms, and shoulders."[2] One result of this sexism was that women who joined religious orders were required to remain cloistered, that is cut off from society, a requirement that would only be waived at the end of the seventeenth century.

The varieties of religions of Europe in the sixteenth and seventeenth centuries

While the vast majority of sixteenth-century Europeans were Christian, the presence of significant Muslim and Jewish minorities must not be overlooked.

Islam in Europe

Within one hundred years of the founding of the religion of Islam by the prophet Muhammad (570–632), the new faith had spread like wildfire through Arabia, the eastern Mediterranean, and North Africa. When engaged in the conquest of Europe, however, the Muslim armies swept through the Iberian Peninsula from North Africa only to run into an immovable object in Charles Martel, a member of the Merovingian dynasty of the Franks. The Battle of Poitiers (732) marked the end of Muslim expansion in Europe. During the subsequent eight centuries, the Muslim faith would coexist with Christianity in the kingdoms and territories that would eventually become the united Kingdom of Spain under the aegis of the 'Catholic Monarchs' Ferdinand and Isabella at the end of the fifteenth century.

The One, Holy, Catholic, and Apostolic church was the established church of the newly-unified Spain of the year 1500. The kingdom's conquering monarchs had completed the centuries-long reconquest of Muslim Spain by Christian forces by defeating the Kingdom of Granada's defenders in 1492, and forcing their Moorish people into subjection. The Moors were the descendants of the North-African Muslim people who had conquered Spain in the eighth century. Copying an existing Roman model of repressive machinery, the monarchs established the Spanish Inquisition charged it with ensuring religious orthodoxy in the realm. Spanish inquisitors were particularly concerned with wiping out all traces of Islam, the religion of the Moors, the newest subjects of the realm, as well as Judaism. Neither the Muslim nor the Jewish faith was encouraged and orthodox Catholic belief prevailed in the land of King Ferdinand and Queen Isabella.

Judaism in Europe

The same intolerance and outright repression was true for the Jews of Europe. The religion into which were born Jesus of Nazareth and the Apostles of the Christian Church had suffered since the holy city of Jerusalem and its holy Temple were razed by Roman troops in 70 C.E., and the region ransacked anew in 135 C.E. in the wake of political rebellions in Palestine. The loss of the Jewish homeland had been compounded by the early estrangement and separation that occurred between Jews and Christians. Indeed, the latter acknowledged Jesus as the promised messiah, and chose to follow his teachings in spite of the refusal of the majority of Jews to do so. Christianity developed separately from Judaism. When the former had become the preferred religion of the Roman Empire after 313 C.E., its leaders showed no particular ties to their former coreligionists.

Jews nevertheless prospered in the Iberian Peninsula after the fall of Toledo to Muslim forces in 711. Jewish philosophers, mystics, scholars, and poets flourished alongside Muslim colleagues. Aristotelian scholar Moses Ben Maimon (1135–1204), known as Maïmonides to Christians, was a prime representative of this. These Jewish authorities were consulted and frequently cited by Christian thinkers who belatedly tried to reestablish contact with ancient learning. A mystical tradition also continued alongside the more rationalist one.

This was a brief episode in tolerance, and thereafter Jews all too frequently became the victims of vicious religious persecution, especially during the Middle Ages, as Christians strategically accused them of having killed Jesus, the Son of God. The dispersal of the Jews to the four corners of the world would have been the punishment imposed by God for their act of deicide. This anti-Judaism, known as anti-Semitism since the nineteenth century, was also fuelled by the particularism of Jews who frequently refused to assimilate into the dominant culture and religion of the various countries.

While remaining distinct in the practice of their religion, Europe's Jews had usually participated in their respective societies before the eleventh century C.E. Thereafter however, in the wake of the religious frenzy associated with the Crusades, Jews were deliberately segregated by the majority Christian population in the West. They were outlawed, forced to live in reserved areas or ghettos, restricted to financial activities, and required to wear distinctive garb such as a pointed hat and a visible badge on their clothing. This social segregation led to psychological segregation, an uneducated populace tending to consider them guilty of any and all calamities that befell their society.

At various times in the latter centuries of the Middle Ages, Christians held Jews responsible for a variety of catastrophes and crimes including wars, epidemics, ritual assassinations, the poisoning of water fountains, and various forms of sacrilege. Jews were massacred in Germany in 1096 and 1147; they were expelled from their homelands of England in 1290, France in 1394, Spain in 1492 and Portugal in 1496. The official church also joined in the campaign, adopting segregationist measures at the Fourth Lateran Council in 1215, and allowing the Roman and Spanish Inquisitions to make Jews into targets of choice. One result of these persecutions was the emigration of large numbers of Jews to eastern Europe, a region which then became their major habitation.

The religious fragmentation of Christianity that followed the Protestant Reformation of the sixteenth century did not change this endemic anti-Judaism by Christians, as Catholics, Protestants, and Orthodox continued to treat Jews as pariahs of society. These marginalized and segregated Jewish communities gradually codified their rules of living, leading to an emerging rabbinic jurisprudence, which coexisted with a long-standing mystical tradition. In the context of the Enlightenment of the eighteenth century, Judaism will be challenged to adapt to its times by Moses Mendelssohn (1729–1786), an acculturation that will be strongly resisted by the Hasidic (pious) Jews.

The Protestant Reformation

The Protestant Reformation of the sixteenth century ensured the definitive religious fragmentation of Europe down to our own day.

Before the Protestant Reformation, despite the presence of Jewish and Muslim minorities, the church appeared united in doctrine, faith, and government. However, once the impact of Martin Luther (1483–1546), John Calvin (1509–1564), Henry VIII (1491–1547) and other reformers was felt after 1517, Christianity would never be the same. A constantly lengthening list of diverse and dissenting churches and denominations emerged, including Lutheran, Reformed, Anglican, Presbyterian, and Mennonite to name only a few.

This fragmentation of the Christian church resulted from the new theology taught by Martin Luther and most of the Protestant leaders; a theology that acknowledged the Bible as the exclusive source of God's Revelation and denied the authority of the church in the definition of matters of faith. Each individual Christian was urged to read the Bible, God's Word and, with the assistance of the Holy Spirit, was free to understand in his or her own wisdom, God's teachings. This soon translated into a growing variety of interpretations and different understandings of the Scriptures, and resulted in the formation of a growing diversity of churches. Protestant leaders like Luther and Calvin had rejected the authority of pope and ecumenical council, and had rejected most sacraments of the Catholic Church, retaining only Baptism and the Eucharist, while giving a different meaning to the latter. They emphasized the power, majesty, glory, and centrality of God in the faith of the Christian, and downplayed or rejected the value of most human activities and practices in the process of Christian salvation. This meant that a wide range of religious customs, practices, and devotions were excised by the Protestant reformers. Among these rejected religious practices were the mandatory celibacy of the clergy, the existence of religious orders of men and women, pilgrimages, the value of relics, the cult of the saints, and the infallible authority of the church.

Among the values and customs promoted by the Protestant leaders were the dignity and responsibility of lay Christians, the regular preaching of the Word of God, the legitimacy of the secular world as the place to achieve one's salvation, the dignity of married life, and the centrality of the Bible in the life of the Christian. However, it was the denial of the authority of pope, council, bishop, and priest – in sum of the church – that had the most direct and immediate impact on the structure of united Christendom.

Fig. 4.   Martin Luther. Engraving by C.E. Wagstaff from the painting by Hans Holbein. National Archives of Canada, c-008907.[3]

The Catholic Reformation

As one third of the Christians of Europe severed their communion with Rome and founded autonomous churches during the sixteenth century, Catholic Church leaders finally realized that energetic action was required to stop the hemorrhage. By the time of Luther's death in 1546, a time when King Henry VIII of England had already broken the English church's communion with Rome and when John Calvin was still building his religious strength in Geneva, Catholics had finally managed to convene an ecumenical council in the town of Trent in northern Italy. There it was that the diverse reforming efforts that had been made by various reformers during the previous decades finally coalesced into a general plan of reform for the international Catholic Church. Indeed, the Council of Trent which met off and on over a period of eighteen years (1545–1563), was in many ways the Catholic response to the Protestant Reformation. It charted the course of Catholicism until the middle of the twentieth century.

At Trent, both the doctrinal and disciplinary reform of Catholicism was undertaken. Key doctrines that had been challenged by the Protestant reformers were addressed: teachings bearing on the grace of God, on the freedom of the Christian, on the meaning of sacraments and of the Eucharist, on the ministerial priesthood, on the value of good works by Christians, and on the role of the church in God's plan of salvation. Sweeping disciplinary reform was also undertaken, including new policies and regulations on the training of clergy, the residency of bishops and pastors, liturgical celebrations, and the importance of preaching. In the decades following the Council of Trent reforming popes and bishops would maintain this thrust by endeavouring to have the rules observed, and by new initiatives such as the publication of a new Roman catechism and a new Roman Missal, the publication of a new Code of Canon Law, and the reform of the calendar by Pope Gregory XIII (1502–1585) in 1582 that gave us the calendar that is still in use today (the Gregorian calendar).

DIVERSITY WITHIN CATHOLICISM

In spite of the best efforts of Catholic leaders, reform would be long awaited in some quarters. This was due to many factors, such as the inertia of the local church, the impediments created by secular rulers who were used to exploiting the church for their own gain, the illiteracy of many clergy, the lack of religious education among the laity, and the

conflicting interests of some churchmen who proved reluctant to abandon their previous lifestyles. For example, a number of clergymen
cohabited with women, in spite of church regulations to the contrary,
and the reformed Catholic Church demanded that they live celibate
lives.

Another factor impeding church reform was the general lack of
autonomy of the Catholic Church. Although the pope had been in fact the
supreme ruler of Catholicism during the thirteenth century, the subsequent
two hundred years had served to erode his authority. Appearances
notwithstanding, at the time of the Reformation of the sixteenth century
the pope in fact had less control over the Catholic Church than did several
monarchs of Europe, rulers such as King Ferdinand (1452–1516) and
Queen Isabella (1451–1504) of Spain, King Francis I (1515–1547) of France,
King Henry VIII (1509–1547) of England, or the successive emperors of
the Holy Roman Empire. Since the thirteenth century, nation states were
arising as the newest form of political organization in Europe, at the
expense of the old Holy Roman Empire which was becoming more and
more of a hollow shell. While gathering and uniting diverse vassals and
subjects under their sovereign rule, the emerging kings of several emerging
nations in Europe also ensured that the Christian church of their realm
fell under their sway. By the sixteenth century, the Church of France, the
Church of England, and the Church of Spain, to name only a few, were
under the thumbs of their respective monarchs. Nobody, not even the
pope, could effect significant change in the churches of these countries
without the consent and assistance of the Crown.

So it was that political, social, and ecclesiastical circumstances made
for a continuing diversity within European Catholicism. When coupled
with the dynamism, or lack thereof, of various church leaders, it becomes apparent that the Catholic Church was anything but uniform on
the eve of the settlement and evangelization of Canada.

RELIGIOUS REVIVAL IN SEVENTEENTH-CENTURY FRANCE

During the century that separated Luther's launching of the Reformation in 1517 and the first permanent settlement of Québec in 1608, like
most European countries France was profoundly shaken and changed
by the Protestant and Catholic Reformations. The country divided into
a small but important and active Protestant (Reformed or Huguenot)
minority, and a Catholic majority that persecuted its minority. The two
religious parties fought through the Wars of Religion (1559–1598) and

the Thirty Years War (1618–1648), each witnessing and committing atrocities in the name of Christ, and this despite the Edict of Nantes of 1598 which decreed religious toleration for Protestants throughout the realm. Simultaneously, a major religious revival swept the country in the seventeenth century, a phenomenon that played a major role in the settlement and evangelization of Canada.

Just as France was founding its colonies of Acadia (1604) and Québec (1608), spiritual renewal got underway in a France that was only then getting around to implementing the decrees of the Council of Trent. The foremost leaders of this renewal were François de Sales (1567–1622) who was bishop of Geneva from 1602, and Pierre de Bérulle (1575–1629). François became the best known leader of French spirituality, having helped in the founding of the Visitandine nuns in 1610, and having written the very popular *Introduction to the Devout Life* (1609) and *Treatise on the Love of God* (1616). François taught the possibility of becoming saintly in all walks of life by the mere fulfillment of one's duty, providing it was done in the love of God and neighbour. The love and mercy of God thus came to the fore in a French spirituality where peasants, artisans, soldiers, kings, and maidens were called to Christian perfection trusting that it was within their grasp. This new theology undermined the prevalent doctrine of the day that salvation was reserved for a select few.

Bérulle, founder of the congregation of Oratorian priests in 1611, taught spirituality as being centred on the sovereign majesty of God, thus ensuring that the virtues of adoration and piety were to be foremost in the life of the Christian. This majestic and all-powerful but remote God could only be reached through his son Jesus the Christ, for mere human beings were considered incapable of doing so on their own. Therefore, Bérulle worked to place the Incarnate Word of God at the centre of his theology. This spiritual road required much self-denial and asceticism in order for the disciple to become worthy, requirements that proved less popular than those taught by François.

As the teachings and spirituality of these leaders spread far and wide, a host of new religious congregations of both men and women were founded in order to implement church renewal. Male groups already in existence included the sixteenth century's Jesuits, Capuchins, and *Récollets*. They were supplemented by new brotherhoods such as Bérulle's Oratorians, Vincent de Paul's (1567–1660) Lazarist Fathers, Jean Eudes' (1601–1680) Congregaton of Jesus and Mary

(Eudists), and Jean-Jacques Olier's (1608–1657) Gentlemen of Saint-Sulpice (Sulpicians).

The Catholic reform impulse in France included the founding of a most secret group that would profoundly influence the Canadian colony. The *Compagnie du Saint-Sacrement* (1627–1665) was established by Duke Henri de Lévy as a society of piety, apostolate, and social service. Its membership was restricted to influential, wealthy, and devoted men and women, both clerical and lay, who wanted to work discreetly in the interests of the Catholic Church. Many of the leaders of the early Canadian church were members of the *Compagnie*.

The four most important congregations of men active in early Canada were the Society of Jesus (Jesuits), the *Récollet* Friars, the Capuchins, and the Sulpicians. As was the case for the women, all were products of the renewal of the Catholic Church during the sixteenth and seventeenth centuries.

The Society of Jesus had been founded by the Spaniard Ignatius of Loyola (1495–1556) on the eve of the Council of Trent; the order was given papal approval in 1540. It rapidly became the Catholic Church's preferred instrument in a number of areas of endeavour including the founding and directing of colleges, the repression of Protestant teachings, and the evangelization of heathen lands. Jesuits, who would play the leading role in the evangelization of Canada and North America, soon became the most able, influential, and powerful order in the Catholic Church. They were the quintessential product of the Catholic Reformation. Indeed, by the early 1600s, Jesuit Father Pierre Coton (1564–1626) was the principal advisor on religious affairs to French King Henry IV, in addition to being his personal confessor.

The Jesuits, the new 'shock troops' of the church, who were highly disciplined and exceptionally well educated, added to the usual vows of poverty, chastity, and obedience a special vow of personal obedience to the pope. Moreover, their rule enabled them to be highly mobile as they wore no distinctive religious habit and were not required to recite the Holy Office in common at fixed daily hours as other monks were required to do. This remarkable band of educators and missionaries numbered more than one thousand men within twenty years of their founding, and more than 8,500 at the turn of the seventeenth century, on the eve of their coming to Canada. By that time, the Jesuit brotherhood was represented throughout Europe, the Americas, and in many countries of Africa and Asia including India, Malaya, Brazil, the Congo, Japan, Ethiopia and China. Ten years later, when Jesuits first set foot in Acadia in 1611, the order included fifty Jesuit houses that sheltered 1,200 men in France alone. By 1640, the French Jesuit establishment had grown to seventy houses and two thousand men. This powerful, determined, and dynamic religious order would set an indelible stamp on Canada.

Women had long been engaged in the religious life, but usually in cloisters, that is to say removed from daily life in society. So it was that after Angela Merici founded the order of St. Ursula, an important teaching order of women, in Brescia, Italy, in 1535, it was transformed into a cloistered order upon its development in France after 1612. By 1677, these cloistered nuns, who took solemn vows, directed three hundred convents in France alone. Ursulines were among the first nuns to set foot in Canada in 1639, the very first contingent of French nuns to leave their homeland for distant shores. They would do so in the company of a handful of nursing sisters, drawn from the growing number of religious women committed to social service during the religious revival in seventeenth-century France. Others included the Sisters of Charity founded by Vincent de Paul in 1633 and the nursing sisters that would come to Montréal in 1659 to assist Jeanne Mance. All of these religious women were part of sisterhoods that were founded during the reforming years of the sixteenth and seventeenth centuries.

A Eurocentric world view

Three fundamental factors determined the nature of the relationship between Europeans and the new nations encountered in America. First were the economic, political, and social reasons that drove these European Christians to find America, reasons such as the quest for riches and new resources of gold, spices, fish, and furs. A second factor was the profound uncertainty of the Europeans' own identity, an insecurity that resulted from the social, political, economic, and religious turmoil of the late Middle Ages. A third factor was the doctrine and theology of medieval Christianity, a teaching that divided the people of the world into the basic categories of Christian and heathen. The Christians were 'us,' the people chosen by God and called to salvation. All others needed to be evangelized and converted to Christianity. It was debatable whether these heathen, these others, had rights or even souls.

The long series of disasters and seemingly insoluble problems that bedeviled Europeans from the fourteenth to the sixteenth centuries are central in explaining the pessimism, the fear, the guilt, the cynicism, and the desperate search for salvation that characterized the Christian churches of the sixteenth and seventeenth centuries. Nor are these same factors to be forgotten in explaining the religious revivals of the seventeenth century, be it in England or France.

At the time of the 'discovery' of America by Columbus in 1492 and the later exploration and settlement of Canada by Europeans, these same Europeans were less and less certain of their own identity, because their own sense of being at home, the place that founded their view of the world, was more and more being doubted. Human beings are driven to "anchor meaning in place,"[4] yet Europeans weren't quite sure of the value of where they were, and consequently of who they were! They felt that they were adrift in an uncertain world. Lacking a secure identity and confidence in themselves, when they encountered others, outsiders, especially people who seemed very different from themselves, they were inclined to dominate them and impose their own customs and beliefs upon them as a means of reaffirming their own shaky foundations, or of recovering the identity that seemed to be slipping away from them.

So it was that new Frances, new Englands, and new Spains dotted the Americas after 1500. In imagining who these new people of the New World were, Europeans were inclined to invent an identity for them, without being overly concerned with discovering their real identity, the one resulting from the Amerindians' own sense of place and history. This was because the recognition and respect of the latter would have forced the Europeans to question their own identity, an exercise that they avoided instinctively. So it was that the profound insecurity of the European discoverers became a determining factor in their perception and their behaviour towards the new nations they encountered. Just as important, however, was the ideological framework in which they placed these new nations. This framework was defined by the church.[5]

From the thirteenth to the sixteenth centuries, papal thought on aboriginal rights developed gradually as Christians encountered people different from themselves, including Jews, Muslims, and various aboriginal nations both inside and outside Europe. These encounters resulted from the crusades, and from expansion and exploration into eastern Europe and Africa. Pope Innocent IV (1243–1254) initially affirmed but simultaneously relativized the heathen's "natural rights to possess property and to exercise political power."[6] Pope Innocent subordinated the infidel's rights to the right of the church to evangelize and make disciples of all nations. Other Catholic commentators of his day went so far as to deny the infidel any natural rights, justifying thereby any conquest by Christian powers, as was the case in the African conquests by the Portuguese in the fifteenth century. Whatever their particular position, all church spokesmen from the thirteenth century onwards were primarily concerned with the rights of the church resulting from its mission to evangelize. This remained the framework of the discussion until the sixteenth century.

Upon Columbus' landfall on the island of Hispaniola in 1492, his patrons, King Ferdinand and Queen Isabella, wanted legal jurisdiction over the new territories. They could not, however, claim ownership by right of discovery because the law of the day required that the country in question be uninhabited for such a claim to be valid, and Columbus had been greeted by native inhabitants. The monarchs therefore asked Pope Alexander VI (1431–1503) to grant Spain exclusive rights to evangelize the new people and simultaneously to adopt whatever measures might be necessary to achieve that objective.[7] This was the purpose of the papal bull *Inter Coetera* issued in 1493, a bull which forbade Portugal from setting foot in the new hemisphere west of the imaginary North-South line drawn from the North to the South pole one hundred leagues west of the Canary Islands. In light of the church's primary duty to evangelize all nations[8] the pope justified his decision by arguing that if they were to be evangelized, the native people had a right to the protection of the pope; since the latter was unable to provide such protection, he delegated his power to the Spanish crown whose duty it became.

In this, most Spaniards understood the papal bull as granting Spain, not protector's rights with a view towards evangelization, but rather exclusive ownership and dominion over all of the lands in question. This interpretation was challenged by Father Bartolomé de Las Casas (1474–1566) who witnessed the horrific exploitation of the native people by Spanish conquerors and settlers in Latin America. Las Casas became the most celebrated defender of the rights of the native people, maintaining that the papal documents of donation gave the crown a mission to evangelize in the territories in question. It was thus subject to church law. In fact, however, the agreement between the pope and the Spanish crown to delegate to the latter the supervision of the work of the church in the new world, the *real patronato* system, made the church into a tool of the state. Dominican Friar Antonio de Montesinos (d. 1530) had been instrumental in turning Las Casas into a determined critic of the Spanish exploitation of Amerindians. The preacher denounced the colonists' atrocities and defended the humanity of the Amerindians. The latter were subject to the *encomienda* system established by the Spanish, a system that differed little from slavery. Failing to obtain improvements in the colonies, Las Casas and some like-minded colleagues intervened in Rome. Pope Paul III then issued a series of documents defending the dignity and liberty of Amerindians. The most important of these was the bull *Sublimus Deus* promulgated on 2 June 1537. It defended the freedom and dignity of Amerindians who were acknowledged as being human beings, spoke of their natural right to private property, and forbade their enslavement under pain of excommunication from the church. The main reason behind the papal pronouncement was clearly the urgency and importance of the evangelization of Amerindians. Given that the scandalous behaviour of the Spanish colonists was showing the church in a very bad light and alienating native people, the pope felt that evangelization would become more difficult if not impossible. He therefore urged more civilized behaviour.

It was with this concern for evangelization that the pope spoke in favour of human rights, the latter being understood as a necessary condition for the former. "'Go ye and teach all nations.' He said all, without exception ... We ... consider ... that the Amerindians are truly men ... We define and declare by these our letters ... that ... the said Amerindians and all other people who may later be discovered by Christians are by no means to be deprived of their liberty or the possession of their property, even though they be outside the faith of Jesus Christ; and that they may and should freely and legitimately enjoy their liberty and the possession of their property; nor should they be in any way enslaved; should the contrary happen, it shall be null and of no effect."[9]

Although the official position of the Catholic Church was clear, in Spanish colonies among others, the interests of the church often clashed with those of the state. Royal patronage in Spanish crown lands prevented the church from enforcing its teaching, a teaching which conflicted with the interests of colonists and conquerors.

A stronger or a weaker Christianity?

On the eve of the encounter between Europeans and the Amerindians of Canada, Christianity was much diversified. This diversity was simultaneously institutional, national, doctrinal, theological, and social, and all of this both within and without Catholicism and Protestantism. It will rarely suffice to discuss what Christians are doing, without immediately specifying which specific Christians one is discussing. Yet these divided Christians are still one in other respects. Did this revolution in sixteenth-century Western Christianity weaken or strengthen the Christian church?

A divided Christian church

By the beginning of the seventeenth century, the institutional diversity of the Christian church was such that one may legitimately wonder if it was still possible to speak of one church. To the long-standing division between the Eastern Orthodox and the Catholics which dated back to the eleventh century, there had now been added the profound division in Western Christianity between Catholics and Protestants. Both of the latter were in turn divided for political, theological, social, and economic reasons.

The Protestant family of Christians had given birth to a growing number of denominations and sects including, but not limited to, the Church of England, the Lutheran Church, the Reformed Church of Geneva, the Reformed Church of France, the Presbyterian Church of Scotland, and the churches of the Mennonites, the Hutterites, and the Zwinglians. Most of these churches harboured dissenting groups, many of which soon emerged as distinct denominations in their own right, groups such as the Baptists, the Puritans, the Society of Friends (Quakers), and the Methodists.

Catholics were also divided, although they stood united in authority and discipline around the teachings and the church structures endorsed by Rome. In addition to diverse liturgical rites found among Catholics of the East and West, divisions were between competing religious orders and congregations, the numbers of which matched those of the Protestant denominations, or between church officials over questions of revenue or privilege; sometimes divergent theologies and spiritualities rent the Roman Catholic Church asunder, as was the case in the fight between Jansenists and Jesuits in seventeenth and eighteenth-century France. Indeed, in order to understand the religious history of New France, one must understand the differences between a Jesuit, a *Récollet*, and a Sulpician, an Ursuline and a nursing sister, a bishop and a priest, and a Gallican and an ultramontane. In the Catholic colony of Canada, disagreements rarely if ever centred on points of doctrine or theology, the issues separating the Catholics and the Protestants. The debates and most bitter disagreements usually arose out of the conflicting interests of different parties in the church and reflected the tensions and dissension existing within the parent countries.

Religious, theological divisions were further exacerbated and frequently overridden, by national rivalries. Europeans came to Canada at a time when their countries of origin were engaged in long-standing campaigns to put the *nation* at the heart of their people's identity, and the monarch at the centre of the nation, usually at the expense of the Christian faith, the foundation of the medieval identity. This meant that as the power of diverse monarchs waxed in their respective kingdoms the power of the church waned. So it was that the kings of England, France, and Spain, to name only the three European powers most engaged in North America, had effective control over their national and colonial churches. The pope was all too frequently left on the sidelines, as were the diverse Protestant churches. National rivalries all too frequently compounded religious divisions.

Religious, theological, and national causes of division within Western Christianity were compounded by economic and social ones. This was particularly evident in some of the Anabaptist churches such as the Mennonites and the Hutterites whose formation represented an exceptional social project and a rejection of the new all-powerful nation state. It also appears in the long-standing hierarchical separation and class divisions between the upper clergy (bishops) and the lower clergy (priests) in Catholicism.

A united Christian church

Yet, in spite of their perennial arguing, feuding, and fighting, in many ways these same Christians remained united. Indeed, Catholics and Protestants, Jansenists and Jesuits, Englishmen and Frenchmen all worshipped the same God, followed the same Jesus, acknowledged the Bible as God's revealed Word, agreed on some basic doctrines, shared many social attitudes, and believed in the necessity of an established church in their respective countries. Although this reality was often lost sight of in subsequent years, it is necessary to remind ourselves of it in our time when the growing presence of other religions in our society raises new questions about the relationship of Christianity to these other religions and to society at large.

Protestants and Catholics never questioned the central importance of the Bible as the revealed Word of God. While Protestants usually denied the infallible authority of the church in defining matters of faith, and stressed the exclusive authority of the Bible as a source of God's revelation, Catholics acknowledged the same authoritative Bible but taught that the church was the sole authoritative interpreter of both the letter and the spirit of God's Word. While this difference was considered a major one down to the mid-twentieth century, recent developments in historical and theological scholarship demonstrate a softening of the hard edges of the respective positions of both Catholics and Protestants.

While engaged in their lengthy family feud that began in the sixteenth century, Catholics and Protestants tended to forget that they shared many fundamental doctrines. They accepted the doctrinal definitions of the ecumenical councils of the early centuries of Christianity, statements that declared the distinct three persons of Father, Son, and Spirit in one God, and the union of fully human and fully divine natures in the one person of Christ. They agreed that Jesus was the one sent by his Father to redeem humankind, which is to liberate people from the sinful condition that tainted their existence. They agreed that Jesus rose from the dead three days after his death, ensuring thereby the resurrection of his chosen people after their death, and their life everlasting in the joyous bliss of the divine presence. They agreed that someone could only be saved by a purely gratuitous act of God, that is to say that a human being could not *earn* his or her eternal life by his or her own merits. They agreed that one became a member of the Christian church through baptism, a rite acknowledged as necessary for all Christians, and one that was usually acknowledged as valid regardless of the denomination in which it had been administered.

Catholics and Protestants also shared a common belief in the necessity of each state having an established church, that is to say an official religion that was supported by the state. This necessity was considered foundational for any state. In the wake of the Protestant Reformation, when governments divided in their loyalties to either the Catholic Church or one of the Protestant ones, it was agreed that the head of state would choose the established church, and the population of that state would be required to abide by that choice or leave the country, thus ensuring that each country remain uniform in its religious allegiance. Generally speaking, the idea of freedom of religion would have to await the Enlightenment of the eighteenth century and the American and French Revolutions.

The reverse of this coin was the shared belief in the illegitimacy of religious dissenters. Catholics believed that outside the church there was no salvation; and that church was the Roman Catholic one. So it was that Queen Mary of England had some three hundred Protestants put to death between 1555 and 1558 when they refused to recant. Protestants rebelled against this church and set up their own distinct ecclesiastical organizations; leaders such as Martin Luther proclaiming principles such as the necessity of freedom for the Christian, and the sole authority of the Bible, all the while damning, frequently in abusive and obscene language, the leadership and many of the teachings of Catholicism. Yet these same Protestants could not tolerate religious pluralism any more than the Catholics could. Luther himself condoned the massacre of rebellious peasants in 1525, and of Anabaptist religious rebels in Münster in 1535, feelings that were shared by other Protestant leaders such as Calvin and Ulrich Zwingli. In Geneva, Calvin directed the burning at the stake of several religious dissenters, including Michael Servetus in 1553. Together, Protestants and Catholics hunted down Anabaptists.

This agreement between Catholics and Protestants to persecute heretics, including each other, extended to other religious dissenters, such as Jews, Muslims, and witches. Indeed, in the year 1600, medieval ideology was still dominant in Europe. Dissenters had no rights because they held erroneous beliefs, the toleration of which could draw down the wrath of God on those who condoned or tolerated them. There was a measure of unity between Catholics and Protestants in this.

Did diversity strengthen or weaken Christianity?

Did the Christian church grow weaker or stronger as a result of the fragmentation that was described above? The answer depends in part on one's definition of the church, and in part on the portion of their spiritual resources that Christians devoted to fighting their religious enemy, Protestant, Catholic, Jew, or Muslim.

If by church one means a unified institutional structure with a central government, a clear hierarchy of powers, and an effective chain of command, then it is clear that the Protestant Reformation was a major obstacle to the establishment of such an institution, by Catholics or Protestants. One of the main tenets of Protestant theology was the reiteration of the direct personal relationship between the individual Christian and God, and the simultaneous weakening of the authority and place of the church in that relationship. The importance of mediation between the Christian and God was reduced by the Protestant reformers. Protestants denied the value of sacraments as Catholics understood them, that is to say as visible and effective signs of God's grace. This greater individualism favoured by Protestant theology served to weaken the communal nature of Catholicism, wherein the Christian community held much greater sway, be it in the authority of the priest, the power of the church to interpret and define doctrine, or the disciplinary rules that were applied.

However, if by church one means not the institution, but the community of the saints, of the virtuous, of those who live under the sign of the Gospel, then it is not at all clear that the Protestant Reformation weakened Christianity. The case can be made that the Protestant Reformation resulted because of intensified Christian concern, and then provoked a reaction among Catholics that was also driven by evangelical concern. The intense rivalry and competition that ensued would have been another manifestation of the renewed Christianity that characterized all Christian churches in the West. In spite of all its wrongs, abuses, and exaggerations, this revitalized Christianity would have been instrumental in discovering and promoting Christian values that may otherwise have remained hidden and undeveloped. In support of this thesis, it is to be remembered that most if not all of the leaders of the developing civilization of the scientific revolution of seventeenth-century Europe and of the Enlightenment of eighteenth-century Europe were Christians. The new values of brotherhood, equality, and freedom, whether of religion, of conscience, of thought, or of association, values that became the badge of distinction of the American and French revolutions, can all be based on Christian sources. In this view, the Reformations and their resultant religious diversities became the springboard for the expansion and strengthening of Christianity, in spite of its concomitant institutional fragmentation.

Those who hold the first view are inclined to focus on the diminished capacity of the fragmented church as an institution to act in a concerted way in response to the major issues of our time, be it in the matter of Third World famine and underdevelopment, environmental disasters, and the growing gap between rich and poor in our society. Indeed, Christians must now negotiate consensus; nobody is in a position to impose anything. Those who hold the second view are more inclined to focus on the liberty that is guaranteed all Christians by the divided institutional structures, be it in matters of belief or of practices within and without the churches. In fact, the coexistence of multiple churches and denominations may be imposing democratic values on Christians who, willy-nilly, are compelled to negotiate with each other and take serious account of the other if they want to achieve anything together. Does this not amount to a stronger Christianity?

The historical record does not allow us to resolve this debate at the present time. On the one hand it is clear that fragmented Christian institutional structures have diminished the quality of Christian response to various major challenges over the years; on the other hand has that same fragmentation not driven Christians to adopt more energetic responses? If on the one hand, institutional fragmentation has forced Christians to talk to one another, is it not also true on the other hand, that these same divisions and debates have represented a great waste of time and energy, resources that could have been utilized more productively elsewhere?

It was this united/divided Christian church that undertook the evangelization of Canada!

Suggested readings

Carroll, James. *Constantine's Sword. The Church and the Jews.* Boston & New York: Houghton Mifflin, 2001.

Le Roy Ladurie, E. *L'Ancien Régime.* Vols. I and II, Paris: Hachette, 1991.

Lindberg, Carter. *The European Reformations.* Cambridge Mass: Blackwell Publishers, 1996.

Rapley, Elizabeth. *The Dévotes: Women and Church in Seventeenth-Century France.* Montréal & Kingston: McGill-Queen's University Press, 1990.

CHAPTER 4

The Encounter between Amerindians and Europeans

Amerindians flourished undisturbed by Europeans until about the beginning of the second millennium. When contact occurred thereafter, it would gradually become apparent that the intruders from across the North Atlantic were driven by motives very different from those of the Amerindians. Explorers, fishers, traders, settlers, and missionaries all participated in the initial contacts, and all shared in the praise or blame that was incurred in the process.

Europeans discover the Americas

The earliest reliable evidence of a European presence in North America dates back to about 1000 C.E. when ancient Scandinavian seafarers, the Norse, extended their Greenland colony onto the coasts of Newfoundland and Labrador. Incontrovertible evidence of such a settlement has been found at L'Anse aux Meadows on the northern tip of Newfoundland, a site that has been declared a world heritage site by the United Nations. It seems that these colonies were very short-lived because of the hostility that developed between native people and the newcomers. During the subsequent half millennium, although further fur trading and contacts may have occurred, there is no convincing evidence of it.

Beginning late in the fourteenth century, Europeans began exploring anew. Initially supported by funding from Genoa, subsequent exploration grew out of the enterprising spirit of the Portuguese who were seeking new resources in fish, spices, slaves, and gold. They sent ships down the west coast of Africa and westwards into the Atlantic where they discovered in turn the Canary Islands before 1400, the Madeira Islands by 1420, and the Azores in 1427. Eventually, in 1488, the Portuguese navigator Bartholomew Diaz rounded the Cape of Good Hope on the southern tip of the continent of Africa.

It was also in a quest for new sources of riches derived from spices from the Orient that late in this same fifteenth century the kings of Spain and of England commissioned the Italian navigators Christopher Columbus and John Cabot respectively to seek new lands. Columbus discovered the Caribbean in 1492, while Cabot was the first to report on the northeast coast of North America in 1497. Simultaneously, fishers from Bristol in England, Normandy, Brittany, and the Basque country set sail to the west in order to discover new fishing grounds. They came upon the Grand Banks of eastern North America, one of the richest fishing areas in the world. From 1500 onwards, the region was being visited by a growing number of fishing boats every year, and various European countries such as Spain, Portugal, France, and England played leading roles in the exploitation of the region's resources.

This growing European presence off the coast of eastern North America was made possible not only by the enterprising spirit of various kings and explorers, but also by the major improvements in the technology of the sixteenth century. Ships were longer and more maneuverable; carried more masts and more effective sails that permitted the use of side winds; had more decks and could thus carry more cargo. Improved mapmaking and better navigational instruments allowed for longer and safer voyages. In addition, because of the accumulation of capital by various trading companies, a growing number of entrepreneurs had the means to underwrite the construction of large ships, the hiring of crews, and the undertaking of time-consuming and expensive voyages with a view to conducting profitable trade.

Once North America was discovered, the next step was to find a passage through it to the seas of the Far East in order to engage in more profitable trade. With this in mind, various European powers commissioned explorers such as Gaspar Corte-Real (1500–1501) who explored Canada's eastern coast for Portugal, and Juan Ponce de Leon who in 1513 explored the southern coast of the U.S. for Spain. Once Magellan had circumnavigated the globe in 1522, it was apparent that no sea passage existed between the Atlantic and the Pacific between Florida and the southern tip of South America. Thereafter, explorers sought a strait through North America. This was the commission the king of

France gave to Giovanni da Verrazzano in 1524; the latter explored the eastern seaboard of the U.S. for naught.

It was with a similar purpose that Jacques Cartier went to explore the Gulf of St Lawrence and then the St Lawrence River beginning in 1534. During his second voyage of 1535–1536, he wintered at Québec after having visited Montréal (Hochelaga) during the autumn. Cartier returned to Canada in the employ of Roberval in 1541, leading a group of some 150 settlers. They returned to France after one winter, having suffered the loss of more than thirty of their people to Amerindian attacks. The latter were perhaps less than pleased at Cartier's having kidnapped a dozen of their youth during his previous voyages between 1534 and 1536. Then Roberval arrived in the summer of 1542, reestablished Cartier's recently-abandoned settlement at Québec, and in turn decamped after only one winter of misery and cold. Thereafter, France would wait more than a half-century before any further attempts at colonization in Canada.

Meanwhile the Portuguese, Breton, and Norman fishers intensified their activities around Newfoundland, the Strait of Belle Isle, and Cape Breton becoming two of their primary areas. The English became more and more involved on the Grand Banks, while the French moved into the Gulf of St Lawrence.

Throughout the sixteenth century, while fishing was the primary activity of the growing number of European ships, a secondary activity was trading with the Amerindians who were encountered ashore. Upon his first voyage in 1534, Cartier had met Iroquoian Amerindians at Baie des Chaleurs and Gaspé; they sought iron hatchets and knives in exchange for their furs. Until 1580 the main centre of this trade was in the Strait of Belle Isle where fishers visited regularly, particularly the Spanish Basques; then it moved upriver to Tadoussac at the mouth of the Saguenay River. Thus by the eve of French settlement in Canada, Tadoussac had become North America's foremost centre for trade, some ships dedicated exclusively to fur trading appearing after 1580.

By 1600, when the French were seriously contemplating founding permanent settlements in Canada, there had already been a century of frequent, but seasonal, contact with Amerindians. The latter had become familiar with a number of European tools and implements which they obtained in exchange for the furs which Europeans sought more and more persistently in order to meet a growing demand in the European market. The founding of permanent colonies at Port Royal in 1605, and especially at Québec in 1608, marked the beginning of a new phase in Amerindian-French relations.

The diverging agendas of Europeans and Amerindians

Aside from random and scattered comments by some earlier explorers like Cartier, written information of any substance about the encounters between Europeans and Amerindians on Canada's east coast dates from the beginning of the seventeenth century at the earliest. This was when the young Paris notary Marc Lescarbot in Port Royal (1606–1607), Jesuit Father Pierre Biard in Acadia (1611–1613), and Governor Samuel de Champlain in Québec (1608–1635), described and commented on their encounters with Amerindians. The latter soon discovered that the new immigrants to their country were very different from all the other nations that they had dealt with.

When they came to Canada, the Europeans were bent on acquiring goods and on imposing their cultural values, religious values included. Such an agenda clashed with that of the Amerindian people for whom most goods were intended to be shared, and for whom religious values, being fundamental to one's cultural heritage, were also to be shared.

The agenda of the Franco-Europeans

Contrary to the Amerindians with their egalitarian social organization, the French, like most Europeans came from a hierarchical society, one where every human being was pigeon-holed in a particular social, economic, and religious class. In France, one could belong to the aristocracy, the clergy, the bourgeoisie, or the peasantry; one could be a free man or a slave, king or subject, rich or poor, man or woman, faithful, heretic or infidel, saint or sinner. The particular combination of labels that any of the king's subjects wore entailed a wide range of social consequences.

This sense of hierarchy was so deeply ingrained in French culture that it determined one's attitude and behaviour towards others, before any personal considerations were taken into account. For example, a child was always to be educated in a set manner, a nobleman had to be treated with due courtesy, a clergyman was due a series of privileges, an unrepentant infidel or a witch could be put to death, and a baptized Christian of whatever ethnic origin enjoyed a number of social privileges that unbelievers did not.

This sense of hierarchy enjoined respect for the authority of those in power. For example, Amerindians decided to go to war by consensus, each warrior remained free to return home whenever he desired, and their war chiefs were elected because of their proven courage in battle. In other words, an Amerindian warrior only obeyed his war chief if he chose to, and because of the respect he had for the man's proven military worth. By contrast, the French armies were composed of conscripts forced into service and bound to remain in service until released; they were commanded by officers appointed by the king, who selected them from the ranks of the aristocracy, and frequently did so not on their military merits, but rather on the basis of their financial and political contributions to the crown. In other words, the soldier had to obey an officer, even if the latter was manifestly incompetent and unworthy.

The same authority structure applied in religious affairs. The French Catholic faithful were usually born and baptized into the Catholic Church, and spent their entire lives under the religious guidance and supervision of clergy whom they had no say in selecting or dismissing. One became a cleric by ordination, a sacramental rite administered by a bishop to those whom he chose. The bishop's authority was strong. In fact, one of the central thrusts of the reformation of the Catholic Church in France during the seventeenth century was to reinforce the authority of bishops under the pope. Through its bishops and priests, the Catholic Church taught its people the way to salvation, and did not hesitate to condemn harshly unacceptable behaviour. Everyone was expected to obey superiors, obedience being promoted as one of the prime virtues of the good Christian. Members of religious orders even made a special vow of obedience.

Contrary to Amerindian egalitarianism in matters spiritual, the French were thoroughly hierarchical. In the church pecking order, clergy were understood to stand above ordinary faithful, priests above other clergy, and bishops above priests. Members of religious orders were said to have chosen the way of perfection, a state of life that was held to be superior to all others. Among religious, those who chose the monastic life were considered the best of the best. Then gender and social values coloured the church hierarchical structure. Women religious were usually supervised by male clerics, and the poor frequently belonged to religious orders that were distinct from the orders of the rich. Hierarchical values and their concomitant authority structures permeated the Church of France. The French could neither approve nor accept the contrasting egalitarian world of Canada's Amerindians.

Since seventeenth-century Europeans also considered themselves to be superior to Amerindians, this sense of superiority proved to be another basic cause of misunderstanding, injustice, and conflict between the French and the Amerindians.

On the face of it, this sweeping cultural confidence that the French had in their own superiority resulted from their technologically more advanced society. This confidence, however, resulted in turn from a conviction that their greater advancement in technology and civilization was due to the fact that as Catholic Christians, they had cornered the market on truth. In other words, they simply 'knew better' because they had received Christian Revelation, whereas the Amerindians had not. Therefore, it was their duty to preach the Gospel to the Amerindians and to take every possible means to convert them to Christianity. Like all pagans and infidels, Amerindians were to be dealt with kindly, but firmly; and if necessary, financial and political leverage could be employed to achieve religious ends.

As is often the case with leading world powers, the seventeenth-century French were not inclined to distinguish readily between their religion and French-European culture. What was considered good for France was understood to be good for Christianity and vice versa. Both tended to blend into one policy towards the Amerindians. This French ethnocentrism and sense of cultural superiority was then reinforced by the Christian theology that prevailed at the time, a theology that categorized all religions and all doctrines in terms of intellectual truth and error. Only the truth could make one free and lead one to salvation. And only the Catholic Church taught the full truth in matters religious. Christianity was by definition the only true religion; outside of the church there was no salvation. Therefore all other religions were erroneous to varying degrees, and the further removed they were from Catholic Christianity, the more erroneous they were. The religions of the Amerindians were so far removed from Christianity that they could hardly be included on the Christian scale of truth. These religions were condemned outright as mere savagery and witchcraft. This conviction of having a monopoly on the truth grounded the belief of the French in their superiority. It prevented them from developing any meaningful understanding of Amerindian spiritualities because the latter were categorized as false from the outset. It was the same conviction that underlay the arrogance of all Europeans of the period, an arrogance that was both ethnocultural and religious.

In the eyes of the French, as of the British and the Spanish, this ethnocultural and religious superiority legitimated their conquest and subjugation of various Amerindian tribes. Whenever deemed necessary by the French, the Amerindians were induced or forced into ceding land and entire regions to the newcomers. Although the French never indulged in such behaviour on the scale of their British rivals to the south, the reason was most likely that the small French population of Canada did not need any more land than it had. In trade, the French did not prove any more generous than they had to be as they endeavoured, like all traders, to obtain the most for the least.

Religious conquest was also very much part of the agenda of the French. The Catholicism that issued from the Council of Trent and the seventeenth-century reformed Church of France constituted a powerful, aggressive, and conquering religious force. Militant apostolic workers such as the Jesuits felt that God had entrusted them with the mission of evangelizing the world, a task that they undertook with zeal, talent, and determination. In spite of daunting hardship and obstacles, the Jesuit missionaries remained dedicated to their chosen Amerindian missions throughout the Americas. The Amerindians were to be converted to the true religion, at whatever cost. In this, the missionaries enjoyed the full support of the French crown.

Since the days of Francis Parkman who wrote a century ago, it has been commonplace to judge the behaviour of the French in North America more leniently than that of the British and Spanish. Time and again, historians have cited Parkman's famous words: "Spanish civilization crushed the Amerindian; English civilization scorned and neglected him; French civilization embraced and cherished him."[1] Whatever the truth of Parkman's conclusion, it must be remembered that during the French regime in Canada, the French were never numerous, consisting of tiny settlements that were few and far between. Indeed, by the time of the British conquest and after 150 years in Canada, French Canadians numbered only about 60,000. Their numbers never threatened Amerindian control of the land, given that their main area of settlement, the valley of the St Lawrence, had been devoid of permanent Amerindian residents when the French arrived in the seventeenth century. Moreover, the fur-trading French and the Amerindians needed each other, whereas the colonizing and numerous British contested with the Amerindians as rivals for the land. It is likely that the greater harmony that characterized French-Amerindian relations resulted more from these different social and economic situations than from any innate French or British cultural characteristics. In ideological and cultural terms, French cultural and religious arrogance was alive and well in the seventeenth century.

An example of such arrogance was the kidnapping of Amerindians, a practice that had begun with some of the early European explorers of the sixteenth century. Corte-Real did so in 1501 in order to sell his captives as slaves in Portugal. The following year, three Amerindians in native costume were presented to the court of King Henry VII in England, and seven Amerindians were brought to Normandy in 1509. It was noted earlier that Jacques Cartier kidnapped a dozen Amerindians during his two first voyages between 1534 and 1536. Given that these victims were usually seized against their will and usually died in Europe, it is not overly surprising that some Amerindian tribes became hostile to the French. In the light of such behaviour, it is not easy to accept Parkman's judgment that the French "embraced and cherished" the Amerindians. It may be said that Europeans generally, and the French in particular, came to Canada in a quest for 'gold, glory, and God.' Their hierarchical and authoritarian culture clashed with the egalitarian consensual one of the Amerindians.

The agenda of the Amerindians

In their dealings with the European newcomers, the Amerindians were primarily interested in obtaining iron cutting tools, such as knives and hatchets, and decorative ornaments made of copper or tin. Metal cooking pots, articles of clothing, blankets, and eventually brandy and muskets also became objects of exchange. All these items were traded for furs. As the years wore on, the Amerindians came to rely more and more on these European products, to the point that by the 1630s they felt that they could not do without them. This was not only because of the greater efficiency and durability of metal products, but also because of the great advantage provided by guns in both hunting and war. Indeed, in inter-tribal war such as that between Huron and Iroquois, the party with the firearms was almost guaranteed victory. Once French settlement began in the seventeenth century, however, and more specifically once the Jesuit missionaries were in place, the Huron trading partners of the French were told that in order for trade to continue they would be required to allow the missionaries to reside with them in their villages. French colonial officials were making Christian evangelization a necessary condition of continued trading.

In addition, those Amerindians who were baptized Christians were given preferential treatment by the French in several ways. When engaged in trading at Québec and Trois-Rivières, Christian Amerindians could obtain goods at the same prices as did French traders, whereas non-Christian were charged significantly more. When exchanging presents with Amerindian trading partners, the French gave more presents to Christian Amerindians than they did to others. Indeed, in Huron villages, Christians were treated with special generosity, being given gifts of food, blankets, etc. Christian Amerindians were granted more honours by French officials and traders, and were acknowledged as the preferred spokespersons in negotiations. Moreover, after 1643, Huron traders were publicly separated by the French into distinct Christian and non-Christian groups whenever they traded at Québec and Trois-Rivières. After 1641, when the French began selling firearms to Amerindian allies, this official discrimination also applied. They would only sell the coveted weapons to baptized Amerindians, thereby providing Amerindian men with strong motivation to seek baptism. Even the dullest of observers soon could not help but notice that there were distinct and important economic, political, and military privileges associated with becoming a Christian.

In spite of the above incentives, the conversion of the Amerindians to Christianity was a long, slow, and difficult process. Other than the random work of itinerant missionaries among various tribes like the Mi'kmaq and the Algonquin, it was the concerted efforts of the Jesuits among the Huron between 1634 and 1650 that took centre stage in the story of missions in Canada. During the first three years of Jesuit residence in Huronia (1634–1637), only one healthy adult was baptized, all other baptisms having been administered to the sick and dying. As late as 1641, after seven years in the country, and after having been insulted, threatened, beaten, and stoned, Father de Brébeuf could report only sixty Christian Hurons in his congregation. But the tide was turning. Indeed, the missionaries reported to their superiors that between 1640 and 1643, they had baptized one hundred Hurons each year, the number increasing to 150 annually thereafter. By 1646 the same missionaries reported 500 Hurons professing the Christian faith, and the numbers and rate of conversion increased thereafter to the point that in 1649 one Huron in two was Christian. Hurons were converting to Christianity by the hundreds. In 1649–50, the last terrible year of misery and deprivation in Huronia, the Jesuit Father Superior Paul Ragueneau reported three thousand baptisms.

In fact, until the destruction of their nation by their traditional adversaries became imminent, the majority of the Huron people remained faithful to their traditional religion. The traditionalists successfully resisted the efforts of the Jesuit missionaries, at least until 1646. Thereafter, they began to lose ground rapidly before the threatened destruction of their society. The devastating Iroquois onslaught made the Huron people lose confidence in their traditional spirits. In desperation, a growing number turned to the God of the Christians.

A similar tale of Christian missionary activity unfolded among the Five Nations Iroquois. There, among the long-standing enemies of the Huron and the French, the Jesuits had only managed to establish their first resident mission in 1656. The mission of Sainte-Marie de Ganentaha among the Onondaga lasted only two years until the French fled surreptitiously in the spring of 1658, after learning that the Mohawk planned to massacre them. Thereafter, the Jesuits managed to send missionaries to each of the Five Nations between 1668 and 1688, the period of peace between the Iroquois and French that resulted from the peace agreement of 1667.

The French never gained the economic ascendancy over the Iroquois that they had enjoyed over the Huron. As a result most Iroquois felt no economic necessity to convert. Also, given that the Iroquois obtained their firearms from the English on the Hudson River, they felt no military necessity to convert to the religion of the French. In fact, the Iroquois were divided into pro-French and anti-French factions. Many who belonged to the pro-French faction were in fact Huron refugees who had been accepted into the depleted ranks of the Five Nations subsequent to the destruction of Huronia. It was this pro-French faction that made up the bulk of those who moved to the Jesuit-run Amerindian village of Laprairie after the peace of 1667, the village that eventually settled at Kahnawake (Caughnawaga) in 1716 after four displacements.

The conflicting agendas of the Amerindians and the French emerge clearly upon analysis of the story of their encounter in Canada during the sixteenth and seventeenth centuries. The specific place of the missionary in this encounter remains to be considered.

The missionaries encounter the Amerindians

Although Christian missions will be studied in Chapter 5, because of the major role of the missionaries in the early encounter between Europeans and Amerindians, brief consideration of their objectives and role is warranted here.

Let us begin by restating the obvious: the primary objective of all missionaries was evangelization; all other considerations whether national, cultural, economic, or political were secondary. However, Christian evangelization of Amerindians immediately raised the question of the degree of European civilization that should accompany it. Whereas all missionaries including the *Récollets*, the Québec Seminary priests, the Sulpicians, and the Jesuits were intent upon evangelization, they frequently differed on the degree of civilization that they felt was desirable in order to achieve that objective. As will be noted later, all the French missionaries to early Canada soon realized that some degree of civilization of the Amerindians was desirable and necessary; they did not agree on the extent of such civilization.

In the process of converting Amerindians, the *Récollets* preferred to enjoy the benefits of civilization more than did the Jesuits. This is indicated by the few Amerindian missions undertaken by the *Récollets*, and by their tendency to stay within French posts when in Amerindian country. In Canada, the *Récollets* usually served as chaplains to the French, and not as missionaries to the Amerindians.

The Jesuits attributed less importance to European civilization in the process of evangelization. In fact, Jesuits looked askance at many of the bad habits of their French coreligionists and sought to insulate their Amerindian people from them. They did not seek the founding of large colonies in Amerindian areas; indeed they feared them. Jesuits founded separate villages for Christian Amerindians, were more open-minded towards others, and tolerant of cultural differences. Much of our knowledge of Amerindian life and societies is drawn from the correspondence of Jesuit missionaries. The latter excel in providing detailed, oftentimes sympathetic and understanding descriptions of the ways of the Amerindian people they served, acknowledging the latter's virtues and qualities, and frequently making comparisons with some of the less than admirable ways of their French coreligionists. At times the Jesuits noted that some of the behaviour of the Amerindians was more Christian than that of the French. The Jesuits clearly gave priority to evangelization over civilization.

The negative side of the Jesuit campaign of evangelization was aimed at the destruction of the native religions. Jesuits forbade members of their flock to use dreams as guides, to use charms for good luck, to consult shamans, and to participate in public feasts and celebrations because of their religious significance. They were not to comply with findings and decisions based on divination, were not to rebury their dead at the periodic Feast of the Dead,[2] were to work towards establishing distinct Christian cemeteries, and were not to fight alongside traditionalist warriors in battle.

The positive side of the Jesuit campaign was the teaching by word, deed, and example of the fullness of Christian doctrine and practice in its French Catholic form. This meant continual preaching, catechism teaching, personal counsel, works of mercy, and the administration of sacraments whenever possible. In Huronia, once the Christians became sufficiently numerous in some villages after 1645, Christian public expression included crosses carved on trees, processions, public prayers, and the reciting of Bible stories in lieu of Huron myths at public events. This led to quarrels with traditionalists and divisions within Huron society.

Aside from sporadic visits of a few clergymen to the coasts of North America during the sixteenth century, visits such as those of the Church of England chaplain Robert Wolfall to Baffin Island in 1577 and of the three clergymen who accompanied Pierre du Gua de Monts' first expedition to Acadia in 1604–05, the first encounter of any significance between a Christian clergyman and Amerindians was that of the secular priest Jessé Fléché in Port Royal in 1610. When the colony of Port Royal was re-established in 1610 by Jean de Biencourt de Poutrincourt, a colleague of the first founder de Monts, de Poutrincourt was required by the terms of his contract with the French crown to evangelize the Amerindians of Acadia in the Catholic faith. Intent upon appearing to comply with this requirement, he was not eager to do more Catholic evangelization than was necessary to satisfy the letter of the law. De Poutrincourt was concerned lest the dreaded Jesuits manage to set foot in Acadia, an area over which he held a commercial monopoly. Indeed, because of their power, zeal, and dedication, Jesuits could be troublesome companions for an entrepreneur solely interested in commercial gain. Indeed, the Jesuits had had two of their men waiting to embark since 1608, but de Poutrincourt managed to set sail from Dieppe on 25 February 1610 without the Jesuits on board. De Poutrincourt felt that he could best keep them at bay in France, by showing the French government that their services were not needed, given that another missionary was in place. With this in mind, he recruited the secular priest Jessé Fléché to serve as a missionary in Acadia.

In order to better convince the court that Jesuits were not needed in Acadia, upon his arrival in Port Royal in the spring of 1610, Fléché immediately set out to baptize as many Amerindians as possible, thereby casting the de Poutrincourts, father and son, in a favourable light. So it was that on 24 June 1610, within one month of having set foot on the shores of the Bay of Fundy, Father Fléché baptized Mi'kmaq chief

Membertou and his family. Before returning to France one year later, Fléché had baptized more than one hundred Amerindians.

In France, the Jesuits had only managed to overcome the obstruction of the Protestant owners of the commercial charter, and gain passage to Acadia, by having a wealthy and pious friend of theirs, the Marquise de Guercheville, first lady in waiting to the queen, buy shares in the commercial company and then give them to the Society of Jesus. Upon arriving in the tiny settlement of Port Royal on 22 May 1611, Jesuits Pierre Biard and Enémond Massé were scandalized at the irresponsible behaviour of their priestly predecessor in baptizing any and all.

In 1611, it was Jean de Biencourt, the son of de Poutrincourt, who was in command of Port Royal. From the outset, the Jesuits were embroiled in controversy with de Biencourt, arguing over a wide range of issues such as the place of burial of Chief Membertou, the punishment of a man accused of rape, and various civil matters. This led Father Biard to excommunicate de Biencourt, who retaliated by forbidding the missionaries to visit Amerindian bands distant from the post, while simultaneously refusing them passage on board ships returning to France. The continued wrangling during 1611 and 1612 led the Jesuit benefactress de Guercheville to purchase a controlling interest in the trading company, to discredit the de Poutrincourt family, and to charter and equip a ship that removed the Jesuits and their mission from Port Royal and led them to found a new mission on Mount Desert Island, across the Bay of Fundy at the mouth of the Penobscot River. This was the mission of Saint-Sauveur, the fledgling mission that was attacked and razed by New England Captain Samuel Argall two months later in July 1613, thereby sealing the fate of the first Jesuit mission in Canada. Four months later, Argall would deal in similar fashion with Port Royal.

Despite the discreditable relations between the various French players in this Acadian story, the story of the encounters between the Amerindians and the missionaries revealed both the friendly disposition of the Amerindians and the missionary policy of the French. Father Fléché's hasty group baptisms of dozens of Amerindians were a reminder of earlier times in the tribal lands of Europe, a policy that would rarely be repeated in Canada. The Society of Jesus adopted a very different policy.

The Jesuit missionaries began by establishing friendly relations with the native people, a policy that would become a mainstay of their work in Canada. They also undertook to learn the languages of the

Amerindians, another practice that would become standard Jesuit policy in the missions of North America. Moreover, the friendly relations and the learning of native languages was only possible because the Jesuits decided that they should live with the Amerindians, rather than remain isolated in the French outposts. In addition, upon arriving on the scene, the Jesuits roundly condemned the missionary policy of Father Fléché, insisting that a minimum of instruction in the Christian faith be required before administering baptism. The broad strokes delineating French Catholic missionary policy were thereafter in place. This friendship and respect for the Amerindians would stand as the bedrock upon which rested all other elements of the policy of the missionaries.

Although driven by the evangelical mandate to go forth and teach all nations in the spirit of Christian love, the work of the early French missionaries with the Amerindians was fraught with the pitfalls that resulted from the encounter of totally different cultures and religions. Although the Jesuits had not counted on the overwhelming difficulties involved in the evangelization of Canada's Amerindians, they adjusted as best they could. While always showing respect for the Amerindians and a willingness to be their friends, they also counted on the trading alliance between the French and the Hurons, among others, as a basis to facilitate their mission. They reinterpreted their own theology as much as they could, while learning Amerindian languages and residing among the Amerindians, all in the hope of making the Gospel relevant to Amerindians. In fact, when considered in the context of seventeenth-century European Christianity and in that of the activities of other teams of missionaries in Canada and elsewhere, the Jesuits proved exceptionally skillful in adapting their Christian mission to Amerindian cultures.

Suggested readings

Axtell, James. *After Columbus: Essays in the Ethnohistory of Colonial North America*. New York: Oxford University Press, 1988.

——. *The European and the Amerindian: Essays in the Ethnohistory of Colonial North America*. New York: Oxford University Press, 1981.

——. *The Invasion Within. The Contest of Cultures in North America*. New York: Oxford University Press, 1985.

Bailey, Alfred G. *The Conflict of European and Eastern Algonkian Cultures,*

1504–1700: A Study in Canadian Civilization. Toronto: University of Toronto Press, 1969.

Charlevoix, François-Xavier de. *Histoire et description générale de la Nouvelle-France.* 3 volumes. Paris: Nyon Fils, 1744, new printing Éditions Élysée, 1976.

Delâge, Denis. *Le pays renversé. Amérindiens et européens en Amérique du nord-est 1600–1664.* Montréal: Boréal Express, 1985, 1991.

Dickason, Olive Patricia. *The Myth of the Savage and the Beginnings of French Colonialism in the Americas.* Edmonton: University of Alberta Press, 1984.

Grant, John Webster. *Moon of Wintertime. Missionaries and the Amerindians of Canada in Encounter since 1534.* Toronto: University of Toronto Press, 1984.

Jaenen, Cornelius. *Friend and Foe. Aspects of French-Amerindian Cultural Contact in the Sixteenth and Seventeenth Centuries.* Toronto: McClelland & Stewart, 1976.

Jennings, Francis. *The Founders of America. From the Earliest Migrations to the Present.* New York: W. W. Norton & Company, 1993.

Jennings, Francis. *The Invasion of America: Amerindians, Colonialism, and the Cant of Conquest.* Chapel Hill: University of North Carolina Press, 1975.

Las Casas, Bartolomé. *History of the Indies.* New York: Harper & Row, 1971.

Muldoon, James. *Popes, Lawyers, and Infidels: The Church and the Non-Christian World 1250–1550.* Philadelphia: University of Pennsylvania Press, 1979.

Reid, Jennifer. *Myth, Symbol, and Colonial Encounter. British and Mi'kmaq in Acadia, 1700–1867.* Ottawa: University of Ottawa Press, 1995.

Sagard, Théodat Gabriel. *Histoire du Canada et voyages que les frères mineurs récollects y ont faicts pour la conversion des infideles.* 4 vols. New edition. Paris: Librairie Tross, 1866.

Trigger, Bruce G. *Natives and Newcomers: Canada's Heroic Age Reconsidered.* Kingston & Montréal: McGill-Queen's University Press, 1985.

Trudel, Marcel. *The Beginnings of New France 1524–1663.* Toronto: McClelland & Stewart, 1973.

CHAPTER 5

Missions of Many Kinds

What is Christian mission?

Evangelization in early and medieval Christianity

Deriving from the Latin *missio* and its verb *mittere*, meaning *to send*, the word *mission* has had multiple meanings in Christianity. In theology it has variously designated the mutual relations between the divine persons, the mandate given by God the Father to his Son, and that given to the Holy Spirit when he was sent to the apostles on the day of Pentecost. For most Christians, however, *mission* signifies communicating the Gospel to those who have yet to receive it.

The Christian concept of mission is grounded in the Old Testament teaching that all the people of the earth are ultimately called to share in the blessings promised to Abraham: "The Lord said to Abram, 'Go from your country and your kindred and your father's house to the land that I will show you. I will make of you a great nation, and I will bless you ... I will bless those who bless you ... ; and in you all the families of the earth shall be blessed.'"[1]

It is also grounded in the history of the Jews who, beginning in the third century B.C.E., engaged in proselytism in the eastern Mediterranean and Mesopotamia. Some Jews having translated their sacred scriptures into Greek,[2] the monotheism, moral teachings, and values of the Jews became accessible to outsiders. It was among these Jewish proselytes that the early Christian church made many of its first converts.

While there are many indications in the life of Jesus that he intended his mission to be universal, it was only after his death that some of his followers first taught the Gospel to non-Jews.[3] Indeed, Paul will be required to struggle to convince his Christian colleagues of the merits of proclaiming the Gospel to pagans without requiring that they submit to the Jewish requirement of circumcision.[4] In fact, it was Paul who developed the Christian theological grounds for mission. Opposing those of his Christian colleagues who wanted the church to remain tied to Judaism and its requirements, Paul argued that Abraham's blessing had been passed on to all nations by Christ who served as intermediary.[5] Paul argued that the resurrection of Christ marked the beginning of a new era, a "new creation" that demolished the wall of separation between Jews and Gentiles.[6] Therefore mission derived from the unique place of Christ in the history of salvation.[7] It was the overflowing love of Christ that made mission mandatory. Paul wrote: "Woe to me if I do not proclaim the Gospel."[8] The early Christian church was in total agreement, as the resurrected Christ is cited instructing his apostles as follows: "Go therefore and make disciples of all nations, baptizing them in the name of the Father and of the Son and of the Holy Spirit and teaching them to obey everything that I have commanded you. And remember, I am with you always, to the end of the age."[9]

The above oft-quoted passage from Matthew's Gospel summarized in a nutshell the attitude of the Christian church during the following fifteen centuries. It was the duty of the entire church to proclaim the Gospel (good news) or evangelize; the latter was not a specialized task reserved to special emissaries and limited to the initial communication of the Gospels. Evangelization or *mission* was the work of the church in its entirety, be it in preaching, proclaiming the Gospel, providing spiritual guidance, or leading communities in worship. The gathering of new people into the church was more often than not the result of a kind of spiritual contagion, rather than that of organized campaigns of recruitment.

Evangelizing the New World

This changed after Columbus landed in the Caribbean in 1492. Lacking the means to direct the evangelization of distant America, church authorities entrusted the evangelization of its inhabitants to the monarchs of Europe who were directing the discoveries of these new lands. Evangelization then became a specialized activity entrusted to these lay patrons, who in turn recruited religious orders to whom the task was delegated. The evangelical work of the church in the Americas became that of Dominicans, Franciscans, Jesuits, and others, all working under the thumbs of the governments of Spain, Portugal, and France, and charged with proclaiming the Gospel to Amerindians. When regular Catholic dioceses were formed in the Americas, their bishops did not have jurisdiction over the mission territories that remained the exclusive preserves of the religious orders.

This system of specialized and segregated evangelization remained in place, even after the Holy See established a central office for missions in Rome in 1622. This central Vatican office, the *Congregation De Propaganda Fide*, gradually took over the supervision of Catholic missions worldwide, thereby continuing the policy of keeping evangelization outside the jurisdiction of ordinary church ministers. The pope was primarily concerned with keeping in check the authority of lay patrons, usually the kings of Europe. He did not want evangelization to revert back into the hands of ordinary bishops.

In fact, it was only at Vatican Council II (1962–1965) that the Catholic church would revert to the policy of the first fifteen hundred years of Christian history, and make evangelization a responsibility of all the churches and of all the faithful.

Evangelizing Canada

So it was that from the time of its founding in the early seventeenth century, the church in Canada fell under the dual authority of the King of France and of the pope, the degree of power of each over the church changing over the years. Missions in Canada were usually directed by religious orders, the Jesuits in particular, whose superior in Québec enjoyed an authority equal to, and at times greater than, that of the bishop of Québec.

The context for the evangelization of Canada proved a most favourable one. It was noted above that Canada was settled during the major religious revival of seventeenth-century Catholicism in France. This meant that many of New France's explorers, settlers, and rulers were influenced by the heady religious wine that flowed in the home country. For example, Governor Samuel de Champlain, the founder of Québec (1570–1635) was a devout Catholic, as was Governor Paul de Chomedey de Maisonneuve (1612–1676), the founder of Montréal. These rulers were advised by a dynamic contingent of clergy who belonged to a varied list of religious orders or dioceses. All were supported by a legion of religious sisters who founded and staffed hospitals, schools, and services for the poor. They were also assisted by a number of lay people who adopted exceptional methods of personal sanctification, or devoted their lives to the works of the church – people like Jeanne Mance (1606–1673) who founded the first hospital in Montréal, or Kateri Tekakwitha (1656–1680), the Mohawk woman whose conversion to Christianity fulfilled the missionaries' fondest dreams. Clearly, nobody could ask for a more favourable setting to undertake the evangelization of a new land.

The missionary personnel: the men

Both men and women were engaged in evangelizing New France, although the women were primarily involved in providing social services within the white settlements themselves. Except for a handful of diocesan priests, members of religious orders bore the brunt of missionary work to Canada's Amerindian people. In descending order of importance, the societies of male missionaries were the Society of Jesus (Jesuits), the *Récollet* (*Récollet*) Friars, the Gentlemen of Saint-Sulpice (Sulpicians), and the priests of the Seminary of Québec. Given that the latter's missionary work was mainly conducted in the Mississippi River valley, it will not be discussed here.

The Récollet *Friars*

After the failure of the Jesuit mission in Acadia in 1613,[10] the *Récollet* Friars were the first religious order to return to New France, but to Canada rather than Acadia. Like that of Acadia, the Canadian colony had also been established by the trader Pierre du Gua de Monts who had obtained a trading monopoly in the St Lawrence River valley in 1608. Thereupon, he had organized the founding of the trading post of Québec, under the command of his lieutenant Samuel de Champlain. The latter, a devout Catholic, sought missionaries who could provide religious services to the tiny settlement and would evangelize the Amerindians of the region. The *Récollets* answered his call in 1615.

The *Récollets* were a reformed branch of the Franciscan Observants, the storied mendicants founded by Francis of Assisi in the thirteenth century. During the Catholic Reformation of the sixteenth century, the Franciscan Observants, the largest order in the Catholic Church, had subdivided under the pressure of various reformers. This led to the founding of the Capuchin friars in 1529, a Franciscan offshoot that practised a more ascetic lifestyle. Half a century later, in France, it also led to the founding of the *Récollets*, another Franciscan offshoot that valued poverty most highly.[11]

Having settled on the right bank of the St Charles River at Québec, the three *Récollet* priests and one brother were mainly concerned with the evangelization of Amerindians, despite their limited number.[12] Father Joseph Le Caron proved to be their foremost missionary. Upon his arrival in Québec in 1615, he undertook the long and arduous journey to the land of the Huron Amerindians on Georgian Bay in south-central Ontario. Closely followed by Champlain, both men wintered in Huronia, returning to Québec the following spring. After spending one year in France (1616–1617), Father Le Caron returned to Canada to evangelize the Montagnais Amerindians on the north shore of the St Lawrence below Québec. In 1623 he again canoed upriver to Huronia, thirteen hundred kilometres from Québec, in company with two *Récollet* colleagues, Father Nicholas Viel and Brother Gabriel Sagard. It was Sagard who later wrote a famous book describing the land and the people he discovered on his journey.[13] Except for another year 1625–1626 that he spent in France, Le Caron remained in Canada until the country was lost to the English in 1629.

The *Récollets* never numbered more than four men in Canada, a mere handful that tried to minister to the small Québec trading post, evangelize the Amerindians, and run a school for Amerindian children established in 1620.[14] They soon realized that the task was beyond their means; for example, between 1616 and 1622 Huronia was devoid of any missionary, while the Amerindians below Québec had only one missionary in their midst during the winters, in the seaport of Tadoussac. Therefore, in 1624 the friars decided to ask for reinforcements from France. When it was apparent that no more men were available from their own order, they asked influential friends to seek out the assistance of missionaries from other orders. It was Duke Lévy de Ventadour, the founder of the *Compagnie du Saint-Sacrement*, who obtained the services of the Society of Jesus for them.[15] Lévy had purchased the title of viceroy of New France in 1625, and was therefore in a position to be of assistance. Another reason for seeking assistance was the friars' disenchantment with the directors of the trading post of Québec whom they accused of obstructing their work. Given that the post was part of a monopoly granted by the crown to a particular trading company, and given that the company in question was owned and directed by Protestants, the de Caën family, the *Récollets* felt that the behaviour of these Protestant traders was reprehensible. The friars

Fig. 5.   Jesuits welcomed by the *Récollets*.[16] Charles William Jefferys. National Archives of Canada, c-028332.

rejoiced at the arrival of Jesuit reinforcements in 1625. Both orders would cooperate closely during the following four years of joint ministry in the colony.

If harmony characterized the first fourteen years of *Récollet* ministry, discord was more typical during their subsequent history in New France. After the 1629 takeover of Canada by David Kirke sailing under the flag of England, the country was returned to France in 1632. Thereupon, the *Récollets* hoped to return to their Canadian mission, only to discover that the government of France refused them authorization to do so. Instead, their erstwhile allies at Québec, the Jesuits, were granted exclusive ecclesiastical jurisdiction in the colony. Although the latter had not conspired in any way to exclude the *Récollets*, the friars convinced themselves that they had; they would thereafter bear a long-standing grudge against the disciples of Loyola, an antipathy that would poison the relations between the two missionary orders for many years after the *Récollets* returned to Canada in 1670.

Meanwhile, a handful of *Récollet* missionaries had worked in Acadia between 1619 and 1624, and again from 1630 to 1645. Capuchin friars also worked there between 1632 and 1667, but in distinct and rival trading posts. This, however, proved to be an even more difficult mission, because of the commercial, family, and national interests that clashed in that colony, until the English raider Thomas Sedgwick conquered it in 1654.[17]

The *Récollets* were brought back to Canada in 1670 by the colony's Intendant Jean Talon, with the specific purpose of foiling the work of the Jesuits, the influential missionaries whom Talon resented. The friars would prove only too willing to cooperate with their benefactor in his various and sometimes devious enterprises. In addition to reoccupying their old mission house on the St Charles River at Québec, the friars were appointed by Bishop François de Laval (1623–1708) to missions in Trois-Rivières, Percé on the Gaspé Peninsula, the St John River in New Brunswick, and Fort Frontenac (Kingston) on Lake Ontario. They were also the crown's preferred chaplains in various garrisons throughout New France.

During the last fourteen years of Bishop Laval's administration of the diocese of Québec (1670–1684), the friars managed to become embroiled in several ecclesiastical disputes in the colony. After the bishop had obtained an annual royal subsidy on their behalf, intended to replace their customary begging from door to door, the friars pocketed the grant and continued to beg.[18] Bishop Laval dismissed one of their men for indiscreet preaching and also refused to allow the *Récollets* to open a convent in Montréal. Then, reneging on their promise, the friars opened the chapel of their hospice in Québec to all faithful, thereby competing with other clergy for the revenues of the settlement. Outraged, in 1681 the bishop suspended all of the friars from exercising any ecclesiastical function in his diocese. The decree was in effect until 1684, the year of Laval's departure for France.

The Society of Jesus

Jesuits had first set foot in the French colony of Acadia in 1611, a region encompassing most of today's Atlantic provinces of Canada in addition to the state of Maine in the United States. It had first been settled by the French in 1604 when Pierre du Gua de Monts (1558–1628) obtained from King Henry IV the trading monopoly in the area in exchange for establishing sixty settlers per year in the new colony and winning over the native people to the Catholic faith. The Protestant de Monts was thus committed to spreading the Catholic faith. Although two priests and a Protestant minister had accompanied the initial settlement, their stay in the post of Port Royal on the Bay of Fundy was short-lived. The minister died, and both priests had returned to France before the colony was abandoned in 1607. Upon the reoccupation of Port Royal in 1610, the secular priest Jessé Fléché accompanied the expedition which was led by de Monts' colleague, Jean de Biencourt de Poutrincourt. Fléché's astounding missionary behaviour was noted above,[19] as were the difficulties the Jesuits encountered in dealing with de Biencourt. This first experiment in Jesuit missions in Canada was ended by the cannons of Samuel Argall in 1613.

Respected, admired, and feared as they were by most Catholics and Protestants, the Jesuits set an indelible stamp upon New France. Their work in Acadia has been recounted above.[20] In response to the invitation by the *Récollets* and Lévy, the superior of the Jesuit province of Paris designated three priests and two brothers to go to Canada. They were fathers Charles Lalemant (superior), Énémond Massé, and Jean de Brébeuf, and brothers François Charton and Gilbert Buret. They sailed from Dieppe on 24 April 1625, arriving in Québec on 15 June. They immediately set out to implement their strategy of evangelization.

While building a residence across the St Charles River from the *Récollets*, the Jesuits supported their hosts in their campaign to wrest control of the colony from the hands of the Protestant rulers of Québec.

They were strongly motivated to do so when they witnessed the open circulation of a slanderous pamphlet in the tiny settlement of Québec, a document that slandered the Jesuits of Paris with the full encouragement of Guillaume de Caën, the head of the trading company. Nor were they pleased when the company refused to allow them to ship supplies to their Québec mission in 1627, thus forcing the cessation of construction work on their new residence. The power of the Jesuit band was such that within two years of their arrival they had obtained from the French government of Cardinal Richelieu legislation that put an end to the interference by the Protestant company.

On 29 April 1627, the Company of New France, also known as the Company of One Hundred Associates, was created by royal charter. This new company purchased all of the rights to the colony of Canada, including a fur-trading monopoly. In return, it had to meet a number of conditions. Only Frenchmen and Catholics would be allowed to settle in Canada; more than four thousand settlers were to be brought to the country in the subsequent fifteen years; during the same fifteen-year period, the company was to cover the costs of worship services and obtain the services of three priests in each of the colony's settlements; new settlers were to be provided with cleared land, seed, and necessary lodging and sustenance for three years; and Amerindians who became Christians were to be considered natural-born Frenchmen. The crown and the church had now supplanted the previous Protestant commercial entrepreneurs in the running of the colony.

In spite of the necessary three-year delay (1629–1632) in implementing these measures because of the takeover of the colony by Kirke, these evangelical purposes became part of colonial policy after 1632. And given that for the next twenty-five years, the Jesuits were the only group of clergy in Canada, they were able to run their missions and direct the church of the colony with the support of the state, and without the opposition or competition of Protestants. In fact, the quarter-century between 1632 and 1657 became a golden age for the church in Canada, the high-water mark of the reformed Catholicism of France, an age of mystics and martyrs.

While rebuilding their residence of Notre-Dame-des-Anges on the St. Charles River, beginning in 1632 the sons of St. Ignatius launched a dynamic campaign of evangelization both within and without the settlement. By 1637 twenty-three priests and six brothers were at work in Canada, launching an epic story that lasted a generation. Directed by Father Paul Le Jeune, Jesuit missionaries worked with the itinerant

Montagnais hunters,[21] with the Hurons near Georgian Bay,[22] in the new settlement of Trois-Rivières,[23] on Miscou Island on the Baie des Chaleurs,[24] along the east coasts of New Brunswick and Nova Scotia, and at the new college which they founded in Québec in 1635.[25] The school for Amerindian boys which they founded at Québec in 1636 failed after a few years, the first example of several unsuccessful attempts by the Europeans to launch schools for Amerindians.

In an attempt to separate the Christian Amerindians from the corrupting influence of white society, the Jesuits established a series of distinct Amerindian villages or reservations, similar to the *reducciones* they established in South America. The first of these was founded at Sillery near Québec in 1637. Over the next few years, between one and two hundred Christian Algonquins and Montagnais lived there between winter hunting seasons which they spent in the forests. This reservation would fail after several years. Other Amerindian villages were on *Île d'Orléans* (1651) and at Lorette (1673) near Québec where the remnants of the Huron nation would retire. After the peace of 1668, the Jesuits founded an Amerindian village at La Prairie (1669) in the interests of Christian Mohawks. It moved four times to become Sault St Louis (1676) and later Caughnawaga (1714); more recently it was renamed Kahnawake. Saint-François on the Chaudière River (1683) was founded to serve the Christian Abenakis, and La Montagne in Montréal was a Sulpician post, later moved to Oka on Lac-des-Deux-Montagnes where the Ottawa River flows into the St Lawrence; recently, it was renamed Kahnesatake. Another Amerindian reservation would appear in 1755 farther up the St Lawrence River, the Catholic mission of St Regis, now renamed Akwesasne.[26] The most celebrated of the Jesuit missions was that to the Hurons which they undertook in 1626 when Father Brébeuf first journeyed upriver to evangelize the nation visited earlier by Father Le Caron. Brébeuf stayed with the Hurons until his recall to Québec in 1629. Following his return to Canada, in 1634 Brébeuf was appointed head of the renewed Huron mission of Sainte-Marie on the shores of Penetanguishene Bay on Georgian Bay.

Subsisting on a frugal diet of crushed Amerindian corn boiled in water (*sagamité*), sometimes enriched with dried fish, the missionaries lived in an Amerindian cabin, sleeping on a bed of bark. Beginning at 4:00 a.m., their daily schedule included meditation, Mass, the reception of Huron visitors, the teaching of catechism, and regular visits to cabins in search of those who were dying in order to baptize them. The latter part of the day included the recitation of prayers, the writing of letters, the study of languages, and discussion of the events of the day.

During the first five years of their ministry, the missionaries had to cope with the results of epidemics of smallpox and influenza that swept through the Huron country in 1634, 1636, and 1639, reducing the Huron population by almost two thirds, from 30,000 to 12,000 people. Previously unknown, the devastating diseases had arrived in the land of the Huron with the missionaries. Moreover, as the latter baptized all the dying people that they could find, it appeared to some Amerindians that the missionaries were in fact killing their victims, baptism constituting the *coup de grâce* delivered by the magician in the black robe. The fact that the missionaries did not succumb to the diseases proved to the same Amerindian critics that the Black Robes managed to protect themselves, while dealing out death to the Huron people. Some favoured putting the Jesuits to death, although they did not manage to convince their nations of this. Amerindian shamans, the local spiritual leaders, were also profoundly disturbed by the missionaries and their message; they encouraged their people to get rid of them.

When Father Jérôme Lalemant took over as head of the Huron mission in 1638, he not only organized the first census of the people, but also centralized Jesuit work in one post that would serve the entire region that included not only the Huron people, but also the Petuns of the Bruce peninsula, the more northerly Nipissings, and the Neutrals on the north shore of Lake Erie. This was Fort Sainte-Marie.[27] Built in 1639 on the Wye River, it constituted a miniature French village in the wilds of central Canada. Fort Sainte-Marie included residences for priests and lay workers, a chapel, a workshop, a hospital, a cemetery, a forge, and a farm with animals and cultivated fields. It had palisades with two bastions dominating the defensive perimeter. At the height of its activity in 1649, Fort Sainte-Marie sheltered sixteen priests, four religious brothers, and twenty-two lay workers[28] employed by the mission. The fort lasted ten years, being burned to the ground by the Jesuits themselves on 14 June 1649, because of the threat of an imminent assault by the enemy Iroquois who had been raiding and ravaging the surrounding area for several years.

After spending one year (1649–1650) hiding from the marauding Iroquois on adjacent St Joseph Island (Christian Island), the Jesuit missionaries and a starving remnant of three hundred Christian Hurons abandoned the area for Québec in 1650. After a short stay on Île d'Orléans they and other later arrivals put down roots at Lorette in 1673. The proud Huron confederacy was no more, as the remainder of their people scattered far and wide throughout central Canada, many becoming members of other Amerindian nations, particularly the Mohawk.

The next episode in the Jesuit story was written south of Lake Ontario, in the land of the Onondagas, another of the five nations that made up the Iroquois confederacy which, from the beginning of the colony, had tended to side with the Dutch and English enemies of the French.[29] The Jesuits got their first chance to send missionaries into the land of the Iroquois after 1653, when Father Simon Le Moyne began a series of annual visits to the Iroquois in the hope of establishing a lasting peace. Le Moyne's efforts resulted in the Onondaga accepting the founding of a Jesuit mission in their midst. In 1656 the Jesuits built a large mission station on the Oswego River south of Lake Ontario, hoping to repeat their former exploits among the Huron. It was called Sainte-Marie de Gannentaha. However, the mission was short-lived. In March of 1658, hearing of an imminent assault and intended massacre by the Onondaga, who would have been inspired to do so by the Mohawk, the French surreptitiously vacated the post and fled back to the St Lawrence. The Iroquois mission was no more.

In the wake of this second failure of a major missionary post in a decade, several Jesuits went back to France, marking the end of their most intensive missionary efforts in New France. Ten years later (1668), in the wake of a peace agreement that resulted from punitive raids by French troops in the land of the Iroquois, they would establish missions in each of the five Iroquois nations. These new missions lasted twenty years, until renewed hostilities between the French and the Iroquois in 1687 forced their closure. Subsequently, Jesuit missionary efforts among the Iroquois centred on the Christian villages or reservations noted above.

The final chapter in the Jesuit missionary story began in 1660 when Father René Ménard (1605–1661) was sent to explore Lake Superior, a region that had been abandoned since the Iroquois war against the Hurons. Travelling in the company of a band of Ottawa Amerindians who were returning to their homes in today's Michigan, Ménard was lost after wintering on the south shore of Lake Superior. Father Claude Allouez (1622–1689) took up the challenge four years later. In 1665 he founded the mission of the Holy Spirit at Chagouamigon at the south-western end of Lake Superior, in the neighbourhood of two villages of refugee Hurons and Algonquins. Starting from there, Father Allouez evangelized the immense basins of Lakes Superior, Michigan, Huron and Erie; he preached the Gospel to two dozen bands of Amerindians during a period of twenty-four years. This giant among missionaries founded a mission at De Père, Wisconsin, before establishing his headquarters at the new Jesuit residence at Sault Sainte-Marie, at the junction of lakes Superior and Huron. There it was that Allouez addressed the assembled chiefs of fourteen Amerindian nations on 14 June 1671, on the occasion of French emissary Daumont de Saint-Lusson's taking possession of the western country in the name of France.

Allouez ranged far and wide in his efforts to reach as many Amerindian nations as he could. In 1670 he had entered the country of the Illinois Amerindians southwest of Lake Michigan, in the company of Father Claude Dablon (1619–1697), another giant among missionaries. A Jesuit colleague, Jacques Marquette (1637–1675), in the region since 1668, founded a mission at Michilimackinac, at the entrance to Lake Michigan, and then, in 1673, set off in the company of the Canadian explorer Louis Jolliet to discover the Mississippi. Marquette died in the region in 1675. Several other Jesuit missionaries were active in the region of the upper great lakes before the end of the seventeenth century.[30] Their ministry was continued further afield in the land of the Illinois nation, on the Illinois River, by Father Jacques Gravier (1651–1708) among others, and then on the upper Mississippi River in the eighteenth century by both Jesuits and Seminary priests from Québec.[31]

Without a doubt, Jesuits were New France's foremost missionaries.

The Gentlemen of Saint-Sulpice

A third group of male clergy engaged in Christian missionary work in Canada were the Gentlemen of Saint-Sulpice, a band of diocesan priests founded in 1641 in the suburban parish of Saint-Sulpice in Paris. In founding his new brotherhood, Jean-Jacques Olier (1608–1657) had as a primary objective the forming of an elite band of priests dedicated to the staffing of Catholic seminaries for the better education of Catholic clergy. This was at a time when the Church of France was undertaking to abide by the Council of Trent's requirement that all dioceses have their own seminary for the training of clergy. Impressed by the quality of Olier's spirituality, a growing number of reform-minded priests joined him, thereby launching the new brotherhood.

The new society, known as the Gentlemen of Saint-Sulpice, was distinctive in several ways. First was the fact that these ordained diocesan priests lived together like members of a religious order, but never took religious vows themselves. Their common life was simply one of the means they chose to enhance their priestly ministry. Another distinctive trait was that the men who joined the new brotherhood frequently belonged to the more aristocratic and wealthier class of French society; a number of them had led other successful careers before opting for the priesthood and the brotherhood. Given that they were not required to take the vow of poverty and to give up their personal ownership of property and wealth, several Sulpicians were personally wealthy. This would have a bearing on their ministry in Canada.

In the mid-1650s, a decade after the founding of Montréal, the post's governor Maisonneuve and his trusted assistant Jeanne Mance were not satisfied with the religious services available at their post, services that had always been provided by the Jesuit fathers. They felt that the number of priests assigned to their post was inadequate, and that the Jesuit superior in Québec was uncomfortably close to the colony's leaders, men who seemed to consider Montréal a rival to Québec. Thereupon, the Montréal leaders resolved to seek different clergy for their post. While visiting France from 1655 to 1657, acting on behalf of the Society of Montréal, the company that owned the island and directed its destinies, Maisonneuve obtained the agreement of Olier to send priests to Montréal. The choice of Sulpicians was easy because Olier himself had been closely associated with the founding of the colony in 1641. Moreover, the brotherhood of priests that he had founded was proving very successful; in 1657, Sulpicians were entrusted with the management of seven seminaries in France. Three priests and one deacon made up the first contingent sent to Montréal in 1657; Father Gabriel de Queylus (1612–1677) was their superior; when forced to return to France in 1661, he was succeeded by his associate Father Gabriel Souart (1611–1691).[32] Both men were personally rich, and used their wealth to benefit the local church.[33] While Sulpicians would prove most important in the leadership and development of the church in Montréal and of their seminary there, they also sent a number of their men to work in Acadia.[34] They also played a more limited but important role in missionary outreach to the Iroquois Amerindians on Lake Ontario, and to those residing on the reservation at Oka.

Once the Mohawks had been subdued by the raids in 1666 of the Carignan-Salières Regiment led by Lieutenant General Prouville de Tracy and peace had been established, the Jesuits founded missions among each of the Iroquois five nations. It was also during this year of 1668 that the Sulpicians founded a mission station at Quinte on the north shore of Lake Ontario (1668–1680), having been invited to do so by the Iroquois who had established some villages in the region. Two Sulpician priests landed there in October 1668, and a third arrived the following year.[35] The mission was subsidized by the Sulpicians of Paris. However, various factors such as the migration of the Amerindian residents, the founding of nearby Fort Frontenac in 1673, and internal squabbling among Sulpicians led to the closing of the mission of Quinte in 1680.

The missionary personnel: the women

The five congregations of women active in New France were the Ursulines, the Hospital Sisters of Québec, the Hospital Sisters of Montréal, the Notre Dame Sisters, and the Sisters of Charity of Montréal. Because of an arbitrary order by Bishop Saint-Vallier, the Hospital Sisters of Québec's Hôtel-Dieu Hospital were separated in 1692 to form a sixth distinct congregation, the nursing sisters entrusted with the new Québec General Hospital. While the sisters were primarily occupied with ministering to the educational and health needs of the French in the main settlements, they always served everyone without discrimination, and many, the Ursulines and Sisters of Notre Dame in particular, made special efforts to meet the needs of Amerindian children.

The Ursulines

The early history of this order of cloistered nuns was outlined above.[36] One of its members in the convent of Tours, Marie Guyart (1599–1672), would lead the first contingent of nuns to land in New France. Guyart had been widowed at the age of nineteen, when the mother of a young child. Her brief but unhappy marriage to Claude Martin had left her longing for happiness. After spending more than a dozen years earning her living as a business manager and having experienced a religious conversion,[37] she sought a cloistered life of prayer. In January 1631, Marie left her elderly father and twelve-year-old son Claude in the care of her sister, and entered the cloister of the Ursulines of Tours. Upon pronouncing her vows in 1633, she chose the religious name of Marie de l'Incarnation.[38]

A series of dreams had showed Marie the vast country of Canada and suggested to her that she go there to build a school for the glory of God. Her reading of the *Relations*, the edited letters of Jesuit missionaries that were widely distributed in France, convinced her that her calling was to serve in New France. When Madame de La Peltrie came knocking on her door, God's will became manifest to Marie.

Marie-Madeleine de Chauvigny de La Peltrie (1603–1671) was another fine example of the tidal wave of mysticism and Christian zeal that was sweeping through French Catholicism in this first half of the seventeenth century. Drawn to a life of prayer and good works, and inspired by the reading of the Jesuit *Relations*, the thirty-three-year-old widow decided to dedicate her considerable fortune to the interests of Canada's Amerindian people. When she fell seriously ill, she vowed to God that if he restored her health, she would personally go to Canada and build a convent and school for the benefit of Amerindian girls. De La Peltrie was cured overnight. Her spiritual adviser informed her of the similar interests of the Ursuline nun from Tours. De La Peltrie thereupon went to Tours and the two women agreed on a joint project. Guyart would lead, and de La Peltrie would underwrite. After recruiting two other Ursuline sisters, one from Tours and the other from Dieppe, the four women set sail from Dieppe on 4 May 1639.

Upon arriving in Québec on 1 August 1639, Marie and her band occupied a small house in Québec's lower town, planned the construction of a new convent on the heights of Québec,[39] and opened a boarding school for French and Amerindian girls. Students' fees were paid in kind, be it butter, venison, pork, or firewood. The number of boarders gradually grew to more than one hundred who were taught the basic skills of writing, reading, and anything else deemed worthy of learning for a young woman.

During their first quarter-century in Québec, more than one hundred Amerindian girls were enrolled in Marie's school. However, much to the Ursulines' chagrin they did not manage to 'civilize' a single one, despite their valiant efforts. Indeed, Sister Marie among others had mastered Amerindian languages, and written dictionaries and catechisms in the Algonquin and Iroquois languages. Nevertheless, she wrote in 1668 that it had all been for naught, as the Amerindian children did not rest easy or take well to French methods of education and discipline. When they felt homesick, the children simply escaped back to their parents in the forest.

The Hospital Sisters of Québec

While de La Peltrie and Guyart were planning their school, another pious benefactress was preparing for the founding of a hospital in Québec. The Duchess d'Aiguillon, a niece of Richelieu, had secured a plot of land in Québec for the establishment of a hospital. She then obtained the services

Fig. 6.   Hôtel-Dieu Hospital of Québec in 1850.[41] Drawing by Charles William Jefferys. National Archives of Canada, c-069810.

of three nursing sisters from Dieppe;[40] Marie Guenet (superior), Anne Le Cointre, and Marie Forestier were all in their twenties when they boarded the same ship as the Ursulines. For the first six months after their arrival in Québec, they were compelled to care for the numerous French and Amerindian victims of the smallpox epidemic that was sweeping through the colony. Then they founded their first hospital at Sillery on the outskirts of Québec, but the threat of Iroquois raids forced them back into town. There it was that in 1646 they occupied a new building, the historic Hôtel-Dieu hospital. For more than 350 years since that time the sisters have been caring for the physical and spiritual health of their patients.

The Hospitalers of Montréal

The New Jerusalem that the colony of Montréal was intended to be had a hospital within two years of its founding. Indeed, in 1644, Jeanne Mance (1606–1673), a pious laywoman from the Province of Champagne in France, had founded a hospital with the funds provided by the benefactress Angélique Faure, the widow of the former superintendent of finance of France, Claude Bullion. The wealthy Faure asked Jeanne Mance to establish a hospital in the colony, at her expense. She also asked that her identity be kept secret. En route to Canada, Mance was awaiting embarkation at La Rochelle when she happened to meet Jérôme Le Royer de la Dauversière (1597–1659) in the church of the Jesuits. Le

Royer was the man who, in concert with Olier, had founded the Society of Montréal, the company that owned and directed that colony. Mance accepted Le Royer's invitation to become nurse and bursar of the Montréal expedition, which was under the command of Paul de Chomedey de Maisonneuve (1612–1676).

With guaranteed funding, Mance proceeded to establish her hospital, assisted by a few laywomen. However, overwhelmed by various responsibilities and feeling that the institution would be better served by religious sisters, Jeanne went to France in 1658 seeking help. In addition to obtaining more funding for her hospital, in 1659 she returned to Canada in the company of three nursing sisters from the Hospitalers of St. Joseph of the city of Laflèche. Their congregation had been founded by the same Le Royer de la Dauversière in 1636 in answer to directives from God. As a supplementary reward from God, Jeanne experienced a miraculous cure of a broken arm when she laid her disabled limb alongside the heart of the deceased Father Olier; the relic rested in the Sulpician chapel in Paris. The Montréal Hôtel-Dieu Hospital would thereafter come under the control of these nursing sisters of St. Joseph.

The Notre-Dame Sisters

A close friend of Jeanne Mance in Montréal was Marguerite Bourgeois (1620–1700) who had come to Canada in 1653 from her native Troyes where she had come to know Maisonneuve's sister; she even met the governor of Montréal himself in 1652. Inevitably Marguerite heard about Canada. She decided to come to teach school in Montréal. After a delay of five years due to the fact that the colony had very few children at that time, she managed to open her school in April 1658.

The success of her school required that she obtain assistance. In 1659, she returned from a journey to France with three new teachers in addition to a servant. This allowed the pious Marguerite to diversify her services. She became the leading hostess entrusted with welcoming eight hundred orphaned girls,[42] the so-called '*filles du roi*,' that the crown sent as marriageable women to the colony in the decade before 1672. Bourgeois met the girls dockside, took them into her home, taught them the duties of housewife, and then arranged for them to meet the settlers, many of whom were desperately seeking a wife in the woman-poor colony. The matter was usually settled within two weeks of a girl's arrival.

In 1671, Bourgeois obtained royal letters patent that secured the continuity of her band. In 1676 they were acknowledged by Bishop Laval as a congregation of 'secular girls,' dedicated to teaching and subject to the religious authority of the bishop. This was followed by rapid growth of the group, as they opened a boarding school in Montréal, a housekeeping school, and a series of small parish schools in the countryside; they even opened a school in the town of Québec. Bourgeois resisted efforts by Bishop Saint-Vallier to merge her band with the Ursulines. On 1 July 1698, her women pronounced vows of poverty, chastity, and obedience, thereby becoming a full-fledged religious congregation.

The Congregation of Notre Dame was distinctive in that it was not a cloistered one, as just about all others were until that time. This meant that the sisters were free to travel in the exercise of their diversified apostolate, and could do so dressed in the same clothing as other women of their day. Upon Bourgeois's death in 1700, forty women were part of her community that was destined to become one of Canada's most important teaching congregations of women. Marguerite Bourgeois was declared a saint by Pope John Paul II when he visited Canada in 1984.

The Sisters of Charity of Montréal

The last group of sisters that appeared in the colony was that of another widow. Marie-Marguerite Dufrost de Lajemmerais (1701–1771) was born in Varennes, New France, into one of the colony's leading families. In 1722 she married François d'Youville with whom she had two surviving sons. The marriage was not a happy one; one reason was Youville's involvement in the brandy and liquor trade. After her husband's death in 1730, Marguerite became more and more involved in charitable works, in particular the care of poor and sick women. Beginning in 1737, in the company of a handful of like-minded 'sisters,' the widow Youville sheltered these women in her home. In 1745, Marguerite and four colleagues formally undertook to share their lives and their property in the interests of the care of the poor.

At this time, the leaders of the Montréal colony were at a loss as to what to do with the Montréal General Hospital, an institution that suffered from bad management and was on the verge of bankruptcy. The General Hospital had been founded in 1692 by the brothers Charon as an institution dedicated to the care of destitute men, eventually including orphans and all other males in need. In 1747, Marguerite d'Youville and her six companions agreed to take it over. Within a few years they had succeeded in making a success of the venture, in spite of numerous difficulties including excessive debts and a disastrous fire. Thereafter, the institution would welcome patients of both sexes. In the process, in 1755 the women adopted the name of Sisters of Charity of the General Hospital, although a more common name for many years was that of Grey Nuns. One hundred years later, the congregation would launch a major expansion into the four corners of North America and the world, becoming one of the Catholic world's largest nursing and teaching congregations of women.[43] On 9 December 1990, the founder Marie-Marguerite Dufrost, the widow d'Youville, became the first Canadian-born Christian to be declared a saint by the Catholic Church.

The evangelization of Canada's Amerindians

Imbued with a strong sense of mission, these varied personnel of the Canadian church undertook the evangelization of Canada's Amerindian people. How did they understand their mission? How did the Amerindians respond?

The point of view of the clergy

The official Catholic view on the status of Amerindians was outlined above: like all other people, Amerindians were the children of God created in His image and likeness; they had souls and were called to acknowledge Christ; they were not to be enslaved. The church's primary duty in their regard was to evangelize them; upon their conversion, they were to be considered equal to any other Christian. Just as important in the view of the clergy was the belief that Christianity was the only true religion, and Catholicism the only true church in Christianity. Any and all other religions, those of the Amerindians included, were false religions. One of the missionary's foremost duties was to cause all traces of such erroneous doctrines and practices to disappear. It was also noted above that given the church's lack of the necessary means of evangelization of these distant Amerindians, it had delegated its powers to various monarchs of Europe. This system of *patronage* also applied to France.[44] The crown of Spain had most assuredly abused its power of patronage over the church, shamelessly promoting royal and commercial interests in the name of the Gospel to the point that the Gospel ran the real risk of being totally discredited in the Spanish colonies of Central and South America. How did France behave in this regard? To what extent were the missionaries in Canada conscious of the distinction between the interests of the Gospel and those of their commercial and royal patrons? Did their missionary strategy give precedence to evangelization or to civilization? Were there differences among them in this regard?

Without doubt Canada's first missionaries, both *Récollet* and Jesuit, considered that their task was primarily one of evangelization. This was why Fathers Biard and Massé in Acadia in 1611 immediately launched into the study of the language of the Amerindians they wanted to evangelize, and proved critical of the behaviour of some of the Frenchmen of the settlement. This was why the *Récollets*, upon their arrival in Québec in 1615 sent men to meet and live with the Montagnais and with the Hurons. This was why the Jesuits founded Fort Sainte-Marie.

However, this policy was soon modified to one that combined evangelization with a partial acculturation to French civilization. It was with this in view that a chain of distinct villages for Amerindian Christians was founded, reservations that would serve to keep the French at bay while initiating their residents to some elements of French culture. This was the motivation behind the numerous efforts of the missionaries to found schools for Amerindian children. Marie Guyart's Ursulines founded a school for Amerindian girls in 1639, and prepared various texts in the Amerindian languages; the *Récollets* opened a school for Amerindian boys as early as 1620; the Capuchin friars in Acadia did likewise in the 1630s; the Jesuits had theirs in 1635; the Sisters of Notre Dame in 1658; even the first nursing sisters in Québec opened a school, as the Sulpicians did in Montréal. While the first generation of missionaries were primarily concerned with the exclusive proclamation of the Gospel, they were soon followed by others who aimed at evangelization combined with some acculturation.

After half a century of experience and sincere effort, the missionaries had come to the realization that their hope of converting Canada's Amerindians to the Christian faith was impossible to realize as long as these same Amerindians followed their traditional lifestyle in their traditional lands. Therefore, by the time Canada was changed from its status as a commercial protectorate of chartered entrepreneurs to that of a royal colony directly administered by the crown (1663), the missionaries agreed that if they were to succeed in converting the Amerindians, they needed first to acculturate them to some degree into the ways of the French. This was the view of both Bishop Laval and Sister Marie de l'Incarnation in 1668. When being pressed by the government to open schools to Frenchify Amerindian children, the latter wrote: "It is ... very difficult, if not an impossible task to Frenchify or to civilize them. We have had more experience than anybody else, and we have noticed that among one hundred of those who passed through our hands, we hardly succeeded in civilizing one. We find them docile and clever, but when we least expect it, they jump the wall and go to join their parents in the woods, where they find more pleasure than they do amid all the attractions of our French houses. Such is the Amerindian character. They will brook no restraint. If they are constrained, they become melancholic and ill. Moreover, the Amerindians have an extraordinary love for their children. When they learn that they are sad ... we must return their children to them."[45]

Their previous policy of evangelization was first modified into a policy of selective acculturation with evangelization. Far removed from the scene, throughout these years the government of France's policy was aimed primarily at acculturating the Amerindians. The government only came around to the view of the missionaries in the mid-1680s.

The changed policy of the missionaries did not translate into their abandonment of the Amerindians to their fate at the hands of commercial or selfish interests. As the era of mystics and martyrs was coming to a close after 1663, the policy of the clergy was to facilitate the partial acculturation of the Amerindians in order to convert them to Christianity. As noted above, schools were one means of implementing this policy. The establishment of Amerindian reservations was another, as was the clergy's fight against the brandy trade. In spite of the fact that the first reservation at Sillery had by this time failed, in the second half of the seventeenth century a string of new reservations for Christian Amerindians were founded in various parts of the colony,[46] villages that soon became important centres of Amerindian life in Canada for the Mohawk, the Algonquin, the Abenaki, the Huron, and others.

In these villages, missionaries evangelized the Amerindians, while their leaders in Québec and Montréal sought to obtain the interdiction of alcoholic beverages in the Amerindian trade. Beginning in the 1650s, French brandy became a scourge in the Amerindian settlements, because few Amerindians who drank did so with moderation; they sought complete intoxication, which all too frequently resulted in horrific behaviour including rape, murder, orgies, and spousal and child abuse. Once the brandy ran out, many found themselves destitute and unable to provide for themselves or their families, leading to misery and starvation. Bishop Laval and the clergy fought assiduously against the brandy trade, but in spite of some temporary victories in the early 1660s when the bishop excommunicated anyone who engaged in the trade, it became a losing battle after 1668 when the colony's government authorized the trade with the Amerindians.[47] The consumption of alcoholic beverages was a side of French culture that the missionaries sought to eradicate among the Amerindians.

Amerindians were especially vulnerable to the effects of alcoholic beverages because of a combination of genetic, psychological, social, and religious reasons. Genetically, Amerindians lacked an enzyme that helped to break down alcohol; psychologically, drunkenness could be a weapon that made possible any and all actions; socially, some wanted to forget their worsening lot, their dispossession by the Europeans; religiously, some deliberately sought inebriation in order to facilitate the dreaming that permitted contact with the spirits. Whatever the reason or combination thereof, drunkenness was a plague that ravaged the Amerindian communities.

Canada's first missionaries were simultaneously agents of the Gospel and agents of the French crown. While promulgation of Gospel values were foremost in their scale of priorities, they were of the view that such values could only be implemented among the Amerindians by means of some acculturation to the ways of the French. In fact, religion and culture were closely intertwined.

The point of view of the Amerindians

In contrast to their European visitors who were driven by commercial gain, insecure identities, and the Christian mandate to evangelize, the Amerindians had a radically different view of the world. This was explained in Chapter Two. Their reaction to the missionaries was based fairly equally on trust, fear, and manifest self-interest.

The trust appears in the extraordinary courtesy and hospitality Amerindians showed to the first French visitors that they encountered, in the great respect and solidarity that developed between many missionaries and Amerindians, and in the exemplary conversions to Christianity that occurred. The stories that underline the openness and trust of the Amerindians when first encountered abound in the literature of explorers and missionaries. Jacques Cartier told of the welcome he received from Amerindians at Gaspé upon his first landing, and of the assistance of others on the St Lawrence River. We read of the first French post in Acadia, Port Royal, being preserved intact by local Amerindians for a full three years between 1607 and 1610, while the French had abandoned the place. *Récollet* Brother Gabriel Sagard wrote of the hospitality of the Amerindians at the western end of Lake Ontario that his exploring party received in 1623. The same trusting attitude by Amerindians appears in the many instances of lifelong friendships that developed between specific missionaries and the Amerindian bands to whom they had chosen to devote their lives. With rare exceptions, these missionaries were the only Europeans to commit their lives and efforts to the welfare of the Amerindian people; they were rewarded by the love and trust of their charges.

Exemplary conversions, such as those of Kateri Tekakwitha also indicate the degree of trust some Amerindians could give to the missionaries. It would be naïve to dismiss arbitrarily such conversions as inauthentic, or as exclusively driven by other than spiritual considerations. A number of Amerindians must have become Christians as a result of a most authentic spiritual experience.

However, along with the trust went fear, a fear based upon the cultural identity of the missionaries and upon their religious agenda. The missionaries were white men, who could be perceived as agents of the French crown, a power that wielded firearms and had shown that it did not hesitate to use them against the Amerindian people. Missionaries could provoke fear, just as any other French emissary could. Missionaries were also feared as enemies of Amerindian religions. Since evangelization was the primary objective of the missionaries, that implied repression of any and all other religions. Toleration of other religions, systems of erroneous teachings in the eyes of the missionaries, was not a virtue in seventeenth-century Christianity, and Jesuit and other missionaries did not seek to disguise their hostility towards the religious beliefs and practices of the Amerindians. However, to attack Amerindian beliefs was to attack their entire culture and way of life because the Amerindian spiritualities, or religions, explained the origin of the world, and gave meaning to each of its important dimensions including birth, coming of age, the identity of the tribe, suffering, success in the hunt, relationships, etc. When the missionaries criticized, ridiculed, demeaned, or fought Amerindian spiritualities, they were attacking Amerindian cultures at their root. To abandon belief in the spirits incorporated in a particular Amerindian tradition was synonymous with abandoning one's Amerindian culture and one's identity. Few were capable of effecting such a profound life change without paying the price of such a loss of identity, which all too frequently was equivalent to opting for a meaningless life.

This was why most missionaries usually failed to baptize Amerindians, except those who were at death's door. So it was that after their first seven years (1634–1641) in Huronia, Father Brébeuf's Jesuit band could only point to a meager crop of converts, a total of sixtyChristians; it had taken three years (1634–1637) before they had succeeded in baptizing their first healthy adult.[48] And the Hurons were a friendly nation. This changed in the wake of the growing military onslaught by the Iroquois after 1642. When the devastating raids intensified after 1647, the Huron people were dying. Then it was that they turned to Christianity in droves, once their culture and way of life – indeed their very existence – was threatened. By 1649 one Huron in two was Christian, and one year later, after the terrible year spent as refugees on Christian Island, Father Paul Ragueneau reported three thousand baptisms. Given that the traditional spirits could not protect them, the Huron would try the spirits of the French.[49]

Along with the trust and the fear, self-interest operated among the Amerindians in their attitudes toward missionaries. Amerindians knew that if they wanted to enjoy the favour of trade with the French, and the rewards that that entailed, they had to show hospitality to the French missionaries. At times, the Governor of New France explicitly told them as much. Also, when everything began to unravel for various Amerindian nations, for example during the Huron catastrophe of the 1640s or when the French forces crushed the Iroquois armies in the 1690s, the spirits of the French seemed to be more powerful than the spirits of Amerindian tradition. Some concluded that it would be opportune, and advantageous, to join the winners. Finally, given the tradition of sharing that was general among Amerindian nations, many Amerindians were inclined to welcome missionaries for the various goods, foodstuffs, or even weapons that their presence would entail.

The legacy of Christian missions

The Census of Canada for the year 1991 shows that over 400,000 – more than 80% – of Canada's Amerindian people identify themselves as Christian, while only 10,000 declare that they hold to one of Canada's Amerindian or Inuit religions. This overwhelming presence of Christianity is in many ways the result of the missionary work of the evangelizing seventeenth century, because this was when entire Amerindian tribes and nations in Canada chose to adhere to the Catholic Church. This was the case for the Huron, the Mi'kmaq, the Algonquin, and a goodly number of the Mohawk who settled on the reservations around Montréal. The arrival of Protestant missionaries in the wake of the British conquest, and the intense Protestant and Catholic missionary campaigns of the nineteenth century, would be the other major factor in the Christian evangelization of Canada's Amerindian people.

Generally speaking, the tribes evangelized by the French became Catholic, and those evangelized by the English became Protestant. Given that English missionary efforts were few and far between in the seventeenth and eighteenth centuries, and given the political domination of France, the majority of that period's Amerindians of Canada ended up adhering to the Catholic Church. Both the French Catholic and the British Protestant missionaries taught a Christian faith couched in the trappings of European civilization. Much of the traditional Amerindian spiritualities, closely tied as they were to Amerindian cultures, disappeared.

The fact that the evangelization of Amerindians did not make much allowance for Amerindian cultures and that it implied much imposition of Euro-Canadian cultures, has resulted in a profound ignorance of Amerindian spiritualities among Canadians. A second result has been the development of some religious syncretism among some Amerindians, as will be shown later. A third result has been that the Christianity that was promoted among the Amerindians has not been as meaningful as it could have been because it was less adapted to the culture of the Amerindians. And all these consequences derived from the European assumption that Christianity was the only true religion, and the corollary that Amerindian spiritualities did not deserve respect. They also derived from the assumption that European civilization supported a superior culture, one that deserved to dominate and replace Amerindian cultures. These fundamental assumptions were only meaningfully challenged after the mid-twentieth century.

Suggested readings

Bédard, Marc-André. *Les Protestants en Nouvelle-France*. Québec: Société historique de Québec, 1978.

Blackburn, Carole. *Harvest of Souls: The Jesuit Missions and Colonialism in North America, 1632–1650*. Montréal & Kingston: McGill-Queen's University Press, 2000.

Campeau, Lucien. *La mission des jésuites chez les Hurons 1634–1650*. Montréal: Bellarmin, 1987. English translation by William Lone and George Topp, Bridgetown, N.S.: Gontran Trottier, 2000.

Carlen, Claudia. Ed. *The Papal Encyclicals 1740–1981*. Wilmington, N.C.: McGrath Publishing Company, 1981.

Choquette, Robert. "French Catholicism Comes to the Americas." Charles H. Lippy et al. *Christianity Comes to the Americas 1492–1776*. New York: Paragon House, 1992.

Green, Leslie and Olive Dickason. *The Law of Nations and the New World*. Edmonton: University of Alberta Press, 1989.

Jetten, Marc. *Enclaves amérindiennes: les "réductions" du Canada, 1637–1701*. Sillery: Éditions du Septentrion, 1994.

Landry, Yves. *Orphelines en France pionnières au Canada. Les filles du roi au XVIIe siècle*. Montréal: Leméac, 1992.

Simpson, Patricia. *Marguerite Bourgeois and Montréal, 1640–1665*. Montréal & Kingston: McGill-Queen's University Press, 1997.

Stogre, Michael. *That the World May Believe: The Development of Papal Social Thought on Aboriginal Rights*. Sherbrooke: Éditions Paulines, 1992.

Walls, Andrew F. *The Missionary Movement in Christian History: Studies in the Transmission of Faith*. n.p.: Orbis Books, 1996.

CHAPTER 6

The Development of the Catholic Church

The Catholic Church is primarily organized on a territorial basis. It is governed by the pope in Rome and by bishops who are understood to be successors of the apostles. Under the leadership of its bishop, a regional church is usually staffed by priests and deacons, some of whom are members of religious orders. However, throughout its two millennia of history, the church has developed and changed many aspects of its structure and government to accommodate itself to new and changing needs in a wide variety of cultures and times. In Canada, from the seventeenth century to the present, the Catholic Church has been torn between the centralizing demands of first French, and then Roman authorities on the one hand, and the aspirations to autonomy of Canada's Catholics on the other hand. The central importance of church structures in the evangelization of the country becomes apparent in the history of the diocese of Québec, church finances, the Seminary of Québec, the schools, and the church institutions dedicated to health care and social work.

The organization of the Catholic Church

As the number of members in the early Christian church grew, the latter adopted forms of organization that facilitated its worship and apostolate. From the first century C.E. to the present, the organization of the Catholic Church has usually been based on territorial divisions, but at times it has also been based on personal ministries and on specific functional considerations that do not lend themselves to territorial structures. An example of a personal ministry in lieu of a territorial one is the personal prelature or world-wide episcopal powers granted to the head of the Opus Dei secular institute. An example of church organization based on functional considerations is that of the military vicariate in Canada, whereby Catholics in the armed forces are ministered to by chaplains who answer to Canada's military vicar, a bishop who has special jurisdiction over armed forces personnel and military bases wherever they may be.

These special cases notwithstanding, the Catholic Church has two basic types of territorial organization, one for regular established churches, the other for mission territories. Both coexist alongside *ad hoc* structures established to facilitate administration at a given time.

The territorial organization of established churches

Territorial divisions are the primary ones in the organization of the Catholic Church, and since the fourth century, the basic cell in that organization has been the parish. The regional grouping of parishes, or the diocese, headed by a bishop, is the second level of territorial division. Just as parishes are grouped together to form dioceses, in like manner the latter are grouped together to form ecclesiastical *provinces*, administrative units established to facilitate church administration and coordination of activities in specific regions.

The territorial organization of mission churches

It was noted in Chapter 5 that from the sixteenth to the mid-twentieth centuries the Catholic Church considered missionary enterprises to be a distinct part of the mandate of the church, whether it was in the personnel entrusted with missions or in the management of missionary policy by the Roman *Congregation de Propaganda Fide*. During those five hundred years, territorial organization reflected this duality in the understanding of evangelization. This occurred when a country or a region that was either being evangelized for the first time by Catholic missionaries (e.g. Canada) or had passed into the hands of some other religion or Protestant church (e.g. England), was designated as an apostolic vicariate, or in some cases as an apostolic prefecture. Once these missionary territories, organized as apostolic vicariates, had developed sufficiently to sustain themselves both in personnel and financial resources, the Holy See made them into dioceses, thereby promoting them to the regular level of ecclesiastical organization.

The management of the Catholic Church

The basic organizational structure outlined above was staffed by a variety of people, some more important than others. Although the importance of the roles of each changed over time, it was the members of the clergy, namely the bishop, the priest, and the deacon, and particularly the first two, who have always held the dominant role in Catholicism. The authority of the clergy varied greatly over time, depending on the prevailing interpretation of the New Testament and of the tradition of the church, and also on the circumstances that prevailed in various regions at various times.

The priest was understood to be an associate of the bishop in his ministry, and held his evangelical authority from the latter. While empowered by his ordination to celebrate Mass, hear confessions, preach, and baptize, he was only allowed to do so by permission of the bishop who had jurisdiction over the territory in which he was working.

The role of deacon had been important in early Christianity. Deacons were those entrusted with material things, such as collecting alms and distributing them to the needy. In most areas, the ecclesiastical order of the diaconate fell into disuse for many centuries, including the period under study here. Candidates to the priesthood were ordained deacons, but merely as a stage on their way to the priesthood. This major order was restored to use by the Second Vatican Council in 1965. Whether bishop, priest or deacon, the clergyman occupied a wide variety of offices in the Catholic Church. These ranged from that of pope to that of parish assistant priest, and included those of presidents or secretaries of various Vatican offices, of heads of regional churches (archbishop/metropolitan) or of local churches (bishop/ordinary). Although the diaconate is only beginning to reemerge as a full-time order in the church of the late twentieth century, there are already deacons in parish ministry, in diocesan administration, and elsewhere.

Religious orders in the church

The religious life is one of three *states of life* in the Catholic Church, the other two being celibacy and marriage. Religious men and women do not marry; they make public vows of poverty, chastity, and obedience, and usually live in community with their colleagues in brotherhoods and sisterhoods that are incorporated by church law. From the outset, these distinctive orders and congregations have developed their own corporate personalities, spiritualities, and forms of apostolate within Catholicism.

As is the case for celibate and married Christians, members of religious orders seek their sanctification and salvation on the basis of their baptism, reinforced by vows and life in community. Their way of life is distinctive in that their spiritual journey is intended to be a living witness to the greater love of God by forsaking ownership of property, marriage, and liberty of personal autonomy. While some members of religious orders remain in the lay state, that is to say that they are not ordained, religious brothers and sisters for example, others, only men, receive Holy Orders, thereby joining the ranks of the Catholic clergy. Until recently, the religious state of life was considered the most perfect of the three states acknowledged by the Catholic Church, a more perfect way than those of mere celibacy and marriage.

In church law, religious brotherhoods and sisterhoods are designated as either religious *orders* or *congregations*, depending on whether their members make *solemn* or *simple* vows. This technical canonical distinction will be disregarded in this book; the words *order* and *congregation* will be used interchangeably.

There have been and are today many types of religious orders, including the monastic, the mendicant, the canonical, the apostolic, the clerical, the contemplative, the secular, and some groups that do not make vows but resemble a religious order in every other respect. The type of religious order is determined by the purpose of the founders in establishing the community.

Religious life began with the founding of *monastic* groups in the deserts and wilds of the Middle East, in Egypt and Syria in particular, during the third and fourth centuries C.E. These monks were fleeing the cities and society of their day, seeking solitude and mortification with a view to getting closer to God. Some individuals obtained the sought-after personal sanctification in total isolation and indulged in extreme forms of asceticism; these were the hermits that have always existed in the church. However, it was soon apparent that isolation was not for everyone; most monks then began living in groups, in communities, albeit in relatively isolated areas. Rejecting the life of the hermit, the majority of monks eventually adopted a balanced daily schedule, made up in equal parts of prayer, work, rest, and sustenance, the way of Saint Benedict of Nursia (480–543 C.E.) in the Italian peninsula. This Benedictine rule became foundational for religious life; in fact Benedictine monasticism was the only form of monastic life in the West between the eighth and the twelfth centuries. Monasticism has continued to the present, a number of Benedictine and Cistercian[1] monasteries being found in Canada.

A second form of religious life that appeared in the Middle Ages was that of *canons*, secular (diocesan) priests attached to a bishop's church, the cathedral. Some of these priests chose to live together in poverty and chastity, thereby leading a semi-monastic life. One example of these were the Augustinian Canons, an order that has also continued to the present, in Canada and elsewhere. This form of religious life where members lived together *as if* they were members of religious orders, but without making the vows, was also copied by other groups in the modern period. This was the case for the Sulpician,[2] and also for the Eudist Fathers who were important in Atlantic Canada after 1890.

A third form of religious life that appeared in the thirteenth century was that of the *mendicant friars*, originally including the Franciscans[3] and the Dominicans,[4] and then extended to include the Carmelites,[5] the Hermits of St. Augustine,[6] and the Servites.[7] The name *mendicant* came from the fact that the members of these orders were originally forbidden to own property personal or in common; they had to beg or work for a living. However, the ban on the ownership of common property soon proved unworkable, and after much debate it was waived by papal authority.

In the modern period, many religious *congregations*,[8] as opposed to orders, appeared in Catholicism. They distinguished themselves by their apostolic objectives, that is to say they were founded with a view to bearing witness to Jesus by working directly with people by preaching, teaching, nursing, or other types of apostolic work. Most of the religious men and women active in Canada belong to this category of religious.

A final category of the religious life is the more recent *secular institute*, a type invented in the twentieth century and characterized by its members remaining in secular professions or trades. Whereas members of traditional religious orders not only live together but usually work in fields that are directly church-related (e.g. teaching, missions, nursing), and do so while wearing a distinctive religious habit, members of secular institutes are employed as individuals in secular society, and dress like anyone else.

The best known of these new secular institutes is Opus Dei, founded by the Spanish priest José Maria Escriva in the 1930s,[9] and made into a personal prelature in 1982. Other contemporary movements dedicated to the apostolate are the Neo Catechumenate (NC), Communion and Liberation (CL), and Focolare. Focolare was founded in 1943 by Chiara Lubich, Communion and Liberation was founded in 1954 by the Milanese priest Don Giussani, and the Neo Catechumenate was founded in 1964 by Kiko Arguello and Carmen Hernandez. These new societies or secular institutes are sometimes dedicated to one specific objective, such as devotion to Mary for Focolare, or the spread of Christian knowledge for CL; in some cases the objective is much more sweeping, nothing less than rebuilding the church from within for NC. While they claim to be lay societies, they include both laity and clergy in their ranks, and the leadership is more often than not dominated by the clergy.

In church law, religious orders of women have much the same standing as orders of men. One distinguishing characteristic is their non-clerical status, that is to say that because women cannot be ordained in the Catholic Church, none of the women religious are ordained, contrary to the situation of many male religious who are ordained. A second distinguishing characteristic of women religious is that they usually work in social service agencies, in teaching, nursing, or care for the poor. A third characteristic is that until recent times, their congregational life was more often than not under the ultimate control of male clergy who were appointed ecclesiastical superiors of the orders of women. The women's movement has changed that. Finally, their numerical importance among full-time church workers increased dramatically during the nineteenth and twentieth centuries. Indeed, in 1800 women religious were usually half as numerous as male clergy, but by the year 1900 the reverse was true and remained true throughout the twentieth century.

Power shifts in the management of the church

Just about every form of government from the democratic to the totalitarian has existed at one time or another in the Catholic Church. Diversity was the order of the day during the first century after the death of Jesus, church authority resting for the most part in the persons of the apostles themselves, those who had been personal witnesses to Jesus' life and teaching.[10] As churches were founded far and wide in diverse settings, and as the passage of time eroded the living memory of Jesus, it was found necessary to adopt standard forms of organization and government for the churches. This was done in the second and third centuries, with much authority coming to rest in the hands of the head of each local church, the bishop. Further expansion of Christianity and the end of persecutions in the fourth century led to greater organization and centralization; the authority of the pope was reinforced, while bishops added large numbers of new clergy to assist them in their ministry in expanding dioceses that now encompassed thousands of faithful. This led to democracy being weakened as church officers consolidated their power within the church; the clerical class was born. In fact, the clergy would remain to our own day the dominant class within the church, usually enjoying not only a greater *degree* of power, but also a different *kind* of power within Catholicism. For many years during the Middle Ages, Catholic theologians did not consider the laity capable of apostolic action.

While the clergy consolidated its control over the church, it was challenged by the state, a menagerie of different rulers that ranged from local warlords to kings and emperors. In fact, from the beginning much of the shifting of power in the history of the church did not occur within the church itself, but rather as a result of the frequent shifts in the balance of power between church and state over matters like taxation, the collection of revenues, military service, power of appointments, etc.

At the time of the founding of the Canadian church, the French crown held the upper hand over the church in the shifting rules of sharing authority. The rules that applied to Canada were the result of the Gallicanism that had developed in France since the thirteenth century; this was the political philosophy that dominated in the Concordat of Bologna that ruled church-state relations in France since 1516. In that document King Francis I and Pope Leo X agreed that the king would nominate his chosen clergy to key church positions such as abbot of a monastery or bishop or archbishop of a diocese, and the pope would confirm the appointments providing certain basic rules were respected. This translated into state control over the management of the church. In addition to the French crown controlling the church of France, the latter's clergy was divided into the same classes that divided French society. Bishops were usually drawn from the aristocracy, while the lower clergy or priests belonged to the lower classes. By extension such divisions left their imprint on the church in Canada.

Gallicanism

From its inception two thousand years ago, the church always had to deal with questions and disagreements pertaining to its own government. Christians perennially disagreed on how to distribute power between the centre and the periphery of the church; indeed Catholics have not always agreed as to where the centre was, because of differing understandings of the nature of the church. Because of their theology, some felt that the primary seat of power should be the local congregation, or the regional church, while others felt just as strongly that it was the international centre of the church, Rome, that should have decisive authority. While such disagreements over church organization crystallized in the many Protestant denominations that were organized along different lines,[11] the opinions were at times just as varied within Catholicism.

Gallicanism is used to denote the particular form of nationalism of French Catholics, an attitude that amounted to the belief that the Catholic Church in France was French before being Roman, insuring thereby the autonomy of the Church of France before Roman authority, but simultaneously entailing dependence of the church on the French State. Deriving from the name of the ancient Roman province of Gaul (France), the word Gallicanism had varied meanings. In its *ideological* connotation it designated a mindset, much like that of a nationalist, whereby all things pertaining to the church were seen first from the point of view of a Frenchman. In its *ecclesiastical* connotation, it described the attitude of French Catholics who put the rights of the French church before those of the Holy See. In its *legal* connotation, Gallicanism designated the specific laws, customs, and traditions that existed to ensure the rights of the Church of France. These pertained to the interests of the king, of parliaments, of bishops, or of other bodies.

This centuries-old French tendency to put the interests of the Church of France ahead of those of the church's international headquarters in Rome had traditionally been opposed by another understanding of the Catholic Church, one that sought to centralize church authority in Rome. Since the nineteenth century, the latter understanding was designated as *ultramontanism*.[12] Ultramontanes were those Catholics who sought the independence of their church from state authorities by entrusting the primary power of decision in their church to Roman authorities.

In their aspirations for national autonomy for their national church within Catholicism, the Gallicans were no different than most other

Catholics of their day. Indeed, it was noted above that the unified kingdom of Spain from the turn of the sixteenth century had extensive jurisdiction over its church. The Holy Roman Emperor Joseph II, who ruled from 1765 to 1790, ruled his church with little deference to the pope. In England, kings had been building the foundations of extensive control over the church since the fourteenth century. In many respects, Gallicanism was a typical product of the age of the Renaissance.

Gallicanism had developed in medieval Europe beginning in the eleventh century, in reaction to the reforming and centralizing efforts of Pope Gregory VII who was in office from 1073 to 1085. Gregory worked to wrest control of the church from the German Holy Roman Emperor, and to free bishops from the control of the same and his vassals. The pope was intent on reclaiming the independence of the church from secular rulers in order to be able to reform churches ridden with abuses. In the process, the pope claimed absolute doctrinal and jurisdictional authority over all churches, thereby denying not only the power of the state, but also the traditional authority of bishops in their own right. This forced an alliance between heads of state and many bishops, both concerned to protect their rights within the church. The polarized ideological tug-of-war between pope and Emperor came to a head at the turn of the fourteenth century between King Philip IV (the Fair) of France and Pope Boniface VIII; each claimed a divine mandate for their supreme authority. While the pope claimed to be the source of all power in the church, and claimed the right to judge the behaviour of heads of state,[13] kings countered with their claim to hold their authority directly from God, while bishops claimed that their episcopal authority derived directly from Christ through their ordination, and not from the pope. As kings of emerging nation-states like England and France consolidated their authority in their own kingdoms, they continued the alliance with the bishops of their realm, each seeking to protect their authority from the centralizing tendencies of Rome.

In this context of emerging nationalism, kings and bishops of France developed a tradition of 'liberties of the Church of France,' a series of rights and customs that were enshrined in the *Pragmatic Sanction* of Bourges issued by King Charles VII in 1438. This was then superseded by the Concordat of Bologna of 1516, and finally by the *Declaration in Four Articles* adopted by the Assembly of the Clergy at the request of the French government of King Louis XIV in 1682. The latter document declared the independence of the king from the church in all secular and material matters, recalled the decrees of the Council of Constance (1414–1417) on the supreme authority of ecumenical councils in the church, reaffirmed the legitimacy of the customs of the Church of France, and declared that any decisions of the Roman pontiff in matters of faith were only valid if they were consented to by the church.

So it was that the church of Canada was founded at a time when Gallicanism was at its peak in the France of Louis XIV, a time when the majority of French Catholics, whether reform-minded or not, considered the church to be first Christian, then French, and finally Roman. An ecclesiastical problem was usually settled in Paris,[14] and only indirectly, if at all, in Rome. The Gallicanism of seventeenth- and eighteenth-century France was complicated by its close association with Jansenism, a harsh and rigorous movement in French spirituality that began around 1640, the year of publication of the book *Augustinus* by Cornelius Jansen. Five tenets drawn from the book were condemned by Pope Innocent X in 1653 as favouring a form of natural or supernatural determinism whereby the Christian would have been unable to observe God's commandments without special divine assistance; but once divine assistance was given, the Christian would have been unable to resist. Rome was of the view that such teachings denied the freedom of the Christian. Jansenist theology tended to be pessimistic about human beings, seeing sin as all-pervasive, and consequently adopted harsh and rigorous teachings. Jansenism continued to bedevil the Church of France until the Revolution of 1789, the movement being the subject of another papal condemnation in 1713. Frequently, all church adversaries of papal centralization and authority were inclined to collaborate in their opposition to Rome. So it was that Gallicans were often identified with Jansenists because both resisted papal authority.

Although not officially present in Canada, Jansenist ideas in the form of theological and spiritual pessimism and rigor can be found in the teachings of a number of churchmen, and particularly in the compendium of church teachings[15] published by the second bishop of Québec, Jean-Baptiste de Saint-Vallier (1687–1727). The foremost adversaries of Jansenism in France and Canada were the Jesuits. Tending to be optimists, as opposed to pessimists, in theology the Jesuits had a much more positive view of human beings in their relationship with God and in their role in salvation. From the outset in the 1640s, Jesuits had opposed the teachings of Jansen and his disciples, and had become the foremost targets of Jansenist criticism.[16] These diverging theological outlooks often clashed, for example when Jesuits promoted frequent reception of communion by the faithful, because of their belief in the fundamental goodness of redeemed Christians. In opposition, Jansenists wanted the faithful to receive the Eucharist as seldom as possible, because of their belief in the fundamental unworthiness of Christians, even when redeemed. The controversy between Jansenists and Jesuits was sustained in France for nearly 150 years.

In Canada, such theological differences were bound to affect the relationships between Jesuit missionaries and other clergy, the Sulpicians for example. These theological conflicts had a way of compounding problems resulting from other differences, those pertaining to canonical jurisdiction for example. Moreover, given the particularly strong attachment of Jesuits to the pope, the followers of Ignatius tended to be perceived at best as suspect, at worst as enemies by the Gallican Catholics who were at loggerheads with the Holy See.

So it was that Gallicanism proved a bone of contention in the church of early Canada, serving to sew discord and mistrust in the ranks of the clergy, and to reinforce theological tendencies towards harshness and rigor in moral teachings. It was this territorial and hierarchical church, conditioned by the dominant mindset of the adherents of Gallicanism, and those of ultramontane persuasion, that established the first institutions of the church in early Canada, namely the diocese of Québec and its parishes, the financial structures, the Seminary of Québec, the schools and colleges, the hospitals, and the services for the relief of the poor.

Early Canadian church institutions

The diocese of Québec

There was no bishop in Canada during the first fifty years of French settlement (1608–1658). First the *Récollets*, then the Jesuits were entrusted with the Canadian mission,[17] and managed it themselves, the religious superior serving as ecclesiastical head of the colonial church, under the authority of the superior general of the order; indeed, the Society of Jesus was one of the large religious orders which were mainly autonomous in mission territories. In 1646, because of pressures brought to bear by Rome, the Society of Jesus had agreed to acknowledge the authority of the archbishop of Rouen over the church of New France. The archbishop had become used to granting ecclesiastical faculties to clergy who were sailing to New France from his port city, the main port of embarkation for the New World. So it was that from

1646, the Jesuit superior in Québec held the title of vicar general of the archbishop of Rouen. The Jesuits had considered severing this connection, but did not do so before 1658.

Before the arrival of the Sulpician Fathers in Montréal, the Jesuits had enjoyed an ecclesiastical monopoly in Canada for a quarter century. They decided that the time had come to obtain the appointment of a bishop in Canada. In addition to the difficulties caused by the alleged meddling of the archbishop of Rouen, they were concerned that the new Sulpician clergy would balk at Jesuit control, and possibly endeavour to have their own man appointed to Canada. It seemed to make eminent sense to obtain the appointment of a bishop of their own choosing. In fact, the founders of Montréal had preempted the Jesuits in seeking the appointment of a bishop in Canada, one of their persuasion of course. Even before the first Sulpician priests set foot in Canada in the summer of 1657, their patrons in France had already taken steps to have Father Gabriel de Queylus, the superior of the Sulpician mission in Canada made a bishop. This was in January, 1657. However, they had not foreseen the powerful Jesuit influence at court. In fact, Regent Anne of Austria[18] offered to have a Jesuit appointed as bishop of New France, but the Society of Jesus refused; instead, they suggested that François de Laval be appointed. This was done, in spite of the fact that the Sulpician party had obtained the endorsement of de Queylus by the Assembly of the French clergy.

The Montmorency family, to which Laval belonged, had distinguished itself in French military and ecclesiastical affairs for a thousand years; the clan had roots going back to ancient Gaul of the fifth century. One of his two sisters was a nun, and one of his five brothers a Benedictine monk. François himself had donned a cassock at the age of eight upon entering the Jesuit College of La Flèche for a ten-year stay (1631–1641). He then studied theology at another Jesuit school, the College of Clermont where he was ordained a priest in 1647. Already the beneficiary of a small fixed income as canon of his uncle's cathedral church of Evreux, François assumed administrative duties in the same diocese after his ordination. Six years later (1654), he resigned the position to enter a hermitage at Caën, a house where a number of mystics, both priests and laypeople, prayed and led an ascetic life of good works in order to better achieve salvation. Laval devoted himself to serving the sick and the poor.

Laval was not a Jesuit, but a faithful follower of their ways. He appreciated the holiness and virtue of the Jesuits, and even claimed that

Fig. 7.   François de Laval.[19] Engraving based on a painting by Claude Duflos. National Archives of Canada, c-005183.

they were the ones who taught him to love God. For many years he had hoped to be sent to the missions, possibly in the Far East, but that was not to be. He was informed that his Jesuit friends had proposed to both the royal and pontifical courts that he be appointed first bishop of New France.

Rome was of two minds about the appointment of Laval. On the one hand, it agreed with the Jesuits that the tie with Rouen should be severed, thereby checking the Gallican party, but on the other hand the Holy See did not want to return to the older policy whereby the Jesuits had sole control of a mission field, a policy that Rome was slowly working to change since the creation of the central office of the *Propaganda Fide* in 1622. Both parties found a compromise solution in the appointment of Laval as apostolic vicar of the apostolic vicariate of New France. By making the territory into an apostolic vicariate rather than a diocese, it would be easier for Rome to demand that its head answer directly to the pope, rather than to the leaders of the Church of France; the rules of the Concordat of Bologna need not apply, thus ensuring the independence of the church. Meanwhile, Laval would be an ordained bishop, with the all the powers that were required to lead the church in Canada.

On 3 June 1658, the pope issued bulls appointing François de Laval apostolic vicar of New France. The archbishop of Rouen was not pleased; nor was the parliament of Rouen which condemned the measure. The archbishop countered by obtaining from the Assembly of the French clergy that all bishops in France refuse to ordain Laval on the grounds that the terms of his appointment were prejudicial to the interests of the Church of France. In concert with the royal court and the Jesuits, the Holy See responded by having Laval ordained secretly in a church that was not subject to French jurisdiction, that of the monastery at Saint-Germain-des-Prés. This was on 8 December 1658. Religious exemption had its uses. Although the controversy dragged on for some time, Laval was now a bishop. After having sworn loyalty to the king, he sailed to Canada in the spring of 1659.

François de Laval set foot in Québec on 17 June 1659. His apostolic vicariate, which covered all of New France, was immense in size and included tens of thousands of Amerindians who were not members of his church, but only three thousand Catholics. Québec was the main settlement with some 1,200 souls in its general area. During his first two years in the colony Laval was bedeviled by the ongoing jurisdictional struggle with the Gallican party, represented by Father De Queylus of Montréal. The latter had not accepted Laval's appointment, and resisted it by various means, until he was definitively ordered back to France by the king in October 1661. The archbishop of Rouen had finally and grudgingly to accept that he had lost that battle to the pope. Thirteen years later, in 1674, the threat of Gallican control having receded, Laval asked for and obtained from the Holy See the promotion of his apostolic vicariate to the rank of diocese of Québec. Meanwhile, from 1665 he discovered that the royal government was bent on reducing the power of the church in Canada, convinced as it was that the clergy held the people of Canada in spiritual and moral bondage. For the rest of his administration, Laval would need to struggle continuously to implement his model of the church against colonial officers who were determined to dominate religious affairs, just as the crown did in France.

During his twenty-five-year administration, Bishop Laval made his episcopal see into the real centre of his church, much as the Council of Trent had directed. Laval gave short shrift to the numerous traditional rights and privileges that had accrued to various elements in the church, be they those of pastors, canons, parishes, or religious orders. In the Church of France for example, once a parish was officially established according to the law, it became a legal corporation in its own right, with rights and responsibilities in matters of property and management. It was only with the greatest of reluctance, and when forced to do so by royal directive, that Laval would establish such permanent parishes in Canada. He preferred to create temporary parishes that did not enjoy legal incorporation, and thereby preserve his full authority to manage them. Exceptions to this policy were the parish at Québec erected as a permanent parish in 1664, and then another thirteen parishes erected in 1679 and 1684, because of a royal edict that required it.

The same was true for pastors, because if the latter did not hold office in a legally incorporated parish, their appointment remained as a grace and favour of the bishop. Laval could appoint and dismiss them at will, whereas he was required to bring a legally-established *curé* to court, and show cause in order to obtain his dismissal. Indeed, given Bishop Laval's ultramontane understanding of the church, church leaders and therefore bishop and pope, should enjoy all the necessary powers to manage a church that remained independent of the state. He always worked to achieve that objective.

Financing the church

The Catholic Church rarely subsidized its activities from a central fund. Whenever a new church or mission was established, it was understood that the founders must find the means to sustain their enterprise, and not rely on funding from Rome. In New France, 40% of the revenues of the diverse church institutions were provided by the crown in the form of subsidies to cover the deficits in the operating budgets of various social services such as hospitals and colleges. In addition to these subsidies by the crown, the church of New France had other forms of revenue to support its ministry. For a thousand years, in many countries of Europe churches had been financed by means of the tithe, a tax paid by the faithful and representing one tenth of the produce of their land. In countries with established churches, such as Canada, church law became civil law, the tithe being required under pain of both ecclesiastical and civil penalties. The tithe had not been instituted in New France before 1663, Jesuit and other missionaries living instead off the revenues of their own orders, supplemented by Sunday collections. However, upon New France's becoming a royal colony in 1663, Bishop Laval decreed the creation of the tithe. Because of disagreements between the bishop and the officers of the crown, and because of the refusal of the people to pay, the new tax was not implemented for another four years, the final rate being set at one twenty-sixth of the produce of the land, a rate that would remain permanent through colonial times.

In addition to the revenues generated by Sunday collections and the tithe, another source of revenue for the church was the various benefices to which some of the clergy held title. It was noted above that Laval himself held such a benefice in the cathedral church of Evreux from the age of fourteen; he also received a modest income from other French benefices. Some of the other French clergy in Québec and in Montréal also held benefices in France; moreover, as was noted above some Sulpicians were wealthy in their own right, while Catholic philanthropists such the widows de La Peltrie and Bullion underwrote their own favourite charities.

Another source of income was real estate, particularly the seigneuries owned by the various religious corporations in New France, the latter including the diocese of Québec, the Seminary of Québec, the hospitals, and religious orders. The various church institutions increased their holdings in the colony over the years, from 10% of the seigniorial lands in 1663, to fully 25% by 1759. These lands were sometimes purchased outright by these institutions, or received as grants from the crown.

By the end of the French regime, the church of Canada was financially secure. However, it should be remembered that this apparently wealthy church was running all of the colony's educational and health-care institutions, in addition to its various missions and churches. Few if any clergy became wealthy as a result of their work in Canada.

The Seminary of Québec

One of Bishop Laval's more noteworthy actions was the building of a seminary at Québec, and a very distinctive one at that. While on a visit to France in 1662–1663 the bishop ordered the founding of the Seminary of Québec. This was consistent with his belief in the need for a strong, independent, and exemplary church. In addition to implementing one of the directives of the Council of Trent by establishing a training institution for prospective priests, Laval made the seminary into the headquarters of his diocesan church, serving much the same purpose as the mother-house of a religious order. In addition to training clergy, Laval's seminary would also house a pool of clergy to serve the diocese's parishes and missions, and would collect all diocesan revenues and then redistribute them according to need. It would also serve as a refuge for tired or ailing priests, in addition to being the bishop's residence. In fact, by this act Laval was going a long way towards organizing the clergy of his diocese along congregational lines, resembling in many respects the life of a religious order. Then, on 29 January 1665 Laval affiliated his new school for clergy with Paris's Seminary of Foreign Missions, an institution that had been created at the same time. The bishop wanted to ensure that the Seminary of Québec would always be supplied with qualified staff and adequate financial resources.

The Seminary of Québec played an important role in the history of the Canadian church, in spite of the fact that Laval's successor Bishop de Saint-Vallier made it into an ordinary seminary, limited to its educational mandate. In addition to training priests, at the turn of the eighteenth century the seminary sent some of its men on missions to the distant Mississippi valley and to Acadia. After being forced to close for a few years during the British Conquest of Canada, it reopened in 1765 with the additional mandate of providing a general classical secondary and college education for young men.

Other educational institutions

Education was held to be a primary apostolic responsibility, second only to evangelization, in fact an opportune means of evangelization. This was an important field of activity for several of the religious orders of men and women that worked in New France. There were continuing, though not always successful, attempts to establish schools for Amerindian, or Amerindian and European children, that of the *Récollets* in Québec in 1620, that of the Ursuline sisters in Québec beginning in 1639, that of the Capuchin friars at La Hève and Port Royal in Acadia after 1633, and that of Bishop Laval at Québec in 1668.

The schools founded for the French children were much more successful. Boys were served by the College of Québec founded by the Jesuits in 1635, an institution that lasted until its enforced closure by the British at the time of the Conquest. This work was assisted by the Seminary priests who founded some elementary schools in the Québec region in the late seventeenth century. In Trois-Rivières, a settlement midway between Québec and Montréal, the *Récollets* directed schools for boys while they were in charge of the parish between 1671 and 1683, and 1693 and 1777. In Montréal, boys were initially served in the coeducational schools of Marguerite Bourgeois, between 1658 and 1668. In the latter year, Sulpician Father Gabriel Souart (1611–1691) founded a school for boys which continued in operation until the end of the French régime.

Girls were also well provided with schools by the various congregations of sisters. In Québec, the Ursulines were the leading educators from 1639, assisted temporarily at the outset by the Hospitallers. The same Ursulines also opened a school in Trois-Rivières in 1697. Marguerite Bourgeois made her community into the leading teaching order in the colony, founding schools in Montréal (1658), Trois-Rivières (1664), Québec (1686), and other rural settlements. In fact, education would remain a leading form of apostolic activity for the Canadian church until the 1960s.

Health care and social work

A major factor in the development of the Catholic Church in early Canada was the handling of all public health care and social work. Health care was a primary area of apostolic activity for Canada's early church, as were most social services such as the care of the poor. As was noted above, Québec had its first hospital in 1639 when the nursing sisters from Dieppe founded the Hôtel-Dieu hospital, an institution that is still serving its community after more than 350 years.[21] Half-a-century later it was supplemented by the Québec General Hospital

Fig. 8   Capuchin friar in Acadia, 1633.[20] Henri Beau. National Archives of Canada, c-011979.

founded in 1692, and staffed by the same congregation of sisters. Montréal was even more fortunate, having its first hospital as early as 1644, only two years after the founding of the settlement. This establishment by Jeanne Mance was later (1659) to be staffed by a band of nursing sisters from Laflèche, while being designated in turn as the Hôtel-Dieu of Montréal. This would also be supplemented in 1694 by another institution, the Montréal General Hospital founded by the brothers Charron.

We know, however, that it was a congregation of women founded in Montréal towards the end of the French régime that made Montréal famous in the field of health care.[22] The widow d'Youville's Sisters of Charity took over Montréal's General Hospital in 1747, and transformed it into one of the country's best hospitals, an institution that would in time become the cradle of a number of other hospitals across North America.[23] This was the time when a *general hospital* was an institution that frequently sheltered not only the sick, but also many of the needy in society, including orphans, the elderly, poor men and women, or handicapped people who could not provide for themselves. When such services to specific groups (e.g. orphanages, homes for the elderly, etc.) began to be provided in specialized institutions in the nineteenth century, it was usually the same congregations of sisters who ran them. While running the schools and the hospitals, the Canadian clergy also established bureaus for the poor in Québec, Trois-Rivières, and Montréal. These served as relief centres and employment agencies. Clearly, the church was proving indispensable to early Canadian society.

Church developments in the eighteenth century

For much of the seventeenth century, the development of the Catholic Church in Canada was something its leaders and members would be proud of. Numbers of generous missionaries bent every effort to evangelize Amerindians in the farthest reaches of New France, from Acadia to the Mississippi, from the Ohio River to Hudson's Bay; Bishop Laval was providing firm and competent leadership to a church enriched with devoted sisters and dedicated priests; the church was providing the colony with all of its educational, health, and social services; and all of this was done with a view to the greater glory of God, and in a spirit of self-denial and Christian charity. However, this conquering evangelical thrust seemed to falter at the turn of the eighteenth century and remain elusive thereafter. Missionaries were fewer and seemingly less dedicated; beginning in 1685, successive bishops of Québec more often than not seemed either inept leaders – Saint-Vallier is one example – or unworthy clergy who put their personal interests above those of the church.[24] The age of mystics and martyrs had come to an end.

Suggested readings

Bosher, John F. *Business and Religion in the Age of New France, 1600–1760. Twenty-two Studies*. Toronto: Canadian Scholars' Press, 1994.
——. *The Canada Merchants, 1713–1763*. Oxford and New York: Oxford University Press, 1987.
Eccles, W.J. *Essays on New France*. Toronto: Oxford University Press, 1987.
Jaenen, Cornelius. *The Role of the Church in New France*. Toronto: McGraw-Hill Ryerson, 1976.
Johnston, A.J.B. *Life and Religion at Louisbourg, 1713–1758*. Montréal & Kingston: McGill-Queen's University Press, 1996.

CHAPTER 7

Theology, Beliefs, Customs, and Piety

The missionary church of New France understood the Gospel in terms of the Catholic theology that prevailed in the home country, and practised the Christian faith as its French fathers and mothers did, all the while developing some of its own particular customs and devotions. While Canada's Catholics founded and undertook pilgrimages to a number of shrines in Canada, including a major shrine and pilgrimage centre at Beaupré downriver from Québec, the missionaries founded a number of Amerindian Christian villages where an intense piety was practised; several of these villages would last until the present.

Doctrine and theology

The Catholic Reformation of the sixteenth and seventeenth centuries had added ultramontanism with its strong rigorist tendencies to the long-standing Gallican mindset of French Catholics. In the seventeenth century, this rigorism, with its underlying pessimism regarding the capacity of human beings to do good, was challenged by the more trusting and optimistic theology of St François de Sales.

Crosscurrents in French theology

In the European theologies of the sixteenth and seventeenth centuries, both Catholic and Protestant, it was generally agreed that all human beings were undeserving of God's blessings, sin was prevalent even among Christians, and only divine intervention made it possible for some Christians to be liberated from the valley of tears that was the world. This pessimistic view of the situation of the Christian drove most theologians to conclude that most people, Christians included, would be damned for all eternity; only a minority would be saved. While the eternal bliss of heaven was the carrot that was used to incite Christians to work harder to obtain salvation, the horror of everlasting hell was the stick used to drive them in the same direction. As was noted in Chapter 3, this view was reinforced by the social and political maelstrom that had been Europe's lot since the fourteenth century. God was punishing his people for their sins. Fear and anxiety thus became standards of religious feelings in Europe, and numbers of clergymen capitalized on this fear, warning of divine retribution if people did not mend their ways. Natural calamities such as floods, famines, earthquakes, and wars were said to be God's punishment administered to a stubborn and sinful flock.

Although the Council of Trent (1545–1563) had called for reform of the church, it was only fifty years later that the call was answered in the Church of France. During this first half of the seventeenth century, one resource was made up of new religious orders including the Ursuline sisters and the powerful Society of Jesus. Another was the new theology taught by the bishop of Geneva, François de Sales (1567–1622). François, the author of *Introduction to the Devout Life* (1609) and *Treatise on the Love of God* (1616) became the foremost leader of a major spiritual renewal in France. François acknowledged the value of austerity and prayer, as the church had long taught. However, he innovated by teaching the possibility of personal sanctification for all Christians, in all walks of life, by the simple but conscientious fulfillment of their duty, providing this was done in the love of God and neighbour. He taught that any and all were called to Christian perfection, and could achieve it, whether they be soldier, housewife, labourer, or scholar. François was in fact a Christian optimist, turning his back on the pervasive pessimism that permeated the prevailing theology of his day, and seriously undermining the view that salvation was the preserve of the few while damnation was that of the many. Another leader of this renewal was Pierre de Bérulle (1575–1629), the founder of the congregation of the Oratory (1611). Bérulle's teaching was centred on the sovereign majesty of God, and on the Christian's foremost duty of piety and adoration. Given God's majesty, the only way to him was through his son Jesus. The mystery of the Word of God becoming flesh thus became the crux of his theology.

Just as the theologies of Bérulle and St François de Sales grew in their influence over the Church of France, a major challenge to the latter's teaching emerged upon the publication of *Augustinus* (1640) by Cornelius

Jansen (1585–1638). The theological pessimism that permeated the book was consistent with the dominant mindset of European Christianity described above, but not consonant with the new theology of Bérulle and François de Sales that had been taken up by the Jesuits. The latter became the foremost adversaries of the Jansenist party that formed in France in a controversy that bedeviled French Catholicism for 150 years. Both parties were fighting for the minds and souls of the French faithful. In the wake of François de Sales, the Jesuits looked with benevolence upon the Christian, considering that baptism and reconciliation with God through Christ made one into a fundamentally good child of God whose sins had been removed and replaced by divine grace. Such fundamental goodness justified the practice of frequent reception of communion; the Jesuits therefore campaigned for the generalization of such a practice in the Church of France. Nor did Jesuits require that the faithful necessarily confess their sins every time they wanted to receive the Eucharist; such a requirement presumed that the faithful were always in a state of sin, whereas the Jesuits felt that the honest faithful Christian remained in God's love and avoided sin. This theological dispute over doctrine soon became one over moral teaching. With its visceral distrust of humankind, the Jansenist party felt compelled not only to restrict the faithful's access to the Eucharist because allegations of unworthiness, but also to compose a series of regulations aimed at confining the behaviour of Christians to a very narrow road. This became known as moral Jansenism, a form of Catholic Puritanism.

These crosscurrents in seventeenth-century French theology then meshed with the rigor that prevailed among all those Catholics intent upon implementing the program of the Council of Trent. Rigorism can be taken as synonymous with moral Jansenism, or Puritanism. However, it was not exclusive to Jansen's party, but could be found among a growing number of Catholic clergy after the middle of the seventeenth century. Indeed, one could be a Jesuit and therefore opposed to Jansenism, but simultaneously very stringent in one's moral requirements. In Canada, the doctrine of Jansenism did not gain a foothold, but moral Jansenism or rigorism had several outstanding representatives, including Bishops Laval and Saint-Vallier.

The teaching of Bishop Saint-Vallier

During his prolonged absence in Europe (1700–1713), Jean-Baptiste de Saint-Vallier, second bishop of Québec (1687–1727), published a *Catéchisme*

(1702), and a *Rituel* (1703) for the guidance of his clergy and faithful. Because of Saint-Vallier's authoritarian and fractious temperament, many of his clergy in Canada were less than enchanted with his management of the diocese of Québec. This was especially true of the Jesuits who had just lost a dispute with the bishop before the royal court over their jurisdiction in distant missions. Seeking revenge against the quarrelsome bishop, the Jesuits seized upon Saint-Vallier's new publications, and prepared a blistering theological criticism of them. Their spokesperson Jesuit Father Bouvart of Québec argued that the writings contained a variety of heresies including Arianism, Pelagianism, Jansenism, Lutheranism, and Calvinism.[1] Bouvart had grossly exaggerated. Although the *Catéchisme* and *Rituel* needed better editorial work, they could not legitimately be accused of the heresies in question. Saint-Vallier obtained the support of the Sorbonne's Faculty of Theology in the dispute, and in the same year published a revised edition of the *Rituel* (1703) in order to remove some of the more problematical elements from it.

Although orthodox, Saint-Vallier's publications were unabashedly rigoristic, however. For example, in the question-and-answer catechism, to the question regarding the comparative number of the damned and the saved, the answer was unequivocal. There would certainly be more people in hell than in heaven, because the road to damnation was broad, while that leading to eternal life was narrow. Nevertheless, the theology of the Council of Trent was taught, including the basics of Catholic doctrine on God, the church, the sacraments, fasting, and liturgical celebration. The books never became bestsellers in Canada, but they remained the standard reference writings on these subjects for the Canadian church until well into the nineteenth century. They contributed to setting a stamp of moral Jansenism on Canada's church that would last until the Second Vatican Council in the 1960s.

Bishop Saint-Vallier's rigorism was based on the fundamental suspicion of all things human, because man was by definition a sinner; only God was worthy of trust. This led to stringent teachings and regulations including a ban on any theatrical productions, on dancing whenever both sexes were present, and on denunciations of immorality that smacked of exaggeration. This mindset was infectious. For example, while the bishop was being held prisoner in England (1704–1709) as a result of his being captured on the high seas, some of his associates in Québec decried alleged widespread immorality and licentiousness in Canada. One Father Glandelet wrote that it had become normal in Québec to see numbers of visibly pregnant girls, and that one person had told him that half of Québec had become a bordello.

Beliefs and religious customs of Early Canadians

Canadians of the seventeenth and eighteenth centuries continued a number of religious beliefs and practices that they had learned in France, while doing so in a fashion that would in time become more and more particular. This Canadian distinctiveness was partly the result of the ecclesiastical, social, political, and geographical context of the country.

The Canadian context

From the perspective of the history of religions, Canada's story during the French régime can be divided into two distinct phases, that preceding and that following the year 1663.

Before 1663, Canada had been a French colony made up of vast spaces inhabited by scattered Amerindian nations, with only a handful of French settlers, soldiers, and missionaries that were huddled in a few settlements along the St Lawrence River. From the founding of the first colony in Acadia in 1604 until the takeover and occupation of the St Lawrence colony by the Kirke brothers in 1629–32, the country had sheltered handfuls of both Catholics and Protestants because the entrepreneurs that were exploiting the trade in Canada were more often than not Protestants who were required by law to ensure a Catholic presence. Upon founding the Company of New France in 1627, Richelieu's government excluded Protestants from Canada. The state-supported church that followed between the years 1632 and 1657 had been a Jesuit monopoly, a time that corresponded with an intense religious revival in France.

That was the Canada in which mysticism, miracles, and martyrdom nearly became everyday occurrences. Indeed, wonders never ceased in the Canada of Jean de Brébeuf, Isaac Jogues, and Marie de l'Incarnation, to name only a few. Strong church government was exercised by the superior of the Jesuits in Québec who, in the absence of any bishop or rival claimant to clerical control, simultaneously ruled the church of Canada and his own Jesuit mission territory without challenge. This homogeneous church government was supported by colonial authorities who enforced a wide range of church moral and ecclesial directives ranging from the observance of the Sabbath to the ban on trading brandy with the Amerindians. For example, on 29 December 1635, public notices and prohibitions were posted on a pillar in front of the church in Québec. They announced penalties against blasphemy, drunkenness, and failure to attend Mass and religious services on holy days.

From the 1630s to the 1660s and beyond, it was considered normal to have visions, to hear voices from God, to receive divine instructions, or a mandate for an ecclesial project, or to read warnings from God into calamities such as disastrous fires or the earthquake of 1663 in the St Lawrence valley. Such a context ensured that any such claim by an individual would at least be granted a favourable hearing, if not necessarily endorsed. In such a context, what in another time would be understood as dreams or expressions of one's subconscious, easily became visions and voices from God, the Virgin, or some other heavenly personage.

Individual cases were so numerous as to defy easy description. Marie de l'Incarnation had led the founding group of Ursuline sisters to Québec in 1639 as a result of a series of divine instructions received in dreams during the preceding years. Her primary financial backer and companion, the widow Marie-Madeleine de La Peltrie, had likewise determined to fund a school in Canada because of a miraculous cure she had experienced in 1635. Simultaneously, Jérôme Le Royer, a tax-collector in Anjou, France, experienced visions that instructed him to found a congregation of nursing sisters and then send them to Canada to work for the welfare of the Amerindians. From 1659, his band of sisters, the Hospitalers of St. Joseph, would staff the Hôtel-Dieu hospital in Montréal, an institution founded by the pious lay woman Jeanne Mance (1606–1673) in 1644. The latter had in turn been the beneficiary of a miracle when, while on a visit to France in 1658–1659, her broken arm was cured.

This was also the time of the famous Canadian martyrs, eight men including seven Jesuits who were put to death for their faith during the 1640s and as a result were declared saints by the Catholic Church. Some died among the Iroquois south of the St Lawrence, while most others were victims of these same warriors during their raids on the Huron people. As was to be expected, the reverse of this intense religiosity was that some individuals were accused of sorcery before the courts, and one was even put to death for this in 1661. This was never an important part of the religion of New France, however, as only five accusations of sorcery occurred; such accusations never occurred subsequently.

After 1663, a number of changes in the Canadian context led to changes in the religious practices in the colony. In the ten years between 1663 and 1673, a system of royal government with an intendant and a governor replaced the previous government by chartered commercial companies. Also, the French population in Canada doubled, rising from 3,000 to more than 7,600. This was the result of a more favourable settlement policy by the government, of the arrival in 1665 of the 1000 men of the Carignan-Salières regiment, and of the coming to Canada of several hundred *filles du roi*, orphans or impoverished young women who were wards of the French state; the latter were sent to Canada to help alleviate the shortage of women in the colony.

The sudden doubling of the population and the arrival of hundreds of rough and ready soldiers made for a weakening of church influence in the colony, and an increase in the number of illicit activities, including sexual indiscretions, excessive drinking, and generally licentious behaviour. Nevertheless, miraculous and mystical occurrences did not end overnight. Sister Marie Barbier of Marguerite Bourgeois' *Dames de la congrégation* claimed to perform miracles after her entry into the sisterhood in 1679. The merchant's daughter Jeanne Le Ber became a recluse from the age of seventeen until her death at age fifty-two in 1714. The Mohawk woman Kateri Tekakwitha (1656–1680) established a reputation for exceptional holiness in the Christian Amerindian village run by the Jesuits near Laprairie.

Nevertheless, in the latter part of the seventeenth century, the heady, intense mysticism of the earlier period was on the wane. As the population grew rapidly, largely due to natural increase, the clergy seemed more concerned with wrangling among each other than with evangelism; this in turn contributed to a diminishing and then stagnating number of clergymen after 1700, a situation caused both by the absence of Bishop Saint-Vallier and by the reduced number of Jesuits sent to Canada. The ratio of priests to people dropped from one for eighteen faithful in 1640 to one for 184 in 1760. Although there had always been more clergy in the towns than in the countryside, the situation worsened in the first half of the eighteenth century. Only one parish in five had a resident priest in 1730.

Popular attitudes to morality and religion

While the more numerous and diversified population and the diminishing numbers of clergy contributed to the gradual weaning of the faithful from the influence of the church, it was only very gradually that the people desisted from some of their religious practices. Outside the towns of Québec, Montréal and Trois-Rivières, many Canadians had never been extensively 'churched.' In 1683, Intendant Jacques De Meulles wrote that three quarters of Canada's inhabitants did not attend mass four times a year and often died without the sacraments. He opined that, as a rule, their religious education was on the same level as that of the Amerindians. The situation was no different in *Acadie*, one observer qualifying the life of Acadians as "dissolute, libertine, and vagabond."[2]

As was the case in the mother country, a strong cult of relics existed in seventeenth-century Canada. The fragments of the bodies of various deceased Christians, reputed to have lived exemplary Christian lives, were in much demand both as personal possessions and as objects of veneration in churches. The latter held them in ornate boxes or reliquaries, and displayed them during special services and processions for the edification of the faithful. The case of the miraculous cure of Jeanne Mance over the heart of the deceased Jean-Jacques Olier was noted earlier.

Another example of the miraculous powers attributed to holy relics was the use that was made of the remains of fathers Jean de Brébeuf and Gabriel Lalemant. Upon abandoning the mission in Huronia in 1650, Jesuit Father Paul Ragueneau had disinterred the bodies of his deceased colleagues, dried their bones, and carried them back to Québec. These bones became relics as the reputation for holiness of the two missionaries grew over the years. Their curative powers were invoked by Sister Catherine de Saint-Augustin of Québec who added some pulverized bones of Brébeuf to a beverage she fed to a sick heretic she was intent on converting. In another case, bent on obtaining a miraculous cure, a Jesuit missionary had several sick Amerindians drink the water in which the bones of Brébeuf had soaked. In similar fashion, some religious images and objects were held to hold supernatural powers. This could be an image of the Virgin used to cure the sick, or one of the holy family attached to the steeple of the cathedral of Québec in 1690 to repel the assault of Admiral William Phipps from New England.

In Catholic understanding, the entire world, including people and nature, was the creation of God. Although any and all were subject to be drawn away from God by the devil, any and all were equally subject to become the place for a special manifestation of God's grace. Therefore, it stood to reason that God's children called upon him to give special attention to fields, homes, crops, marriage beds, ships, voyages, church bells, and any number of other objects, activities, and people. This was why special blessings were plentiful in the church of early Canada. Frequently, holy water was used for this, water that had been blessed by a priest as a visible token of the grace of God being conveyed to the person or thing being blessed. Early Catholic Canada was perceived by the faithful as a world that was constantly subject to and needful of God's blessings.

The religious images found in Canada represented many of the characters found in the Catholic calendar of saints; these images existed in metallic or paper form. Scapulars were also found. They were pendants made of cloth representing in miniature what had originally been one of the garments worn by monks. Some of the faithful in Canada wore a scapular around their neck, with one image representing the Virgin, another the Sacred Heart, or some other holy figure. It was in this late seventeenth century that a new religious devotion called the *novena* originated. It consisted of the daily fulfillment during nine consecutive days of set works of piety such as the recitation of certain prayers, the hearing of Mass, or the visiting of churches. In return, the practitioner was rewarded with indulgences and hopefully the fulfillment of an expressed wish.

Confraternities

Beginning in 1656, a series of confraternities were founded in New France. Confraternities were lay associations of piety, usually established at the suggestion of the clergy, and intended to promote lay devotion to Christ and the chosen patron saint of the group.[3] The latter became the model of the members who sought personal conversion through the imitation of the patron's virtues, the receiving of the sacraments, the recitation of prayers, and the fulfillment of various works of charity such as the visitation of the sick and of prisoners. Some of the confraternities were segregated by gender. Many recruited large numbers of faithful, although not enough is known about the degree of participation of the membership. Indeed, in some cases pastors automatically enrolled all of their parishioners in some of the confraternities of their parish. In return for their efforts, members of confraternities received indulgences and the satisfaction of having done more than was required in the interests of obtaining salvation. In the eyes of the clergy, confraternities were one of the ways used to steer the faithful along the narrow path to salvation.

Holy places and pilgrimages

French as well as Amerindian Canadians acknowledged some places as sacred, that is as venues where God, the Virgin, or spirits were encountered and where wonders happened. In early Canada, several such places existed, the earliest and foremost being the shrine dedicated to St Anne at Beaupré on the north shore of the St Lawrence some thirty-five kilometres below Québec. Anne, the mother of the Virgin Mary, had been honoured in some Christian churches since earliest times. Her popularity increased after the twelfth century, and the Holy See extended her feast to the universal church in 1584. It is celebrated on 26 July. The feast took strong root in Brittany, France, whence it was carried to Canada by the Breton sailors for whom St Anne was their designated protector against the perils of the sea. In their long sailing voyages to Canada, which lasted four to six weeks if not more, these rough-hewn men knew that landfall was not the end of their troubles, because navigating up the Gulf and the St Lawrence River with its many shoals constituted a more perilous adventure than crossing the North Atlantic. The rapids at the narrows below Québec at Beaupré constituted one of the most dangerous places on the river, a place where the sailors never failed to ask for St Anne's assistance, just as Amerindians considered it a special place to encounter spirits. Upon passing this last hurdle on their way upriver from France, ships fired cannon shots to celebrate their safe arrival.

There it was that in 1658 a chapel was built on land given for the purpose by the settler Étienne Lessard. Two years later it was replaced by a church. Shortly thereafter, a group of shipwrecked sailors attributed their rescue to the intervention of St Anne. Indeed, miracles were beginning to occur at Beaupré. Sister Marie de l'Incarnation reported in 1665 that at that sacred place the blind recovered their sight, the sick their health, and the paralyzed their ability to walk. The news spread far and wide and the church dedicated to St Anne at Beaupré became the site of pilgrimages. The faithful made special voyages there to pray God through the intermediary intervention of Mary and her mother, and to ask for exceptional divine intervention to cure them of their illnesses. The shrine of St Anne de Beaupré was born. While some pilgrims returned year after year, others came from the furthest corners of the colony to implore the intercession of Mary's mother. Its lone pastor reported in the 1730s that the shrine was sufficiently busy to keep three or four priests occupied with hearing confessions, celebrating Masses, and leading the pilgrims in prayer.

Fig. 9.   Church at the shrine of St Anne de Beaupré in 1876. National Archives of Canada, PA-148905.

At St Anne's shrine, a growing number of pilgrims left mementos of God's answering their prayers. These included numerous gifts to the church, but also paintings that were commissioned by grateful pilgrims whose prayers had been answered. They were called *ex voto* paintings given that their patrons had vowed to commission them if God gave them a favourable answer. In 1670, Bishop Laval donated the first relic of St Anne to the shrine, one that he had obtained from France. The following year, the Hurons came to Beaupré on a pilgrimage, inaugurating the widespread devotion to Mary's mother among Canada's Catholic Amerindians.[4] Over the years, the pilgrimages continued at Beaupré; new churches being constructed in the late seventeenth century, in 1876, and in 1976. In 1960, Pope John XXIII donated a relic. It is estimated that the now internationally-renowned shrine receives a million and a half visitors yearly in this early twenty-first century.

While St Anne de Beaupré was far and away the major shrine in early Canada, it was not the only one. Others were at Ancienne Lorette, at the Jesuit house of Notre-Dame-des-Anges in Québec, at the chapel of Notre-

Dame-de-Bon-Secours in Montréal, at the church of Notre-Dame-des-Victoires in Québec's Lower Town, and at Oka outside Montréal.

After fleeing to Québec from Huronia in 1650 and 1651, beginning in 1673 the Huron people settled a short distance outside Québec on land obtained for them by the Jesuits. The settlement was named Lorette in commemoration of the town in Italy that was dear to their missionary, Father Pierre Chaumonot (Calvonotti). In 1674, the first chapel of the new mission of Notre-Dame-de-Lorette was constructed and blessed to serve an Amerindian population that numbered between 150 and 300 in the following years. Only good Christian Amerindians were welcomed at Lorette, Father Chaumonot frequently noting their admirable Christian virtues. The result was that French settlers, including Governors Frontenac and Denonville, soon began to journey to Lorette to pray in the place of holiness. Within a generation, however, brandy traders succeeded in penetrating the Amerindian village and tarnishing its reputation for virtue. Nevertheless, pilgrims kept coming, even after the Amerindians had moved from the initial Ancienne Lorette to nearby Loretteville (Jeune Lorette) and built a new chapel there in 1730.

The chapel of Notre-Dame-de-Bon-Secours in Montréal was built by St Marguerite Bourgeois in 1678 to house the statue of the Virgin that she had brought from France in 1672. Rebuilt and restored on several occasions, the chapel is the oldest church in Montréal, and is still a shrine for pilgrims. It contains *ex votos* that date back to the early years of the colony. The Church of Notre-Dame-des-Victoires on the Place Royale in Lower Town Québec was another of Canada's oldest shrines, although most of today's visitors are no longer pilgrims but tourists. Built in 1688, it was given its present name to commemorate two French victories over British invaders in 1690 and 1711. It became a special place of pilgrimage for sailors. Finally, beginning in 1740, the Sulpician fathers and their Amerindian parishioners built a Way of the Cross on Oka mountain at the Christian Amerindian village on the Lake of Two Mountains west of Montréal. It served as a shrine for Christian Amerindians of the greater Montréal area.

The piety of early Canadians was also reflected in hundreds of wayside crosses that dotted the landscape of the colony. Beginning with the explorer Jacques Cartier who erected a large cross when he landed at Gaspé in 1535, Canada's French explorers and settlers used crosses both to mark their claims of possession of the country and to honour God in their villages and at various crossroads. Reporting on his journey down the St Lawrence from Montréal to Québec in August, 1749, the Swedish scientist and keen observer Pehr Kalm wrote: "There are several crosses put up by the road side, which is parallel to the shores of the river. These crosses are very common in Canada, and are put up to excite devotion in the traveler. They are made of wood, five or six yards high, and proportionally broad. In that side which looks towards the road is a square hole, in which they place an image of our Savior, the cross, or of the holy Virgin, with the child in her arms; and before that they put a piece of glass, to prevent its being spoiled by the weather... They put up about ... [those crosses] all the instruments which they think the Jews employed in crucifying our Savior ... A figure of the cock, which crowed when St. Peter denied our Lord, is commonly put at the top of the cross."[5]

For early Canadians, the world was God's garden where he roamed at will. Therefore, it stood to reason that he could, and did become manifest in a wide variety of persons and places. These were the saints, the objects closely associated with them, and the special sites where God chose to demonstrate his care and benevolence for his people. Such privileged manifestations were to be expected because God's intention was always to liberate his people from their sins, and receive those of good will into his eternal life of bliss. The faithful's role was first to confess their sins, to ask for divine assistance in living according to God's will, to recognize the chosen individuals and places where God appeared, and to show their gratitude for these manifestations by appropriate gestures. The latter included prayers, the reception of the sacraments, the observance of God's law, the undertaking of pilgrimages, and in some cases the commissioning of *ex votos* in thanks for favours received. The world of early Canadians was a sacral world under the watchful eye of God.

Amerindian Christian villages

When Catholic missionaries first came to Canada in the early seventeenth century, their first evangelization of the Amerindian people was made by individual missionaries who joined specific Amerindian bands in their villages or camps. Those who evangelized the Algonkian people who sustained themselves by hunting and fishing, by necessity became itinerant missionaries who travelled in the forests and on the rivers and lakes with the people they sought to evangelize. This was the case of the first *Récollet* and Jesuit missionaries on the north shore of the St Lawrence below Québec. The missionaries who evangelized the more sedentary and agricultural Iroquoian people like the Huron resided in a cabin in an Amerindian village while working to obtain the conversion of their charges to the Christian faith.

However, whether he was sedentary or itinerant, the missionary soon realized that he was working under an enormous disadvantage, not so much because of the physical hardships and inconveniences, although these were major obstacles in themselves, but primarily because Amerindian spiritualities were woven into the very fabric of Amerindian daily life. In order to change these spiritualities, to replace them with the message of the Gospels as he felt he must, the missionary was required to challenge the myths, the stories, and the daily customs of the entire nation or tribe he was dealing with. In a word, in order to evangelize success-fully, the missionary had to attack and undermine the culture of the Amerindians he was dealing with. He had to destroy their understand-ing of the world, in order to replace it with another. Not all missionaries sought to effect such cultural replacement with the same intensity. In fact, the Jesuits proved more willing to adapt particular elements of Amerindian life and custom to the Gospel they preached, while Sulpicians and *Récollets* proved to be less so. Nevertheless, all agreed that in the end the accultura-tion of the Amerindians would facilitate their evangelization.

In the light of the minimal results obtained during their first attempts at evangelizing Amerindians, the missionaries concluded that their ob-jective could be achieved more easily if the hard-won Amerindian con-verts could be protected and nurtured in a more favourable environment than was the typical Amerindian village or encampment. The idea of a Christian Amerindian village, one reserved for Christian Amerindians only, was born. In addition to the celebrated Fort Sainte-Marie Among the Hurons, these included Sillery, Cap-de-la-Madeleine, Loretteville, Kahnesatake (La Montagne or Oka), Kahnawake (Sault-Saint-Louis or Caughnawaga), Saint-François on the lower Chaudière River, and Akwesasne (Saint-Régis) near today's Cornwall. These several villages for Christian Amerindians that came to be founded in Canada during the French régime were not established on land to which the Amerindians held title, but rather on land belonging to the clergy, whether Jesuit or Sulpician. The Crown ceded the land to the clergy for the purpose of establishing a Christian Amerindian village there.

The story of Fort Sainte-Marie was told earlier;[6] some of these other

missions are worthy of note as special projects aimed at better evangelizing Canada's Amerindians. The first such village was founded by the
Jesuits at Sillery on the outskirts of Québec in 1637, another founded
later at Cap-de-la-Madeleine near Trois-Rivières. In the 1640s the Sillery
mission harboured about forty Christian families and a number of other
traditionalists drawn from the neighbouring Algonquin and Montagnais
nations to whom the Jesuits endeavoured to teach agricultural methods
that would replace their traditional livelihood as hunters and fishers.
Indeed, intensive hunting had depleted the game in the region's forests, forcing the Amerindian people to find other means of subsistence.
Problems of disease, alcohol, an Iroquois raid in 1655, and a devastating
fire soon spelled disaster for the mission. The number of inhabitants
diminished, leading the Jesuits to open the land to white settlement in
the 1660s. However, beginning in 1676 Abenakis settled there, replacing
the earlier Montagnais and Algonquin, thus ensuring a rebirth of the
Amerindian community that lasted until the early 1740s.

On Sillery and Sainte-Marie had set the pace, several Amerindian
Christian communities were founded. As was noted above, from 1673
Lorette was the refuge of the remnants of the Huron nation that had
temporarily settled on Île d'Orléans after 1650. Another village for Christian Amerindians, the mission of Saint-François-de-Sales, was founded
in the region of Québec near the mouth of the Chaudière River to serve
the Abenakis. To serve the western Abenakis, the mission village of
Saint-François-du-Lac (Odanak) was founded in 1700 on the Saint-
François River near Lake Saint-Pierre, a part of the St Lawrence River
above Trois-Rivières. Shortly thereafter, most of the Amerindian residents of Sillery were removed to Bécancour on the river of the same
name, south of Trois-Rivières, thus creating another community.

On the Jesuit seigneurie of Laprairie, across the St Lawrence River
from Montréal, a handful of Christian Mohawks and Oneidas settled
after 1668, at the invitation of Father Pierre Raffeix. During the following years, numbers of others joined them, disenchanted with the un-
settled conditions in the Iroquois villages, conditions caused by factors
such as the large numbers of newly-adopted members of the tribes, the
problems related to alcohol abuse, and the tensions between the rival
camps of Christians and traditionalists. The Amerindian village at
Laprairie received a major influx of new residents in the 1690s when the
majority of the Mohawks moved there from their traditional homes,
after suffering military setbacks in war. Over the years, the mission

village moved from Laprairie westward to Kahnawake (Sault-Saint-Louis or Caughnawaga) on Lake Saint-Louis.

In Montréal, the domain of the Gentlemen of Saint-Sulpice, in 1676 the priests founded an Amerindian Christian village on the slopes of Mount Royal; it was known as La Montagne, and welcomed both Algonquins and Iroquois. In order to remove their charges from the all-too-readily available alcohol offered by white traders, the Sulpicians moved their mission from La Montagne to Sault-au-*Récollet* and then, in the wake of the Crown's grant of a seigneurie to the Sulpicians for that specific purpose, in 1721 the Sulpicians moved their Amerindian village to Lac-des-deux-Montagnes at the junction of the Ottawa and St Lawrence rivers. Along with its older population of Iroquois and Algonquin, the new mission of Kahnesataké (Oka) welcomed some 900 Nipissing, Fox, Pawnee, and Sioux refugees from the wars of recent years who had gathered at nearby Sault-au-*Récollet*.

The last of the Christian Amerindian villages founded during the French régime were further up the St Lawrence River from Montréal. On the site of today's Ogdensburg, New York, in 1749 the Sulpicians founded the mission of Oswegatchie for the Iroquois. Nearby, across the St Lawrence River from Cornwall, Ontario, in 1755 the Jesuits founded the mission of Akwesasne (Saint-Régis), a site that stood at the junction of the future provinces of Ontario and Québec, and of the State of New York.

During their better years, many of these Christian Amerindian villages bore witness to an intense Christian life. In the 1640s, the mission at Sillery was highly disciplined. Converts were subject to ecclesiastical penances, including public floggings for certain offences. Native captains elected by the Amerindian residents enforced the rules, while the more devout among the Amerindian converts were enrolled into sodalities. In the Huron Lorette, where drunkenness was punishable by imprisonment or expulsion, one man and one woman called *dogiques* were elected by their peers to supervise both secular and sacred affairs. In addition, several communities had male and female catechists for the religious instruction of the people.

In many Christian villages, daily prayers were recited at the close of each day, while Sundays were marked by a variety of liturgical services, processions, sermons and instructions. Hymns were composed and sung, and churches were brightly and lavishly decorated. A variety of pious associations were founded by the missionaries, including sodalities and confraternities. This was the context in which the woman Kateri Tekakwitha, of mixed Mohawk and Algonquin stock, established her reputation for sanctity during her residence at Sault-Saint-Louis between 1677 and 1680. She even indulged in mortifications which included self-flagellation and sleeping on a bed of thorns, practices which were not considered morbid at the time.

Concluding remarks

The religion that was practised in early Canada was the majority-faith of France transplanted into a very different setting. The Protestantism present during the colony's first quarter-century (1604–1629) was outlawed after 1627, and the crusading faith of Catholic reform was implemented by the Jesuit-led missionary church for the next quarter-century (1632–1657). This was the age of mystics and martyrs, men like Jean de Brébeuf and Gabriel Lalemant who were put to death in Huronia in 1649. On 29 June 1930, they were declared saints by Pope Pius XI, along with six other men who had died in the missions of New France, namely René Goupil (1642), Isaac Jogues (1646), Jean de LaLande (1646), Antoine Daniel (1648), Noël Chabanel (1649), and Charles Garnier (1649). While Jesuit missionaries were being put to death, Sister Marie de l'Incarnation simultaneously ran her congregation of Ursuline sisters and engaged in an ongoing dialogue with God through exceptional mystical encounters.

Beginning in the 1660s, this heady, intense, and passionate Christianity slowly changed into the more mundane, ordinary, and unexceptional religion that became manifest after 1700. Petty clerical bickering and religious indifference came to overshadow the Christian faith, love, and dedication of earlier times. Nevertheless, in spite of this less-than-admirable trend, some continued to bear witness to the Gospel in outstanding ways. This was the case of the teaching Sisters of Notre Dame and their founder Marguerite Bourgeois who was declared a saint by Pope John Paul II in 1984. It was the case for the nursing sisters of Charity of the Montréal General Hospital and their founder Marguerite Dufrost, the widow d'Youville, who was also declared a saint by Pope John Paul II in 1990.

During these 150 years of changing Christianity, Canadians understood the world as created by God, managed by God, and led by God towards a glorious destiny where sin and death would be overcome, and a life of everlasting bliss would be the reward of God's faithful children. Those who turned their backs on God would inherit a life of eternal torment. Like their clerical leaders, the faithful wrestled with the question of the relative numbers of the saved and the damned, most giving the edge to the latter. Their leading spokesman in Canada was Bishop Saint-Vallier. Their theology was more hard-edged and pessimistic, focusing as it did on the ubiquity of sin, and the terrors of God's judgment.

Some seventeenth- and eighteenth-century Catholics, however, foresaw a more glorious future and were growing in numbers. This latter party included the Jesuits who tended to speak more emphatically and frequently about hope, love, mercy, trust, and forgiveness. Theirs was a gentler and loving mindset, one more driven by loving trust in God than by fear. This party represented the wave of the future in Canadian Catholicism, one that would gradually gain ground on the prophets of doom.

By all accounts, the religious practices of Canadians were not only clergy-driven, but very much a part of daily life and understanding. The *ex votos* in the shrines, the pilgrimages in the tiny colony, the wayside crosses that dotted the landscape, the membership in confraternities – all testify to a faith that permeated everyone's understanding. To be sure, not all French Canadians behaved in a fashion that could draw down the clergy's blessings upon them; in fact, in the eyes of the bishops, so many Canadians misbehaved that their prospects of salvation would have been dim at best. One must remember, however, that Canada's bishops, Laval and Saint-Vallier in particular, tended to be grim, determined, and joyless taskmasters. They came out of an older school of theology and reform where a good Christian was expected to suffer, by necessity or by choice, in order to gain heaven.

Many Amerindian Christian villages were sooner or later ravaged by the spread of alcohol abuse among the residents, a disease that destroyed some entire communities. During the years when this infection was kept at a distance, however, these Christian Amerindian villages frequently lived and practised exemplary forms of Christian piety. Indeed, when circumstances were favourable, Amerindians took very well to the colourful and dramatic rituals and liturgy of Catholicism. Incense, statues, hymn-singing, sacred stories, processions, pilgrimages, holy water, holy images, all highlighted a faith that was intense, all-encompassing, and meaningful. The intensity of the religious faith of Christian Amerindians was reinforced by the cultural conversion and/or trauma these same Amerindians experienced when abandoning their traditional ways in order to become Christians. They had to abandon not only a series of beliefs, but had to turn their backs on a way of life, a world view integrated with their traditional spiritual understanding.

In fact, when faced with the militant evangelizing of the missionaries, Amerindians reacted in three different ways. Initially, when their Amerindian communities were still strong, most resisted the intruders and their message, rallying around their traditional way of life and spiritualities. This reaction is manifest in the history of the Jesuit mission of Huronia from 1634. Secondly, when it became apparent that the Amerindian way of life was seriously endangered as a result of war, disease, or a combination thereof, one of two reactions became typical. One was to convert to Christianity outright, abandoning the traditional ways. The other was to reject the missionaries and retain the ancestral, traditional way.

Thirdly, some Amerindians confronted with both militant evangelism and an uncertain future for their way of life, chose the path of dimorphism, that is to say electing both Christianity and the traditional ways. Many observers and scholars feel that this may well have been the reaction of large numbers of Amerindians, simultaneously claiming to be Christians and continuing to practise their traditional spiritualities. Indeed, the exclusiveness claimed by the Christian faith was an unusual concept for Canada's Amerindian people who traditionally felt that there was a wide range of spirits in the world and just as many ways of communicating and honouring them. It was not the Christian faith to which Amerindian traditionalists objected. It was its claim to exclusivity, its demand that the Christian Amerindian reject his traditional religion.

While there is no doubting the sincerity of the religious conversion to Christianity of many Amerindians, there is also no doubting the fact that many became Christians when they saw their traditional world disintegrating around them. They chose Christianity in order to survive as a people. They either chose it exclusively as the missionaries required, or as another way alongside their traditional religion. Ironically, the Catholic Christianity they chose as their collective life raft would serve a similar purpose for French Canada in the wake of the British Conquest.

Suggested readings

Boglioni, Pierre and Benoît Lacroix. Eds. *Les pèlerinages au Québec.* Québec: Presses de l'Université Laval, 1981.

Choquette, Robert. "French Catholicism Comes to the Americas." Charles H. Lippy et al. *Christianity Comes to the Americas 1492–1776*. New York: Paragon House, 1992.

Cliche, Marie-Aimée. *Les pratiques de dévotion en Nouvelle-France*. Sainte-Foy: Presses de l'Université Laval, 1988.

St. John, Leonard. *The Novalis Guide to Canadian Shrines*. Ottawa: Novalis, 1994.

CHAPTER 8

The Church, the British Conquest, and the *Québec Act*

In stages between 1710 and 1790, New France disappeared and was replaced by a new British colony that, in time, spanned the entire northern half of North America. This radical change in the political destinies of Canada was highlighted by the Conquest itself (1760), followed by two constitutional laws adopted by the Parliament of Great Britain, namely the *Québec Act* (1774), and the *Constitutional Act* (1791). However, while Canada's government was now British and Protestant, its people remained French and Catholic. The Christian church in Canada continued to serve its people as best it could while adapting to its new English and Protestant sovereign.

The British Conquest

At the beginning of the eighteenth century, the French Crown controlled most of the North American continent, from the Gulf of Mexico to Hudson Bay, and from Acadia to the Illinois country in the Northwest. England, France's foremost rival in the region, had a tenuous foothold in Newfoundland, but a powerful presence in the Thirteen Colonies of the Atlantic seaboard, a compact group of rich and thriving settlements that were sixteen times more populous than New France.

The unravelling of the French empire in North America began when England conquered Acadia in 1710, but especially upon the end of the War of the Spanish Succession when the Treaty of Utrecht in 1713 consigned major portions of the French empire to England. Through it, Louis XIV's government was forced to pay off the English for military losses in Europe. That was when Hudson Bay, Newfoundland, and peninsular Nova Scotia, the main part of Acadia, passed into English hands. France retained possession of the St Lawrence colony and of what was left of Acadia, namely Prince Edward Island (*Île Saint-Jean*), Cape Breton Island (*Île Royale*), and New Brunswick.[1] The boundary between French Acadia and English Nova Scotia ran through the Chignecto peninsula, near present-day Amherst.

For thirty years thereafter, while peace prevailed between England and France, each built up its North American strength for the fighting that was bound to break out again between the two world powers. This was when the major fortress of Louisbourg on Cape Breton Island was constructed by France as a new centre of the fishing trade, and as the primary anchor of its defenses in the region. When fighting resumed during the War of the Austrian Succession (1740–1748), besieged Louisbourg fell to a seaborne assault from New England in 1745. The fortress was returned to France by the peace treaty of Aix-la-Chapelle in 1748.

A climate of war continued to prevail when British and French armies clashed in the Ohio River valley in 1754. This marked the beginning of the fighting officially designated as the Seven Years' War (1756–1763).[2] This struggle that ended French dominion in North America included the deportation of the Acadians between 1755 and 1763, the second fall of Louisbourg (1758), the fall of Québec to British forces led by General Wolfe (1759), the fall of Montréal to another British army (1760), and the resulting capitulation of Canada.

The church and the Conquest

The Conquest of Canada was the culmination of a half-century of conflict between England and France, and the beginning of another half-century of struggle between the Catholic Church of Canada and her new colonial masters. The fifty years preceding 1760 had been difficult ones for the church in Canada, and the invasion by the British, particularly the bombardment of Québec in 1759, did nothing to improve the situation. Once in control of the country, Great Britain allowed freedom of religion to Catholics, but also undertook to ban some religious orders, to restrict the rights of the church, and to establish the Church of England in the new colony. England's policy was expressed in a series of documents written after 1760. Because of the Conquest, new challenges faced the Catholic clergy in all areas of endeavour. The central institutions of the church were all threatened, including the bishop's office, the religious orders, and the institutions of education. The way the church responded to these challenges determined its fate in Canada then and to the present day.

The state of the church on the eve of the Conquest

The state of Catholic theology, customs, and piety have been noted above,[3] as was the ineffective leadership of the church for most of the half century preceding the British conquest. And this at a time when the British had already conquered much of Acadia and were giving the Acadian Catholics a taste of the treatment Canadians could anticipate if and when Britannia took over the central colony on the St Lawrence.

There was no bishop in Québec for twenty of the forty years between 1700 and 1740, and when a bishop was in residence he was usually ineffective. This leadership vacuum translated into low numbers of clergy, low morale among them, festering administrative and disciplinary problems, and diminishing influence of the church on the government of the colony. The first of the absentee bishops had been Saint-Vallier[4] who had sailed to France in 1700 in order to counter his Jesuit rivals in the missions of the Mississippi River. While there, Saint-Vallier published his *Rituel*, and then took ship back to Canada in 1704 only to be taken prisoner on the high seas by the English who held him prisoner for five years. Upon his release in 1709, the unhappy bishop discovered to his dismay that the French court refused to allow him to return to Québec, because of the numerous and sustained complaints of many of the colony's clergy, both male and female. It took Saint-Vallier another four years to convince the government to permit his return. Upon his arrival in Québec in 1713 after a thirteen-year absence, the bishop took up residence in the General Hospital, led a life of austerity, and proceeded to denounce both clergy and faithful for their alleged wantonness and mediocrity. The disgruntled bishop was not much loved when he died on 26 December 1727. He had been bishop of Québec for forty-two years, nearly half a century characterized by absenteeism, legal wrangling, and personality conflicts between the bishop and his clergy and flock. Saint-Vallier was not lacking in personal virtue, but in the leadership skills that were necessary to inspire collegiality and collaboration.

In 1728, the Canadian church desperately needed a strong bishop, but would have to wait another thirteen years to obtain one. Another three ineffective churchmen occupied the see of Québec in succession

Fig. 10.   A wayside cross on the Lachine Road in 1866.[5] Francis Ann Hopkins. National Archives of Canada, c-002737.

before Bishop Pontbriand[6] arrived in 1741. The first was the Capuchin friar Louis-François Mornay[7] (1727–1733) who refused to come to Canada yet continued to hold the title of bishop of Québec and collect the revenues that went with the position. His coadjutor (1727–1733) and then successor (1733–1739), Pierre-Hermann Dosquet, actually spent four years in Québec out of his twelve years as a bishop. The French court finally managed to purchase his resignation in 1739, and nominated François-Louis Lauberivière[8] (1739–1740) to succeed him. On 8 August 1740, Lauberivière had the misfortune of dying of a disease contracted on board ship, only twelve days after setting foot in Québec.

The bishop's office was more effective during the administration of Henri-Marie Dubreil de Pontbriand (1741–1760) who resided in Canada continually from his arrival on 29 August 1741 until his death on 8 June 1760. Pontbriand wanted to reform the institutions of his diocesan church, much in need of attention because of the many years of neglect. He had to contend, however, with the difficult social and economic conditions that prevailed in his diocese, due to several years of crop failures and the persistent war that marked the local and international scene during most of his twenty years in office. The situation was compounded by abuses and mismanagement of the colony's affairs during the years of Intendant François Bigot (1748–1760) and the periods of famine that struck the colony in 1752, 1757, and 1758.

In spite of disagreements with some of the clergy, Pontbriand governed his diocese with a strong hand, subject however to the pleasure of the royal court. Indeed, Pontbriand had sworn an oath of allegiance to the court, and was in effect an officer of the crown from whom he received an annual stipend of twelve thousand French pounds. He had various buildings restored, including the bishop's house and the cathedral, both of which had been allowed to become run down. By 1758, the bishop was convinced that the colony would be lost to the English, and was fearful of what this entailed for Catholics. The situation in Acadia was far from reassuring for Canada's Catholics.

During the fifty years after the English conquest of Nova Scotia in 1710, things had gone from bad to worse for its French Catholic population. The Treaty of Utrecht in 1713 had acknowledged the freedom of religion of the people with the usual condition of "as far as the laws of Great Britain allow." After 1713, British authorities in Nova Scotia always sought to obtain an unconditional oath of allegiance from Acadians, while the latter insisted on only taking the oath if they were not required to take up arms against France, and if they remained free to practise their Catholic religion. The deadlock between the two parties was ended in 1755 when Governor Lawrence of Nova Scotia ordered the deportation of the Acadian population in order to give their lands to English settlers.

There were two distinct groups of Catholic clergy working in Nova Scotia after 1710, the priests ministering in the Acadian parishes and the missionaries to the Amerindians. Both groups ended up hunted down by British forces, but only the latter deserved to be because of their loyalty to the French crown. The priests who served the Acadian parishes in Port Royal and the Minas Basin were either *Récollets*[9] or Sulpicians[10] who were instructed by the bishop of Québec to show unquestioned loyalty to their new British sovereign. The pastor of Grand Pré, Father Chauvreulx, took the oath of loyalty to the English king in 1749 and advised his 3,000 parishioners to do so as well. At the same time, the pastor of Port Royal, Father Desenclaves did likewise. Nevertheless, both were later arrested and deported along with every other priest in Nova Scotia.

The missionaries to the Amerindians of Nova Scotia were based in the French Acadian territories that surrounded Nova Scotia, were salaried by the French crown, and worked not only to evangelize the Amerindians but also to keep them loyal to France. These included Jesuits who directed two missions, one to the Abenaki on the Penobscot and Kennebec rivers in today's state of Maine, and another to the Malecite Amerindians on the St John River in today's New Brunswick. On the Kennebec, Father Sébastien Râle (1627–1724) urged his people to resist the English until he was killed in an English raid in 1724. His scalp was taken and sent to Boston for bounty. The story was similar at the Jesuit mission at Meductic on the St John River where missionaries evangelized their charges while supporting their fight against the English.[11]

The missionaries to the Amerindians of Nova Scotia were initially led from Louisbourg by the Canadian priest Antoine Gaulin (1674–1740). Gaulin had been working in Acadia since 1698. After the founding of Louisbourg in 1717, he established a mission for the Mi'kmaq at Antigonish around 1720. Gaulin retired to Québec in 1732. He was succeeded in his Amerindian missions by two French priests who would become notorious in the English annals of Nova Scotia. Both were sent by Paris' Seminary of Foreign Missions. Father Jean-Louis Le Loutre (1709–1772) was a missionary to the Amerindians of Nova Scotia who would end up with a price on his head. After his arrival in Louisbourg in 1737, he worked with the Mi'kmaqs at Shubenacadie, near today's Truro in the heart of Nova Scotia. He kept his flock loyal to France in the war against England that broke out in 1744. Upon his return from three years in France (1746–1749), Le Loutre resided at French Fort Beauséjour on the contested Chignecto peninsula that divided Nova Scotia from Acadia. He became the nemesis of British forces in his effective support of the Mi'kmaq against the British. Father Le Loutre fled the country when Fort Beauséjour fell in 1755, but was captured on the high seas by the British who held him prisoner for eight years. Father Pierre Maillard (1710–1762) arrived in Louisbourg in 1735, mastered the Mi'kmaq language, and toured various Amerindian villages in Nova Scotia, Cape Breton, and Prince Edward Island. When hostilities broke out in 1744, he made himself indispensable to French authorities by keeping the Mi'kmaq loyal to France, and by participating in their raids on English posts. After the second fall of Louisbourg in 1758, he spent one year hiding in the forests with several fugitive Acadian and Amerindian families. Then, in November 1759, he accepted the peace settlement offered by English authorities, and spent his three remaining years of life working as a salaried English agent charged with keeping the peace with the Amerindians. Ironically, he was given a solemn funeral service organized by the government of Nova Scotia, whose legislature had decreed the perpetual imprisonment of Catholic priests only three years earlier. Upon Father Maillard's death, there was not a single Catholic priest left in Nova Scotia.

The immediate effects of the British invasion

Other than the destruction of the Fortress of Louisbourg after 1758, Québec was the only place to suffer extensive material damage from the British conquest. The two-month British siege of 1759 completely destroyed one third of the town's houses, and many others had to be torn down afterwards. Most of the religious institutions along with the fortifications were located atop the escarpment, and thus bore the brunt of the bombardment. The cathedral, the seminary, the parish rectory, and the chapel of the bishop's residence were completely destroyed. The chapels of the Ursulines, of the Jesuits, of the *Récollets*, and of the Seminary were partially damaged. However, in the surrounding area damages were much more limited, the most notable being on the south shore of the St Lawrence, downstream from Lévis. At Trois-Rivières, only one of twenty churches was destroyed, while in the region of Montréal, only four of forty-eight churches were damaged.[12]

Upon occupying Québec in September 1759, the British army took over both the Hôtel-Dieu and the convent of the Ursulines to serve as hospitals for the troops. It then repaired the Ursuline chapel and used it for Church of England worship for one year; then the conquerors made the chapel of the *Récollets* into their house of worship from 1760 to 1796. The Ursulines regained possession of both their convent and their chapel in 1760. In addition, the British established their main military warehouse in what had been the Jesuit College until its closure in 1759. That institution would never reopen.

During the siege of Québec, all the teaching and nursing sisters had sought refuge in the General Hospital which was somewhat removed from the centre of the town. These 113 women, who constituted more than half of all the sisters in Canada, were equally divided among the three congregations of Ursulines and Hospitalers from the two nursing institutions.[13] Another seventy-seven sisters worked in Montréal, while

Fig. 11.   View of the bishop's house and the ruins looking from Upper to Lower Town Québec in 1761. Richard Short based on engraving by J. Fougeron. National Archives of Canada, c-000352.

fourteen Ursulines laboured in Trois-Rivières, for a total of 204 sisters in Canada. With few exceptions, these women were of Canadian birth.

The male clergy in Canada were equally divided between nearly one hundred diocesan or secular priests and eighty-four members of religious orders. In 1759, the latter included thirty Sulpicians, twenty-five Jesuits, twenty-four *Récollets*, five Seminary priests, and the Spiritan Father Maillard in Nova Scotia; the vast majority of these men were born in France, with the exception of the *Récollets* who were Canadian in a proportion of 70%. Fully 80% of the secular priests were of Canadian birth. Within five years, however, fifteen of the religious clergy would return to France, leaving the secular clergy with a growing majority. The days of French domination of the church in Canada were decidedly numbered.

Within a year of the fall of Québec, the effects of the Conquest were becoming apparent. The problems of the church would increase exponentially upon the death of Bishop Pontbriand on 8 June 1760, two months before the capitulation of Montréal. How could the church rebuild without a leader? How could a French-speaking Catholic bishop be appointed from an occupying power that was both the enemy of France and Protestant?

British religious policy, 1759–1765

Upon the capitulation of Montréal in September 1760, the British army had full control of Canada; it would remain in charge until civil government was implemented on 10 August 1764, subsequent to the 1763 Treaty of Paris whereby Canada became a colony of Great Britain. During these years of military rule, from 8 September 1760 to 10 August 1764, the colony was divided into three independent military districts, each ruled by a military commander who answered to General Amherst in New York. James Murray was in command of the Québec region, Ralph Burton of Trois-Rivières, and Thomas Gage of Montréal. When Murray was appointed civil governor of the entire colony, renamed the Province of Québec, the command of the military was no longer within his jurisdiction.

The religious policy of the conqueror was made explicit in a series of documents spanning the six years between 1759 and 1765. They are, in order: the Articles of Capitulation of Québec (18 September 1759), the Articles of Capitulation of Montréal (8 September 1760), the Treaty of Paris (10 February 1763), General James Murray's commission as governor (21 November 1763), the instructions to Murray (7 December 1763), and the legal opinions of law officers of the crown issued in June 1765, opinions whereby the penal laws of Britain were said not to apply to Canada.

During these years, and again in the wake of the *Québec Act* of 1774, British religious policy was Janus-faced. On the one hand the Articles of Capitulation of 1759 and 1760, the peace treaty of 1763, and the *Québec Act* of 1774, all public documents, spoke of freedom of religion for Canada's Catholics, while on the other hand, various commissions and instructions issued privately to the governors of Québec directed them to hold the church on a tight leash, to restrict its freedom as much as possible, and to do everything they could to promote the interests of the Protestant religion. Of the eleven Articles of Capitulation of Québec, Article 6 deals with religion. In response to the requests of the commander of the defeated French garrison, the British commander replied: "The free exercise of the Roman religion is granted, likewise safeguards to all religious persons, as well as to the Bishop, who shall be at liberty to come and exercise, freely and with decency, the functions of his office, whenever he shall think proper, until the possession of Canada shall have been decided between their Britannic and most Christian Majesties."[14]

A year later, on 8 September 1760, Montréal capitulated. Governor Vaudreuil presented a list of fifty-five Articles of Capitulation, to which the British commander Jeffrey Amherst responded. Given that all parties foresaw the likelihood that Great Britain would retain possession of Canada, several of the articles dealt with matters of religion. General Amherst reserved for the king the decision to continue or not the compulsory payment of tithes and refused to permit the French court to appoint a new bishop,[15] but did endorse the following articles on freedom of religion: "The free exercise of the Catholic, Apostolic, and Roman religion, shall subsist entire, in such manner that all the states and the people of the towns and countries, places and distant posts, shall continue to assemble in the churches, and to frequent the sacraments as heretofore, without being molested in any manner, directly or indirectly.[16] The chapter, priests, curates and missionaries shall continue, with an entire liberty, their exercise and functions of cures, in the parishes of the towns and countries."[17]

Amherst had no reservations whatsoever in granting religious women full rights and privileges, given that they never meddled in politics, provided necessary nursing and teaching services in the colony, and had always treated English patients in their hospitals with the same regard as any other patient. Moreover, the sisters were all Canadian, with few ties to the alien nation of France. Therefore the British commander endorsed Vaudreuil's request in Article 32: "The communities of nuns shall be preserved in their constitutions and privileges; they shall continue to observe their rules, they shall be exempted from lodging any military; and it shall be forbid to molest them in their religious exercises, or to enter their monasteries: safe-guards shall even be given them, if they desire them."[18]

However, he refused to show the same benevolence to the male religious, preferring to reserve that decision to the king.[19] Nevertheless, both female and male religious orders were allowed to preserve their property. "All the communities, and all the priests, shall preserve their movables, the property and revenues of the seigniories and other estates, which they possess in the colony, of what nature soever they be; and the same estates shall be preserved in their privileges, rights, honours, and exemptions."[20]

The third official document expressive of British religious policy during these years was the 1763 Treaty of Paris, which ended the Seven Years' War between France, Great Britain, and Spain. The question of religious rights in Canada was addressed summarily in only one article of this treaty: "His Britannic Majesty ... agrees to grant the liberty of the Catholic religion to the inhabitants of Canada: he will, in consequence, give the most precise and most effectual orders, that his new Roman Catholic subjects may profess the worship of their religion according to the rites of the Romish church, as far as the laws of Great Britain permit."[21]

Given that Catholicism was proscribed in Great Britain at the time, the condition "as far as the laws of Great Britain permit" was not reassuring to Canada's Catholics. The fundamental law became equivocal at best. The fate of the church in Canada would depend entirely on the subsequent decisions of the British government and its colonial officers.

The fourth document in our series bearing on religious policy was the governor's commission issued to Murray on 21 November 1763. Therein, the new governor was granted "full power and authority to collate any person or persons to any churches, chapels, or other ecclesiastical benefices within our said province, as often as any of them shall happen to be void."[22] While such a clause was standard in the mandates given to colonial governors, it is not known if London wanted Murray to invoke these powers in Canada.[23]

The instructions issued to Governor Murray on 7 December 1763 constitute the fifth document dealing with religious policy, and the most explicit one. There, for the first time, was the more or less explicit expression of how Great Britain intended to honour her ambiguous treaty obligations in the matter of the religious freedom of Canadians. While directing the governor to observe the treaty obligation of respecting the "religious freedom," the king's instructions so circumscribed this freedom as to make it barely tolerated. Indeed, the British policy appeared to be toleration of Catholicism, while every measure was adopted to establish and promote the Church of England in Québec.

28. Whereas we have stipulated, by the ... definitive Treaty of Peace ... to grant the liberty of the Catholic religion to the inhabitants of Canada, and that we will consequently give the most precise and most effectual orders, that our new Roman Catholic subjects in that province may profess the worship of their religion, according to the rites of the Romish church, as far as the laws of Great Britain

permit; it is therefore our will and pleasure, that you do ... conform with great exactness to the stipulations of the said treaty in this respect.

29. You are, as soon as possible, to summon the inhabitants to meet together ... in order to take the oath of allegiance, and make and subscribe the declaration of abjuration ...; and in case any of the said French inhabitants shall refuse to take the said oath, and make and subscribe the declaration of abjuration ... you are to cause them forthwith to depart out of our said government....

31. You are as soon as possible to transmit to us, by our commissioners for Trade and Plantations,[24] an exact and particular account of the nature and constitution of the several religious communities of the Romish church, their rights, claims, privileges and property, and also the number, situation and revenue of the several churches heretofore established in our said province, together with the number of priests or curates officiating in such churches.

32. You are not to admit of any ecclesiastical jurisdiction of the see of Rome, or any other foreign ecclesiastical jurisdiction whatsoever in the province under your government.

33. And to the end that the Church of England may be established both in principles and practice, and that the said inhabitants may by degrees be induced to embrace the Protestant religion, and their children be brought up in the principles of it; we do hereby declare it to be our intention, when the said province shall have been accurately surveyed, and divided into townships, districts, precincts or parishes ... all possible encouragement shall be given to the erecting of Protestant schools in the said districts, townships and precincts, by settling, appointing and allotting proper quantities of land for that purpose, and also for a glebe and maintenance for a Protestant minister and Protestant schoolmasters; and you are to consider and report to us ... by what other means the Protestant religion may be promoted, established and encouraged in our province under your government ....

37. And to the end that the ecclesiastical jurisdiction of the Lord bishop of London may take place in our province ..., we do think fit, that you give all countenance and encouragement to the exercise of the same, excepting only the collating to benefices, granting licenses for marriage, and probates of wills, which we have reserved to you, our governor, and to the commander-in-chief of our said province for the time being.

38. And we do further direct, that no schoolmaster ... be henceforward permitted to keep school, without the license of the said Lord Bishop of London.[25]

Finally, on 10 June 1765, law officers of the crown issued their opinion on the contradictions between the terms in the peace treaty, the articles of capitulation, and the penal laws of Great Britain against Catholics. They were of the view that the treaty obligations were binding and superior to statute law, thereby ensuring that the penal laws would not apply in Canada; this became official British policy in Québec. British policy and the instructions to the governor were clear. It remained to be seen how these would be interpreted and implemented by Murray.

CATHOLIC REACTION TO THE CONQUEST

Compromise and accommodation became the watchwords of Catholics in responding to the threats and challenges posed by the British Conquest. A fundamental problem that had to be addressed at the outset was that of obtaining the appointment of a bishop of Québec. After the Acadian Catholics had been dispersed, Canada's faithful watched and waited. For the sisters it was business as usual, as the British army of occupation sought to accommodate them in every way. It was the male clergy that were most affected by the British takeover of Canada. During the first four years of British rule, fifteen of the eighty-four regular priests in Canada availed themselves of the British permission to return to their homeland. Since the British did not allow these religious orders of men to recruit any new members, they were destined to disappear. So it was that the last *Récollet* friar died in 1813, while the planned demise of the Society of Jesus in Canada and elsewhere was accelerated by a papal decision of 1773 to disband the powerful order. The fact that the date of death of the last Jesuit in Canada occurred as late as 1800 could only have happened because the colonial government allowed the Jesuits to remain in office until their deaths. This left the Sulpicians who were also supposed to die out, but were given a new lease on life after 1790 when some French royalist Sulpicians who had been granted political asylum in England, were allowed to come to Canada. The survival of the Montréal community of priests was thus ensured.

The lack of a bishop after 1760, coupled with the closure of the Seminary of Québec between 1759 and 1765, served to thin out the ranks of the secular clergy as well, so that by 1766, the total number of priests in Canada was down to 138, from the 180 that had been in place in 1758. Even after the appointment of a new bishop in 1766 the numbers of priests would not increase because more were dying than were being ordained.[26] In fact, the shortage of clergy that became manifest in the 1760s would persist until the 1840s.

One of the thorniest issues of contention that the Catholic leaders faced was the appointment of a bishop of Québec, an appointment that was necessary if the Catholic Church was to survive. Indeed, a church without a bishop was a church without priests, and therefore without sacraments, preaching, and other essential services. On this issue there was an impasse between royal and papal jurisdictions, because any Catholic bishop had to be appointed by the pope and the recognition of a bishop appointed by the pope was prohibited by King George III's coronation oath and English statute law.

Upon the death of Bishop Pontbriand in 1760, in conformity with prevailing church law, the chapter of the diocese of Québec had appointed a vicar general to manage the church in each of the regions of the diocese, namely Montréal, Trois-Rivières, Québec, in addition to the more distant areas.[27] Foremost among these vicars was Jean-Olivier Briand (1715–1794) who was entrusted with the Québec region. Upon the signing of the Treaty of Paris, they began working in earnest to obtain the appointment of a bishop. Given London's prohibition of any appeal to Rome, it was decided to revert to the old law that had prevailed in France before 1516,[28] a practice whereby the chapter elected a candidate for episcopal office. The chapter's chosen candidate was Father Étienne Montgolfier (1712–1791), superior of the Montréal Sulpicians.

Duly designated (15 September 1763) and bearing a petition to King George from his clerical colleagues, Montgolfier travelled to Europe, obtained the required authorizations from both Rome and London, but then discovered before being ordained bishop that Governor Murray would prefer Father Briand as the new bishop. Conscious of the importance of maintaining the good will of the governor, Montgolfier was back in Québec by September 1764 where he was replaced as the bishop-elect by Father Briand. Briand journeyed in turn to London, and after many delays obtained the consent of British officials to a stratagem whereby Briand would be secretly ordained a bishop in a private chapel in France, and with the approval of Roman authorities, would return to London to swear an oath of allegiance. This was done, it being understood that such a discreet approval by the court of St James was not to be construed as establishing a precedent for the approval of the Catholic faith. So it was that the Holy See issued bulls in favour of Bishop Briand, while London merely acknowledged him to be the "superior of the clergy." The new bishop stepped ashore in Québec on 19 July 1766.

In spite of London's directives to the contrary, from the beginning compromise and accommodation were the *modus operandi* in Québec, on the parts of both the governor and the church. The clergy was on solid theological ground here, because Catholic theology required that the faithful be loyal to their country's legitimate sovereign. So it was that upon the death of George II in 1760, the clergy in the Montréal area adorned their hats with black mourning crêpe. On 1 February 1762, Vicar General Montgolfier issued a general directive[29] to the clergy ordering the clergy of his Montréal district to sing a *Te Deum* in the churches to celebrate the marriage and coronation of King George III.[30] The name of the king would later be inserted into the canon of the Mass by Bishop Briand. In addition, the church accepted the burial of some Protestants in Catholic cemeteries and the celebration of Protestant worship in some Catholic chapels.

General Murray reciprocated in kind. In addition to paying a modest stipend to the head of the Québec church and to the missionaries to the Amerindians, on 5 June 1762 he penned a lengthy and detailed report on the state of the Québec region wherein he strongly recommended that no attempt be made to alter the Catholic religion in Canada, that a bishop be appointed, that the seminary be reopened, and that some means be found to assist in the reconstruction of the cathedral.[31] He even suggested that assistance be found to endow the restored episcopal see. Although Murray noted that the Jesuits were unloved and could be allowed to disappear, he recommended that their property be used to subsidize the bishop's office and the diocesan chapter. He considered the *Récollets* to be harmless, while noting that the congregations of women were held in the highest esteem by the Canadian people. Murray wrote to the minister:

1. The Canadians are very ignorant and extremely tenacious of their religion, nothing can contribute so much to make them staunch subjects to his Majesty as the new government giving them every reason to imagine no alteration is to be attempted in that point.
2. Care was taken under the former government to keep up a great part of the clergy French, especially the dignified part: to prevent

the further importation of these, it would be necessary to encourage the natives to engage in the profession, which cannot be so well done, except the see is filled up, as without a bishop there can be no ordination: some difficulty will attend this, as it is unendow'd tho' hereafter means may be found of making up this deficiency.

3. A like difficulty occurs in relation to the chapter; their number indeed might be reduced by letting the vacancies lie dormant, if some provision cannot be made for them as will hereafter be proposed.

4. An expedient to assist the people in rebuilding their great church, would much ingratiate their new masters with them.

5. The Jesuits are neither loved nor esteemed in general, and this order may be easily removed whenever the government shall think proper without giving offence, out of part of their estate provision might be made for the bishopric, and chapter which would ease the crown of further expenses on that head.

6. The *Récollets* is an order of mendicants, as they depend upon charity for subsistence, they are careful not to give offence; probably should they find the inhabitants upon the present change, cool towards their order, they will of themselves seek a better living somewhere else.

7. The seminary educates the youth, and fits them for orders, it will be necessary to preserve and encourage this house on that account ...

8. As to the communities of women they are much esteemed and respected by the people, the narrowness of their circumstances will probably prevent their being filled up so easily as in former times ...

9. There are some French Protestants in this country ... It would be a great comfort to these, if a church was granted for their use, and some French clergyman of sound sense and good character, with a tolerable salary, was invited to settle among them.[32]

This generosity by the commanding general and governor of Québec continued until his definitive departure from Canada in the summer of 1766. Murray's commission of November 1763 had empowered him to appoint pastors of parishes, and his instructions of December 1763 had given him sweeping powers over the Catholic Church in Canada. He chose to disregard most of them, while assisting the Canadians in their efforts to obtain the appointment of a bishop. Murray liked the Canadians while realizing that their church was the most reliable and stable institution in the country. This consideration would become even more important in the subsequent years leading up to the rebellion of Britain's thirteen colonies on the Atlantic seaboard. Murray's successor in Québec, Guy Carleton (1724–1808) was appointed lieutenant-governor and administrator of the Province of Québec on 7 April 1766; Murray retained the title of governor until Carleton was appointed in his place on 12 April 1768.

Like his predecessor, the new governor liked and trusted the Canadians, and chose to work with them in managing the colony. He cooperated with Bishop Briand in obtaining the appointment of a second bishop, a coadjutor who would automatically succeed to the episcopal see of Québec upon the death of the resident bishop, thereby assuring the succession. This was achieved in 1772, in spite of the ever delicate problem of obtaining a papal appointment when it was expressly forbidden by British policy. In return for Britain's accepting the appointment, Briand accepted the candidate chosen by Governor Carleton.[33] Bishop Briand helped Carleton in his efforts to reconcile Canadians to the British. At the request of the governor, on 15 October 1768 he wrote to his priests urging them to be loyal to their new sovereign, to be grateful that they had a governor who was so supportive of their religion, and to take care not to offend any Protestants among them. The latter were only to be addressed as *Protestants* or *separated brethren*.[34]

This policy of compromise and cooperation between the English Protestant governor and the French Catholic bishop was opposed by Francis Maseres who served as attorney-general of Québec from 1766 to 1769, and by the Board of Trade and Plantations which was striving to have the official directives pertaining to the church implemented, but to no avail.[35] They were countered by Carleton, who was seconded by both the attorney-general and the solicitor-general of England.[36] In fact, Carleton was in England from 1770 to 1775, arguing in favour of establishing in Canada a centralized system of government similar to the one the country had been used to as a French colony. This would keep republican ideas at bay and help keep Canadians loyal to Britain, while giving the government greater control over the church, as was customary in the Gallican tradition.

During the governor's five-year absence in England, his lieutenant Hector Theophilus Cramahé (1720–1788) ran the colony; he adopted his superior's ways in matters of religion. Cooperation was the order of the day. For example, on 23 June 1773 he wrote to the Earl of Dartmouth, one of the king's principal secretaries of State:

It has ever been my opinion ... that the only sure effective method of gaining the affections of his majesty's Canadian subjects to his royal person and government, was, to grant them all possible freedom and indulgence in the exercise of their religion, to which they are exceedingly attached, and that any restraint laid upon them in regard to this, would only retard, instead of advancing, a change of their ideas respecting religious matters; by degrees the old priests drop off, and a few years will furnish the province with a clergy entirely Canadian; this could not be effected without some person here exercising episcopal functions, and the allowance of a coadjutor will prevent the bishop's being obliged to cross the seas for consecration and holding personal communication with those, who may not possess the most friendly dispositions for the British interests.[37]

The *Québec Act* and its aftermath (1774–1776)

Governor Carleton gained most of what he wanted in London. The bill that was adopted by Parliament in 1774 restored in Canada a system of government and law very similar to the one that had prevailed under the French crown. The *Québec Act* that came into effect on 1 May 1775 constituted a milestone for Canadians, a threat for the newly-arrived English merchant class, and a bad omen for the rebellious English settlers to the south. However, within the year it was followed by detailed instructions to Carleton that were intended to nullify most of the perceived gains of the *Act*.

The Québec Act, *1774*

In addition to extending the Province of Québec to the Ohio and Mississippi rivers, the *Québec Act*, 1774, revoked the policy of anglicization that had been in place since the royal Proclamation of 7 October 1763. Such a policy had never been implemented since, with few exceptions, the early colonial officers in Canada had been fluent in French and had usually administered the colony in French. This was true for Generals Murray, Gage,[38] Burton,[39] and Haldimand,[40] just as it was for Lieutenant-governor Cramahé among others. The new constitutional law recognized anew the "free exercise of the religion of the church of Rome, subject to the king's supremacy."[41] The Catholic clergy were empowered to collect the tithe from Catholics only, thereby limiting the rights that had existed in law since 1760; the government could support Protestant ministers by imposing the tithe on Protestants. The traditional British oath of allegiance that had been enacted in the days of Queen Elizabeth I was replaced by an oath shorn of all objectionable religious elements, and bound Catholics exclusively to political loyalty to King George III. Property and civil rights were confirmed for all Canadians, religious orders excepted, and the civil law of the country would henceforth be the laws and customs of Canada, namely the *coutume de Paris* that had prevailed in New France. This meant that British common law did not apply in Canada. In criminal matters, however, British law would prevail. Moreover, the *Québec Act*, 1774 did not allow either for an elected assembly or for *habeas corpus*, a fact that worried its critics. The governor was authorized to appoint a legislative council for the colony.[42] Governor Carleton's party had clearly won the day. The British government was in effect giving the Canadian Catholics almost everything they wanted.

The instructions to Carleton (1775)

But then the other face of British policy appeared, the one that reflected the aspirations of the Board of Trade. On 3 January 1775, detailed instructions were issued to Governor Carleton regarding his administration of the Province of Québec under the new constitutional law that would take effect on 1 May following. It would only be the exercise of the Roman religion that would be tolerated and no other privileges; any correspondence or appeal to foreign ecclesiastical authorities was strictly forbidden; the exercise of episcopal power, the ordination to the priesthood, and the appointment of pastors were subject to the license and permission of the governor; only Canadians were eligible to church appointments; churches were to be shared between Protestants and Catholics where necessary; all church officers were to swear the required oath of loyalty to the crown; all Christians of whatever denomination were entitled to burial in church properties; the British royal family was to be prayed for in all churches; the governor had the right of visitation of all religious congregations and seminaries; no new members could be admitted into the religious congregations of men; upon the death of the last Jesuit, the Society of Jesus was to be suppressed and dissolved as an order, and its properties entrusted to the crown; Protestant ministers and schoolmasters were to be supported in every possible way, adequate stipends and allowances, parish allotments and parsonages included.

Just as had been the case in 1763, the British government appeared to take away with one hand what it gave with the other in matters of religious freedom. Catholics were to be free to exercise their religion, but under the tight control of the government. The intention was clear: Catholicism was to be tolerated but the Church of England was to be established.

The aftermath (1775–1776)

However, Governor Carleton had other ideas.[43] He simply continued his long-standing policy of cooperation with the Canadians and disregarded the instructions from London. He was better able to do so by not reconvening his Legislative council after having received the instructions from London. On 10 March 1775, Bishop Briand reported to a French bishop:

> Religion is perfectly free in this diocese: There are no constraints on my ministry. The governor likes and appreciates me; the English honour me. I rejected an oath that was proposed to me and the British Parliament has changed it and made it such that all Catholics can take it: in the bill which authorized our religion, they have however used the word "supremacy"; but we do not swear by the terms of the bill: I spoke of this to his Excellency our governor who replied: "Why should you care about the bill? The king will not use this power and he agrees and even claims that the pope is your superior in matters of faith but the bill would not have passed without that word. No one intends to interfere in your religion. And our king will not meddle with it as much as does the king of France: no one asks you to acknowledge that supremacy, as you see it in the oath: So swear and think what you wish."[44]

As they rejoiced over the religious freedom they enjoyed, Canadians soon had the opportunity to show their gratitude to their friendly governor. Upon the adoption of the *Québec Act, 1774*, the first American Congress (1774) had protested its granting of legal emancipation to a religion that had allegedly proven guilty of hypocrisy, murder, bloodshed, persecution, and oppression throughout the world. Within months of its incendiary declaration, the same Congress asked Canadians to join it in the rebellion against British tyranny while promising to respect their Catholicism. Bishop Briand and his colleagues were not convinced of the trustworthiness of their American neighbours. Hostilities broke out between British troops and American settlers at Lexington and Concord, Massachusetts in the spring of 1775. Governor Carleton was concerned, especially after British forts at Crown Point and Ticonderoga, New York fell to the rebels in May, 1775. In response to Carleton's request, Bishop Briand and Vicar General Montgolfier in Montréal issued a sermon and a directive to their clergy in support of the government and against the American invaders of Canada. They underlined the goodness and gentleness of George III's government, and directed the faithful to be loyal and supportive of their government and their king. In spite of temporary success in occupying Montréal in November 1775, the rebel army failed to make any significant gains in Canada. Its siege of the fortress of Québec during the winter of 1775–1776 ended in a disastrous rout. By the summer of 1776, the Americans were back home.

Most Canadians remained neutral during the fighting. One reason for their lack of involvement was the clergy's role in condemning any supporters of the rebels, under pain of excommunication from the church. The guilty were thereby excluded from the sacraments, required to make a public apology for their treason, and obtain the forgiveness of their king, before the bishop would readmit them to the church. It was without the support of the Canadians that the Americans proclaimed their new republic in 1776.

Upon the birth of the United States of America, the nature of the relations between church and state in Canada had already been well defined in both theory and practice. Despite numerous instructions to the contrary, British governors of Canada from Murray to Carleton, including Haldimand, chose to allow a great deal of freedom to the church in return for having their way in the selection of the bishops. It was a policy of pragmatism. Although there would be some deviation from this policy in the early years of the nineteenth century, thereafter other governors acknowledged its wisdom. In effect, Canada's Catholics had achieved emancipation more than fifty years before their coreligionists in Great Britain.

Suggested readings

Brunet, Michel. *Les Canadiens après la conquête, 1754–1760*. Montréal: Fides, 1955.

Burt, Alfred Leroy. *The Old Province of Québec*. New York: Russell and Russell, 1933, 1970.

Choquette, Robert. "French Catholicism Comes to the Americas." Charles H. Lippy et al. *Christianity Comes to the Americas 1492–1776*. New York: Paragon House, 1992.

Moir, John S. *Church and State in Canada 1627–1867*. Toronto: McClelland & Stewart, 1967.

Neatby, Hilda. *Québec: The Revolutionary Age, 1760–1791*. Toronto: McClelland & Stewart, 1977.

Shortt, A. and A. G. Doughty. Eds. *Documents Relating to the Constitutional History of Canada, 1758–1791*. Second ed. Ottawa: King's Printer, 1918.

Trudel, Marcel. *L'Église canadienne sous le régime militaire 1759–1764*. Montréal: Institut d'histoire de l'Amérique française, 1956.

CHAPTER 9

Revivals in the Late Eighteenth and Early Nineteenth Centuries

Upon the Province of Québec's effective redefinition as an alliance between a French Catholic population and an English Protestant sovereign, and in the wake of the subsequent American War of Independence (1775–1783), more than 36,000 settlers fled the rebellious southern colonies to seek refuge in Canada. They were the Loyalists whose arrival in Canada would lead to yet another set of constitutional rules for the country.

Although they had been preceded by a handful of Protestants in Québec and by a few thousand in the eastern colonies after 1750,[1] the coming of the Loyalists marked the first arrival of large numbers of Protestants in the country. During the late eighteenth and early nineteenth centuries, these new Protestant Canadians simultaneously founded or reinforced a variety of denominations while undertaking the evangelization of the new frontier. Simultaneously, Canada's Catholics launched their own form of religious revival by launching Canada's church into a crusade for the conversion of the continent. Not to be outdone, even Canada's Amerindians experienced their own religious revival at the turn of the nineteenth century.

The origins of Protestantism in Canada

The presence of a few hundred Protestants in New France, of a Church of England cleric among the Arctic explorer Martin Frobisher's expedition to Baffin Island in 1577, and of a few Catholic and Protestant clergy in Lord Calvert's settlement of Ferryland on Newfoundland's Avalon peninsula during the 1620s represent the first stirrings of Protestant Christianity in Canada. All these missions were short-lived, as were others by naval chaplains or wandering friars who visited the fishing stations on the Newfoundland coast during the seventeenth century. After the British Conquest, Protestant military chaplains appeared in British garrisons in Acadia and Québec.

A significant Protestant presence in Canada had to await the mid-eighteenth century when 5,000 Protestant settlers from Britain, Switzerland, and Germany set foot in the new British port of Halifax in 1749 and 1750. They were of Lutheran and German Reformed tradition; many of them settled in Lunenburg. They were followed between 1760 and 1765 by 8,000 settlers from New England, drawn by the promise of free land and religious freedom for dissenters. Similar motives attracted a number of Protestant and Catholic immigrants from the British Isles, who settled in various parts of Nova Scotia, Cape Breton, and Prince Edward Island. It is estimated that the region had a total population of some 18,000 by 1775.[2] Newfoundland was also experiencing steady growth as new permanent residents arrived from the southeast of Ireland and the English West Country, including Anglicans and Protestant dissenters[3] in addition to Catholics.[4]

The beginning of the American War of Independence in 1775 signaled the onset of the migration to Canada of more than 35,000 refugees from the new republic in the south. While 7,000 of these United Empire Loyalists travelled overland to Canada via Lake Champlain or Niagara, fully 30,000 settled in Nova Scotia north of the Bay of Fundy, the territory that would become the distinct Province of New Brunswick (1784). This initial wave was followed, after 1791, by thousands of 'late Loyalists' who were drawn by the land and opportunities in Canada. This surge continued until immigration from the United States was curtailed by the War of 1812. The Loyalists created a critical mass for Protestantism in Canada, a tradition whose small numbers had formerly led to marginalization.

In many respects, the United Empire Loyalists were the losers in the American War of Independence; the men and women who had chosen to stay loyal to England when the rebellion broke out. Upon the victory of the rebels, they felt compelled to flee northwards to the British colony of Canada, in many cases urged to do so by the seizure of their property in the new republic and by the inequitable treatment they received at the hands of the new government. Indeed, those who had not supported the independence movement were less than welcome in the United States. They were also drawn to Canada by the free land that was available to all loyal British subjects from the new republic.

Although defeated politically and economically, the Loyalists felt a shared loyalty to Great Britain. They also shared an experience of free democratic society that would affect their political and social life in Canada. These Loyalists were a varied lot, the majority being farmers, tradesmen, soldiers, or frontiersmen of various religious traditions. The majority was Protestant, but some Catholics, Amerindians, and Jews were also present.

The organization and governance of Protestant churches

Because of the choices made by the leading Protestant Reformers of the sixteenth century, men such as Martin Luther, John Calvin, Henry VIII, John Knox, and Menno Simons for example, or because of other choices made later by subsequent Protestant leaders such as John Wesley or William Booth, to name only a few, the Protestant churches are very diverse in their forms of organization and government. The Protestant Reformers rejected the traditional episcopal form of church government because the Catholic doctrine of priesthood on which it rested was set aside. In its place, Protestants taught that the clergyman was a preacher of the Word of God and not a priest who offers sacrifice to God. Consequently, the bishop, a fully developed priest in Catholic teaching, had lost his *raison d'être*. In his place, together with God's Word – the Bible – stands the minister, servant of that Word in the interests of the community of believers, the church, all of whose members are priests because of their Baptism.

Because Protestant theology on the one hand no longer acknowledged the special elevated status and consequent authority of the ministerial priest, and on the other hand recognized the priesthood of all believers, various Protestant leaders organized their churches in such a way that authority within them rested with the community, or with the elders, or with a committee of ministers, or with ministerial supervisors, or with various combinations thereof. In other words, the theological foundations supporting a ministerial priesthood and bishops were removed, and replaced by a theology underlining God's presence among the faithful. The door was thus opened to various forms of church governance structures that did not rest upon the ministerial priesthood.

This leveling and democratizing movement in the Protestant

churches which was of theological origin was then reinforced by the fact that Protestant churches had no international centre of government with jurisdiction over all churches. Moreover, from the outset, the Protestant churches were very different from one country to another. Without the doctrinal and institutional unity of Catholicism, there was no way to make the Protestant churches either uniform or united, because just about everything worked against them: national origins, languages, political rivalries, theological differences, and the sheer variety of Christians' tastes and opinions. Moreover, Protestant principles insisted on the freedom of interpretation of God's Word. This resulted in a growing diversity in Protestant church organization and government.

Closest to the traditional Catholic model of church government was that adopted by the Church of England, or Episcopal Church, a church which under Queen Elizabeth I struck a balance between Catholicism and Protestantism.[5] Bishops were retained as were many Catholic customs and practices, albeit sometimes somewhat altered in meaning because of the concomitant importation of Protestant ideas. Other Protestant churches, such as some Methodist and Lutheran also preserved the office of bishop but with altered meaning. In these traditions, the bishop was an overseer but not a chief priest. Protestant churches that stood in the tradition of John Calvin's ideas, and they would eventually constitute the majority in English-speaking countries in particular, did away with priests and bishops for the reasons noted above. Among others, these churches include the Presbyterian Church, most Methodist churches, the United Church of Canada, the Reformed or Calvinist churches, the Baptists, the Pentecostals, and many others. In these churches, authority is acknowledged as resting ultimately in the community of the faithful where the Spirit of God resides. This authority is expressed through various representatives, elected or appointed. They sit on local, regional, national, and sometimes international bodies where they debate and set policies and make decisions for their churches. So it was that many Protestant churches in Canada developed more democratic forms of government than did the Catholic Church.

Establishing Protestantism in Canada

During this half-century between 1750 and 1800, Canada's newly-arrived Protestants, as well as the British Crown, immediately undertook to make Protestantism the official religion of the country which meant making the Church of England into the established church of Québec, Nova Scotia,[6] Newfoundland, and Upper Canada. They failed in Québec, but succeeded in Nova Scotia, and partially succeeded in Newfoundland and Upper Canada.

Atlantic Canada

Nova Scotia, conquered by the British in 1710, and in the process of expelling its Acadian population after 1755, became a royal colony in 1758. Its council decided in 1757 not to allow "popish recusants" to vote in the forthcoming elections for the province's first legislative assembly. During its first session in 1758, that legislature declared the Church of England to be the state religion of the colony, but that 'free liberty of conscience' would be the rule for Protestant dissenters, a promise that was reiterated the following year by Governor Lawrence. The same legislation of 1758 made perpetual imprisonment the penalty for Catholic priests found exercising their ministry in Nova Scotia. "Every popish person, exercising any ecclesiastical jurisdiction, and every popish priest or person exercising the function of a popish priest, shall depart out of this province on or before the twenty-fifth day of March, 1759. And if any such person or persons shall be found in this province after the said day, he or they shall, upon conviction, be adjudged to suffer perpetual imprisonment."[7]

After becoming a distinct province in 1769, the legislative assembly of Prince Edward Island restricted the rights of Catholics much as Nova Scotia had done, and also made the Church of England into its state religion (1802). New Brunswick adopted a series of measures that restricted the rights of Catholics, measures that included the denial of the franchise and the imposition of the oaths of abjuration and supremacy. In Newfoundland, until 1779, official British policy had been to extend liberty of conscience to all "except Papists." In that year, because of the war with France and the fact that half the population was Irish, Britain instructed the governor to treat the Catholics like all others, but the governor chose to ignore the directive. It was only after the Treaty of Versailles (1783) that in 1784 a new governor extended religious and political liberty to Catholics.

Although these discriminatory measures were sometimes amended, and were frequently ignored, official policy in Atlantic Canada was to establish the Church of England, tolerate Protestant dissenters, and outlaw Catholics, much as the laws of Great Britain required.[8] Official religious discrimination in Atlantic Canada only ended upon the adoption of Catholic emancipation legislation by the Parliament of Great Britain in 1829. The colonies were then told to harmonize their own laws with the new imperial legislation.[9]

Upper Canada

The Loyalists who entered Canada after 1775 were given lots in Québec's eastern townships, on the upper St Lawrence River, on the north shores of Lake Ontario and Lake Erie, and in the vicinity of their entry points at Niagara and Detroit. The number of these early migrants that settled in Ontario is estimated at some 7,000 souls.

These English-speaking and, in the majority, Protestant settlers soon discovered that their Province of Québec was French-speaking and Catholic, with a population of 90,000 souls that was almost ten times larger than the English-speaking Protestant one. Moreover, Québec's civil law was the *coutume de Paris*, whereby land was occupied on the seigniorial system, rather than on the British system of free and common soccage.[10] In addition, the province had no representative assembly, a democratic institution to which the immigrants from the south had grown accustomed. The Loyalists asked for constitutional change in order to redress these grievances and gain control over their own political affairs.

The result was the Constitutional Act of 1791, an amendment to the *Québec Act*, 1774, which divided the Province of Québec into two distinct provinces, that of Lower Canada and that of Upper Canada; creation of the latter was intended to satisfy the demands of the new Loyalist settlers. A four-tier governing structure was put in place, each province having an elected assembly of not less than sixteen representatives, an appointed legislative council of seven members, a lieutenant-governor and a common governor for both provinces.

Seven of the fifty articles in the *Act* of 1791, articles 35 to 41, dealt with religious matters. The *Québec Act*'s stipulation regarding the right of the Catholic clergy to collect the tithe from Catholics only was reiterated, along with its companion directive that British authorities could require that the rest of the population pay the tithe for the support of the Protestant religion and the maintenance of the Protestant clergy. The royal instructions to the same effect that were issued to governors Carleton and Haldimand of Québec from 1775 were confirmed, it being stipulated that these instructions to favour the Protestant religion continued in force in both Lower and Upper Canada. According to the *Act*, in both provinces land was to be reserved for "the due and sufficient support and maintenance of a Protestant clergy," land that was to correspond to one-seventh of all the land that had in the past, or would in the future be granted by the Crown.[11] In addition to granting these enormous "clergy reserves," the government of the colony was empowered "to constitute and erect, within every township or parish which now is or hereafter may be formed, constituted, or erected ... one or more parsonage or rectory ... according to the establishment of the Church of England; and ... to endow every such parsonage or rectory with so much or such part of the lands so allotted and appropriated as aforesaid."[12]

In addition, the head of the colony's government was authorized to appoint Church of England clergy to all vacancies in such churches which were under the jurisdiction of the Bishop of Nova Scotia.[13] No penal legislation against Catholics or Protestant dissenters was included in the *Act* of 1791, although there were other discriminatory policies such as the one restricting to the clergy of the Church of England the right to officiate at marriages. In fact, the Church of England was established in Upper and Lower Canada. Huge tracts of land were reserved for its benefit, the governor could create any number of parishes and rectories at will, and he was authorized to appoint only Church of England clergy to them.

If Canada did not end up with the Church of England as a full-blown state religion, it was not for lack of trying by the government of Great Britain in the last quarter of the eighteenth century. The policy of establishment ran aground on the shoals of political, ethnic, social, economic, and religious diversity. In the Province of Québec the shoals were linguistic and religious. In all of the colonies, the immigrants that were arriving from the United States and the British Isles by the tens of thousands during the first half of the nineteenth century were in some cases accustomed to democratic institutions which in the former case codified separation of church and state in its constitutional documents, and in most cases were disinclined to accept a state-supported Church of England.

The development and renewal of Protestantism

By 1800, several thousand Protestants were settled in each of Canada's provinces, and a growing number of denominations were in place or about to arrive. The theology that underlay these churches was a collage of the theologies of the Reformation of the sixteenth century, of the rational supernaturalism of the seventeenth and eighteenth centuries, and of the pietism of the eighteenth.

These changing theologies were also a reflection of the economic, political, and social turmoil that characterized the turn of the nineteenth century, a period marked by the developing industrial revolution, the American Revolution (1775–1783), the French Revolution and Napoleonic empire (1789–1815), and the migration of people in ever increasing numbers towards the industrial and manufacturing centres in Great Britain, the United States, and Canada.[14] It was in this context of rapidly changing environments that a series of revivals occurred in British, American, and Canadian Protestantism, revivals driven by the evangelical thrust that cut through Protestant denominations in the eighteenth and nineteenth centuries.

Protestant denominations

In early nineteenth-century Canada, English-speaking Protestants usually came from Great Britain or the United States. Those of British origin belonged to the Church of England or to one of the dissenting Protestant churches such as the Presbyterian, Methodist, or Baptist. The law in all the regions of Canada strongly favoured the Church of England, but it would become more and more difficult to implement such discriminatory laws as the first half of the century unfolded. The challenge came from a growing majority of Protestants who belonged to denominations other than the Church of England. Some of these denominations had originated in Great Britain from the beginning of the seventeenth century when, in the wake of the Puritan challenge to the established church, dissenting churches like the Baptist[15] and the Quaker[16] had emerged. One hundred years later, another group of disgruntled members of the Church of England led by the Reverend John Wesley founded the Methodist church, a denomination that became very important in Canada.[17] The Canadian Protestants who came from Scotland belonged to that country's established church, the Church of Scotland, or to one of its secessionist branches.[18] Theologically, Irish Protestants were no different from their English and Scots neighbours.

While similar to their British cousins in many ways, the Protestants who came from the United States were distinctive in other ways. Given that American Protestantism was originally imported from Great Britain, its denominations were usually identical to the British ones, including Methodists, Baptists, and Quakers.[19] These denominations, however, were distinctive with respect to their relative importance in America, and in the socio-political values that they had developed in the American setting. One example of the differing relative importance of denominations is that of the Baptists whose members in the United States were mainly Southern and frequently Black. Another is that of the Congregationalists, a denomination that proved to be very important in New England, from whence the Canadian group came.[20] The Canadian denominations of American origin were also distinctive in the degree to which they prized democratic rights, in their egalitarian thrust, and in their belief in freedom in a setting of diversity and competition.

The largest Protestant denominations in Canada in the early nineteenth century were the Church of England, the Church of Scotland or Presbyterians, the Methodists, the Congregationalists, and the Baptists, the latter being primarily located in the Atlantic colonies.[21] Several other smaller denominations developed alongside these including the Lutherans, the Quakers, the Mennonites,[22] the Moravian Church,[23] the Unitarians,[24] the Universalists,[25] the Disciples of Christ,[26] and the 'Irvingites.'[27]

Although the number of Anglicans in Canada in 1800 is less than certain, they were identified with the small elite that governed the colonies. By mid-century, however, they had acquired a more popular base; for example they had become the largest denomination in Upper Canada. Although they regretted the growing unpopularity of their constitutional privileges, Anglicans stood together in a church that remained administratively united, unlike their leading Protestant rivals. Indeed, during the first half of the nineteenth century, the institutional fragmentation of both Presbyterians and Methodists hindered their development as denominations. Although these divisions were usually imported into Canada and were caused by differences of discipline and polity, and not doctrine, nevertheless the five or more branches of each denomination could not easily coordinate their ministry.

So it was that most of Canada's Protestants, then as now, belonged to a handful of denominations, while a minority divided their fellowship among a large number of much smaller churches.

Protestant evangelicalism

Evangelicalism is a term that has had diverse meanings in different parts of the world. The word derives from the Greek and Latin terms for 'Gospel,' and is sometimes used to designate all Protestant churches because of their teaching that the Bible constitutes the exclusive source of Revelation. In Germany and Switzerland, the Evangelical Church is both Lutheran and Reformed in its theological tradition.

In Great Britain, the United States, and Canada, the term *evangelicalism* designates a movement within the Protestant churches. Evangelicalism emerged in the British context of the eighteenth century, an age of prevalent rational supernaturalism whereby God was understood and obeyed in very rationalistic ways. This age of reason and enlightenment led the Church of England, among others, to preach and witness to a most reasonable Christianity, a kind of religion that did not satisfy a growing number of faithful. In reaction to this reasonable Christianity, more affective forms of belief appeared with the pietistic movement in Germany and the evangelical movement in Great Britain, because numbers of faithful wanted a religion that spoke more to their hearts than to their intellects. They wanted an independent church, not one that was co-opted by the Crown. Some of these British evangelical Christians became part of the emerging Methodist denomination, while others remained in their original church while working to redirect its ethos and spirituality.[28]

So it was that British evangelicalism was not the name of a particular denomination, but represented a movement within a growing number of denominations that would run like a thickening thread through the entire length of English-speaking Protestantism from the eighteenth century to the present. There were Anglican evangelicals, but also Baptist, Methodist, and Congregational ones. As the evangelical movement grew in strength in the nineteenth century, it created its own distinctive agencies, for missions or education for example, thereby provoking growing opposition from other members of the same churches.

In the United States evangelicalism put on the face of religious awakenings. There were two Great Awakenings in American Protestantism during the eighteenth century. The First Great Awakening began in 1726 in New Jersey, affected the Dutch Reformed, the Presbyterian, and Congregational churches, and over the next thirty years spread to all the American colonies. It was led by the Reverends Jonathan Edwards (1703–1758) and George Whitefield (1714–1770), the latter a close associate of John Wesley. The Second Great Awakening began at the turn of the nineteenth century among the Congregational churches of New England, and then spread throughout the land, particularly among Presbyterians, Methodists, and Baptists.[29]

This evangelicalism that cut across denominational lines displayed a number of distinctive characteristics. Evangelicals of the early nineteenth century were Protestant Christians who believed in the transforming power of faith in Christ, thus standing apart from the Christian rationalists of their day who gave short shrift to God's Providence and intervention in human affairs. Evangelicals believed in miracles when it was less than popular to do so. Evangelicals wanted to bring their churches back to the doctrines of the Reformation of the sixteenth century. These doctrines included that of the sole authority of Holy Scripture, belief in its verbal inspiration by God, in the salvation of the Christian by faith in God through Christ, in the necessity of redemption and atonement[30] by Christ's death, in a Second Coming of Christ,[31] in the pervasiveness of sin, and in the necessity of personal conversion. In fact, the necessity of a personal experience of conversion became a badge of distinction for evangelicals, frequently a *sine qua non* for admission into a denomination or into the ministry. This conversion was understood to be instantaneous and gave the Christian a conscious assurance of faith in Christ.

Evangelicals were an earnest and zealous crew of Christians, who felt that it was urgent to preach the Gospel everywhere. While most established clergy limited their preaching to the usual Sunday services in churches, evangelicals preached in taverns, on docks, and at the entrances to mineshafts and factories. The urgency they felt rested on a sense of perpetual crisis. They favoured a heroic morality rather than a prudential one; the middle of the road was not for them. They played down the importance of ritual and liturgy in church services, while insisting on the key importance of preaching God's Word in a vital and colourful style. In a Protestantism that had rarely been known for its missionary activities, evangelicals launched major missionary programs that rivaled those of the Catholics in the nineteenth century. They were at the cutting edge of social reform, leading the campaigns for the abolition of slavery and for the adoption of factory laws to protect women, children, and the oppressed of all kinds.

Like their Reformation forefathers, evangelicals manifested a strong suspicion of Catholicism. They led the fight to stop the re-establishment of the Catholic hierarchy in England in the 1850s, as well as the resistance to the Tractarians or Oxford movement within the Church of England after 1835.[32] Evangelicalism was in many respects a return to the sources of Protestantism, and to the Reformation, one tenet of which was its strong faith in a sovereign God who saved the depraved sinner through the loving sacrifice of his Son Jesus; all that was required to gain access to this redemption was faith. Faith was a gratuitous gift from God, frequently granted in an instantaneous moment of conversion; thereafter, the Christian was to lead a life of holiness.

Protestant revivals

Sinners were drawn to this redeeming encounter with God by hearing his Word. Given the unsatisfactory attitude and teachings of many established denominations, evangelicals frequently organized their own venues for preaching. These were the revivals that renewed nineteenth-century Protestantism. The latter were "outbursts of mass religious fervour... stimulated by intensive preaching and prayer meetings."[33] The revivals tended to be very emotional and boisterous in Canada.

An initial revival occurred in Nova Scotia between 1776 and 1783, the years of the ministry of Henry Alline (1748–1784). This native of Rhode Island came to Nova Scotia with his parents in 1760, in the heart of the First Great Awakening. The family settled near Falmouth in the Minas basin area, where Henry at the age of twenty-seven had a conversion experience on 26 March 1775. This resulted from his opening the Bible and reading Psalm 38, which led to the redeeming love of God melting his soul and telling him to preach the Gospel. After resisting the calling for more than a year, he gave in, found peace and spiritual certitude, and began preaching in the Minas basin. After three years of this, in 1779 he was ordained an evangelist by three of the local congregations, and began preaching farther afield. Between 1779 and 1783, Alline travelled on horseback, by boat or on foot through most of settled Nova Scotia, New Brunswick, and Prince Edward Island. From his base with his family in Falmouth, the itinerant preacher visited the most isolated parts of the province where the recently-arrived Yankee settlers suffered from economic hardship, the insecurity of the uprooted, and the absence of most denominations. He founded a handful of *New Light* congregations, but did not concern himself with institutional considerations, so that his congregations remained unstable at best. He died while visiting New England in early 1784.

Alline's work was typical of revivalists. He emphasized the necessity of being born again, of an instantaneous new birth resulting from a conversion experience and leading to the recognition of Christ as one's personal saviour. He led his flock in prayer and song, composing several hymns himself. He urged his listeners to participate in the prayer meetings, drawing upon himself the accusation of opponents in the established church that he was guilty of leveling the church, of promoting an unwanted egalitarianism. Their opposition was reinforced when they heard Alline repeatedly preach that God was primarily love, thereby challenging the traditional Calvinist theology which emphasized God's justice and punishment of sinners.

Although short-lived, this first revival in Canada had a significant impact on rural Protestantism of Atlantic Canada. The *New Light* churches did not survive as such, most of them merging into the Baptist denomination after 1800 in the heady context of the Second Great Awakening. Evangelical zeal was being channeled onto a narrower path by denominational norms and structures.

Other revivals included one among the Methodists of Nova Scotia, and a number in Upper Canada, where they usually took the form of camp meetings.[34] The first had occurred at Cane Ridge, Kentucky in 1801. They were open-air gatherings that lasted several days, much like the Scottish 'long communion' meetings where several days of prayer had culminated in the serving of the eucharist to tables of communicants. Methodists were the first to organize such a lengthy 'camp' meeting at Dundas, Upper Canada in 1805; they made these meetings their own in Canada. A circuit of such meetings would exist in Ontario, their popularity waxing and waning periodically throughout the nineteenth century. Camp meetings were usually noisy, emotional, and intense. Hundreds of participants gathered in a field surrounded by one or more platforms or wagons on which preachers stood to urge the flock to repentance and conversion. Those in attendance frequently experienced conversions and spiritual rebirths; they were born again. In the process, it was not unusual to witness swooning and trembling, amid the singing and exhortations that filled the usual three or four days of the event. Methodist preacher Nathan Bangs described one of the first camp meetings held in Upper Canada:

> At five o'clock Saturday morning a prayer-meeting was held, and at ten o'clock a sermon was preached on the words, 'My people are destroyed for lack of knowledge.' At this time the congregation had increased to perhaps twenty-five hundred, and the people of God were seated together on logs near the stand, while a crowd was standing in a semicircle around them. During the sermon I felt an unusual sense of the divine presence, and thought I could see a cloud of divine glory resting upon the congregation ... I ... descended from the stand among the hearers; the rest of the preachers spontaneously

followed me, and we went among the people, exhorting the impenitent and comforting the distressed; for while Christians were filled with 'joy unspeakable and full of glory,' many a sinner was weeping and praying in the surrounding crowd. These we collected together in little groups, and exhorted God's people to join in prayer for them, and not to leave them until he should save their souls. O what a scene of tears and prayers was this! I suppose that not less than a dozen little praying circles were thus formed in the course of a few minutes. It was truly affecting to see parents, weeping over their children, neighbors exhorting their unconverted neighbors to repent, while all, old and young, were awe-struck. The wicked looked on with silent amazement while they beheld some of their companions struck down by the mighty power of God, and heard his people pray for them... During this time some forty people were converted or sanctified.[35]

During these heady days of revival, wonders never ceased. Preachers received directives from heaven, opponents were often punished for refusing their assistance, and warnings of impending disasters and invitations to repentance were heard. This invasion by the Holy Spirit was no doubt helped along by several characteristics of the society of the day, which included the isolation felt by many rural folk who craved the socializing associated with camp meetings, and the opportunity the latter offered to women and youth to express themselves by participating in testimonies. The spirit of revivalism made for very lively religion, at a time when both churches and society were usually drab and unexciting.

This diversified and vibrant Protestantism of the late eighteenth and early nineteenth centuries was built on the twin pillars of denominational fidelity and evangelical fervour. Evangelicalism and the heritage of the Reformation were the unifying forces that effected a Protestant commonality, one that acknowledged the existence of a divine order where God was sovereign; he ruled history and had revealed his will in the Bible; human beings were all inveterate sinners whose only chance for salvation was the result of Christ's death on the cross; those Christians who believed and obeyed God's will would be rewarded with eternal life in heaven, while those who disbelieved and disobeyed would burn in Hell for all of eternity. This common Protestantism was constantly challenged by the forces of fragmentation that it carried within itself, forces that were doctrinal, spiritual, political, ethnic, economic, and social. At times like the early nineteenth century, these forces were dominant, as Methodists, Presbyterians, Baptists, and others each divided into several denominations; a century later, the forces of unity would take over.

While awakenings and revivals in Protestantism were carried on the wave of evangelicalism, the revival of nineteenth-century Catholicism became the foremost objective of the ultramontane movement.

Catholic renewal

Christian churches were always in need of reform, at least in the eyes of some of their members. During the 'enlightened' eighteenth century, just as was the case for the Church of England among others, the Catholic Church had become infected with the virus of rationalism. In France, the leading Catholic country to affect Canada's religious life, the rational supernaturalism of the age was coloured by the often virulent anti-Catholicism and secularism of the so-called *'philosophes,'* men like Denis Diderot (1713–1784) and François-Marie Arouet (1694–1778), better known as Voltaire. In putting an end to the *'ancien régime'* in France, the Revolution that broke out in 1789 also marked the beginning of a century-long struggle between the revolutionary, secularist, lay forces in French society on the one hand, and the Catholic, monarchist, and conservative forces on the other. Throughout the nineteenth century, this leading Catholic country would see-saw between governments controlled by one party or the other, republican or monarchist/ imperial. It was in this context of a divided country that some French Catholic liberals undertook to reform their church in the early nineteenth century. Their achievement and the reaction thereto, directly affected the Catholic Church in Canada which had close ties with French Catholicism.

Catholic ultramontanism

The renewal of the Catholic Church in the nineteenth century would be the work of a group of Catholics called *ultramontanes*. The ultramontane movement began in France, and then spread to other European countries and to Canada. By the mid-nineteenth century, ultramontanism was the driving force in the renewal of international Catholicism, a force that would have sweeping effects in Canada and elsewhere. Ultramontanism was a major renewal movement that began in early-nineteenth century

French Catholicism. The word literally means 'beyond the mountains,' and designates those French Catholics who looked beyond the Alps, the mountains that separated France from Italy, towards Rome for the answers to their church problems. These ultramontanes did not accept the strong control exercised by the government over the Church of France, a system of state control that had formerly been called Gallicanism, and that had been continued under Napoleon and under the restored monarchy after 1815. Ultramontane Catholics sought an independent church, one that was not – for all practical purposes – a department of state, a church that could evangelize freely, denounce the government if necessary, freely recruit and educate clergy without government control, and freely establish and run schools at all levels.

In order to free their church from stifling government control, the reform-minded ultramontane Catholics turned towards Rome, on the assumption that the sway of the government of France over the Church of France could only be held in check by the countervailing power of the Holy See. So it was that with a view to obtaining greater liberty in France, the ultramontanes sought to give the Holy See greater control over the Church of France. It remained to be seen whether the result would be liberation or servitude.

Ultramontanism had been growing in popularity since the seventeenth century and through the eighteenth as various movements that favoured church nationalism (e.g. Gallicanism, Jansenism, Josephism) lost favour with disenchanted Catholics. When Gallicans were perceived as supporters of the French Revolution and the various horrors that were associated with it during the 1790s, many of France's Catholics turned to the alternative that was ultramontanism. The leader of the movement was Father Félicité de Lamennais (1782–1854). Growing up during the troubled revolutionary years, Félicité had lost his faith until, with the assistance of his brother Jean-Marie who was a priest, he had a conversion experience and became a devout Catholic at the age of twenty-two. In 1816, at the age of thirty-six, he became a priest, albeit somewhat reluctantly.

Lamennais gave a great deal of thought to the state of the church in France. As early as 1808 he published a book critical of individual reason and its associated rationalism and atheism, arguing in favour of the necessity of a strong and autonomous church. From his country retreat of La Chênaie, his base of operations during subsequent years, Lamennais surrounded himself with a handful of like-minded friends and reformers. Beginning in 1818 he published the first volume of his most celebrated book entitled *Essai sur l'indifférence en matière de religion*.[36] There he underlined the importance of the church community, the equation of Catholicism with the religion of all mankind, the desirability of a theocracy, and the importance of the pope as international leader of all. He later (1829) demanded the full separation of church and state, the freedom of education from state control, and the freedom of the press. To promote his ideas, primarily his foundational one of the centrality of freedom for Christianity, he founded associations, established the celebrated newspaper *L'Avenir* (1830–1831), and gathered around himself talented associates like Charles de Montalembert and Henri Lacordaire.

Félicité de Lamennais' ideas, particularly his campaign for freedom, worried a number of French bishops as well as the new pope Gregory XVI (1765–1846) who took office in 1831. Gregory surprised Father Lamennais by condemning his liberal ideas in the encyclical *Mirari Vos* of 15 August 1832. Upon Lamennais' response in the celebrated book *Paroles d'un croyant* (1834) wherein the pope's authority was said not to include the political sphere, Gregory condemned it in the encyclical *Singulari Nos* of 25 June 1834. Father Lamennais thereupon left the church, and eventually abandoned Christianity.

The two encyclicals that condemned Lamennais' ideas marked a turning point in the history of ultramontane Catholicism. Until that time, the movement had been associated with the liberal ideas defended by Lamennais' party, including freedom of the press and freedom of education. Lamennais' group wanted freedom to build a strong and independent church, without the limitations and constraints imposed by government control. The pope's intervention announced the refusal of the Catholic Church to be associated with these liberal ideas that had issued forth from the American and French Revolutions. Thereafter, the Catholic Church became visibly identified with the forces of reaction, whether it be in politics, religion, culture, and intellectual endeavours, and would remain so identified for the next hundred years and more.

On the political, intellectual, and theological fronts, the nineteenth century was engaged in a great struggle between the forces of liberalism and conservatism. In politics, liberalism was synonymous with republicanism, separation of church and state, freedom of the press, the possibility of divorce, and a range of other policies that resulted from the belief in the fundamental freedom of the individual citizen. Sometimes liberalism showed a doctrinaire face, supporting secular and anti-clerical programs in the belief that the clergy was too influential, in education for example. In matters intellectual, liberalism was associated with several thinkers who challenged the religious foundations of western society and the historical foundations of Christianity. Among others, the philosophers Friedrich Hegel (1770–1831) and Karl Marx (1818–1883), the historian Leopold von Ranke (1795–1886), the philosopher-historian David Friedrich Strauss (1808–1874), and the naturalist Charles Darwin (1809–1882) all challenged the foundations of Christianity. In theology, a series of challenges added to those initiated by Strauss, Marx, and Darwin. While Friedrich Schleiermacher (1768–1834) proposed a new way of doing theology in German Lutheranism, Johann Adam Möhler (1796–1838) led the way in seeking reform of German Catholicism.

When Catholic ultramontanism was hijacked by Rome and became reactionary after 1832, a series of contextual factors helped it to develop into a powerful movement of centralization, uniformity, and strong discipline within the Catholic Church. One side of the ultramontane coin was the defensive reaction to the above-noted forces of liberalism which threatened the privileged position of the church in society. The other side of that coin was the campaign to centralize the government of the Catholic Church, to reinforce the authority of the pope, and to make Catholic belief and practice uniform throughout the Catholic world. The long century of reactionary Catholicism that stretched from the 1830s to 1960 would be characterized by a very conservative and anti-liberal mindset, fear of the modern world, distrust of the human being generally, and depreciation of scholarship and research. While claiming to tolerate those whom it considered to be in error, the ultramontane church did not show much indulgence to the erroneous teachings themselves. This same Catholic Church sought the independence of the church, the reinforcement of the clergy's numbers and power, and the conversion of the world through intensive missionary efforts. Ultramontane Catholicism adopted colourful ritual and devotions, elaborate worship services, and taught a very severe moral code wherein obedience was the foremost virtue, and sexual misbehaviour the leading sin.

Ultramontanism in early-nineteenth-century Canada

The ultramontane wave that would sweep through Catholicism from the mid-nineteenth century had two ports of entry into Canada. The first was Lower Canada (Québec) and the growing number of clergy there who espoused the ultramontane view. The second was the Irish-Catholic community that arrived in the country in the middle decades of the century.

Jean-Jacques Lartigue, bishop of Montréal from 1836 to 1840, was the first Canadian churchman to promote ultramontanism in Canada. In his capacity as auxiliary bishop of Québec, in charge of the district of Montréal (1820–1836), from the outset Lartigue stood for a church independent both of the government and of the *Parti Canadien* that represented the new lay elite in Québec. This lay element fought for greater political rights and an increased role in society for itself, thereby supplanting the clergy in its role of intermediary between the people and the colonial government.[37] Lartigue was an opponent of Gallicanism and its policy of independence for local churches, a devoted admirer of the pope, and a believer in the supremacy of papal authority in the church. While his clergy stood by the people in their striving after greater political autonomy, Bishop Lartigue opted for a middle course between their aspirations and those of the government. His support of papal authority facilitated this.

By the time of Lartigue's death in 1840, the foundations of ultramontane Catholicism were laid in Canada. Its development became the responsibility of his successor Ignace Bourget (1799–1885), bishop of Montréal from 1840 to 1876. Bourget would prove to be the foremost leader of the ultramontane forces in Canada.[38]

Renewal in Amerindian religions

The religious beliefs and customs of Canada's native people were studied in Chapter 2, and the religious consequences of the encounter between Amerindians and Europeans were considered in Chapter 5. The growing number of Canadians coupled with their dominating ideologies and advanced technology resulted in increasing pressures for changes in the cultures and spiritualities of Canada's Amerindian peoples. Until the early nineteenth century, these forces were held in check by the limited number of Europeans and the vastness of the country; most Amerindians were still protected by relative isolation from the white man. After 1800, however, the number of immigrants to Canada grew by leaps and bounds, and the assimilationist pressures on the religions of the Amerindian people grew commensurately. As the nineteenth century wore on, it became more and more difficult to sustain the myths, beliefs, stories, customs, and rituals that made up the religions of Canada's Amerindian people, spiritualities that were intimately tied to the entire social and cultural fabric of the diverse nations and tribes.

It was in this context of increasing pressures by Canadian civilization and increasing difficulty in finding spiritual solace and meaning in Amerindian religions, that there emerged among the Iroquoians the religion of the longhouse, a reform of traditional Amerindian spirituality, founded by the Seneca Ganiodaio (d.1815) or Handsome Lake in 1799. That was when Ganiodaio began to have a series of visions that led to the reform of his own alcoholic tendencies and provided him and his followers with a new sense of purpose in life. His Good Message urged his followers to return to selected traditional practices, while making their own some of the beliefs and customs of the white man.

The religion of the longhouse spread from its cradle in upper New York State to the Grand River reservation in Upper Canada where it won the allegiance of 20% of the residents by 1860; the other 80% were Christian, a proportion that was sustained for a century thereafter.[39] Numbering 700 faithful in the 1890s on the Grand River reserve, three and then four longhouses serving the Cayuga, Mohawk, and Onondaga tribes were dedicated to the religion. The majority of longhouse followers resided in the lower Grand River valley.

Despite Ganiodaio's openness to accommodation, his followers made his movement synonymous with the refusal to compromise traditional Amerindian beliefs and customs. These included the languages, the confederacy form of government, the social structure including the matrilineal form of lineage, and the rituals and herbal remedies for healing. It became a religion of protest against encroachment by the white man, and of preservation of traditional Iroquois culture.

In accord with the annual agricultural cycle, the ceremonies of the religion of the longhouse included a mid-winter festival or New Year's celebration in late January, spring rituals of maple sugar harvesting and seed planting, and summer celebrations of the strawberry, bean, and green corn. The ritual year ended with the harvest festivities in the fall when thanksgiving was made to the Creator for his bounty. Ceremonies were organized in each longhouse by the faithkeepers, three men and three women. Ceremonial leaders mastered the proper chants and prayers. While women prepared the food, men, sometimes dressed in traditional Iroquois costume, led dances and songs accompanied by drums and turtle-shell rattles. The latter were prized possessions.

Healing practices and beliefs were widespread in the religion of the longhouse. Many herbal remedies were used and followers could join a number of active medicine societies. Children were introduced to the traditions at an early age. Marriage having always been an informal ritual, men and women usually chose their own spouses. Marriage was then arranged by the kinship groups of the bride and groom. Couples were expected to be faithful to each other. Nevertheless, some did separate, although there was no such thing as legal divorce. The dead were buried in the graveyard of the longhouse. Ten days after death, the death feast was held. Then it was that the spirit of the deceased was believed to depart the body to go to the home of the Creator. Followers of the religion of the longhouse abided by the moral teachings of Handsome Lake by being good children and parents, faithful spouses, and by abstaining from alcohol and gambling. They sought to live in the Amerindian way, and avoided the ways of the Canadians of European origin.[40]

Beginning in the 1920s, the religion of the longhouse spread into the reservations of the Montréal area, where it became the main support for an emerging aboriginal movement. In Akwesasne for example, the religion of Handsome Lake allowed the Mohawk to consolidate the ideological foundations of their cultural heritage, including the hereditary system of government.[41] In the 200 years since its founding, there are still significant pockets of followers of the religion of the longhouse, particularly in southern Ontario where the Grand River reserve has become its centre.[42]

Suggested readings

Bumsted, J.M. *Henry Alline, 1748–1784.* Toronto: University of Toronto Press, 1971.

Chadwick, Owen. The Victorian Church: *An Ecclesiastical History of England.* London: Adam & Charles Black, 1966.

Chaussé, Gilles. *Jean-Jacques Lartigue, premier évêque de Montréal.* Montréal: Fides, 1980.

Grant, John Webster. *A Profusion of Spires.* Toronto: University of Toronto Press, 1988.

Moir, John S. *The Church in the British Era.* Toronto: McGraw-Hill Ryerson, 1972.

Rawlyk, George A. *Ravished by the Spirit: Religious Revivals, Baptists, and Henry Alline.* Kingston & Montréal: McGill-Queen's University Press, 1984.

———. *Wrapped Up In God: A Study of Several Canadian Revivals and Revivalists.* Burlington, Ont.: Welch Publishing Co., 1988.

Westfall, William. *Two Worlds: The Protestant Culture of Nineteenth-Century Ontario.* Kingston & Montréal: McGill-Queen's University Press, 1989.

CHAPTER 10

Missionary Agencies

Both a cause and effect of the revitalized Protestant and Catholic churches were the various missionary agencies that became more important than ever during the nineteenth century. In Catholicism, religious orders had been important since the founding of monasticism in the third century C.E.; nevertheless, during the nineteenth century they would attain a new pinnacle of importance in numbers of orders, numbers of members, the international scope and variety of their work, and the enhanced role of women in their apostolic story. A similar commitment by Protestants was even more surprising, given the rejection of the notion of religious life by most Protestants. This was attributable to the strong support of missions by the Protestant *converted*, the evangelicals who were *born again* to Christian holiness.

Protestant missionary agencies

During the eighteenth and nineteenth centuries, more than a score of missionary agencies were founded in Protestantism, some as denominational agencies, others as inter-denominational organizations, working in the interests of several churches who shared a common evangelical outlook. It was not only the number of these agencies that was surprising, but also their very existence, given the fact that Protestants had not formerly given much importance to missionary outreach. What was also surprising was that a number of these agencies were founded not by clergy, but by lay members of various Protestant churches. The *raison d'être* of these agencies also varied, and included the production and dissemination of religious literature, education, the support of colonial churches, and the organization of missions to the heathen. A number of these British agencies were directly involved in the founding and support of several of Canada's early Protestant churches. These British agencies cannot claim sole credit for Protestant evangelization, because numbers of Protestant missionaries, in both Nova Scotia and particularly in Upper Canada, came directly from the United States. Nevertheless, they played a major role in promoting Protestant Christianity in all parts of Canada, especially in Atlantic Canada and the Northwest.

Eighteenth-century agencies

The Society for Promoting Christian Knowledge (S.P.C.K.) became the forerunner of several others when it was founded in 1698 by Thomas Bray and four laymen of the Church of England. In addition to promoting charity schools in England and Wales, the society's objectives were the dissemination of Bibles and religious literature both within and without Great Britain, and the promotion of Christian knowledge and understanding everywhere. In addition to founding and supporting schools and colleges, the S.P.C.K. established its own publishing house which, to the present day has continued disseminating religious and theological literature. The S.P.C.K. did not belong to the evangelical party.[1]

Only three years after launching the S.P.C.K., the same Thomas Bray founded another society whose purpose was to assist the first in promoting Christian missions in foreign lands. Founded in 1701, The Society for the Propagation of the Gospel in foreign parts (S.P.G.) was an official agency of the Church of England and incorporated by royal charter. It had the dual purpose of providing church services for British people overseas, and evangelizing the heathen in British colonies. During the eighteenth century, the S.P.G.'s primary area of activity was British North America and the British West Indies; it extended its area of endeavour to other continents during the nineteenth century.

In Canada, the S.P.G. proved to be one of the foremost bulwarks of the missionary movement. Its initial efforts were limited, however, given the thinly scattered English-speaking population in pre-1750 Canada. In 1703, only two years after its founding, the society was supporting the Anglican missionary John Jackson in Newfoundland, and would do likewise for Laurence Coughland who worked there between 1766 and 1773. After 1704, the S.P.G. also staffed a mission among the Mohawks, a work that eventually led many of these allies of the British, many of whom immigrated to Canada, to become Anglicans. It also supported an Anglican missionary in Lunenburg, Nova Scotia in the 1760s, as it did three Protestant (Huguenot) ministers stationed in Montréal, Trois-Rivières, and Québec from the 1760s.

After the end of the American War of Independence, the S.P.G. increased its activities in Canada. This was not due to British missionaries, most of whom were reluctant to come to Canada, but largely because more clergy became available from the former southern colonies. This personnel enabled the Church of England to establish more missions, schools, and scholarships. Money was not a problem, since the Church of England clergy and teachers were salaried by the Crown until 1815. In fact, increased parliamentary grants after 1813 and the extensive clergy reserves in the Canadas enabled the S.P.G. and the Church of England to evangelize at will, without financial worries. The other churches were envious of Anglican good fortune. The S.P.G. continued to enjoy the substantial financial support that the state extended to the Church of England in Canada until the 1850s. Although it continued its work during the second half of the nineteenth century, by the year 1900 its commitment to Canada's church ceased; at the time the S.P.G. was providing £9,000 to Canadian Anglican dioceses.

Although the S.P.G. was the leading British agency that supported missions in Canada during the eighteenth century, smaller groups were also at work. One was the London-based Society for the Furtherance of the Gospel. Founded in 1741, it supported the work of the Moravian Brethren in Labrador. After obtaining a land grant of 100,000 acres at Esquimaux Bay, Labrador, in 1771 the Moravians sent a band of German and English missionaries to found a mission at Nain, and then at Okak in 1776 and Hopedale in 1782.

Nineteenth-century agencies: the leading missionary agencies

The turn of the nineteenth century marked the founding of the major evangelical agencies that would promote Protestant Christianity with a vigour that would at least match that of the traditional established churches. These evangelical agencies included The London Missionary Society, The Church Missionary Society, the Religious Tract Society, The British and Foreign Bible Society, The Wesleyan Methodist Missionary Society, The Glasgow Colonial Society, and The Colonial and Continental Church Society. In addition, several denominations created other, auxiliary missionary agencies, for example The Women's Missionary

Society (1880) of the Methodist Church of Canada. There was even an inter-denominational attempt to convert French Canada to Protestantism by means of The French Canadian Missionary Society (1839).

The London Missionary Society (L.M.S.) was the first of the inter-denominational missionary agencies. Founded in 1795, it focused its initial activities on Tahiti, and then on the Far East and Africa, but rarely turned its attention to Canada. The significance of the new agency in our story is that it was created by a group of Wesleyans, Anglicans, Congregationalists, and Presbyterians cooperating in the evangelization of the heathen. This early ecumenism among Protestants was a harbinger of what would become characteristic among evangelical Christians.

The most important Church of England missionary agency to the heathen was The Church Missionary Society (C.M.S.), founded in 1799 by the evangelical wing of the Church of England. In addition to promoting numerous Bible translations and founding and supporting missions in various countries of the world, the C.M.S. became the foremost Anglican missionary agency in Canada's northwest after 1822. From its base in London, England, the C.M.S. collected funds, recruited missionaries, trained them, and sent them into the field, the preferred field being India and the Far East. Most of the missionaries the C.M.S. sent to Canada came from the artisan and lower-middle classes. In its own Islington College, opened in 1825, spiritual pursuits were more important than academic ones, the molding of Christian character taking precedence over scholarly achievements. The society did not train its missionaries in aboriginal languages; most C.M.S. missionaries remaining ignorant of them throughout their careers. In the missions to Canada's Amerindian people, the C.M.S. was the foremost rival to the Catholic Oblates, particularly in the North. By 1895, the English society was spending £18,000 on its missions in Canada, supporting sixty ordained ministers in addition to five lay missionaries.

One of the C.M.S. initiatives was the publication of several magazines designed to bolster the morale of missionaries and to better inform them about church-related events in the world. For example, *The Church Missionary Intelligencer*, a monthly founded in 1849, was distributed to all missionaries in the field, serving to promote the support of the missions by the faithful. It contained book reviews, excerpts from the letters of various missionaries, the histories of mission outposts, and a variety of biblical and theological commentaries. The magazine always reflected the evangelical theology of the C.M.S.

While the C.M.S. was the foremost British missionary society that supported evangelical work in Canada during the nineteenth century, others were The Glasgow Colonial Society (1825), The Colonial and Continental Church Society (1838), and The Wesleyan Methodist Missionary Society (1813). The first, in the main composed of evangelicals, was from its founding in 1825 the primary channel of financial aid to the Church of Scotland in Canada. When it divided in 1843 in the wake of a major disruption led by Thomas Chalmers in the church of the home country, most of its Canadian beneficiaries chose the separating Presbyterian Free Church over the traditional Church of Scotland. Canada's Presbyterians would remain divided until 1875.

The Colonial and Continental Church Society was founded in 1838 by evangelicals in the Church of England who sought to support the apostolate in English colonies.[2] Its involvement in Canada was limited to supporting a handful of ministers.

Britain's Wesleyan Methodist Missionary Society (1813) played a significant role in Canada during the first half of the nineteenth century when it sent missionaries into Atlantic Canada, central Canada, and the Hudson Bay Territories of the Northwest. However, its role diminished at mid-century when it transferred its responsibilities in Upper Canada (1847) and the Northwest (1854) to the Canadian Methodist Conference, which had become an independent body in 1828.

By the end of the nineteenth century, Canada's Protestant churches had become independent, in fact if not always in name; this led to their assuming full responsibility for missionary work in Canada. For example, in 1902 the Church of England in Canada established The Missionary Society for the Church in Canada, the same year that the Methodists founded The Missionary Society of the Canadian Church.[3] Support from foreign agencies, British and American, was becoming a thing of the past.

Converting French Canada

Part of the intensive missionary campaign by Protestants in the nineteenth century was a concerted effort to convert French Canadians from Catholicism to Protestantism. This began in Montréal in the 1830s, but when the effort failed because of strong opposition by the Catholic Church, the Protestant churches shifted their focus to the rural areas of new settlement. While a variety of Protestant instruments were used in Québec, including a series of boarding schools and the bi-monthly newspaper *Le Semeur Canadien* (1851), the leading agents of Protestant proselytism in Québec were Henriette Odin-Feller, The French Canadian Missionary Society, and Charles Chiniquy.

The first noteworthy Protestant missionary to Québec was Henriette Odin-Feller (1800–1868), a Swiss immigrant who arrived in Montréal in 1835 bent on converting the French Canadians. As a young woman in Switzerland, Odin-Feller had come to admire, then join, a group of reforming Protestants who challenged the official Protestant church. Her marriage to Henri Feller in 1822 marked the beginning of five years of personal tragedy, a period when death claimed her daughter, her husband, her sister, and her mother. Thereafter, the young widow became deeply involved in the evangelization efforts of her associates, simultaneously opting for a belief in "believers' baptism."[4] After some of her friends had come to Canada under the sponsorship of the Société des missions évangéliques de Lausanne, the widow Odin-Feller came in turn in 1835, in the company of Louis Roussy.

Odin-Feller spent her first year doing missionary work in the cities and towns of Québec, frustrated by the constant hostility, rejection, and even occasional manhandling to which she was subjected as she went from door to door witnessing to her version of the Christian faith.[5] In 1836, the two Swiss Protestant missionaries decided to settle further afield, in a rural area of new settlement where the Catholic clergy could do little to thwart their efforts. This was the beginning of the mission at Grande Ligne, some sixteen kilometers south of Saint-Jean on the south shore of the St Lawrence River near Montréal. The mission of Grande Ligne, consisting of a chapel and school, was the base for Odin-Feller's activities of preaching, teaching, and colportage until her death thirty-two years later. At that time, the church of Grande Ligne included some 400 members, served by nine chapels and seven ministers.

Madame Odin-Feller's modest inroads into Catholic ranks had been assisted by the disappointment of some 'patriote' Catholics who witnessed the support Bishop Lartigue had given to British authorities at the time of the rebellion of 1837. She then consolidated her hold over her people by her deep spirituality, her medical skills, and the proselytizing of the children enrolled in her school.

Just as Henriette Odin-Feller established her mission, and as Canada suffered under the consequences of the failed rebellion of 1837–1838, most of the Protestant churches in Canada decided to create a new missionary society. In 1839, The French Canadian Missionary Society was organized jointly by the Methodist, Baptist, and Presbyterian churches with the objective of converting French Canadians to Protestantism without favouring any denomination in particular. The Church of England refused to join, as did Odin-Feller, although the latter's theology closely resembled that of the Baptists. The new society's main achievement seems to have been to irritate the Catholic majority, without making any significant inroads into its ranks.

Simultaneously, each of the Protestant churches established boarding schools in order to better proselytize French Canadians. However, their success was also minimal, one reason being that they were usually bilingual schools that welcomed both English-speaking and French-speaking pupils. Moreover, the schools were under the control and supervision of churches that were overwhelmingly English-speaking, thus tending to favour the assimilation of the francophone minority, thereby weakening the latter's ties to the francophone Catholic majority in Québec.

The third leading agent of Protestant proselytism in Québec was the renegade priest Charles Chiniquy (1809–1899). Ordained a priest in the diocese of Québec in 1833, Chiniquy ministered in various parishes while developing his campaign against alcoholic beverages. During the late 1830s and the 1840s, Chiniquy became a leading temperance crusader in Québec, preaching to packed churches throughout the province. The talented and colourful revivalist preacher led growing numbers of his rapt faithful to tearful and joyous repentance from their alcoholic ways and to the taking of temperance pledges. Increasingly, however, his bishop was forced to relieve him of one pastoral appointment after another because of Father Chiniquy's propensity to commit indiscretions with women. It was after one of these misadventures that he was ordered to enter the novitiate of the Oblates in Longueuil in 1846. His stay was short-lived, however, as the Oblates found within a year that the irrepressible clerical firebrand's behaviour was intolerable. Chiniquy thereupon took up again his temperance crusade, in the diocese of Montréal this time, only to be expelled from the diocese by Bishop Bourget in 1851, again because of the supposedly celibate priest's scandalous involvement with a woman.

For the next five years, he ministered to the French-Canadian parish of St Anne at Kankakee in the diocese of Chicago, Illinois. Again, however, his bishop found his behaviour intolerable. Not only was the troublesome priest's popularity with the faithful a threat to other clergy, but he suggested to his flock that they could not entrust their welfare to their Irish bishop. Moreover, the bishop was hearing rumours of further sexual misbehaviour by Chiniquy. The exalted and passionate 'apostle of temperance' was thereupon suspended from his ministerial duties and then excommunicated from the church in 1856 upon his refusal to obey his superior's directives.

Banned from the Catholic Church, a decision that was confirmed in 1858, but with the continuing support of most of his parishioners, Chiniquy then joined the Presbyterian Church in the United States which ordained him to the ministry in 1860. Within two years that church's Chicago consistory had also expelled him because of his rebellious temperament, but within a year the synod of the Canadian Presbyterian Church took him in; therein he remained for the rest of his long life, assuming the mantle of apostle to French Canada. For the next thirty-five years, Chiniquy's preaching consisted of virulent and impassioned attacks on Catholicism and its entire works, including its doctrines, its sacraments, its moral teachings, and its devotions. He accused the pope, bishops, and clergy of every sin and abuse under the sun. His work was so appreciated that he was officially appointed his church's missionary to French Canada in 1873.

From his base in Montréal where he lived with his wife and children, the fiery preacher often indulged in spectacular and provocative gestures, such as in Montréal in January 1876, when he consecrated wafers of bread only to crumble them, dump them on the ground, and trample them under foot in order to demonstrate that the Catholic Eucharist was meaningless.[6] He published a series of pamphlets and bestselling books in the same vein, relishing in the denunciation of alleged moral abuses by priests in the confessional and elsewhere. Among his most notorious publications was the first volume of his memoirs which was entitled *Fifty Years in the Church of Rome* (1885), in which he continued to belabour alleged abuses by the Catholic Church. A measure of the book's success was that by 1892 it had been translated into nine languages, and by 1898 it was into its seventieth edition. His religious testament, published on 23 January 1899, was merely more of the same.

The campaign to convert Canada's French-speaking Catholics to Protestantism was largely unsuccessful. At its peak in 1900, it is estimated that Protestantism counted sixty-five churches and missions and some sixty ministers and evangelists, and a total of 20,000 faithful, or one per cent of the French-speaking population.[7] Given that fully one half of these may have been Presbyterian, Chiniquy's controversial work would appear to have had a measure of success.

Missions in Canada's northwest

Riding the ships, barges, and canoes of the Hudson's Bay Company, Protestant missionaries, primarily Anglican, but also Methodist, Baptist and other, undertook the evangelization of the immense North and West of Canada, an area that encompassed some two-thirds of Canada's ten million square kilometers. They did so beginning in 1820 when the first Church of England minister set foot in Red River. In a century-long head-to-head competition with the Catholics, especially the Oblates, these Protestant evangelizers sought to win over the Amerindian people to their version of Christianity.

The number of clergy remained modest until 1840, some half a dozen men scattered from Rainy Lake in today's northwestern Ontario to Fort Vancouver at the mouth of the Columbia River on the Pacific slope. Afterwards, missionaries became more numerous as permanent stations were founded along the vast network of fur trade posts along the Red, Saskatchewan, Athabaska, Mackenzie, Yukon, Fraser, and Columbia rivers. While the Church of England sought to keep Catholics in check in the land of the western fur trade, the growing European settlements on the southern prairies and British Columbia attracted clergy of an increasing variety of churches. The outcome was that by the turn of the twentieth century, the Church of England, primarily due to the efforts of its C.M.S. personnel, claimed the allegiance of some one-third of the Amerindian and Inuit people of Canada's North and West; Catholics claimed most of the others. Canada's other Protestant churches would be active among European settlements primarily.

Auxiliary missionary agencies

Auxiliary agencies supported the work of the Protestant missionaries. The first to display evangelical colours was The Religious Tract Society, founded in London in 1799 by a group of Anglicans and Nonconformists of evangelical persuasion. As the name indicates, its purpose was to publish religious tracts and literature, which it did in over 200 languages. Only five years later, was founded The British and Foreign Bible Society. It was a response to complaints that the Bible was not being translated and disseminated with the urgency that evangelical convictions demanded. From its headquarters in London, this inter-denominational agency was directed by a lay committee composed of equal numbers of Anglicans and other Protestants. For two centuries it has been engaged in translating, printing, and distributing the Bible in many languages throughout the world, always striving to avoid denominational bias.

Another institution that proved an important buttress to Protestant evangelical missionary activities was the Sunday school. Founded in England in 1780 with the objective of promoting literacy among Britain's poor children on their only work-free day, the schools soon multiplied to the extent that a Sunday School Society was formed in 1785 to support individual schools. It was directed by an equal number of Anglicans and other Protestants. By 1800 a growing number of schools were found in both Great Britain and North America. Beginning in 1803, a series of auxiliary agencies was founded to provide the schools with books and supplies, and to support their largely volunteer teaching staff. The latter was mainly composed of evangelical Christians.

From the outset, Sunday schools included moral instruction as well as Bible readings. Pupils were taught respect for authority and the value of hard work, honesty, and self-discipline. As the government expanded its public school system during the first decades of the nineteenth century, Sunday schools focused more and more on religious education and came to be more often than not under parish or congregational control. Nevertheless, they remained inter-denominational in their control and curriculum, avoiding sectarian controversy and partisanship. After 1843, the Church of England instituted its own Sunday schools, whose organization was thereafter parallel to the nondenominational ones.

In Canada, Sunday schools became an important component in the evangelical Protestant apostolate. Their classes served to promote temperance, missions, and a wide range of church concerns among the children who were educated under their influence.

Catholic missionary agencies

Just as Protestant and evangelical missionary agencies were founded in Protestant countries, especially in Great Britain, a parallel phenomenon was emerging in Catholic countries. In Canadian Catholicism, France played a role analogous to that of Great Britain in Canadian Protestantism. While missionary agencies appeared novel in British Protestantism, the missionary agencies of the Catholics were the religious orders, both old and new, male and female. These brotherhoods and sisterhoods were financially assisted by new organizations dedicated to fund-raising for the missions.

Religious orders

Members of religious orders traditionally justify their chosen style of life by invoking Jesus' saying, "If you would be perfect, go sell all your goods and follow me" (Matthew 19:21). It was explained earlier how this communal life of detachment from personal goods has taken a variety of forms over the centuries. Whenever major renewal movements have swept through the Catholic Church, they have been characterized by the founding of new religious orders. This was the case during the Gregorian reformation of the eleventh to thirteenth centuries that led to the founding of a series of new orders including the Franciscans, the Dominicans, and the Cistercians. The Catholic reformation of the sixteenth and seventeenth centuries also gave birth to new orders including the Society of Jesus, the Capuchins, the Ursulines, and the Sulpicians to name only the more prominent.

The Catholic renewal of the nineteenth century was no different. Centred in post-revolutionary and post-Napoleonic France, the France of the restoration of the monarchy after 1815, the Catholic awakening led to the founding of more religious orders of men and women than at any similar period in the past. There were only 12,000 sisters in the country in 1808, but no less than 128,000 in 1901. These women joined 400 new religious orders of women that were created in the country, in addition to the other orders that had been in place for many years. The majority worked in schools, hospitals, and other social services. Also, in less than a century France had more than made up for its clerical losses. Between 1830 and 1901, the number of men in religious orders in France went from 3,000 to 30,000, and by 1876, the country had one ordained priest for every 654 Catholics, a proportion of clergy of which any prelate could be proud.

Because of the century-long political tug-of-war between revolutionary republicans on the one hand, and conservative monarchists on the other, France's policies *vis-à-vis* the Catholic Church ranged from the very favourable under the monarchs and emperors to the most unfavourable under the republican governments. Periodic revolutions led to periodic discriminatory laws and regulations against Catholic interests, including laws and regulations that sought to restrict religious orders, those of men in particular. Whenever the country went through such periods of discrimination, religious orders sought refuge elsewhere. Canada was a favourite harbour in the successive storms. This became especially true after 1880 when republican governments proved particularly hostile, and remained so until after World War I.

Until 1880, French government policy was usually favourable to Catholics, enabling religious orders to develop almost at will. This was when a series of traditional orders were authorized anew including Trappists, Sulpicians, Eudists, Capuchins, and Vincentians (Lazarists). Other celebrated orders were also re-established without the blessing of the French government, orders such as the Society of Jesus, the Benedictines, and the Dominicans. New orders were founded, the Missionary Oblates of Mary Immaculate (1816) being the most notable for Canadians, but a number of others also appeared at a dizzying pace, including the Congregation of the Holy Cross (1837), The Brothers of Saint Vincent de Paul (1845), and the Fathers of the Blessed Sacrament (1856).

Although the most important migration of French religious to Canada would have to await the early years of the twentieth century, there were contingents of sisters, brothers, and priests that came in earlier times. The first group were refugees from the French Revolution of 1789 who arrived in Canada shortly afterwards. They were mainly Sulpicians and secular priests. The second wave began in 1837 and continued for several years thereafter, and resulted from deliberate recruiting activity by Bishop Bourget of Montréal who desperately sought assistance for his expanding church. Many key orders came to Canada at this time, including the Brothers of Christian Schools, the Oblates, the Jesuits, the Viatorians, and the Holy Cross Fathers. The third wave of religious migrants began after 1880, primarily as a result of French laws and regulations that were contrary to the interests of religious orders. By this time, Canada was not lacking in clergy, and its bishops were therefore more discriminating in admitting these foreigners into their dioceses, particularly in the cities of Canada.

As was the case in France, Canada also witnessed a spectacular growth in the number of its religious congregations during the nineteenth century. While all ten religious orders of men in Canada before 1880 were of foreign origin which then gradually recruited Canadians, fully thirteen of the nineteen congregations of women were Canadian foundations from the outset.[8] Moreover, the latter do not include the seven congregations of women present in Canada since the French régime. Including these last, Canada, more specifically Québec, had ten orders of men and twenty-six congregations of women in place in 1880, a year when most were recruiting growing numbers of new members. These were the troops that filled the ranks of the Catholic missionary crusade in nineteenth-century Canada.

Missionary agencies of men

In assuming responsibility for missions, religious orders traditionally accepted full financial responsibility for them, as well as the burden of staffing, directing, and managing the missions.

The revenues of the missionaries usually came directly from their own congregations, unless some other source of funding became available. The orders generated these funds by using the profits from some of their other more profitable activities, such as boarding schools, wealthy parishes, publications, or various investments. In the nineteenth century, the missionary orders were assisted by auxiliary agencies created in France with the express purpose of collecting money and redistributing it to the missionaries. The most important of these agencies was the French Société pour la propagation de la foi, while the Oeuvre de la sainte enfance provided much more limited subsidies.

Missionaries were driven by the biblical commission to "go ... and make disciples of all nations, baptizing them in the name of the Father and of the Son and of the Holy Spirit, and teaching them to obey everything that I have commanded you."[9] In a time of religious awakening like that of the nineteenth century, the Catholic conscience became highly sensitized to the importance of this mandate. While many orders of men and women were active in Canadian missions during the nineteenth century, foremost among the men were the Missionary Oblates of Mary Immaculate, while Jesuits and secular clergy provided smaller contingents.

The Oblates were founded in France in 1816, under the name of the Missionaries of Provence, a society of secular priests dedicated to evangelizing the neglected poor of the French countryside. In 1826, the institute was given papal approval under the name of Missionary Oblates of Mary Immaculate. Within a few years the founder, Eugène de Mazenod, had transformed his band into a religious congregation with vows. Active in the preaching of parish missions, in 1827 the Oblates added to their duties the running of the diocesan seminary in Marseilles, only ten years before their founder was appointed bishop of the diocese, a post he occupied until his death in 1861. The new congregation based its spirituality on that of the Sulpicians which stressed the dignity and responsibility of the priest, while requiring that each of its members make a special promise of obedience to the pope, thereby becoming one of the first manifestly ultramontane congregations. Oblate moral theology was inspired by Alphonsus Liguori, a teaching that was more merciful and kind than traditional Gallican theology; it made more allowance for human weakness.

Oblates first came to Canada as a result of a chance encounter between Mazenod and Bishop Bourget of Montréal who had stopped overnight in Marseilles during a voyage to Rome in 1841. At the time, the congregation numbered a mere fifty-five men, restricted as it was by the French government regulations adopted in 1828, regulations that made it very difficult to expand its work. When Mazenod discovered that Bourget was looking for new missionary workers for his diocese, he jumped at the chance of opening a new field of endeavour for his men.

Upon their arrival in Montréal in December, 1841, the first six Oblates were entrusted with the parish of St Hilaire on the Richelieu River. This became their base of operations for preaching missions in neighbouring parishes, in the Eastern Townships of Québec, and in the vast Ottawa Valley, areas that were opening up to new settlers from Québec, Ireland and elsewhere. The itinerant preachers often departed their mission stations after having established temperance societies and confraternities of Marian devotion. Eager to get closer to the city of Montréal and because of a generous gift from a benefactor, in August 1842 they were able to move their headquarters to Longueuil. Six years later, their wish was realized when Bishop Bourget entrusted them with the parish of Saint-Pierre-Apôtre in the heart of the city. This would long remain their mother house in eastern Canada. By 1848, the Oblates had already expanded their missionary activities to include the Saguenay River, the St Maurice River, the north shore of the lower St Lawrence, James Bay, Red River, and northern Saskatchewan in the Northwest. Shortly thereafter, they were working in Labrador, the Pacific slope, the Arctic, the northeastern United States, and Texas. Their epic missionary story corresponds to the early settlement of more than half of today's Canada, encompassing all of Canada's North from the Atlantic to the Pacific, in addition to the Ottawa Valley, the Prairies, and British Columbia. By the year 1900, hundreds of Oblates were at work in every part of Canada.

The Catholic theology that grounded Oblate missionary efforts understood the entire universe to be God's creation, men and women to be created in God's image, and every person, place, institution, object, or event as possible venues for the Christian's encounter with God. The gift of God's grace could be received, or God could be encountered anywhere, anyplace, anytime, and through the agency or mediation of anyone. In addition, the Catholic was assured of receiving the gift of God at certain prescribed moments when one of seven prescribed rites of the Church, the sacraments, was administered. Baptism washed away sins, Confirmation gave the gifts of the Holy Spirit, the Eucharist nourished the faithful with the flesh and blood of Christ, Penance (or Reconciliation) delivered God's forgiveness of sins, Marriage put a divine seal on a couple's mutual promise, Holy Orders made the clergyman into Christ's associate, and the Sacrament of the Sick gave God's final blessing to the faithful suffering serious illness.

The entire world, nature and society included, was called to salvation by God through Christ. The missionary was therefore bent on transforming the world, not on condemning and escaping it. While tainted, the natural environment and society were fundamentally good. They only needed to be reformed to become God's garden.

While instantaneous, miraculous, and dramatic conversion of a sinner was always possible, in Catholic teaching conversion was usually held to be a more gradual process whereby the sinner regretted sinful ways, turned to God, and was helped every step of the way by the Church. This conversion was usually triggered by the work of a priest or missionary who proclaimed the Gospel. Once a potential convert appeared among the Amerindians who were being evangelized, the missionary taught him or her the rudiments of the faith, perhaps during two or three weeks, including the sign of the cross, the Creed, and a few prayers such as the Our Father and the Hail Mary. Then the missionary baptized the person on the understanding that baptism would wash away all sins, give God's grace to the new Christian, and make him or her receptive to the nurturing care of the Church, including the further ministrations of the priest and the community. In Catholic theology, conversion was more often than not a process as opposed to an instantaneous event, a process helped along by preaching, catechism, priestly guidance, and sacraments. Baptism, the Eucharist, penance, and the others actually delivered God's grace to the recipient; they were not merely symbols of an internal spiritual event. Such a theology meant that Catholic missionaries were less reluctant to baptize Amerindian converts than were the Protestant missionaries for whom individual conversion of the heart needed to precede baptism which symbolized that conversion.

The Oblates were also typical Catholic missionaries in that their religious life facilitated their work. Canadian missions were almost by definition poor, unable to provide sufficient revenues to sustain a missionary station. The Oblate vows of poverty and chastity meant that their missions could survive on a shoestring, since no wives or children of the missionaries needed to be provided for; moreover, the poverty that was endemic in the missions of the North and West appeared to be providential to the Oblates whose motto was "He has sent me to evangelize the poor." In Canada's northwest, the Presbyterian Alexander Ross wrote in 1855 that the typical Catholic missionary was sent on his way with a mere £10 and the blessing of his bishop. At that time, the Oblate mission of Île-à-la-Crosse in northern Saskatchewan, a station that included four missionaries, survived for a year with only £54 in supplies, including one bag of flour per missionary.

The Oblate vow of obedience also helped to sustain Catholic missions by ensuring that the missionaries' religious superiors always had effective control over the missions. Indeed, the poverty, misery, and isolation of many mission stations in the North and West were difficult to endure at the best of times, given the distance of the posts from civilization and the difficulty of communicating with them. For example, a missionary in the Mackenzie River valley who wrote to his relatives or superior in Europe could only hope to receive an answer two years later. Mission supplies had to be ordered two or three years in advance. A number of the missionaries were driven into clinical depression or other mental illness by the awful burden of total isolation for months at a time. The vow of obedience conditioned the missionary to be more receptive to directives from his superiors, while enabling the latter to transfer their personnel when necessary.

In their work of evangelization, the Oblate missionaries adopted tactics designed to best facilitate the conversion of Canada's Amerindian people. During their education in Europe or Canada, the missionaries received no special training in either knowing or appreciating the cultures and languages of Canada's Amerindian people. However, upon being appointed to Amerindian missionary work in Canada, the Oblate was required first to learn the languages of the Amerindians to whom he was being sent, a schooling usually obtained from veteran missionaries themselves. So it was that Oblate Bishop Alexandre Taché wrote in 1859: "The first thing we do upon arrival amidst a tribe, even before arriving if possible, is to learn its language. Not all missionaries are equally successful, but all soon manage to do without interpreters, and instruct the Amerindians directly, a condition essential to the success of a mission."[10]

When evangelizing many of the Métis, the Oblate had the advantage of already knowing French.

From the outset in the mid-nineteenth century, several Catholic missionaries composed prayer books, hymnals, and catechisms in a variety of Amerindian languages, using the syllabic script that had been invented by Methodist Reverend James Evans (1801–1846) at his station of Norway House in northern Manitoba. The texts were then printed at centres such as Fort Chipewyan, Lake La Biche, Montréal, and Paris. Such work was usually the missionaries' only academic pursuit, busy as most were with fishing, trapping, cabin-building, farming, or driving dog teams over hundreds of kilometres in the wilds of northern Canada.

In some parts of Canada, in British Columbia in particular, Oblate missionaries established a novel system of Amerindian self-management of their own Christian villages. The system was put in place by Father Paul Durieu (1830–1899) who worked in British Columbia for forty years, from 1859 until his death. Durieu used the Catholic ladder, a graphic representation of the story of salvation that began with creation and ended in heaven for the saved, or hell for the damned. The ladder had been invented by an earlier missionary to the Pacific slope, Father François Blanchet, and then further refined by the celebrated Oblate missionary to the West, Albert Lacombe (1827–1916). The ladder showed two roads to eternity, the high, straight, and narrow one of Catholic teaching, and the low, twisted, and easy one of all false religions and teachings.

During his missionary journeys along the lower Fraser River, Father Durieu spent most of his days preaching, teaching catechism, and baptizing children. At a general meeting in the evening, the Amerindians would elect a captain, two soldiers, and two policemen charged with assisting the chief in policing the village according to the rules of the missionary. Oblates in British Columbia felt that the system worked well in assisting their villages of converts in doing the right thing.

Catholic mission stations were of two kinds. The main stations were those where two or more missionaries resided year round and were the base of operations for itinerant evangelists. The more important of these resident centres could include a working farm, a warehouse, a boarding school, a convent, an infirmary, and various other services that were needed to resupply and sustain the mission posts. The secondary stations were those visited by the evangelists on their circuits of posts scattered among the various Amerindian bands. During these circuits, the missionary would devote anywhere from a few days to several months to a given post, before moving on.

The travelling missionaries frequently availed themselves of the transport provided by the Hudson Bay Company (H.B.C.) which ran canoes, barges, dog teams, or pack horses between its numerous trading posts. Given that most mission stations were located in the neighbourhood of a trading post, the Company's network was a godsend to the missionaries. Moreover, the Company frequently helped the missionaries by providing them with free lodging and food, and by providing materials and labour for the building of the missionary's cabin and chapel. In fact, both the Protestant and the Catholic networks of mission posts would have been much more modest, if they had existed at all, had it not been for the gracious support of the H.B.C.

While the Oblates were the foremost missionary agency in nineteenth-century Canada, a number of others were also active. Surprisingly enough, the first priests to penetrate new territories were frequently secular clergy, that is priests who were not members of any religious orders, but who worked for a particular diocese. This had been the case in the 1790s, when French *émigré* priests who had fled the French Revolution and who had just come to Canada from England were in many cases the first priests sent into the wilds of Upper Canada by the bishop of Québec. They travelled up the St Lawrence from Montréal, reporting on the religious needs of new settlements at Cornwall, Kingston, York, and elsewhere. The first priests to evangelize the Ottawa Valley's burgeoning forestry communities after 1815 had also been secular priests sent from Montréal. They stopped at Hawkesbury, Hull, Aylmer, and Fort Coulonge, hearing confessions, baptizing, blessing marriages, and preaching to any and all. The same was true for Canada's Northwest, including British Columbia, which was first evangelized by secular priests sent by the bishops of Québec beginning in 1818.

These initial forays by secular clergy were usually followed by the takeover of the mission territories by specific religious orders. The latter usually did so at the request of the secular clergy itself which was unable to assure continued financial and personnel support for new mission fields. This was the case in the Northwest after 1845 when

Bishop Joseph-Norbert Provencher (1787–1853), a member of the secular clergy, sought and obtained the services of the Oblates as insurance for the future of his new diocese of Saint-Boniface which included most of the Northwest.

The Society of Jesus returned to Canada under similar auspices. Disbanded by papal directive in 1773 but reinstated in 1814, the brotherhood that had provided the giants of Catholic missions during the French régime returned to North America, specifically to the United States, shortly afterwards. Upon the Jesuit superior general Father Roothaan's acceding to Bishop Bourget's request that his men return to Canada, in 1842 an initial contingent of Jesuits took over the parish of Laprairie, the site of their former seigneurie and mission to the Iroquois.[11] Thereupon, Michael Power, the parish's outgoing pastor who had just been made first bishop of Toronto, convinced them to take up again their missions to Canada's Amerindians by sending men to southwestern Ontario. From bases in Windsor and Manitoulin Island, during the second half of the nineteenth century Jesuits expanded their apostolate to include much of north-central and northwestern Ontario, with posts at Manitoulin, Guelph, Sudbury, Spanish, Midland, and Thunder Bay, in addition to the state of Michigan in the U.S.A. Although their numbers in Canada would not match those of the Oblates, Jesuits nevertheless reinvented their presence among Canada's Amerindians.

Missionary agencies of women

While the numbers of religious women doubled in both France and Québec during the first half of the nineteenth century,[12] during the next half-century France's increase was only 35%, while Québec's was fully 1,000%, going from 650 sisters in 1850 to no less than 6,628 in 1900. Most of them were Canadian women, as had been the custom for congregations of women in Canada from the outset. While none of the numerous women's congregations played a role as predominant as that of the Oblates in the missions, among the more active were the Sisters of Charity, the Sisters of Providence, and the Sisters of Saint Anne, all founded and based in Montréal. They were the leading providers of social services, teaching, nursing, and care of the poor.

The founding of the Sisters of Charity of the General Hospital by Saint Marguerite d'Youville has been described above.[13] Until the 1830s, the order had limited its activities to its hospital work in Montréal. However, the growing number of sisters that came with the religious awakening of

that time allowed the directors of the sisterhood to accept more foundations in other cities, and then in remote mission stations. During the
1830s and 1840s, the Sisters of Charity founded hospitals, schools, orphanages, infirmaries, and services to the poor in Saint-Hyacinthe, Québec,
Ottawa, and Saint-Boniface. After 1850, their network expanded rapidly
across the continent, including Edmonton (St Albert), Île-à-la-Crosse in
northern Saskatchewan, Providence on the Mackenzie River, the northeastern United States, and James Bay. Moreover, in many of these places,
an initial foundation, such as a hospital, frequently generated several
distinct institutions such as orphanages, day schools, boarding schools,
and nursing homes. In addition, the order sometimes divided to give birth
to other identical orders that bore different names such as the Grey Nuns
of the Cross,[14] or the Grey Sisters of the Immaculate Conception.[15]

The Sisters of Charity of Montréal were the preferred female cowork-
ers of the Oblates in their rapid expansion across the North-American
continent. Whenever the priests founded a mission that was important
enough to warrant a school or a hospital, they usually asked d'Youville's
community for assistance before inviting any other order to join them.
While the priests ran the mission station, the sisters provided the teaching
and nursing care, with the support of some lay employees.

Another Montréal congregation of sisters that played an important
role in missions was that of the Sisters of Providence. Founded in 1843,
the new congregation was the result of more than a decade of dedicated
work in support of elderly and destitute women by Émilie Gamelin,
née Tavernier. Indeed, during the first half of the nineteenth century,
Montréal had been bearing the ill effects of industrialization and growing immigration of Irish people fleeing their suffering homeland. This
led to a host of social problems, which in turn occasioned the emergence of several groups of lay women bent on providing some relief
to the poor and destitute immigrants, orphans, widows, and others.
One of these groups was led by the widow Gamelin who, under the
urging of Bishop Bourget, in 1843 transformed her band of pious lay
volunteers into a congregation of women who took vows, dedicated
to the service of disabled and elderly women. They were the Sisters of
Providence.[16]

The Sisters of Providence were founded at the beginning of a period of very rapid growth in the number of women who entered the
religious life in Québec. As their numbers grew by leaps and bounds after
1850, they undertook a wide range of activities including day care centres,
orphanages, schools, boarding schools, soup kitchens, etc. Any social

service that was deemed necessary in the new chaotic industrializing world could become one of the forms of the apostolate of the sisters. Inevitably they were also drawn to distant mission territories in Canada.

One of the prime areas of the apostolate of religious sisters in Canada had always been the teaching of children in elementary schools, a work that had been the preferred arena of the Ursulines and the Sisters of Notre Dame since the seventeenth century. The religious awakening of the 1840s and the swelling ranks of the religious life allowed new teaching congregations to emerge. In 1844, with the support of the Oblates and Bishop Bourget, Eulalie Durocher had founded the Sisters of the Holy Names of Jesus and Mary, dedicated to running schools for the young. Only six years later, another teaching congregation appeared, founded by Esther Blondin. In addition to establishing deep roots in Québec, the Sisters of Saint Anne (1850) had soon dispatched a band of women to Victoria, British Columbia (1858), which became their base for a wide-ranging apostolate on the West Coast. Boarding schools and day schools of the Sisters of Saint Anne were soon to be found scattered from the forty-ninth parallel in the South to Alaska in the North.

Indeed, after 1850, the initial limited objectives of many of the congregations of women were abandoned under the pressure of circumstances. Many congregations would thereafter work as general-purpose social service orders, simultaneously founding, running, and staffing day schools, colleges, boarding schools, hospitals, orphanages, and various services to the poor. This was the case for the Sisters of Charity, the Sisters of Providence, the Sisters of Mercy, and a number of others. The rapidly expanding social needs in a given community where a congregation of sisters was established forced them to assume a wider range of duties.

The rapid increase in the number of religious women after 1840 continued unabated. In fact, in the twentieth century between 1930 and 1960 there will be another surge in their numbers, resulting in the extensive network of hospitals, schools, and other social service institutions in which they served Canadian society until recent times.

Conclusion

Missionary agencies were a key component in the evangelization of Canada by both Protestants and Catholics. In Catholicism, these agencies were usually, but not always, religious orders. In Protestantism, because religious orders were not desired, special agencies were founded with specific objectives in mind, objectives such as the supply and training of missionaries, the financial support of missions, the provision of prayer books and other literature, etc. In other words, agencies such as the S.P.G., the C.M.S., the British and Foreign Bible Society, and several others were fulfilling the exact same function in Protestant missions as were the religious orders in Catholic missions. No church, Protestant or Catholic, could have fulfilled their mission without the precious support of these agencies.

Suggested readings

Arnold, Odile. *Le corps et l'âme. La vie des religieuses au XIXe siècle*. Paris: Seuil, 1984.

Berkhofer, Robert F. *Salvation and the Savage: An Analysis of Protestant Missions and American Amerindian Response, 1787–1862*. Lexington: University of Kentucky Press, 1965.

Bowden, Henry Warner. *American Amerindian and Christian Missions*. Chicago: University of Chicago Press, 1981.

Butcher, Dennis L., et al. Eds. *Prairie Spirit: Perspectives on the Heritage of the United Church of Canada in the West*. Winnipeg: University of Manitoba Press, 1985.

Choquette, Robert. *The Oblate Assault on Canada's Northwest*. Ottawa: University of Ottawa Press, 1995.

Danylewycz, Marta. *Taking the Veil: An Alternative to Marriage, Motherhood and Spinsterhood in Québec, 1840–1920*. Toronto: McClelland & Stewart, 1987.

Denault, Bernard and Benoît Lévesque. *Éléments pour une sociologie des communautés religieuses au Québec*. Montréal: Les Presses de l'Université de Montréal, 1975.

Dufourcq, Élisabeth. *Les congrégations religieuses féminines hors d'Europe, de Richelieu à nos jours: histoire naturelle d'une diaspora*. 4 vols. Paris: Librairie de l'Inde, 1993.

Haig, Alan. *The Victorian Clergy*. London: Croom Helm, 1984.

Harrod, Howard L. *Mission among the Blackfeet*. Norman: University of Oklahoma Press, 1971.

Hostie, Raymond. *Vie et mort des ordres religieux. Approches psychosociologiques*. Paris: Desclée de Brouwer, 1972.

Huel, Raymond J. A. *Proclaiming the Gospel to the Amerindians and the Métis*. Edmonton: The University of Alberta Press. 1996.

Jean, Marguerite. *Évolution des communautés religieuses de femmes au Canada de 1639 à nos jours*. Montréal: Fides, 1977.

Langlois, Claude. *Le catholicisme au féminin. Les congrégations françaises à supérieure générale au XIXe siècle*. Paris: Cerf, 1984.

Laperrière, Guy. *Les congrégations religieuses. De la France au Québec 1880–1914*. vols. 1 & 2. Sainte-Foy: Les Presses de l'Université Laval, 1996, 1999.

Laurin, Nicole et al. *À la recherche d'un monde oublié: les communautés religieuses de femmes au Québec de 1900 à 1970*. Montréal: Le Jour, 1991.

MacGregor, James. *Father Lacombe*. Edmonton: Hurtig, 1975.

Mitchell, Estelle. *Les Sœurs Grises de Montréal à la Rivière Rouge, 1844–1984*. Montréal: Méridien, 1987.

Morice, A. G. *History of the Catholic Church in Western Canada*, 3 vols. Toronto: Musson, 1910.

Smillie, Benjamin. Ed. *Visions of the New Jerusalem: Religious Settlement on the Prairies*. Edmonton: NeWest Press, 1983.

Urquhart, Gordon. *The Pope's Armada*. Reading, Great Britain: Corgi Books, 1996.

CHAPTER 11

The Churches and the State

During the first half of the nineteenth century, while the Catholic and Protestant missionary agencies were launching their initial campaigns, the main Christian churches in Canada underwent significant structural changes and rapid development. At the beginning of 1800, only the Catholic Church had large numbers of faithful, some 140,000, mainly in Québec. In the Maritime colonies as in Upper Canada, settlement of any importance was just getting underway, while only a handful of fur traders and their scattered Amerindian clients inhabited the vast Northwest.

By mid-century however, the situation had changed dramatically. In a total population of just over 2.3 million people, there were 983,680 Catholics and 965,055 Protestants belonging to the four leading traditions that were, in order of numerical representation: Presbyterian (310,512), Anglican (303,897), Methodist (258,1570), and Baptist (92,489). In addition, the Protestant group included a number of other small denominations that came to Canada after the War of 1812; these included Universalists, Unitarians, Mormons, Disciples of Christ, and the Catholic Apostolic Church or Irvingites. When the members of all Protestant denominations are taken into account, Canada harboured six Protestants for every four Catholics in 1850.

It was during this period that the relationship between the churches and the state was radically transformed. Whereas in 1800 the laws in all of the colonies that made up Canada either formally established or favoured the establishment of the Church of England as the state religion and discouraged other forms of Christianity, by the mid-nineteenth century most official ties between churches and governments had been severed.

The structure and development of the churches

During the first half of the nineteenth century, the accelerated growth of the population in all the British colonies that would later become Canada was accompanied by rapid development and important organizational changes in the churches. Leading the movement were the Catholic Church, the Church of England, the Presbyterians, and the Methodists. Simultaneously, several denominations underwent an institutional fragmentation driven by diverse regional, theological, and spiritual factors.

The Roman Catholic Church

Canada's sole diocese of Québec was unable to divide into several jurisdictions until the close of the War of 1812. The main obstacle to the earlier creation of more dioceses and bishops was the obstruction of British authorities who, after 1793, were subjected to the constant pressure of the Church of England's founding bishop, Jacob Mountain of Québec; he sought the implementation of the Crown's official policy of making the Church of England into Québec's established church, a policy that had always remained a dead letter. However, the Catholic Church's manifest loyalty to the British Crown, particularly during the War of 1812, ensured a change of heart by London. Beginning in 1817, a series of new Catholic ecclesiastical jurisdictions were authorized, new apostolic vicariates, districts, and dioceses that by mid-century would encompass all of British North America from the Atlantic to the Pacific. Government support for the growing number of bishops would be reinforced by their continuing loyalty to the British Crown during the rebellion of 1837–1838 in Lower Canada. By mid-century, the former solitary but immense diocese of Québec had been subdivided into more than a dozen dioceses, each headed by a bishop responsible for nurturing a growing flock.

   Upon his retirement in 1784, Bishop Briand had been succeeded in turn by L.-P.-F. Mariauchau Desgly (1784–1788), Jean-François Hubert (1788–1797), Pierre Denaut (1797–1806), and Joseph-Octave Plessis (1806–1825). They directed a diocese of Québec whose Catholic population had doubled from 70,000 to 140,000 during the thirty years between 1760 and 1790, and would more than double again in the subsequent thirty years, to surpass 400,000 faithful by 1820. However, during the same period their diocese suffered from a diminishing number of clergy.

Indeed, the number of priests had diminished by 25% between 1760 and 1790, dropping from 196 to 146, a diminishing ratio of priests to faithful that went from one priest for every 350 Catholics to one priest for every 1,000.

Concerned as they were with their diminishing number of church workers, the successive bishops of Québec were just as concerned by the sustained efforts of some of the colonial officials to put the Catholic Church on a British government leash. Indeed, since his arrival on 1 November 1793, Jacob Mountain, founding bishop of the new Anglican diocese of Québec, was primarily concerned with making his church in fact and not only in theory, the established church in the British Province of Québec. Until the beginning of the War of 1812, Mountain enjoyed the support of a handful of key British officials in the colony, especially Attorney-General Jonathan Sewell, Civil Secretary Herman Witsius Ryland, Lieutenant-governor Sir Robert Shore Milnes (1799–1805), and Governor-General Sir James Henry Craig (1807–1811). The Catholic bishops of Québec had their hands full in checking the government's campaign aimed at subjugating the Catholic Church.

With a view to restricting the powers of the Catholic bishop, the Anglican party sought to reserve to the governor the right to appoint pastors in Catholic parishes, a right that was supposedly the governor's since 1763 but that had never been claimed because of successive governors' judgment that it was inopportune to do so. Bishops Hubert, Denaut, and Plessis managed to avoid such a decision, despite financial incentives that were offered to induce them to do so.[1] Mountain, Milnes, and their friends were also disconcerted when their initiative of 1801 to create a network of state-funded schools in every part of the province was successfully resisted at the instigation of Bishop Plessis. Although this Royal Institution for the Advancement of Learning was launched and did manage to create some schools, the latter were intended for the Protestantization and Anglicization of Canada's French Catholics. This objective sealed their fate. The campaign aimed at subjugating the Catholic Church continued unabated until the onset of the War of 1812 between Great Britain and the United States forced the government to focus on more urgent questions.

During those two decades of blatant efforts by Mountain and his friends to bring the Catholic bishops of Québec to heel, the latter had considered dividing their huge diocese in order to better serve its growing population. However, these projects remained stillborn, given the hostile attitude of the government officials who were required to approve any such division of the diocese. But in the wake of the War of 1812, given the demonstrated loyalty of Bishop Plessis and his clergy, the British government changed its policy, having decided that it owed a debt of gratitude to the bishop. A sign of this changed attitude was found in a 2 July 1813 letter of the secretary of state for the colonies, Lord Bathurst, to the new governor of Canada, Sir George Prevost. Therein, Bathurst referred to Plessis as the 'Catholic Bishop of Québec,' a title that could only provoke the ire of Jacob Mountain who understood it to mean that the government was granting official recognition to his religious nemesis. Although, such official recognition would in fact await another five years, Mountain was right in understanding that Bishop Plessis had won an important battle for his church. Thereafter, the tug of war with the Anglican party ended, the British government having recognized that the Catholic Church was the *de facto* church of the Province of Québec. It would no longer seek to obstruct its development, given its oft-proven loyalty to the Crown.

The rapid growth of the British colonies after 1800 made it urgent to divide the diocese of Québec in order to make it more manageable. The long-sought-after division began in 1817 when Rome acceded to the 1815 plea of Father Edmund Burke and created the vicariate apostolic of Nova Scotia with Burke at the helm. Simultaneously, during a voyage to Europe in 1816–1817, Father Alexander Macdonell of Upper Canada had pleaded with British and Roman officials for the creation of new dioceses in the Maritimes and Upper Canada. Macdonell was concerned lest the bishop of Québec have francophone clergy appointed as bishops in these regions. The result was a series of decisions taken by the Vatican in 1818 whereby the region of Prince Edward Island, New Brunswick, and Cape Breton was made into a distinct ecclesiastical district of the diocese of Québec entrusted to Angus Bernard MacEachern, while the newly-created district of Upper Canada was entrusted to Alexander Macdonell. Both Macdonell and MacEachern were ordained bishops.[2] The two new bishops were in fact largely autonomous, but for administrative purposes, each was appointed vicar general, auxiliary, and suffragan to the bishop of Québec.

This preliminary division of the diocese of Québec had been obtained at the instigation of two English-speaking priests who felt that French-speaking Bishop Plessis was not inclined to give them a full measure of justice in his ecclesiastical appointments. When Plessis learned of Rome's decisions of 1818, he immediately asked for the creation of two additional ecclesiastical districts, one in Montréal to be headed by Jean-Jacques Lartigue, the other in the Northwest to be entrusted to Joseph-Norbert Provencher. British authorities gave their consent, and Rome made the additional appointments in 1820.[3]

Whereas Canada's Catholics had only one bishop in 1816, four years later a total of six were authorized by both London and Rome, each entrusted with a distinct portion of the Canadian church. However, these districts were very unequal in size and importance. Indeed, while the districts of Québec and Montréal each included 200,000 faithful, the district of Upper Canada and the district of Prince Edward Island, New Brunswick, and Cape Breton had a modest 15,000 Catholics apiece, Nova Scotia a mere 10,000, and the Northwest only 3,000. Nevertheless, the administrative expansion of the Catholic Church in Canada was under way.

During the rest of the century, the expanded Catholic administrative structure of 1820 was consolidated and extended farther. The primary reason for this was the rapid growth of the population through natural increase and immigration, a growth that required more church services. So it was that areas that were initially created as mere districts or vicariates apostolic became full-fledged dioceses which were then subdivided in turn to create more dioceses. Before Confederation in 1867, the dioceses listed in table 11.1 were created.

The increasing number of dioceses and bishops required that a further level of organization be established, that of the ecclesiastical province or grouping of several dioceses. This process began with the creation of the ecclesiastical province of Québec in 1844, headed by Archbishop Joseph Signay. In fact, the title of archbishop had been granted by the Vatican as early as 1818 to J.-O. Plessis, but the latter was forced to hold his title in abeyance because the British government did not want him to outrank the Church of England's Bishop Jacob Mountain in their British Province of Québec. During these years, the bishop of Québec was the *de facto* supervisor or archbishop of the Canadian church, but he refrained from using his title in public, thus allowing the British officials and the Anglican bishop to save face. By 1844, however, all of the earlier protagonists had left the scene, and the Catholic Church had once again won the gratitude of the British government by resisting the rebellion in Lower Canada in 1837–1838. Canada's first ecclesiastical province, the Province of Québec, was established in 1844 without any undue opposition from government officials. The new province's bishops held their first council in 1851,

Table 11.1   Administrative divisions of the Catholic Church before 1867

Name	Name changed to	Year
Vicariate apostolic of New France	Diocese of Québec (1674)	1658
Prefecture apostolic of Newfoundland	Vicariate apostolic of Newfoundland (1795) Diocese of Newfoundland (1847) Diocese of St. John's (1856)	1784
Vicariate apostolic of Nova Scotia	Diocese of Halifax (1842)	1817
District of Prince Edward Island, New Brunswick, and Cape Breton	Diocese of Charlottetown (1829)	1818
District of Upper Canada	Diocese of Kingston (1826)	1818
District of Montréal	Diocese of Montréal (1836)	1820
District of the Northwest	Diocese of the Northwest (1847) Diocese of St-Boniface (1851)	1820
Diocese of Toronto		1841
Diocese of New Brunswick	Diocese of Fredericton (1852) Diocese of St. John, N.B. (1860)	1842
Diocese of Arichat, N.S.	Diocese of Antigonish (1886)	1844
Diocese of Vancouver Island	Diocese of Victoria (1908)	1846
Diocese of Bytown	Diocese of Ottawa (1860)	1847
Diocese of Saint-Hyacinthe		1852
Diocese of Trois-Rivières		1852
Diocese of London, Ont.		1856
Diocese of Harbour Grace	Diocese of Grand Falls (1964)	1856
Diocese of Hamilton, Ont.		1856
Diocese of Chatham, N.B.	Diocese of Bathurst (1938)	1860
Vicariate apostolic of British Columbia	Diocese of Vancouver (1908)	1863

Source: André Chapeau, Louis-Philippe Normand and Lucienne Plante, *Évêques catholiques du Canada / Canadian R. C. Bishops 1658–1979*, Ottawa, Saint Paul University, 1980.

where they agreed on a series of rules and regulations for the management of their dioceses.

However, the new ecclesiastical province only encompassed the dioceses of the Canadas (Upper and Lower Canada). Those of the Maritimes remaining separate until they were gathered together under the archdiocese of Halifax in 1852. Upper Canada would in turn be organized into the distinct ecclesiastical province of Toronto in 1870 and the Northwest similarly in the province of St Boniface in 1871. In fact, by the middle of the nineteenth century, the administrative structure of the Catholic Church in Canada was largely in place; in subsequent years it would be expanded to include several new dioceses, but not fundamentally altered. At that time, the church was riding the crest of a wave of religious enthusiasm that would generate new vocations to the religious and priestly life by the thousands, and would lead to the founding of scores of new missions and educational and social institutions. For the next hundred years, Catholics would prove to be confident and committed.

The Church of England

Until the mid-nineteenth century, the Church of England in Canada was simply a colonial extension of the mother church from which it received its doctrinal and administrative marching orders. It came to Canada with the British explorers and settlers, especially after the British Conquest of 1760. Beginning with the appointment of Charles Inglis as founding bishop of Nova Scotia in 1787, its administrative structure in Canada expanded modestly throughout the first half of the nineteenth century, and then more rapidly afterwards. From its outset in the sixteenth century, the Church of England had always endured the tension resulting from the theological tug of war between its Protestant and Catholic wings.

Since King Henry VIII separated England's church from Rome in the 1530s, and especially since Queen Elizabeth I (1558–1603) molded the Church of England into a middle way between Catholicism and Protestantism, this established Christian church of the majority of the English cherished the Bible as the sole source of divine revelation, but also preserved an episcopal system of government. The Church of England's liturgy was based on the *Book of Common Prayer,* a compendium of daily prayers, sacramental rites, and biblical readings that was and still is in use throughout the worldwide Anglican Communion, in a variety of editions. The doctrinal stance of the Church of England was summarized in the Thirty-Nine Articles issued under Elizabeth in 1563. Although both the *Book of Common Prayer* and the Thirty-Nine Articles were subject to diverse theological interpretations, they nevertheless reflected the Church of England's doctrine of the primacy of the Bible, and its rejection of what it considered to be Roman Catholic corruption of true Christian doctrine.

Until Charles Inglis (1734–1816) was appointed founding bishop of

Nova Scotia in 1787, there had never been a Church of England bishop in any of the British colonies; Anglican missionaries had all answered to the Bishop of London. Inglis' new diocese included all of British North America, Upper and Lower Canada included. While Inglis remained in his see until his death in 1816, within six years of his appointment his diocese was divided by the creation of a second Church of England see that encompassed all of Upper Canada and Lower Canada.

In 1793 Jacob Mountain was appointed bishop of the new Anglican diocese of Québec where he immediately undertook his ultimately futile campaign to strengthen his church at the expense of Catholics. Indeed, Mountain felt that the Catholic Church was more favoured than the Church of England in Québec. For example, the Anglican bishop was bound by clause 39 of the *Constitutional Act*, 1791, whereby the governor appointed pastors of Anglican parishes, whereas the Catholic bishop remained free to make his own appointments without government interference. Nevertheless, Mountain enjoyed certain advantages. One of these was that because of his title of 'Lord Bishop of Québec,' Mountain sat on the legislative councils of both Lower and Upper Canada, and was also granted, at his request, a seat on the executive committees of both colonies. All was for naught, however, in his campaign to marginalize the powerful Catholic bishop.

The fundamental reason for Mountain's troubles was the mere handful of members of the Church of England in the colony, most of who belonged to the British colonial staff. At the time of his arrival in 1793, Bishop Mountain had only nine working clergy in his entire diocese and fewer churches still, most Anglican worship taking place in commandeered Catholic chapels of the *Récollets*, Jesuits, or others. Indeed, the first Anglican Church in the Canadas was the one built in 1785 on the Six Nations Reservation on the Grand River in Upper Canada. After the turn of the century, and especially after 1815, the situation of his church improved as a growing number of clergy ministered in Upper Canada, and more generous subsidies were received, from the S.P.G. in particular, enabling the bishop to pay his clergy up to £200 annually for their services. In 1826, Mountain was succeeded in the see of Québec by Charles James Stewart. At the time, his vast diocese had grown to include fifty parishes and missions, as many ministers, and sixty-three churches in Upper and Lower Canada. By 1837, he was supported by no less than eighty-five ministers, fifty of whom were in Upper Canada alone.

As the number of Anglicans grew with the growing population of the nineteenth century, the vast Anglican diocese of Québec was subdivided in 1836 to form the district of Montréal headed by suffragan bishop George J. Mountain (1789–1863), the son of Jacob, who within a year succeeded to the see of Québec upon Bishop Stewart's return to England. Montréal would become a diocese in its own right in 1850. Meanwhile, in 1839 Newfoundland was made into a diocese headed by Aubrey George Spencer and Upper Canada was made into the autonomous diocese of Toronto headed by the controversial John Strachan, and in 1849 the diocese of Rupert's Land was created in the Northwest under Bishop David Anderson.

By mid-century, the basic administrative structures of the Church of England in Canada were in place. The seven dioceses (Halifax, Fredericton, Québec, Montréal, Newfoundland, Toronto, and Rupert's Land) were independent of each other, a situation that would gradually change during the second half of the century, when provincial synods emerged after 1856, and then a General Synod was formed in 1893. However, the latter were mainly consultative bodies with little administrative control over the individual dioceses.

It was also during the first half of the nineteenth century that the evangelical movement profoundly divided the Church of England, as well as other denominations. The fortunes of the dual competing theological strands of Catholicism and Protestantism within the Church of England had waxed and waned since the sixteenth century. It was noted above that beginning in the eighteenth century, the growing evangelical movement had simultaneously given birth to the Methodist denomination that separated from the Church of England after 1790, and to a growing evangelical party that stayed within the church, a party that had established distinct missionary and apostolic agencies such as the Church Missionary Society.

In 1833, a new chapter in the rivalry between these two theological strands began when a handful of Anglican divines at England's Oxford University began to preach and publish in support of a more Catholic, or High Church interpretation of the doctrine of the Church of England. Led by John Keble, Edward B. Pusey, and John Henry Newman, the Oxford Movement wanted to revive the interest of Anglicans in many traditional elements of early and medieval Christianity, elements such as the teachings of the Fathers of the Church, the sacraments, the liturgy, and the independence of the church from the state. They spoke of the necessity of acknowledging that the church was a divine institution, that its bishops received their authority in unbroken succession from the apostles, and that the *Book of Common Prayer* was the rule of faith. A series of *Tracts for the Times* begun by Newman in 1833 gathered many supporters for the movement; the series also provoked the ire of Church of England bishops and of Anglicans of more evangelical persuasion who feared that Newman's party was drawing their church into the orbit of Roman Catholicism. Their fear seemed founded when several leading members of the Oxford Movement, men such as W.G. Ward, F.W. Faber, H.E. Manning, R.I. Wilberforce, and especially J.H. Newman, joined the Catholic Church after 1845.

Nevertheless, the majority of the Oxford Movement remained in the Church of England wherein their ideas gained more and more of a hearing, in spite of the opposition of the press, the bishops, and the government. Their emphasis on worship and ceremonial led not only to their being designated as *ritualists,* but also to a renewal of liturgical forms in the Church of England. They also stressed the high dignity of the Christian ministry, the value of the religious life, and the importance of social work. Some proved outstanding in their commitment to the poor. Evidence of Tractarian influence in the churches appeared when Gregorian chant replaced the singing of metrical psalms, when preachers replaced their Geneva gowns with surplices, when holy days were observed, when frequent communion became more widespread, and when daily church services replaced weekly ones. High churchmen also led the way in the revival of Gothic architecture in the churches, an art form with its distinctive stained glass windows and pointed arches.

Inevitably, this intense debate within the Church of England spilled over into Canada where High Church and Low Church parties came to be at daggers drawn. Although most Church of England bishops in Atlantic Canada shared the principles of the Tractarians, in Upper Canada the local catalyst of the internal fight within the church was John Strachan, founding bishop of Toronto from 1839 until his death in 1867. However, Strachan was as much concerned with preserving the traditional social order as he was with the theological principles of the Tractarians. Born in Scotland in 1778, Strachan had come to Canada in 1799 as a school teacher. Raised a Presbyterian, after working as a private tutor in Kingston, Upper Canada, at his request he was ordained a deacon (1803) and a priest (1804) in the Church of England while founding a school in Cornwall, Upper Canada. There he remained until 1812, having married into an influential and wealthy family. He proved to be an outstanding teacher, educating his charges to value their British and Christian identities. He then accepted a pastoral appointment in York (Toronto) where he distinguished himself again during the American invasions of 1813 by showing unwavering courage and patriotism in dealing with the enemy. As a member of Upper Canada's executive council from 1817 to 1836, and of the legislative council from 1820 to 1841, he proved to be a key member of the government, skilled in administration while always advancing the interests of education and of the Church of England. All the while, he ran both his parish and the local grammar school.

Strachan is best remembered for his work in the interests of education in Upper Canada, a role that will be described later.[4] He also played a leading role in the religious history of the colony, always endeavouring to advance the interests of the Church of England, whether in the matter of the clergy reserves, or in countering the growing voluntarism that threatened the privileges of his church. Beginning in 1824 he sought to obtain from the Colonial Office the division of his church's diocese of Québec and his own appointment as bishop of Upper Canada; he would be required to wait fifteen more years for the appointment. Meanwhile, as archdeacon of York from 1827, he trained clergy and visited the widely-scattered parishes and missions of Upper Canada, while running his own parish and school. He was tireless in ministering to the sick and dying during the cholera epidemics of 1832 and 1834, adding again to the debt of gratitude of his flock. He rebuilt St James church in Toronto where he was installed as founding bishop of Toronto in 1839, at the age of sixty-one.

There it was that he exercised his pastoral charge for another quarter-century, continuing his lengthy and exhausting travels throughout Upper Canada. He recommended Newman's writings and the High Church position, while warning against the abuses of both Romanism and Protestant dissent. He founded The University of Trinity College in Toronto in 1852, an institution soon identified with the High Church elements of the church. Within ten years, in the wake of new subdivisions of his diocese to form the diocese of Huron (1857) and the diocese of Ontario (Kingston,1861), dissident Anglicans of evangelical persuasion in turn founded Huron College in London in order to advance their different theological agenda.

By the time of his death in January 1867, Strachan's toryism and High Churchmanship had gone out of style. Nevertheless, he was a giant who vigorously stood for an autonomous and dynamic church in a society that was changing under his very eyes. The High Church position that he defended set its stamp upon many of Canada's Anglican churches.

The Presbyterians

Presbyterianism designates a form of church polity in the Reformed tradition of John Calvin's Geneva wherein the church is governed by *presbyters* (ministers or elders), as opposed to bishops or the congregation. Churches of such a polity were formed in Scotland after 1560, in the wake of the Reformation of the Church of Scotland led by John Knox. The latter was imbued with Calvin's theological ideas and was particularly concerned with eliminating the office of bishop in his Reformed church. Ever since, the Reformed churches of Scotland have been known as Presbyterian churches, whether they be the established Church of Scotland, various dissident groups (Secession churches) that separated from it after 1733, or new denominations that formed in the nineteenth century in Britain, the United States, and Canada. The name *Presbyterian* thus designates both a type of Protestant church, and some specific Protestant denominations.

Presbyterians believe in the spiritual independence of their church from the state, in the primary authority of the Bible as the rule of faith and practice, and in the doctrine expressed in the Westminster Assembly's Confession and Catechisms of 1648, a teaching substantially based on John Calvin's writings. In worship, primary emphasis is given to preaching and hearing the Word of God, while communion service is usually held two or three times a year.

Presbyterian churches are governed by a hierarchy of representative committees or councils made up of both ministers and elected elders or lay representatives. The local parish committee is known as a *court* and is composed of the minister and elders. The regional committee that governs several congregations in a region is known as the *presbytery* and is also composed of ministers and representative elders. Several presbyteries within a large area send representatives to the *synod*. The ultimate legislative and administrative authority is the *General Assembly* which is made up of an equal number of representative ministers and elders elected by the presbyteries.

Presbyterian Christianity came to Canada with the numerous immigrants from Scotland, a primarily-Presbyterian country with a minority of Catholics in its Highlands. Although the odd precursor had set foot in Canada during earlier times, significant numbers of Presbyterians did not appear in this country until after the British Conquest of 1760.

Thereafter, Presbyterians were usually present wherever settlers of Scottish descent were to be found. They brought with them the denominational varieties of their homelands.

Until the mid-nineteenth century, the leading Presbyterian body in Canada was the Church of Scotland. However, after 1733, the latter had suffered fragmentation in the old country as its members divided over the issue of lay control of churches, or lay patronage. This gave rise to Secession Presbyterian churches, which in turn divided into other factions. These competing forms of Presbyterianism were present in Canada, as were others such the American Presbyterians and the Reformed Presbyterian Synod of Ireland. The Church of Scotland was given considerable assistance by the Glasgow Colonial Society which was formed in 1825 and helped provide ministers and resources to the church in the Canadian colony. Beginning in the 1830s, some of the Church of Scotland and Secessionist Presbyterian bodies began merging, only to be challenged anew in 1843 by a major division within the Church of Scotland. That was when the Reverend Thomas Chalmers, driven by his evangelical convictions, led a large number of Presbyterians out of communion with the Church of Scotland and formed the Presbyterian Free Church. Within a few years, the Free Church gathered into itself some two-thirds of Canada's Presbyterians, thereby becoming the leading Presbyterian body to which the others would gravitate. Their 310,512 members of 1851 made them into Canada's largest Protestant denomination. By 1875, Canada's Presbyterians would have reunited into the one Presbyterian Church in Canada.

Methodists

The Methodist movement had been founded in the eighteenth century within the Church of England by the Reverend John Wesley. Methodists were Arminian in theology, believing that all men and women were called to salvation, rejecting thereby the Calvinist doctrine that held that all people were eternally predestined by God to either salvation or damnation. They also stressed the importance of personal prayer and conversion in a Christian life centred on the love of God and neighbour, a life in the Spirit that was manifest in good works and holiness.

Upon Wesley's death in 1791, his followers had separated from the Church of England to found a distinct denomination ruled by an annual *conference* of designated members. This conference admitted preachers to membership, thereby conferring upon them ministerial status, and authorized the administration of the sacraments of baptism and Holy Communion. The denomination was organized into local *societies*, a number of which formed *circuits*, which in turn were grouped together in *synods* located in various districts. The Conference remained the supreme authority. It appointed the chairmen of districts and the supervisors of circuits. During Wesley's lifetime, more than 40,000 Methodists appeared in North America, their presence in Canada dating from the end of the eighteenth century. American Methodism became largely episcopal in that its superintendents were called bishops, although they did not claim to be ordained in the Catholic sense. Although a mere handful in Canada in 1800, by 1851 Methodists were the second largest Protestant denomination in the country, numbering 258,157. Shortly after the emergence of Methodism as a distinct denomination in the 1790s, it suffered a number of divisions into various branches, although the bulk of the membership remained with the founding denomination known as Wesleyan Methodists. Because of the large number of immigrants that came to Canada from Britain and the United States, many of these denominational offshoots were active in Canada during the nineteenth century.[5]

Before the War of 1812 most Methodists in Canada came from the United States, the country's primary source of immigrants; therefore it was only natural that American nationals controlled Methodist church work in Upper Canada. After 1815, however, increasing numbers came from Great Britain as the primary source of immigration shifted overseas. This allowed the British Wesleyan Methodists to dominate their church's apostolate in Maritime Canada and Québec. American and British Methodists put different stamps on the Methodist churches of the regions in which they dominated. On the one hand, the Wesleyans were more conservative. They were inclined to discourage any excessive emotionalism in revival meetings, to favour a more conventional piety, to be more conservative in politics, and to require a better-educated clergy. On the other hand, the Methodists of American origin tended to favour the more emotional revival meetings, and looked with some suspicion on their coreligionists of British extraction. Nevertheless, in 1828 the Methodists of Upper Canada severed their ties with their American church parent, and in 1833 united with the Wesleyans in an effort to end their long-standing rivalry.

Baptists and other Protestants

The Baptists were but a handful in 1800, centred in Maritime Canada where the denomination first took root in Nova Scotia and New Brunswick among the New Light congregations that had been founded by Henry Alline.[6] This remained the primary region of Baptist strength as between 25–40% of the Protestant residents belonged to the denomination throughout the nineteenth century. By 1851 in Canada, Baptists had a respectable 92,489 members, the smallest of the four leading Protestant denominations. Since their founding in early-seventeenth-century Amsterdam and England, Baptists were noteworthy for their practice of believers' baptism, or adult baptism, and their refusal to accept the validity of the baptism of infants. Their church polity was congregationalist in that the local congregation's autonomy was of central importance. Baptists therefore looked askance on any form of national or international union. Baptists also tended to be in the forefront of battles for freedom in church and society.

From the outset, members of this dissenting church divided over the question: "Who is called to salvation?" Just as the Methodists had done, some chose the Arminian answer that all human beings were called to salvation by God. They were designated as General Baptists. However, the majority answered in classical Calvinist fashion, that only God's chosen ones were called to salvation; all others would be damned. They were designated as Particular Baptists. They grew into an important denomination in Great Britain, and an even more important one in the United States where their active evangelism in the nineteenth century made them into one of that country's largest denominations, particularly in the South. In early nineteenth-century Canada, these two long-standing parties within the Baptist communion were known as Free Will Baptists (General Baptists) and Regular Baptists (Particular Baptists). The first was the more open and accommodating group, disposed to welcome into its communion all Christians of good will; the second was the more conservative party, intent on restricting access to its communion to those who were full-fledged members of the church.

By the mid-nineteenth century, the denominational factionalism that had characterized the Methodist, Anglican, Presbyterian, Baptist, and other churches since 1800 seemed to have spent itself. The second half of the century would witness the reunion of numbers of these factions. Just as a united Presbyterian church in Canada was formed in 1875 and further consolidated in 1886, a similar reunion of most Methodist denominations occurred in two stages in 1874 and 1884 to form the Methodist Church in Canada. This more conciliatory attitude among Protestants resulted in part from the changed public opinion in Canada at the time of Confederation, opinion that gave precedence to cultural and political issues; Canada's Protestants were able to come together around a common program of making the Anglo-Protestant Dominion of Canada into the Dominion of the Lord. The will of Protestants to unite also resulted from the disappearance of church establishment and privilege in 1854. Before that time, most Protestant denominations had been engaged in a decades-long struggle to eliminate the state privileges of the Church of England, or to obtain some for themselves. The fight against Anglican privilege had centred on the question of the 'clergy reserves.'

Clergy reserves

In Maritime Canada where the Church of England had been fully established by law, there were no extensive land grants to the state church, at least not on the scale of the grants made in the Canadas. As noted in Chapter 9, in the central colonies of Upper and Lower Canada, the *Constitutional Act, 1791* included clause 36 which was aimed at favouring the Church of England by endowing it with extensive tracts of land, and clause 38 which allowed the founding of Crown-endowed rectories by the governor. Beginning in the 1820s, these clergy reserves became the subject of an intense political debate in both Lower and Upper Canada, but especially in the latter, a debate that was only ended by the secularization of the reserves in 1854. The secularization of 1854 can be taken as the beginning of the separation of church and state in Canada. The *Constitutional Act, 1791*, allowed the governor or lieutenant-governor of either Lower or Upper Canada to reserve one-seventh of all the lands granted in their colonies "for the support and maintenance of a Protestant Clergy."

As much of the Crown land in both colonies was given in grants during the subsequent decades, these clergy reserves amounted to huge amounts of land. For example, in Lower Canada alone, at the outset the most heavily settled colony, clergy reserves totaled some 675,000 acres by 1825. Since Upper Canada was rapidly settled between 1791 and 1850, even more land than the above was reserved for the Protestant clergy. However, until the 1820s, land was so plentiful in the Canadas that this huge gift by the state was not necessarily synonymous with wealth for the beneficiary, because settlers could easily find cheaper land elsewhere and were not compelled to rent or buy clergy reserves. Only in the 1840s, once extensive settlement had driven up land values, would the reserves generate revenues that surpassed the cost of their management. Initially managed by the government, after 1816 the reserves were managed by distinct corporations established for that purpose.[7] The lands graciously given to the Church of England were then rented or sold by the corporations, the proceeds serving to subsidize the work of the church.

However, the insufficient revenues generated by the clergy reserves compelled the British government to otherwise provide for the state church. Given that the government had judged it politically impossible to collect the constitutionally-sanctioned tithe to support the Church of England, the latter was funded by a parliamentary grant made to the Society for the Propagation of the Gospel, a grant that amounted to £15,000 annually between 1825 and 1830 in the Anglican diocese of Québec. When a new reform-minded government in Britain announced its intention to put an end to such subsidies in the 1830s, the Church of England was compelled to find support in other quarters.

Until 1815, it had always been understood that the phrase 'Protestant clergy' used in the *Constitutional Act, 1791* designated the clergy of the Church of England alone, because the latter was the only legally established church in England. Thereafter, however, some supporters of the Church of Scotland argued that their church was the established church in Scotland, was clearly Protestant, and should therefore be made a beneficiary of the clergy reserves, along with the Church of England. This controversy, which erupted around 1820 and continued for the following three decades, was the first major challenge to the monopoly of the Church of England. Beginning in the late 1820s, a second challenge was voiced by those Upper Canadians who opposed any and all state subsidies to an established church. These *voluntarists* considered that the clergy reserves should be secularized and the proceeds given over to non-sectarian education. This party included a number of Christians belonging to a variety of denominations, Baptists and some Methodists for example. They maintained their struggle until victory was theirs in 1854.

In the wake of progressively more acrimonious criticism of the discriminatory but constitutional system of land grants to the Church of England, and reminded of festering unrest in the colonies by the rebellions in both Lower and Upper Canada in 1837 and 1838, Great Britain sought to defuse the looming church-state crisis by legislating a compromise in the clergy reserves controversy. In 1840, new imperial legislation ended the Anglican exclusivity by dividing the *old revenues* of the reserves in a proportion of two to one between the Church of England and the Church of Scotland. *New revenues* would be shared between these two churches on the one hand and other denominations on the other, in an equal proportion, but only once existing charges had been paid.[8] In fact, such revenues, and very modest ones, only became available in 1848. By then political agitation by the voluntarist party resumed with increased intensity. Given that the Church of England and the Church of Scotland each represented no more than 20% of the population of Upper Canada, in effect the settlement of 1840 merely gave one-third of the revenues of the clergy reserves to the Church of Scotland, preserving two-thirds for the Church of England. Sixty per cent of the population remained ineligible.

The separation of church and state

While disestablishment of the churches had occurred gradually in Canada's Maritime Provinces during the late-eighteenth and early-nineteenth centuries, in the Province of Canada it occurred with the legislation of 1854 that abolished clergy reserves.[9] Indeed, beginning in 1848, public opinion in Upper Canada and reform-minded governments were determined to do away with the system of church privilege at public expense. After British enabling legislation in 1853 cleared the way, in 1854 the government of John A. Macdonald voted to abolish clergy reserves while preserving the vested interests of beneficiaries. The sums that would have been paid to various claimants over a set period of years were commuted into a lump sum, which was offered to them as a final settlement of the issue. The individual claimants, clergy for the most part, could then transfer their entitlement to their respective denominations in return for a guaranteed income from the latter for the rest of their lives. In the end, the total value of the reserves was set at £381,971, of which 65% was paid to the Church of England, 28% to the Church of Scotland, 5.4% to the Roman Catholics, and 2.6% to the Wesleyan Methodists. The thorny ecclesiastical and political issue that had bedeviled Upper Canadian politics for more than a generation was thus laid to rest.

Although much less controversial, another plank in the state-support platform of the *Constitutional Act,* 1791, was the one that enabled the governor or lieutenant-governor to create any number of rectories endowed with as much land as was deemed expedient within every township or parish "according to the establishment of the Church of England" (article 38). After the War of 1812, while authorizing the division of the Catholic diocese of Québec, the government had endowed all Anglican rectories in Lower Canada, thus ensuring their financial security. Then, in the midst of intense political debate, in 1836 retiring lieutenant-governor Sir John Colborne signed patents erecting forty-four Anglican rectories in Upper Canada, endowing them with 400 acres each. They remained an Anglican heritage to the present.

The legislation of 1854 was the end of an era in the relations between the churches and the state in Canada. Since the founding of New France and through the British Conquest of Canada, first the Church of France, and then the Church of England had been the established churches of the country. The French Crown had established the church of New France; Nova Scotia, Prince Edward Island and New Brunswick had established the Church of England by colonial legislation; and the English Crown had tentatively established the Church of England in Canada with the *caveat* of the rights of Catholicism expressed in the *Québec Act,* 1774. This establishment included government subsidies of many kinds, in the form of land grants, direct subsidies, and salaries. It also included direct and indirect control of the established churches by government, in the form of nomination bishops, approval of pastoral appointments, approval of church budgets, or of monitoring clerical pronouncements.

While financially benefiting from these government subsidies, the established churches paid a high price in their loss of autonomy, whether financial, political, or spiritual. The established churches became, for all practical purposes, departments of state and their clergy public functionaries. Their flocks were frequently not inclined to be financially generous, knowing that the Crown would provide. While being a major turning point in church-state relations, the legislation of 1854 did not erect an impenetrable wall of separation between church and state in Canada. It was noted above that some churches, chiefly the Church of England and the Church of Scotland, continued to benefit indefinitely from being bought-out by the Crown. Other forms of collaboration and subsidization appeared in the various systems of confessional education that emerged at the time in several provinces of Canada.[10]

Nevertheless, the legislation of 1854 severed the main ties between the Crown and the churches of Canada. Thereafter, perhaps because of their new-found freedom, many of Canada's churches learned to stand on their own financial, political, and spiritual feet. The second half of the nineteenth century would prove to be one of clashing Protestant and Catholic crusaders, each bent on evangelizing and civilizing the new nation that emerged at the time of Confederation.

Suggested readings

Boon, T.C. *The Anglican Church from the Bay to the Rockies*. Toronto: Ryerson, 1962.

Carrington, Philip. *The Anglican Church in Canada: A History*. Toronto: Collins, 1963.

Flint, David. *John Strachan: Pastor and Politician*. Toronto: Oxford University Press, 1971.

Grant, John Webster. *A Profusion of Spires*. Toronto: University of Toronto Press, 1988.

Johnston, A.A. *History of the Catholic Church in Eastern Nova Scotia*. 2 vols. Antigonish, NS: St Francis Xavier University Press, 1960–1971.

Moir, John S. *Church and State in Canada 1627–1867*. Basic documents edited and with an introduction by J. Moir. Toronto: McClelland & Stewart, 1967.

——. *Enduring Witness: A History of the Presbyterian Church in Canada*. Toronto: Presbyterian Church in Canada, n.d.

Semple, Neil. *The Lord's Dominion. The History of Canadian Methodism*. Montréal & Kingston: McGill-Queen's University Press. 1996.

Young, Brian. *In Its Corporate Capacity: The Seminary of Montreal as a Business Institution*. Montréal & Kingston: McGill-Queen's University Press, 1986.

CHAPTER 12

The Evangelical Crusade

The intensity of people's religious feelings waxed and waned over time depending on a variety of personal, social, political, and religious factors. Like the Protestant and Catholic Reformations of the sixteenth and seventeenth centuries, the Catholic revival in seventeenth-century France and the pietism of eighteenth-century German-speaking regions – all of which had arisen unforeseen – evangelicalism emerged in eighteenth-century Britain and the United States and grew throughout the nineteenth century. It was imported into Canada along with the hundreds of thousands of immigrants from those countries.

Rooted in the Calvinism of the Reformation, in the Puritanism of the sixteenth and seventeenth centuries, and in the Methodism of the eighteenth century, British and American evangelicalism crossed denominational boundaries. It gathered together in a like-minded spirit: all those English-speaking Protestants who felt that Jesus the Christ was their lord and saviour, that is to say that he had died on the cross to atone for the sins of humankind and risen from the dead three days later to bring eternal life to those who chose to follow him; that the Bible was God's Word and the place where he revealed himself and his teaching; that they had personally and individually experienced a conversion to Christ at a specific time and place; and that they must bear witness to their saviour and change their society in the process. In the United States, the Second Great Awakening (1795–1835) constituted a major turning point in Protestant theology, and became a launching pad for the development of Protestant evangelical theology in Canada as well.

While the term *evangelicalism* usually designates a religious revitalization movement within English-speaking Protestantism, in this book the word *evangelical* is used to designate both that movement and the parallel movement within Catholicism known as ultramontanism. The reason is that both Protestant evangelicalism and Catholic ultramontanism shared the same fundamental religious outlook.

Common characteristics of evangelical Christians

Catholic and Protestant Christianity in Canada had much in common in the hundred years after 1850. In addition to the basic four characteristics noted above, common traits included a strong faith in God, an understanding that Christian faith was primarily defined as assent to God as first truth, a passion for God's truth, a holistic understanding of Christianity, impatience with intellectualism, and a resolute determination to evangelize society through missionary outreach, confessional schools, temperance campaigns, and control of the public agenda. Beginning in the mid-nineteenth century, there were both Catholic and Protestant evangelicals engaged in a crusade to convert Canadian society, a crusade that would last for a hundred years.

Unlike the Christians of New Testament times who understood Christian faith as a total personal commitment to Jesus as lord and saviour, Christians of medieval and modern times understood Christian faith as being primarily an acceptance of God as Truth. Indeed, in the wake of the foundational ecumenical councils of the fourth and fifth centuries C.E. that had defined the doctrines of the Trinity and of the simultaneously divine and human Christ, the great thirteenth-century theologian Thomas Aquinas had defined faith as the assent given to God as first truth, an understanding that was continued in the writings of most Catholic and Protestant theologians, and in the teaching of the churches until the mid-twentieth century. In the context of the denominational rivalries that characterized Western Christianity after the Reformations of the sixteenth century, this meant that Protestant and Catholic churches gave precedence to right doctrine in determining fidelity to the Gospel. Therefore, churches took great care in ensuring that their faith was accurately defined in doctrinal statements, catechisms, and administrative decisions, while simultaneously condemning any and all dissenters as heretics. Given the varieties of philosophies, theologies, languages, and temperaments, this translated into one of two things. Either doctrinal varieties grew exponentially, as was the case in Protestantism where no centralized administrative religious authority existed, or the doctrinal varieties were leveled into a uniform and all-encompassing creed, as was the case in the highly centralized Catholicism that prevailed from the sixteenth to the twentieth centuries.

As men and women of their times, Christians of the medieval and modern Western world, both Catholic and Protestant, agreed that there was only one truth, God being the ultimate Truth. They believed that it was possible to learn and define that truth, either by research and learning insofar as human truth was concerned, or by divine Revelation inasmuch as God's truth was concerned. However, given the different theological teachings that resulted, among other things, from the Reformations of the sixteenth century, Protestants claimed to take their divine Revelation from the Bible alone, while Catholics claimed to take it from the Bible as understood by the Catholic Church. This fundamental disagreement transformed the common Christian outlook into two warring parties that constantly crossed swords from the sixteenth to the twentieth centuries. In other words, by understanding Christian faith as being primarily founded on intellectual assent to God as first Truth, Christians tied their common faith to the perennial disagreements and varied opinions that characterize intellectual life.

This shared understanding of the Christian faith was accompanied by a common passion for this truth. Indeed, by the turn of the nineteenth century, a growing number of Christians were challenging the rationalism that had come to dominate Christian theology in the wake of the scientific revolution of the seventeenth century and the Enlightenment of the eighteenth century. German pietism, followed by British Methodism had challenged the prevailing theological mindset by insisting on the importance of feelings, of a Christianity of the heart. Then romanticism swept through European literature, a movement represented by Johann Wolfgang von Goethe, François-René Chateaubriand, Samuel Taylor Coleridge, and William Wordsworth among others. In Protestant theology, this renewed focus on a religion of the heart was led by the Lutheran pastor Friedrich Schleiermacher who defined religion as a feeling of absolute dependence. The bastions of the centuries-old theology anchored in human reason were shaken.

This was the result of the Second Great Awakening (1795–1835) in the United States, a profound change in the theology that grounded much of Protestant life. Until that time, Calvinist doctrines had prevailed in most Protestant churches, doctrines with determinist logic such as the total depravity of humankind, unconditional election to salvation by God, limited atonement by Christ, irresistible grace, and perseverance of the saints. When this traditional Calvinism encountered the romanticism and republicanism of America, it changed. The creed of these new evangelicals is summarized in the following passage drawn from the constitution of the American Missionary Association: "A belief in the guilty and lost condition of all men without a Savior; the Supreme Deity, incarnation and atoning sacrifice of Jesus Christ, the only Savior of the world; the necessity of regeneration by the Holy Spirit; repentance, faith and holy obedience, in order to [achieve] salvation; the immortality of the soul; and the retributions of the judgement in the eternal punishment of the wicked, and salvation of the righteous."[1]

The questioning process that occurred during the Second Great Awakening served to define evangelicalism. While professing traditional Protestant doctrines such as those found in the above citation, led by the celebrated revivalist Charles G. Finney (1792–1875), American evangelicals stressed moral ability rather than moral depravity, defined sin as willful rather than constitutional, rejected rationalistic formalism, and stood for social change. For Finney and his followers, "sin was something one did, not something one was."[2] This liberal interpretation of traditional Calvinistic doctrine made much more allowance for human weakness and projected a Christian doctrine that was much more merciful and forgiving of human weakness. In the process, the hard determinism of traditional Calvinism received a fatal blow.

While they focused on a religion of the heart, stressed the importance of feelings in Christian faith, and showed their impatience with intellectualism, many of the new evangelicals, the romantics of Christian theology, felt that the established churches in their respective countries had 'sold out' to the state. Established or majority churches such as the Church of England, the Lutheran church in Germany, or the Catholic Church of France were accused by these new evangelical Christians of having made too many compromises with the state, of being tainted by too many compromises with secular society, of having become too far removed from the authentic Gospel.

In addition, the evangelical understanding of Christian faith was total or whole. They felt that one's entire life, both personal and social, must reflect one's Christian faith. They condemned their coreligionists who were mere "Sunday Christians," while doing "business as usual" during the rest of the week, as if the Christian faith only applied on Sunday. Like the Puritans and the Methodists before them, evangelicals felt that the sure sign that one had become an authentic adult Christian was to have undergone a conversion experience. Like the Puritans who had required such a personal experience in order to become full members of the church, nineteenth-century Methodist evangelicals, among others, required any candidate to the ministry to have experienced such a personal conversion. While the experience of conversion was described in various ways, it always involved an initial phase of self-criticism or confession of unworthiness and sinfulness before God; there followed the visitation of God's blessing or grace which was accompanied by strong feelings of peace, warming of one's heart, or exceptional joy; then the converted expressed the firm resolve and commitment to change his or her sinful ways and bear witness to the Gospel during every waking moment. While the established churches had always acknowledged the legitimacy and value of authentic conversion, they had rarely insisted on its necessity in Christian life, at least not as a sudden, instantaneous experience. By contrast, evangelicals made a specific and personal experience of conversion into the required gateway into an adult Christian life.

Another characteristic of evangelicals was their insistence on the centrality of the Word of God, the Bible, as the foundation of Christian life. In this, they were returning to the central teaching of the Protestant Reformation while challenging the prevailing theology of their times, a theology that they considered overly rationalistic and too far removed from the Word of God. For evangelicals of the nineteenth century, the Word of God was to occupy pride of place in preaching, theology, spirituality, and moral teaching.

For evangelical Christians, the Christian faith was not one element among others in the composition of the person or in the fabric of society. In the eyes of evangelicals, that was the point of view of the established churches, one that allowed the latter to make too many compromises with secular society. For evangelicals, the Christian faith was considered the dominant, central, and overwhelming factor that determined and conditioned everything else in one's personal and social life. This meant that one began by establishing what the Word of God taught on any given subject; then one proceeded to implement that teaching. The Word of God was sovereign and was to rule everything else.

Consequences of evangelicalism in Canadian society

The evangelical sense of the sovereignty of God led therefore to a sense of the sovereignty of the church. Since the days of Emperor Constantine in the fourth century C.E., the Christian church had more often than not been under the thumb of the state led by either emperor or king. During these 1,500 years, the phenomenon of the established church had gradually become the dominant, usually the only, model of the Christian church in existence. The Church of Spain, the Church of France, the Church of England, and other similar state churches were intended to be the only legitimate and authorized churches in their respective realms. They were supported by legislation while dissenting churches were not only discouraged but more often than not the objects of persecution and repressive legislation.

This phenomenon of the established church meant that it was allotted a specific role in society, a role defined by public legislation. Moreover, the leaders of the churches were used to negotiating with the leaders of the civil government, to arrive at joint solutions to various problems that arose. Given that the system of the established church required that the role of the church be defined in relation to that of the State, agreements or compromises were made on a wide range of issues such as taxation of the church and of clergy incomes, government financial support of the church, exemptions from military service for the clergy, the role of the government in the appointment of church leaders, restrictions on the right of the church to comment on public policy, the respective roles of the church and the government in public schooling, marriage legislation, etc.

In the eyes of nineteenth-century evangelical Christians, the diverse agreements between established churches and governments resulted in excessive and unacceptable restrictions on the freedom of the church to preach the Word of God. The established churches were perceived to be shackled, unable to criticize and denounce abuses or to proclaim the Gospel as they should. The solution was to free the Christian church from the clutches of the state by taking the required steps to ensure its autonomy. In English Canada, this meant that evangelicals opposed direct and indirect government subsidies to the churches. They stood for voluntarism, that is to say that churches and their activities should be supported by voluntary donations by their faithful, not by government grants. While the settlement of the clergy reserves question had gone a long way towards meeting this objective of the evangelicals, after 1854 there remained considerable government support for churches. For example, the Church of England enjoyed a large legacy of land that had been granted in earlier years, numbers of clergy who received government subsidies before 1854, continued to do so afterwards, confessional schools both public and separate existed in various parts of Canada, etc. The struggle of many evangelicals for the autonomy of their church would be ongoing.

Another consequence of evangelicalism was that the zeal and earnestness that characterized it was applied not only to individuals in their personal lives, but to society as a whole. After 1850, and particularly after Confederation in 1867, evangelicals set out to transform the Dominion of Canada into the Dominion of the Lord. While French Canada became a Catholic society as will be noted below, English Canada became a Protestant society. The historian N. Keith Clifford wrote: "The inner dynamic of Protestantism in Canada during the first two thirds of the century following Confederation was provided by a vision of the nation as 'His Dominion.' This Canadian version of the Kingdom of God had significant nationalistic and millennial overtones, and sufficient symbolic power to provide the basis for the formation of a broad Protestant consensus and coalition. Not only the major Protestant denominations but also a host of Protestant-oriented organizations such as temperance societies, missionary societies, Bible societies, the Lord's Day Alliance, the YMCAs and YWCAs utilized this vision as a framework for defining their task within the nation, for shaping their conceptions of the ideal society, and for determining those elements which posed a threat to the realization of their purposes."[3]

During the second half of the nineteenth century, evangelicalism grew from an initial revitalization movement within English-speaking Protestantism to become the driving force behind Protestantism in Canada. It made English Canada into a Protestant society with Protestant public schools, and a Protestant public agenda in matters such as alcoholic beverages, immigration, minority rights, and national objectives.

While zeal and earnestness for the proclamation of the Gospel was the obverse side of the evangelical coin, militancy, aggressiveness and intolerance were its reverse side. Driven by their zeal to establish the Kingdom of God throughout the world, evangelicals were impatient with those who disagreed with their conquering and exclusivist rhetoric. In both Britain and Canada, evangelicalism came to the fore in the midnineteenth century in contexts of confrontation with religious adversaries, particularly Catholics. In England, it was the suspected Roman leanings of the Oxford Movement within the Church of England of the 1830s and 1840s that sparked an evangelical reaction, which was in turn reinforced by the so-called papal aggression controversy of the early 1850s, a debate that pulled together into a common front most English evangelicals of whatever denomination in opposition to the Catholics.

At the same time in Canada, after 1835, Protestant evangelicals undertook to convert Catholic Québec to Protestantism. Presbyterians, Baptists, and other evangelicals sympathized with the militant no-popery campaign that was occurring in the United States between 1830 and 1855, a campaign that was highlighted by the publication of Maria Monk's *Awful Disclosures of the Hôtel-Dieu Hospital in Montréal*, the burning of an Ursuline convent in Boston, and a presidential election campaign of the 1850s that was strongly imbued with anti-Catholic rhetoric.

As the Canadian campaign to convert Québec to Protestantism failed, in the early 1850s Upper Canada's Protestants showed increasing resistance to the efforts of the province's Catholics to establish confessional schools. Growing polarization between the country's Protestants and Catholics was highlighted by random riots that set one against the other, and then in the systematic campaign to eliminate Catholic schools in New Brunswick, Manitoba, and the Northwest Territories during the quarter-century following 1870. A similar campaign in Ontario during the 1880s and 1890s did not succeed, a campaign led by Member of Parliament Dalton McCarthy and the Protestant Protective Association. During the latter half of the nineteenth century, evangelical Protestants were not only bent on proclaiming the Gospel, but also on establishing the Kingdom of God in an English-speaking Protestant form. The Dominion of Canada was to become an English-speaking Dominion of the Lord where Catholics and French Canadians were to be kept in their assigned places.

Canada's evangelicals, both Catholic and Protestant, were also very involved in the temperance and prohibition campaigns. Given the uncontrolled and sometimes lethal omnipresence of alcoholic beverages throughout the colonies of British North America, in the 1820s the temperance movement began. At the outset, temperance was precisely that, a movement aimed at achieving moderation in the consumption of alcoholic beverages. While the moderate use of beer, cider, and wine was considered acceptable, strong spirits were the targets of temperance activists who saw in the unholy bottle a scourge that was responsible for violence, family breakdown, and moral perdition. In step with the growing industrialization and urbanization of Canada throughout the nineteenth century, temperance activists soon enjoyed the support of merchants and employers who were concerned with the effects of alcoholic consumption on profits and work habits.

Evangelicals were fond of establishing and joining voluntary associations aimed at achieving their social and religious goals. Just as they founded Bible societies, missionary societies, the YMCA, Sunday schools, and numerous other agencies, as the nineteenth century wore on evangelicals founded countless temperance societies or local chapters of national societies in parishes and towns. The Women's Christian Temperance Union (WCTU), based in Toronto, was one of the better-known societies. Through their local chapters and national executives, such societies organized conferences, speaking tours, conventions, and fundraising campaigns. They lobbied governments to obtain legislative changes and to better enforce the laws that existed. At emotionally charged temperance meetings that resembled religious revival meetings, the audience was urged to mend its ways, convert to teetotalism, and take the pledge never to drink (sin) again. In fact, the commitment of the evangelical Protestants to the temperance campaign was more total than was that of the Catholics. Their commitment to temperance became such that by the turn of the twentieth century, for many Canadians, Protestantism and temperance came to be considered synonymous terms. By this time, the objective was no longer to obtain *moderation* in the consumption of alcoholic beverages, but rather the *prohibition* of the manufacture, sale, and consumption of the dreaded potions. This objective was temporarily achieved in provincial and federal legislation by the end of World War I.

For their part, large numbers of Canada's Catholics also undertook to ban the bottle during the nineteenth century, much as the Protestants did, albeit with their own leaders and societies. In Canada's growing Irish Catholic community, it was the Irish crusader Father Theobald Mathew who inspired the founding of total-abstinence societies in Catholic parishes beginning in the 1840s and 1850s. Among French Canadians, the important religious revival that spread from Montréal after 1840 was accompanied by a strong temperance crusade. As Catholics flocked to their churches by the thousands to hear guest preachers like Bishop Charles de Forbin-Janson in 1840–1841, they were urged to join temperance societies and pledge teetotalism. Bishop Ignace Bourget of Montréal and his episcopal colleagues capitalized on the intensified religious feelings by recruiting skilled preachers dedicated to promoting temperance. One of the more notorious of these was Father Charles Chiniquy who, in celebrated preaching tours throughout Québec between 1848 and 1851, managed to get 400,000 faithful to sign the pledge of abstinence from alcohol. While local chapters of temperance societies emerged throughout French Canada, those who swore to abstain were given black crosses to hang in their homes to remind any and all of their forsaking alcoholic beverages.

Evangelicalism rekindled the fires of both Protestantism and Catholicism in the nineteenth century, launching both Christian traditions on a campaign of world conquest, while imprinting on Canada a stamp that has lasted until very recently. Many elements common to all evangelical Christians were noted above including a faith in God as truth, a passion for this truth, and total devotion to Jesus Christ as saviour, trust in his Word, a holistic understanding of Christianity, and the importance of a conversion experience in Christian life. A number of the social consequences of this evangelical understanding were also noted, consequences which made for much harder-edged Christian behaviour than did the more relaxed and 'reasonable' teachings of the established churches. The strongly-held convictions of the evangelical Christians resulted not only in their achieving greater influence in many areas of social endeavour from temperance to schools, but also in intensifying the conflicts within their ranks. The conflicts between Catholics and Protestants were noted above. However, conflicts also arose between various groups of Protestants, some of whom grew apart from the Protestant evangelical mainstream that was taking shape late in the nineteenth century.

Protestant Diversity

While evangelicalism was like a growing swell running through the sea of Protestantism in the nineteenth century, it spawned other movements that became important contributors to an ongoing diversity within Protestantism. Among the more important were millennialism, and the holiness movement. In some respects these movements were manifestations of evangelicalism, but then moved beyond it to focus on specific aspects of Christian teaching that were not given prominence in mainstream evangelicalism.

Eschatology, Apocalyptic, Millennialism, and Adventism[4]

Millennialism

Nineteenth-century evangelicalism fostered a rebirth of millennialism, a form of Christian belief as old as the church. Rooted in Jewish apocalyptic literature of the time of Jesus, Christian millennialism was primarily based on a reading of the book of Revelation, a part of the New Testament.[5]

In Christianity, the theological doctrines that dealt with death, judgement, heaven and hell, and the final events of history, were known as eschatology. Eschatology answered the question: "What happens after my death?" and provided answers for as long as there has been a Christian Church. The nature of the answers varied, however, according to time, place, character, and circumstance. Indeed, Christians would have to interpret Revelation, the Bible in particular, in order to find out God's teaching on this score.

One of the literary forms found in the Bible was apocalyptic or revelatory literature, wherein God revealed to his faithful truths not otherwise known. Examples of this were the book of Daniel in the Old Testament, and the book of Revelation or the Apocalypse in the New Testament. Such apocalyptic writing was a form of eschatology, one answer to the question: "What happens after my death?"

When the final events of history were believed to be imminent, we were dealing with apocalyptic eschatology. Christians who adopted such a deterministic view of history believed that our world was an evil place dominated by the Antichrist; the end of history as was known was imminent, to occur when the Antichrist engaged in a final cataclysmic battle at Armageddon with the heavenly host of Christ whose victory would establish the Kingdom of God on earth.

The apocalyptic genre of literature was a way of solving the problem of evil. It taught believers that despite the widespread evil and suffering that seemed to dominate and permeate their lives, justice was about to be done to them. The onset of the Kingdom would be God's Judgment Day when justice would finally prevail – when the saints will be rewarded and the wicked punished. Such a doctrine was music to the ears of Christians who were depressed, oppressed, and despairing of seeing better days. It was a source of hope to them, because it promised redress and justice in very short order, albeit at the cost of the destruction of this world. But then, these Christians had usually given up on this world.

> Then I saw an angel coming down from heaven, holding in his hand the key to the bottomless pit and a great chain. He seized the dragon, that ancient serpent, who is the Devil and Satan, and bound him for a thousand years and threw him into the pit, and locked and sealed it over him, so that he would deceive the nations no more, until the thousand years were ended. After that he must be let out for a little while.
>
> Then I saw thrones, and those seated on them were given authority to judge. I also saw the souls of those who had been beheaded for

their testimony to Jesus and for the word of God. They had not worshiped the beast or its image and had not received its mark on their foreheads or their hands. They came to life and reigned with Christ *a thousand years*. (The rest of the dead did not come to life until the *thousand years* were ended.) This is the first resurrection. Blessed and holy are those who share in the first resurrection. Over these the second death has no power, but they will be priests of God and of Christ, and they will reign with him *a thousand years*.

When the *thousand years* are ended, Satan will be released from his prison and will come out to deceive the nations at the four corners of the earth... in order to gather them for battle; they are as numerous as the sands of the sea. They marched up over the breadth of the earth and surrounded the camp of the saints and the beloved city. And fire came down from heaven and consumed them. And the devil who had deceived them was thrown into the lake of fire and sulfur, where the beast and the false prophet were, and they will be tormented day and night forever and ever.

Then I saw a great white throne and the one who sat on it; the earth and the heaven fled from his presence, and no place was found for them. And I saw the dead, great and small, standing before the throne, and books were opened. Also another book was opened, the book of life. And the dead are judged according to their works, as recorded in the books. And the sea gave up the dead that were in it, Death and Hades gave up the dead that were in them, and all were judged according to what they had done. Then Death and Hades were thrown into the lake of fire. This is the second death, the lake of fire; and anyone whose name was not found written in the book of life was thrown into the lake of fire. [6]

The significance of the mysterious thousand-year period discussed in the above passage served as the subject of diverse interpretations among Christians. Christian millennialists were divided into two categories, depending upon whether they made the thousand-year reign in question precede or follow the Second Coming of Christ. *Premillennialists* were those for whom the Second Coming preceded the millennium, whereas for *postmillennialists*, it follows the millennium.

Over the two thousand years of Christian history, the fortunes of millennialism have waxed and waned. In the early church, premillennialism was widespread, as many expected the end of this world and the Second Coming at any time. A number of second- and third-century writers acknowledged as saints by the church were premillennialists, men such as Justin Martyr, Irenaeus of Lyons, and Hippolytus of Rome. However, in time a number of interpreters came to dwell upon the carnal pleasures that the saints would enjoy on earth during the millennium, a development which sparked growing revulsion among Christians against millennial ideas. This disfavour was reflected by St Augustine in the early fifth century and marked the demise of Christian millennialism as an important movement for a thousand years.

Most Christians have been and are postmillennialists, believers in gradualism, that is to say that they perceive the Second Coming of Christ as an ultimate fulfillment through time of a gradual implantation of God's reign on earth. For them, the millennium will precede the Second Coming, meaning that no catastrophic cataclysm was foreseen to punish our world for its sins. Postmillennialists believe that the millennium will be ushered in largely through human efforts that will lead to a gradual transformation of society into a better place. It will be up to them to work as diligently as possible to obtain change in this world; the millennium is theirs to build. In their eyes, this world is fundamentally good, a very good place, albeit flawed in a number of ways. This goodness of God's creation is manifest in human beings, nature, society, politics, business – in every arena of human endeavour. The world is a garden created by God and given to his children for their growth, fulfillment, and enjoyment. For these Christians, the Second Coming of Christ and Judgement Day will come *after* (post) the millennium, once human beings, God's children, have succeeded in preparing the way. These Christians are optimists; they look with favour upon this world; it is their God-given duty to build it into a progressively better place. So it was that many Christians in nineteenth-century Canada felt that in and through their daily lives they were contributing to the building of Christ's Kingdom here on earth, the dominion of the Lord. Because of their gradualist beliefs, then, postmillennialists were usually not newsworthy.

After the Reformations of the sixteenth century, while most Catholic and Protestant churches treated millennial ideas with great reserve, premillennial ideas resurfaced in a number of the more marginal groups such as the Anabaptists on the continent, seventeenth-century English independents, and German pietists of the seventeenth and eighteenth centuries. These ideas then blossomed in Great Britain and the U.S.A. during the nineteenth century, appearing in new denominations such as the Irvingites, the Plymouth Brethren, and the Adventists. All of these groups, albeit small, were active in Canada after the 1830s and 1840s, a time of rapid immigration, growing industrialization, periodic epidemics, a worrisome economic slump during the 1840s, and the political uncertainty associated with the rebellions of Lower and Upper Canada, and the union of the Canadas in 1841.

During the 1830s, John Nelson Darby founded the Plymouth Brethren in England, a group of conservative and puritanical tendency that stressed the autonomy of the local church as well as the imminent millennium. As distinct from most churches that explained the world as gradually progressing towards its fulfillment in Christ, Darby taught that the history of the world was to be understood as a series of dispensations or periods, each characterized by growing tribulations leading to the imminent Second Coming of Christ that would mark the founding of his Kingdom on earth. Darby's millennialism and stress on conversion were instrumental in forging religious alliances that transcended the boundaries of Protestant denominations. In the 1880s and 1890s, this led to a series of Bible and Prophetic conferences held at Niagara-on-the-Lake, Ontario, meetings that among other things, served to rekindle the fires of Protestant evangelicalism.

Adventism

Adventists are premillennialists who believe that the millennium will follow the imminent Second Coming of Christ and extend until the Advent of Christ at the end of time. The Final Judgment of all the living and the dead would then take place. The adjective "Adventist" designates a group of denominations that first appeared in 1831 under the leadership of William Miller (Millerites) who was proclaiming the imminent Second Coming (Advent) of Christ in Dresden, New York. Based on his study of the Old Testament, Miller announced that the said event would occur during the year 1843-44. When this didn't happen, numbers of followers deserted his movement, but Miller himself continued preaching that the Second Coming was still just around the corner. A number of millennial groups spun off Miller's movement, including the Seventh Day Adventists, disciples of Miller who undertook to observe the seventh day (Saturday) as the Sabbath. Seventh Day Adventists are strongly Protestant, ascetic, and millenarian, although they soon discovered that it was best not to be too specific in predicting the time of Christ's return.[7] Seventh Day Adventists practise adult baptism by total immersion, and require from their members strict temperance and abstinence from alcohol and tobacco, while recommending abstinence from tea, coffee, and meat. In 1991, Seventh Day Adventists numbered eight million members worldwide, 52,000 of whom were in Canada.

For premillennialists, the Second Coming, and the accompanying end of the world as we know it, is about to happen in a whirlwind of destruction, disaster, and catastrophe. This makes them very newsworthy. Nevertheless, premillennialists do not agree as to whether the promised millennium that will follow the Second Coming will be spent by the saints on earth or in heaven. If in heaven, then the earth may well be the scene of chaos and catastrophic turmoil in the meantime. However, if the saints are to spend the millennium on this earth, the latter may well become a world of milk, honey, and consummate bliss for the saints.

Premillennialists are a small minority among Christians but periodically a very visible and vocal one. They believe that the millennium is imminent; it will be ushered in by cataclysmic events such as earthquakes, famine, epidemics, and terrible wars; this will lead to an ultimate battle at Armageddon, the victory of Christ's host, the destruction of Antichrist, the day of Judgement by God, and only then the millennium. Given their tragic, pessimistic outlook on this world, they believe, indeed they hope that it will soon cease to exist. In their apocalyptic eschatology, they consider this corrupt world, dominated as it is by the Antichrist, as entering a period of Great Tribulation, while awaiting the victory of Christ.

Premillennialists disagree as to the fate of the saints during this Tribulation. The majority, known as pretribulationists, believes that the saints will be spared from suffering by being miraculously taken up to heaven to be with Jesus; they call this the Rapture of the Gathered Remnant. A minority of premillennialists, the post-tribulationists, disagree, believing that they have to live through the Tribulation. Therefore, they develop a survival mentality, many emphasizing the importance of weapons and military training. They are prone to violence because any opposition they encounter in society can be seen as part of the Tribulation's forces of Antichrist. Some premillennialists stand midway between these two factions; they are mid-tribulationists who believe that they will need to survive part of the Tribulation, until the time when they are either slain or Raptured until they return to fight with Jesus at Armageddon. This was the persuasion of the Branch Davidians who died at Waco, Texas in 1993, in their confrontation with the FBI.

Premillennialists also disagree as to where the saints will be, in heaven or on earth, once the battle of Armageddon has been won, the Second Coming of Christ has occurred, and the millennium has begun.

Those who opt for the earthly venue believe that the final Advent of Christ and the Final Judgment will follow the millennium. They are Adventists. The millennium will be a time when righteousness will spread over the earth which has been removed from the control of the defeated Antichrist.

Holiness

As Protestant evangelicalism developed during the nineteenth century, its fundamental belief in the importance of personal conversion had strongly influenced a number of churches, foremost of which in Canada were the Methodist ones. While some evangelicals believed that a subsequent second conversion, or sanctification was required in order to become a perfect adult Christian, others such as John Wesley believed that the Christian's initial conversion was followed by a gradual progression in the faith, all in order to achieve sanctification or holiness.

As Canadian society moved away from its difficult settlement era with its small rural communities and its attendant emphasis on conversion and revivals, during the second half of the nineteenth century Canadian Protestants began to give more attention to the holiness of life, the sanctification that was to follow conversion. Although revivals continued as a prime form of evangelism in Canadian Protestantism after 1850, they were more subdued in tone, less emotional and strident, reflecting thereby the more settled socio-economic status of the faithful. So began the Holiness movement that by the end of the century would be embodied in distinct denominations, ones that remained evangelical in their fundamental convictions such as the centrality of the Bible and of conversion, but that emphasized right behaviour, right living, and an exemplary Christian life. These new denominations broke away from the Methodist denominations because of their belief in a sudden, one-time experience of sanctification, a kind of second conversion experience. The focus of these evangelical Protestants had shifted from the convert's belief to his experience and behaviour. Conduct had taken precedence over doctrine, a position thoroughly in keeping with the earlier emphases of evangelicalism.

Among the first leaders of distinct Holiness movements were Nelson Burns who founded the Canadian Holiness Association in 1879, and the Reverend Ralph Horner who left the Methodist ministry in the 1890s to found the Holiness Movement Church in Ontario. Holiness teachings and emphasis on Christian activity in daily life were adopted by some denominations such as the Salvation Army, a movement founded in

England by William Booth in 1878. Others were the Mennonite Brethren in Christ, the Free Methodists, and the Reformed Baptists.

Evangelicalism grew and changed during the nineteenth century and would continue to do so during the twentieth. Millennialism and Holiness were two of its offshoots. Paradoxically, ultramontanism may be considered another, although as a movement within Roman Catholicism, it had little to do with Protestantism.

Ultramontanism in Canada

After working for sixteen years (1820–1836) as auxiliary bishop entrusted with the district of Montréal, in 1836 Jean-Jacques Lartigue (1777–1840) became bishop of the new diocese of Montréal. A strong disciple of the French ultramontane authors Félicité de Lamennais and Joseph de Maistre, he believed in the necessity of the autonomy of the church in society and in the primacy of jurisdiction of the pope in the church. During his twenty years as a bishop, constantly seeking to ensure the independence of the church from the state, Lartigue managed to obtain the creation of the diocese of Montréal (1836) and the appointment of Bishop Ignace Bourget (1837) as his coadjutor without consulting or obtaining the approval of the civil government. Lartigue's concern with the independence of the church was also manifest in his disapproval and eventual disavowal of the leaders of the rebellion of 1837–1838 in Lower Canada, in spite of the fact that Louis-Joseph Papineau, the leader of the rebellion, was his cousin. By the time of Lartigue's death in 1840, ultramontane ideas had taken strong root in the diocese of Montréal.

His successor, Ignace Bourget (1799–1885), had been Lartigue's secretary for seventeen years (1820–1837) before being chosen as his coadjutor and designated successor in 1837. Bourget was just as thoroughly imbued with ultramontane ideas as his mentor. Indeed, Bourget was an admirer of Lamennais and de Maistre; he fully shared Lartigue's views on the church in society, and ran the Saint-Jacques theological seminary founded by Lartigue in 1825 along ultramontane lines. Under Bourget's direction, the Saint-Jacques Seminary taught its students the doctrines of papal infallibility and papal primacy of jurisdiction more than forty years before they became doctrines of the Catholic Church at the First Vatican Council in 1870.

During his thirty-six years at the helm of Canada's most important diocese, Ignace Bourget presided over a major religious revival that started in Montréal in 1840, launched an important newspaper *Les Mélanges Religieux* (December 1840), recruited and founded numerous religious congregations of men and women, and successfully struggled to establish and reinforce his authority over rival groups within the Canadian church. Most Canadian churchmen who sought financial assistance or new religious personnel usually made the bishop's house in Montréal their first stop. With considerable justification, some called him the 'Pope of Canada.' He it was who usually prepared bishops' petitions to the Holy See seeking the creation of new dioceses or recommending the appointment of new bishops; he it was who was also entrusted by the Vatican with the task of obtaining the resignation of Bishop Pinsonneault of London, Ontario in 1866. Bourget was a strong churchman and a powerful leader in a church that was militant, powerful, and uncompromising.

As ultramontanism took hold of the Catholic Church in Canada during the second half of the nineteenth century, Bourget was supported by many like-minded bishops, men such as Jean-Charles Prince founding bishop of Saint-Hyacinthe (1852–1860), Alexandre Taché who was bishop (1853–1871) and then archbishop (1871–1894) of Saint-Boniface in Canada's Northwest, and especially Louis-François Laflèche who was coadjutor (1867–1870) and then bishop (1870–1898) of Trois-Rivières during the last third of the century. Although all bishops were not of similar temperament, ranging as they did from the militant and uncompromising Laflèche to the more conciliatory and discreet Archbishop Alexandre Taschereau of Québec (1870–1898), all were cast in a similar mold. Their theological and ideological differences were more of degree than of kind.

The religious revival that started in Montréal in 1840 and presided over by Bishop Bourget was implemented by the clergy, many of whom belonged to religious orders and congregations, either imported from France or created in Canada. In Québec alone in the three-quarters of a century between 1837 and 1914, a total of twenty new congregations of men and thirteen new congregations of women were imported from France, while twenty-one other congregations of women were founded in Canada.

The new religious congregations that appeared in Canada before 1850 were noted in Chapter 10. After 1850, a similar pattern of imports and native foundations continued. Some of the French foundations of men were the Brothers of the Sacred Heart, the Dominicans, the Redemptorists, the Basilians, the Trappists, the Marists, the Franciscans, the Capuchins, and the Missionaries of the Sacred Heart. [8] Some of the

Canadian foundations of women were the Sisters of the Assumption of the Virgin, the Sisters of the Precious Blood, the Sisters of St Joseph of Saint-Hyacinthe, and the Dominicans of the Child Jesus.

With few exceptions, this legion of men and women were of ultramontane conviction. Growing numbers of them would be staffing the Catholic schools, hospitals, and parishes of Canada, teaching the new generations the doctrines and values of ultramontane Catholicism. So it was that Catholic ultramontanism developed its doctrines in Europe, developed strong leaders in Canada in the persons of Bishops Lartigue, Bourget, and Laflèche, and recruited an army of clergy to conquer, occupy, and lead the country and its church. This growing Catholic evangelical movement simultaneously took over both the religious revival that began in Montréal in 1840, and its accompanying French Canadian nationalism. Thereafter, for more than a century Catholicism and nationalism would constitute the twin pillars that supported French Canada's national identity. They were the two faces of the same French Canadian coin.

Reinforcing the ultramontane centre

While ultramontane Catholic forces were developing in Canada, they were also reinforcing their centre in Rome. After having been hailed as a liberal pontiff when he took office in 1846, within a few short years Pope Pius IX was seen as a conservative protector of the status quo. By 1860, he had lost a running battle with the forces of Italian unification who seized the Papal States as part of their project of nation-building. The pope dug in his heels, and urged Catholics the world over to resist the evil forces of liberalism, modernism, and revolution that he considered at the root of all the troubles of his church. Under the leadership of the charismatic Pius IX, Catholics the world over circled their wagons to fend off the attacks of their numerous perceived enemies, a growing legion that included secularists, liberals, rationalists, naturalists, Protestants, unbelievers, etc. Sensational publications such as David Friedrich Strauss' *Leben Jesu* (1835), Karl Marx and Friedrich Engels' *Communist Manifesto* (1848), Charles Darwin's *On the Origin of Species* (1859), and Ernest Renan's *Vie de Jésus* (1863) challenged the ultramontane Catholics in some of their most fundamental beliefs. They responded with vigour and determination in documents that would set the tone of official Catholicism for one hundred years.

The first telling and sensational response from Rome was issued on 8 December 1864. The encyclical *Quanta cura*, accompanied by the *Syllabus of errors* were documents that would stand as the definitive charter of ultramontane Catholicism. The *Syllabus* was published as a catalogue of what the Vatican considered the leading errors of the time. It contained eighty propositions that condemned, among other things, pantheism, socialism, rationalism, and liberalism. Upon the publication of these documents, it was no longer possible to be a liberal-minded Catholic, or even to have any ideas that were not shared by Vatican authorities.

Meanwhile, the Catholic forces that sought both to grant the pope supreme jurisdiction or primacy in the church and to have the pope declared infallible, had been building since the 1840s. Indeed, although the Catholic Church had always accepted the infallibility of the *church*, it had never seen fit to further clarify its position by defining *how*, or through which channels the church demonstrated its infallibility. Moreover, there had never been unanimity on the question of papal primacy, many Catholics of the Gallican tradition being suspicious of an overly powerful papacy. They considered the latter to be an office of international coordination and honorary primacy, rather than one of international government. Consistent with the centuries-old Gallican tradition, many Catholics felt that the national or regional church, be it that of Germany, France, Spain, or of any other country should be entrusted with decisive powers in the government of the church.

Nevertheless, as the 1860s progressed, ultramontane ideas gained ground. Because of the pope's difficulties in Italy, the repeated revolutions in France, the militant anti-Catholicism in countries like Britain and the U.S.A., and the revolutionary intellectual challenges of authors like Marx and Darwin, many Catholics came to feel that an aggressive conservatism and reaction were warranted. A growing number of Catholic clergy, trained in ultramontane seminaries, shared the views of those who supported *Quanta cura* and the *Syllabus*. This enabled their leaders to plan their next step, an ecumenical council whose agenda was to assert both the primacy and infallibility of the pope.

The First Vatican Council opened on 8 December, 1869 with 700 bishops in attendance. After adopting the declaration (constitution), *Dei Filius*, consistent with *Quanta cura* in condemning liberalism, pantheism, etc., the council turned to the more controversial questions of the primacy and infallibility of the pope, issues that were known to divide Catholic churchmen and theologians. The majority ultramontane party included the laymen W.G. Ward in England and L.Veuillot in France, Archbishop H.E. Manning of Westminster and Bishop L. Pie of Poitiers. The minority liberal party included J.H. Newman of England, Ignaz von Dollinger in Bavaria, and Bishop F. Dupanloup of Orléans, in addition to several American and German bishops. The questions of the pope's infallibility and primacy were debated in May and June 1870. Final resolutions were then put to the vote of the Council in July, and adopted with very strong majorities. On the question of primacy, the Council endorsed the ultramontane position in asserting the full administrative jurisdiction of the pope over all the churches of the Catholic world. Gallicanism thereby suffered a fatal blow.

On the question of infallibility, the Council's decision was more nuanced than has generally been acknowledged. On the one hand, the minority liberal party was disappointed in that the pope's infallibility was not tied more closely to the traditional doctrine of the infallibility of the church. Indeed, the pope was said by the Council to be infallible *of himself* and not because of the consent of the church. On the other hand, the hard-line ultramontane party was disappointed in that the Council limited the pope's power of infallibility to matters of faith and morals exclusively, and then only when he chose to speak *ex cathedra* invoking his position as pastor of the universal church. Although some Catholics, such as I. von Dollinger, would leave the Catholic Church because of this decision, the vast majority accepted it and supported it. Indeed, during subsequent pontificates to the end of the twentieth century, Pope Pius XII was the sole pontiff to invoke the power of infallibility, and this on one occasion only, in 1950 when he promulgated the doctrine of the Assumption of Mary into heaven.

Vatican I came to an abrupt end in the summer of 1870 when war broke out between Prussia and France, thereby curtailing the fulfillment of its agenda. Nevertheless, its declarations on papal primacy and infallibility proved to be fundamental in the hardening of the ultramontane position within Catholicism and in signaling the course that the Catholic Church would follow for the next hundred years. The Council stands with the encyclical *Quanta cura* as the foremost symbols of the era of Catholic ultramontanism.

Moral teaching, piety, and devotions of ultramontane Catholics

The moral teaching of the Catholic Church derives from its perception of the human being's relationship to God and the world, an understanding that changes over time. When God is taken to be primarily loving and merciful, and men and women are perceived as free and loving partners in a provident God's grace, the church's moral doctrine reflects these values of mercy, loving, partnership, freedom, and creativity.

When God is understood as being primarily a powerful and stern judge who applies a rigid code, and when men and women are perceived as weak, inconsistent, immature, and untrustworthy children, then the church's moral doctrine reflects values such as discipline, obedience, rigid rules and regulations, submission to legitimate authority, and suspicion of any and all. Then, rather than presenting the world as God's garden filled with beauty and wonders, the church tends to position beauty and wonders in another world, while painting this world as a vale of tears, replete with the snares of the devil. Historical and social circumstances condition which of the above-noted theological tendencies prevail at any given time in the Catholic Church.

Issuing as it did from the troubled and difficult late-medieval and early-modern periods, the traditional Catholicism of the eighteenth and early-nineteenth centuries was harsh and uncompromising in its moral doctrine. Women were walking sources of temptation for the male elect of the Lord, the world was the devil's playground, people could not be trusted to do the right thing, the Eucharist was not to be received too frequently because of the faithful's unworthiness, and absolution was not easily forthcoming for the penitent in the sacrament of Penance. This form of rigorism had been challenged by the theologian and evangelist Alfonsus Liguori (1696–1787), the founder of the Redemptorists. Convinced that the prevailing rigorism of his church served mainly to alienate the faithful, Liguori chose to stress gentleness and simplicity in proclaiming the Gospel. His theological and devotional writings became very influential in the nineteenth century, Liguori being declared a saint in 1839, and a doctor of the church in 1871.

As the ultramontanes tightened their grip on the Catholic Church in the second half of the nineteenth century, their moral teaching reflected these changing moral values among Catholics. The traditional stringent Jansenist moral teaching was slowly set aside, to be replaced by a kinder and more gentle moral theology that was more in tune with the improving social circumstances of Canadian Catholics. By the latter part of the century, although some bishops still condemned the presence of women on stage, none claimed that all theatre was evil as had been the case in colonial times. Confessors rarely refused to grant absolution to a penitent, contrary to former practice. Excommunications became rare in Canada, as the bishops realized that a changing society required modified moral teachings.

The intensified evangelism of Canada's ultramontanes was reflected in the piety and the varied devotions that served as its signposts after 1840. As piety became more Roman, it became more public, colourful, and fervent. As the traditional wayside crosses were again being erected, a series of new devotions to Jesus and Mary appeared, the latter taking centre stage after her appearances to three children in Lourdes, France, in 1858. The rosary was recited more and more frequently, and pastors led their flocks in meditations on the lives of Jesus and Mary. The veneration of the Blessed Sacrament, the Christ that Catholics held to be present in the consecrated wafer of unleavened bread that was displayed on a church altar, became a popular devotion. While some undertook the Forty Hours devotion before the Blessed Sacrament, originally an Italian devotion of the sixteenth century, others joined groups dedicated to the Perpetual Adoration of the Blessed Sacrament that was exposed twenty-four hours a day.

Various religious congregations promoted their preferred devotions. So it was that the Oblates of Mary Immaculate promoted Mary's Immaculate Conception, a doctrine long-held by Catholics and proclaimed as dogma by Pius IX on 8 December 1854; the Redemptorists encouraged devotions to St Anne; the Holy Cross Fathers supported St Joseph; and the Franciscans endorsed devotions to St Francis. Needless to say, each religious congregation had its favourite patron saint whom it promoted. While some faithful wore a scapular, a cloth image of a saint, others erected private altars in their homes, joined confraternities, or engaged in processions, pilgrimages, or novenas.

This intensifying piety was encouraged and reinforced by a series of revivals or missions that took place in Canada beginning with that of Bishop Forbin-Janson. During his fifteen-month preaching tour through central and eastern Canada from September 1840 to December 1841, Forbin-Janson had packed the churches of French Canada with his traditional three-pronged evangelical invitation to sinners to acknowledge their sinfulness, to turn to God and to accept conversion, and then to lead a holy life and sin no more. During these missions, the thousands of faithful who packed the churches confessed their sins to one of dozens of confessors, received the Eucharist, took the temperance pledge, participated in colourful processions, erected large crosses (sometimes 100 feet tall) outdoors as memorials of the mission, and resolved to mend their ways and lead model Christian lives. Bishops like Ignace Bourget continued these missions in subsequent years in various parts of their dioceses, missions that served to evangelize, sometimes for the first time, tens of thousands of people.

The new piety of the new Catholic evangelicalism was also reflected in the liturgical ceremonies that were, like the architecture and the doctrine, intended to copy the Roman model. Catholic worship was made into a sensuous experience with a plentiful and colourful supply of flowers, candles, vestments, ornaments, and incense. Ceremonies were elaborate and long, reinforcing the message of the power and importance of God and his church. Religious feast days were numerous, many requiring attendance at Mass just as on Sunday. Special occasions in the life of the church were also opportunities for joyous celebrations. Such occasions could include a bishop's departure for, or arrival from Rome, the ordination to the priesthood of a young man from the parish, the departure of the zouaves from Montréal for Rome in 1868, or the crowning of the statue of Notre-Dame-du-Cap in 1904. [9] Pilgrimages also grew in importance. While some pilgrims went to international shrines such as Lourdes, Jerusalem, or Rome, others travelled to the old Canadian shrines that were noted earlier, the most important being St Anne at Beaupré; a score of new shrines were created in the nineteenth century, particularly after 1873. Most were dedicated to members of the Holy Family.

The most notable of the new shrines created in the nineteenth century was that of Notre-Dame-du-Cap, at Cap-de-la-Madeleine near Trois-Rivières. It was the brainchild of Father Luc Désilets, pastor of the local parish. During the winter of 1877–1878, Désilets was engaged in the construction of a new parish church, but could not transport his building materials from the south shore of the St Lawrence because, due to a mild season, the river had not frozen that year. After conducting prayers before the local statue of the Virgin, and undertaking not to destroy his old church if his wishes were granted, the pastor saw the river miraculously freeze over in the spring, and remain frozen for one full week, long enough for the building materials to be carried across the ice bridge on the river. Later, the same statue performed a second miracle by opening its eyes before Désilets and two of his colleagues. As word of these wondrous events spread far and wide, Cap-de-la-Madeleine became a major shrine (1883), its miracle-working statue drawing pilgrims from all over North America and beyond.

A few years later, it was a miracle-working Brother in the Congregation of the Holy Cross, Brother André, who became the driving force in the development of another major Canadian pilgrimage centre, St Joseph's Oratory in Montréal, a shrine founded in 1904.

Ultramontanes in Canadian society

As ultramontane Catholics grew in confidence, strength, and control of the Catholic Church in Canada during the second half of the nineteenth century, they became entangled in a series of public controversies that, in the eyes of their liberal adversaries, smacked of undue ecclesiastical interference in cultural and political affairs. While school controversies will be dealt with later, three of the disputes in which ultramontane Catholics flexed their new-found muscle were those that centred on Montréal's *Institut Canadien*, on the *Programme catholique* issued by a group of Catholics in 1871, and on the undue influence of the clergy over voters during general elections.

Montréal's *Institut Canadien* had been founded in 1844 as a centre where the intellectually curious could attend lectures, read books and journals from a well-stocked library and reading room, and discuss and debate various issues of the day. It so happened that the *Institut* gathered together many of Montréal's liberal-minded intelligentsia, a fact that was not lost on Bishop Bourget who, in step with Pope Pius IX, was engaged in a running battle against liberals of all kinds. In fact, with the support of Bishop Bourget, in 1854 Montréal's Jesuits had founded a Catholic Union intended to check the influence of the *Institut*. Then in 1857 Montréal's Sulpicians founded a *Cabinet de lecture*, a rival library, reading room, and conference centre that was in fact better equipped than the *Institut*. However, the *Cabinet* was church-controlled which meant that radical, liberal, revolutionary, or controversial speakers or readings were excluded in favour of much bland devotional literature. In fact, the *Institut* was proving more successful than the *Cabinet*.

Beginning in the mid-1850s, Bishop Bourget challenged the *Institut*, seemingly determined to do away with this liberal thorn in his side that served as a constant reminder that there were other ideas about that differed substantially from the prescribed ultramontane ones. Despite his issuing three pastoral letters against it in 1858, the bishop did not succeed in scaring off most of the *Institut's* members. Determined to crush it nevertheless, Bourget condemned it outright in 1868, forbidding Catholics to remain members under pain of excommunication.

Thereupon, a new complication arose in that upon the death of the printer Joseph Guibord, a member of the *Institut*, his pastor refused to bury him in the Catholic cemetery because of the bishop's excommunication of all unrepentant members of the *Institut*. Aided and abetted by Guibord's *Institut* colleagues, his widow brought the question before the courts, arguing that the deceased's civil rights, including his right to a decent burial, took precedence over the ecclesiastical rights of the local Catholic Church. Indeed, given that Montréal had no secular or religiously neutral cemetery, it was argued that the plaintiff had a prior civil right to be buried in the Catholic cemetery. Over a period of five years (1869–1874) the case was debated and appealed all the way to the Judicial Committee of the Queen's Privy Council in London, the country's highest court at the time. In 1874 the court ruled in favour of the plaintiff, and ordered Bourget to receive Guibord's remains in the Catholic cemetery. Compelled to comply, the bishop nevertheless proceeded to deconsecrate the plot of land where Guibord's remains were interred.

So it was that this protracted dispute between Bourget and the *Institut Canadien* ended with a victory for the latter. In the longer term, however, it was the bishop who occupied the higher ground in that by the mid-1880s, the *Institut* closed because of declining membership. Indeed, by the end of the nineteenth century, it was difficult *not* to be ultramontane in Québec Catholicism.

The fight of ultramontane Catholics against liberal ideas also erupted in the context of provincial and federal elections during the 1870s. The *Programme catholique* was a political pre-electoral manifesto published on 20 April 1871 in the *Journal des Trois-Rivières* in preparation for the Québec provincial general election that was to take place that summer. It was written by a group of ultramontane Catholics, whose leader appears to have been the journalist, essayist, and politician François-Xavier-Anselme Trudel. The *Programme* urged political candidates to undertake, if elected, to change any and all laws that clashed with the doctrine of the Catholic Church as taught by Catholic bishops. The manifesto created a storm of controversy as liberal-minded people condemned its support for ecclesiastical interference in politics, while conservative ultramontane Catholics, Bishops Bourget and Laflèche in the lead, commended the authors of the *Programme* for their right thinking. In the end, the only *programmiste* candidate to be elected was Trudel himself.

In fact, the *Programme* is an excellent example of ultramontane doctrine on the relations between church and state. In the wake of the writings of Veuillot, de Maistre, and Lamennais, ultramontane Catholics began by putting the pope and the church at the centre of things. The church, ruled by a sovereign and infallible pope, was in their eyes the extension of God's activity in this world, a supernatural entity. The church was of divine origin, and held its powers directly from God. It was a perfect society, sent to evangelize an imperfect natural world that included civil governments that ruled imperfect societies, both the governments and the societies being of human origin, only indirectly related to God, and therefore imperfect. This meant that whenever the interests of the state and the church conflicted, the latter's interests had to prevail. Indeed the church was infallible, and Canadian ultramontane leaders such as Trudel, Bourget, and Laflèche tended to extend this infallibility to include political and social matters.

The same issue of the relative authority of church and state surfaced anew in 1874 when Québec bishops led by Bishop Bourget issued a joint pastoral letter condemning liberalism, and supporting the clergy's right to counsel their flocks on their electoral duties. This was in reaction to a new law that condemned the "undue influence" of clergymen in elections, a law that would later lead to litigation in cases where pastors were accused of exercising such "undue influence" in the federal election of 1875. The controversy that surrounded these events eventually led to the Vatican sending a special delegate to Canada in 1877. Archbishop George Conroy's mandate was to calm the waters and restore harmony in Québec where the bishops were set on a collision course with liberal-minded politicians. The resulting stay in public controversy was destined to be only temporary. In fact, controversy continued during the 1880s and 1890s around the issues of the Riel rebellion and the hanging of Riel in 1885, the *Jesuit Estates Act* of 1889, and the Manitoba Schools question after 1890. There could be no agreement between those who wanted the state to be separate from the church, and those of ultramontane persuasion who believed that the state had to be subject to the church.

Conclusion

During the second half of the nineteenth century, both Protestant evangelicals and Catholic ultramontanes were engaged in a crusade to re-establish Jesus Christ and the Word of God as sovereign in Canada. They sought to mold a Canadian society ruled by God's Word. In that sense both Protestant and Catholic parties were evangelical. However, they were hamstrung by their disagreements on what such divine rule implied, for a society ruled by the Catholic Church was most decidedly not acceptable to Protestants, and vice versa.

Their adversaries were the growing number of Canadians who shared the new values that had issued forth from the American and French revolutions of the late eighteenth century, and been promoted throughout the nineteenth century, values that were rapidly taking root in intellectual, political, and social circles. Their adversaries also included a number of ethnic and religious minority groups who feared the threatening swell of evangelical unanimity and intolerance.

Suggested readings

Airhart, Phyllis D. *Serving the Present Age. Revivalism, Progressivism, and the Methodist Tradition in Canada*. Montréal & Kingston: McGill-Queen's University Press, 1992.

Anderson, Benedict. *Imagined Communities. Reflections on the Origins and Spread of Nationalisms*. London/New York: Verso, 1983, 1991.

Bebbington, D.W. *Evangelicalism in Modern Britain*. London: Unwin Hyman, 1989.

Bellavance, Marcel. *Le Québec et la Confédération. Un choix libre*. Québec: Éditions du Septentrion, 1992.

Berger, Carl. *The Sense of Power: Studies in the Ideas of Canadian Imperialism 1867–1914*. Toronto: University of Toronto Press, 1970.

Billington, Ray Allen. *The Protestant Crusade, 1800–1860: A Study of the Origins of American Nativism*. Chicago: Quadrangle Books, 1938, 1964.

Clarke, Brian. *Piety and Nationalism: Lay Voluntary Associations and the Creation of an Irish-Catholic Community in Toronto, 1850–1895*. Montreal & Kingston: McGill-Queen's University Press, 1993.

Daigle, Jean. Ed. *The Acadians of the Maritimes: Thematic Studies*. Moncton, N.B.: Centre d'études acadiennes, 1982.

Houston, Cecil J. and William J. Smyth. *The Sash Canada Wore*. Toronto: University of Toronto Press, 1980.

McGowan, Mark G. *The Waning of the Green: Catholics, the Irish and Identity in Toronto, 1887–1922*. Montréal & Kingston: McGill-Queen's University Press, 1999.

Moir, John S. and C.T. McIntyre. Eds. *Canadian Catholic and Protestant Missions*. New York: Peter Lang, 1988.

Murphy, Terrence and Gerald Stortz. *Creed and Culture. The Place of English-Speaking Catholics in Canadian Society, 1750–1930*. Montréal & Kingston: McGill-Queen's University Press, 1993.

Noel, Jan. *Canada Dry: Temperance Crusaders Before Confederation*. Toronto: University of Toronto Press, 1995.

Noll, Mark A. and George Rawlyk. Eds. *Amazing Grace: Evangelicalism in Australia, Britain, Canada, and the United States*. Montréal & Kingston: McGill-Queen's University Press, 1994.

Noll, Mark A., et al. Eds. *Evangelicalism: Comparative Studies of Popular Protes-*

tantism in North America, the British Isles, and Beyond, 1770–1990. New York: Oxford University Press, 1994.

Palmer, Howard. *Patterns of Prejudice: A History of Nativism in Alberta.* Toronto: McClelland & Stewart, 1982.

Paz, D.G. *Popular Anti-Catholicism in Mid-Victorian England.* Stanford: Stanford University Press, 1992.

Rawlyk, George A. Ed. *Aspects of the Canadian Evangelical Experience.* Montréal & Kingston: McGill-Queen's University Press, 1997.

——. *The Canadian Protestant Experience, 1760–1990.* Burlington: Welch Publishing Co., 1990.

Robson, Robert. Ed. *Ideas and Institutions of Victorian Britain: Essays in Honour of George Kitson Clarke.* London: G. Bell & Sons, 1967.

Robbins, Thomas and Susan Palmer. *Millenium, Messiahs and Mayhem. Contemporary Apocalyptic Movements.* New York/London: Routledge, 1997.

Rousseau, Louis & Frank Remiggi. *Atlas historique des pratiques religieuses.* Ottawa: University of Ottawa Press, 2000.

Ruddell, David-Thierry. *Le Protestantisme français au Québec, 1840–1919: 'Images' et témoignages.* Ottawa: National Museum of Man, 1983.

Senior, Hereward. *Orangeism: the Canadian Phase.* Toronto: McGraw-Hill Ryerson, 1972.

Voisine, Nive and Jean Hamelin. Eds. *Les ultramontains canadiens-français.* Montréal: Boréal, 1985.

Voisine, Nive. *Louis-François Laflèche: Deuxième évêque de Trois-Rivières.* Saint-Hyacinthe: Edisem, 1980.

Westfall, William. *Two Worlds: The Protestant Culture of Nineteenth-Century Ontario.* Kingston & Montréal: McGill-Queen's University Press, 1989.

CHAPTER 13

Alternatives to the Evangelical Crusade

Although each of the two parties of evangelical crusaders became a powerful majority in English-Protestant and French-Catholic Canada respectively, nevertheless significant numbers of Canadians refused to hop aboard their noisy bandwagons that trumpeted the benefits of temperance, the Anglo-Protestant civilization, or the Franco-Catholic nation. These dissenters proposed alternative visions of life and of Canadian society, visions that were based on different interpretations of the Christian faith, on different religious views, or on different ethnic, cultural, and political considerations. The most militant opposition to Canada's evangelically-driven quest for uniformity came from Louis Riel's Métis people in the Northwest.

Why some opposed the evangelical crusades

The opposition to both Protestant and Catholic evangelicalism was driven by a variety of social, intellectual, ideological, and religious reasons, a number of which were the product of modernity, a world view that grew from the sixteenth to the nineteenth centuries. Modernity emphasized the rational and the individual, values that stood in contrast to both the emotional-mystical and the communal emphases of evangelicalism. The evangelicals' focus on faith, the Bible, conversion, and good works struck fear into the hearts of those Canadians who gave precedence to freedom, human reason, and scientific inquiry. The evangelicals' quest for common and uniform standards in matters of prohibition, morality, and church authority over both the state and people's consciences led these dissenting Canadians, both Christian and other, to fear the loss of their cherished personal, political, or cultural rights.

Social reasons

Many were driven to resist the evangelical arguments because of their social conditioning. The industrial revolution that began in eighteenth-century England was sweeping the Western world by the second half of the nineteenth century. The invention of the steam engine had led to the invention of locomotives, steam-driven machinery in factories, steam-ships, and a chain-reaction of technological development that revolutionized industry, manufacturing, transportation, and travel. These radical technical changes caused major upheavals in economies, standards of living, employment, social classes, and the development of large cities surrounding the growing factories that drew labourers from far and wide. Coupled with the population explosion that characterized Great Britain after 1800, hundreds of thousands of Irish, English, and Scots emigrated during the nineteenth century. While numbers left their rural homes for industrial centres such as Birmingham, Liverpool, and Manchester, many others landed in North America. The rapidly industrializing European Northwest had soon worked its magic on the United States and Canada.

Industrialized and urbanized societies with growing numbers of migrant workers made for personal, cultural, and social values that differed significantly from those of traditional, rural, agrarian, and stable societies. Traditional ethnic, cultural, and religious communities broke down because of the dispersion and mixing of people, broken families, and the new geographical, economic, political, social, and religious surroundings. Frequently, young men emigrated alone with the intention of setting aside a small nest egg to pay for the journey of their wives, children, or loved ones at a later date. This meant that industrial centres were inhabited by large numbers of young men who were separated from their families and therefore prone to become restive in the hurly-burly plants and neighbourhoods they inhabited. Some of their neighbours were a growing number of young women who had also come to the growing cities and industrial centres in order to find work.

Many of these migrant workers and young people were destitute; indeed their poverty had been a major consideration that drove them out of their homelands in the hope of finding their fortune. However, more often than not they found themselves toiling in less-than-humane working conditions that included miserly wages, very long hours, unhealthy and unsafe circumstances, and the constant threat of losing their jobs at any time. Many felt that in leaving their rural homes for the industrial cities, they had jumped from the frying pan into the fire. The situation of the immigrants was compounded by the fact that they had also lost their social support network of family, village, neighbour, and church. Indeed, all of these social institutions had yet to develop a solid footing in the new and growing workers' neighbourhoods of the cities of industrialized Canada. For the new workers, rooming houses stood in lieu of friendly neighbours, and reinforced the isolation, loneliness, and despair of too many young men and women.

The parishes and churches of Canada's industrializing cities were soon overwhelmed by the flood of new workers, many of whom sought to overcome their misery by drinking to excess or consorting with women of ill repute. The clergy of the churches had not been trained to deal with the new social challenges; many did not understand the extent of the social revolution that they were witnessing; few understood or spoke the languages of many of the immigrants. Although some Christians, both clerical and lay, did tackle the new social problems head-on, most did not.[1] The latter fell back on their traditional understanding and explanations, thereby alienating many of the new labourers who perceived the churches as being lackeys of Big Business, the enemies of the working poor. These social critics of Christianity would never support evangelical crusades that were aimed at reinforcing the churches.

This same social situation also nourished other opponents of the Christian evangelical crusades, but for different reasons. To those who opposed the churches because the latter seemed to lack a social conscience, were added those who appreciated the greater freedom that resulted from the new society where the grip of the church had been loosened. Indeed, the diminishing control of the churches over the lives of the new working classes in the cities resulted in a greater freedom of lifestyle, of customs, of thinking, of religion. In the rapidly industrializing cities of Montréal and Toronto, it was relatively easy to behave as one chose without incurring the wrath of the local church which remained powerless to intervene. For example, for those Canadians who felt that they should be free to consume alcoholic beverages if they chose to, the temperance campaign of the crusading churches, which was in fact a prohibition campaign, threatened their social freedom. They stood opposed.

Intellectual reasons

In the West, science had developed in the context of modernity, indeed it had become a primary characteristic of modernity. The empirical and

Baconian science that developed from the seventeenth century relied on empirical observation of phenomena followed by conclusions based on the laws of reason.[2] These foundation stones of Baconian science, namely empirical observation and inductive rational argument, were destined to become the distinctive characteristics of the ideologies of modernity that have prevailed in the West until the present.

Traditional religion and Christianity, however, were built on very different philosophical assumptions. While traditional Christians, like modern scientists, sought to better understand their world, unlike the new scientists they found their primary truth in God's Revelation rather than in the empirical observation of natural phenomena. Indeed, the Christian church taught that the mysteries of life were answered by God who spoke through his Word, his Son Jesus the Christ, whose truth was to be found expressed in the Bible and lived in the Christian church. It was the authority of these sources of truth, ultimately God's authority, that commanded obedience to the teachings of the Bible and the church, including its legitimate spokespersons. The Christian ethos was one of acknowledgement of, and obedience to, legitimate authority who express God's teachings.

Beginning in the seventeenth century, this Christian traditional mindset encountered growing opposition from modernity. In the eighteenth century, the new Baconian philosophy with its empirical and rational assumptions became the prevailing mindset among intellectuals in the West. This meant that from their primary bases in England and France, the West's new intelligentsia challenged with increasing confidence a lengthening list of traditional doctrines of the church. Miracles were declared to be impossible, mere imaginings by credulous people; a series of Catholic doctrines were denied outright, including the transformation (transubstantiation) of bread and wine into the body and blood of Christ during Mass; the role of saints and of Mary as mediators before God was questioned; the authority of the church and of its leaders was diminished; the divine inspiration and inerrancy of the Bible were denied. Many of the new scientists either denied the legitimacy of the Christian church or reduced it to the level of any other association or brotherhood. The exclusively rational mindset of modernity excluded the world of wonder that was sustained by traditional Christianity and by religions generally.

It was in this context that the discipline of critical history developed, a method of studying the past whereby documentary evidence and rational demonstration were required in order to establish truth.

Growing numbers of the new scholars revisited the historical record, seeking to document and demonstrate their findings; whenever this proved impossible, they concluded that the truth was impossible to ascertain which made the facts or events at best uncertain, at worst false. For example, historians had demonstated that the historical foundations of the papal States lay in Charlemagne's eighth century rather than in Emperor Constantine's fourth century; the celibacy requirement of the Catholic clergy was shown *not* to be of apostolic foundation; the history of the early Christian church highlighted a church very different from that of the nineteenth century. The same scientific thrust gave rise to a series of new or revitalized scholarly disciplines such as archeology, paleontology, Egyptology, geology, linguistics, philosophy, biblical criticism, literary criticism, etc.

Given the importance of Christianity in the history of the West, these same scholars were soon examining the doctrines, traditions, customs, and origins of the Christian church. Their conclusions were frequently troubling, if not devastating to the defenders of traditional Christianity. The history of the planet earth was shown to be much longer than the six thousand years allowed by biblical chronology, thereby casting serious doubt on the story of the Garden of Eden and of Adam and Eve that is told in the book of Genesis. The biblical story of creation was challenged in the light of growing archaeological evidence of the existence of human beings on earth for hundreds of thousands of years. When the English naturalist Charles Darwin (1809–1892) published his *The Origin of Species by Means of Natural Selection* (1859) and *The Descent of Man* (1871), the educated public received with growing enthusiasm his theory of biological evolution which held that living species were gradually transformed over time because of the effect of their environment, and because of the gradual adaptation of their organs to their use or disuse. The new doctrine of natural selection was soon applied to the evolution of human beings, thereby challenging traditional Christian doctrine on the instantaneous creation of humans by God.

Some interpreters then extended Darwinism to encompass the evolution of nations and ethnic groups, which were then ranked according to racial, psychological, emotional, or other criteria. Christian theologians had long explained the origins of humanity by invoking the myth of Adam and Eve in the Garden of Eden. This allowed them to explain our origins as coming from a single couple, monogenism, thereby supporting the Christian teaching that all men and women belonged to one family; all were children of God. We were all brothers and sisters, irrespective of colour, race, or any other distinction. Now, new racialist ideologues used Darwin's work to teach that human beings originated from several different couples, the theory of polygenism. They suggested that there was no common parentage between the upper races – *us* – and the *lower races*. It just so happened that one moved higher or lower on their scale of human quality in direct proportion to one's distance from London, England. So it was that Europeans were generally classified in the upper tier of races, while Africans, Asians, or Amerindians were much lower down the scale. One variation of this teaching was the doctrine of phrenology, which held that one's intelligence could be measured by the constellation of bumps on one's skull. It just so happened that the lower races invariably lost such competitive measurements with the *upper races*. This social Darwinism, dressed as it was in scientific robes, made some ethnic or racial groups superior to others. As Darwinism spread and gained increasing favour as an explanation of the origins of human beings, the Christian churches found themselves increasingly on the defensive.

Just as disturbing for the churches were the findings of biblical scholars. Traditionally, all Christian churches took the Bible to be the literal Word of God, a text directly inspired by the Holy Spirit, and therefore free of error. Beginning at the time of the Renaissance, particularly from the sixteenth century, scholars had shown the imperfections of various translations of the Bible from the original languages of Greek and Hebrew. Therefore, they sought to produce better translations.

However, it was in the nineteenth century that scholars began to examine carefully the history of the canon, and of each of the biblical books.[3] They showed that the nearly three-score books of the Old Testament and the twenty-seven books of the New Testament each had a history, that is to say that each book was composed by a particular author or editor, at a specific time and place, with a specific purpose. Some books wanted to tell a story, while others contained prophecies or catechetical teachings. While some books were in fact edited collections of pre-existent texts, others were written by one author. Moreover, the names of the authors could not be taken at face value, as ancient customs allowed communities to attribute authoritative names to books they had compiled. Some biblical books borrowed or copied passages from other books; others contradicted each other on one point or another. Finally, historians discovered other Jewish and Christian texts of the early Christian period, texts that were very similar to some of the biblical texts but that were not part of the received canon. Was the final selection of the books to be included in the Bible an arbitrary one? Who chose them? Why were some texts excluded?

These and other questions were made more troublesome by the discovery that the texts of the Bible reflected much of the culture, vocabulary, and concepts of the societies in which they were written, societies that ranged in time from the fifth century B.C.E. to the first century C.E. Scholars found traces, sometimes outright borrowings not only from Jewish and Semitic religions, but also from Egyptian, Mesopotamian, and Roman religions, not to mention Greek philosophy. In the light of the growing mountain of evidence pertaining to the historical development of the biblical books, educated Christians were driven to treat the Bible as they would any other book, which is with a critical eye. But then, what of biblical inspiration? What of the truth of Christianity and of the church which rested in large part on the Book?

Ideological reasons

Some opposed the evangelical crusades of the nineteenth century because of different ideological commitments. The modern period with its growing commitment to Baconian philosophy and rationalistic science had resulted in the American and French Revolutions of the late eighteenth century. The latter had in turn made liberalism and conservatism the leading ideological combatants of the nineteenth century, not to mention atheistic humanism. Born in reaction to the constraints, class divisions, social and economic inequalities, and privileges of the tradition-bound *ancien régime* in Europe, liberalism sought liberty above all else. This meant freedom of the individual, of the press, of conscience, of public assembly, of association, of teaching, of religion, of thought, etc. The growing number of liberal-minded people in the West stood opposed to uniformity and privilege of all kinds. Therefore, they stood opposed to Christian uniformity and church privilege, whether it be in matters of established churches or of state legal and financial support for confessional schools.

Given the resistance to change of the traditionally privileged groups, the Christian churches included, however, most liberal-minded people were driven to organize their own militant and crusading parties aimed at overthrowing the ruling privileged groups. The conflict between liberals and conservatives was thus polarized, each party hardening its position in reaction to the blows dealt to it by the opponent. So it was that the liberals who were allegedly preaching freedom soon sounded just as categorical and inflexible as their conservative opponents. All too often, liberalism became radicalism, while conservatives became more and more reactionary. In other words, in the heat of ideological battle during the nineteenth century, polarization often led to revolutions, directed by either the right or the left.

This either-or mindset set its stamp on religions and churches, just as it did on political and philosophical parties. As evangelicalism, both Protestant and Catholic (ultramontanism), gathered its strength from the mid-nineteenth century, it became more and more conservative, that is to say reactionary, in its policies and doctrines. Among the Protestants where temperance became teetotalism, a growing number of churches in Canada overcame their organizational and denominational differences, and founded a common religio-cultural front to control the public agenda. 'Others,' be they French, Catholic, Asian, or Ukrainian were given much shorter shrift.

While English-speaking Canada put on a progressively more distinctive Protestant face, French Canada did likewise with its very own version of Catholicism. Indeed, the geometric growth in the numbers of male and female clergy in French Canada after 1840 was simultaneously the result and the cause of a phenomenal increase in both church control over the minds of the faithful and in the expansion of Catholic services from the Atlantic to the Pacific to the Arctic. Religious sisters and brothers replaced lay people as school teachers, while Catholic schools were declared to be the only ones to be tolerated in Canada. In their rigid ideological determinisms, Catholic ultramontanism and Protestant evangelicalism were two sides of the same conservative or reactionary coin. Each party had Truth in its possession, and each was bent on controlling the destiny of the country; it was the will of God.

Those with a conservative bent frequently allied themselves with particular ethnic or cultural interests, transforming themselves into defenders of these groups. So it was that while Canada's Protestant churches gradually raised the standard of British, English-speaking imperial loyalty and uniformity, the Catholic Church almost tore itself asunder over the competing ethnocultural interests of Irish English-speaking Canadians and French Canadians.

The ideological fight between liberals and conservatives dominated Western society in the nineteenth century. Given the conservative nature of most religions, most of them would line up on the conservative-reactionary side. This was the case for most Catholic and Protestant churches. Those believers who sided with the liberal camp would end up either leaving or being cast out of their believing community or fighting a long, drawn-out, and losing battle within it.

Religious reasons

In addition to the social, intellectual, and ideological reasons for opposing the evangelical crusades, there were also religious reasons at work. One of the most telling was atheistic humanism, the belief of a number of intellectuals that there was no God. Having posited this as the fundamental and obverse ground of their world view, they simultaneously posited, just as arbitrarily, as the reverse side that one could only believe in the visible, the tangible, and observable. For some of these scholars, the good of humankind, however determined, and not the will of God was the only legitimate goal of our endeavours. For others, all of reality was reducible to matter. The most influential of these forms of atheistic humanism was Marxism. Although the latter had little influence in Canada, nevertheless Marxism and its broader setting of atheistic humanism had considerable indirect influence through their effect on the European intelligentsia whose influence on Canadian intellectual leaders was considerable.

Another religious reason for opposing the evangelical crusades was noted above, namely that by the end of the nineteenth century, millennial and holiness emphases had developed in Protestantism. Protestants in the latter movements seemed less and less willing to accept the increasing social commitment that was developing in the Protestant churches of the turn of the twentieth century.[4] Millennialists and holiness advocates centred their spirituality on the individual believer before God. They were not inclined to join in crusades of whatever kind that required strong collective commitments.

There were also Canadians who avoided the evangelical bandwagon for other religious reasons. The latter included the teachings of other great religions such as Judaism, those of communal Protestants like the Mennonites and the Hutterites, the doctrines of a variety of sects such as theosophy and the Doukhobors, various beliefs such as spiritism, some socio-religious movements such as Freemasonry, Christian social reformers such as Henry George, John Wilson Bengough, and Agnes Maule Machar, and some radicals and nonconformists such as Dr Maurice Bucke, Colonel Robert Ingersoll, and T. Phillips Thomson. In the nineteenth century a number of religious beliefs were simmering, beliefs that would keep their faithful at arm's length from the evangelical crusades mounted by the mainstream churches of English and French Canada.

Christian alternatives to the evangelical crusade

Christians who either stood apart or opposed the evangelical crusades in Canada included liberal Catholics such as those found in the *Institut Canadien* noted above, and liberal Protestants, Christian social reformers, and other Protestants like the Mennonites and the Hutterites.

Liberal Protestantism

Liberal Protestantism represented another Christian alternative to the evangelical crusades in Canada. Broadly speaking, liberal Protestants felt that their Christian doctrinal heritage needed to be adjusted to the cultural and intellectual tenets of their time. Indeed, at any time and place, Christians had to interpret and explain the Revelation of God which they held in faith. Such interpretation required that the received religious doctrines and understanding be reconciled with the customs and ways of thinking of any given society. While most Christians acknowledged this, the degree of adaptation of religious doctrine was frequently hotly debated. In the nineteenth-century Western world, those Protestants who posited cultural criteria and practices as the norms to which religious doctrine was to conform were known as liberal Protestants. By contrast, those Protestants who felt that religious norms were the proper benchmark to which cultural ways were to be adjusted were known as conservative or evangelical Protestants.

Because of the increasing influence of a number of ideologies such as Marxism, socialism, and Darwinism, the debate became more and more heated within both Protestant and Catholic churches. While some liberal Protestants were inclined to label their conservative coreligionists as intellectual fossils or dinosaurs – people who refused to adapt to their times – the conservative Protestant camp returned the favour as they designated the liberals as pseudo-Christians who preserved a mere veneer of Christianity. The same polarization occurred among Catholics where liberals confronted conservatives, sometimes known as integrist Catholics.

By the turn of the twentieth century, liberal Protestants and Catholics had come to be known as modernists, those Christians for whom modernity was the norm and for whom traditional Christian doctrine seemed to be given short shrift, or at least needed to be recast. In many respects, modernist Protestants seemed to hold that the sacred and the profane were one, the latter standing in lieu of the former. Such modernists could be found in several of Canada's leading Protestant churches, with the Methodists leading the pack. These Methodists would carry the liberal Protestant theology of cultural accommodation into the United Church of Canada when it was formed in 1925. Some would exchange their Christian belief in favour of a broad humanism that barely acknowledged the existence of a transcendent order.

Christian social reformers

Other alternatives to the evangelical crusades were those of a number of Christian social reformers, men like the American Henry George, the Toronto satirist John Wilson Bengough, or militant women such as Agnes Maule Machar.[5] Faced with the growing social and economic inequity of the capitalist West of the late nineteenth century, and convinced that such an economic and social order was directly related to traditional Christian teaching, Christian social reformers sought a new theology in order to effect change in the social and economic orders. Although these reformers preferred to march to their own drummer, some of them shared the evangelical fervour and some of the goals of the crusaders.

Henry George's book *Progress and Poverty* (1879) played a seminal role in promoting this search for a new social ethic and a new political economy. George denounced the injustices of the capitalist system, considered that the root cause of the evil was the private ownership of land, and preached in favour of land reform as the solution for Western society's social and economic ills. Indeed, the 1880s and 1890s, the decades when Henry George's sway was greatest, were the years when the ideas of the social gospel were sewn.[6] Christian social reformers were seeking a form of Christian socialism that would correct the abuses and injustices of the prevailing individualistic order. They would work for social salvation through good works.

The Toronto journalist and editor John Wilson Bengough was founding editor (1873) of *Grip*, "the superb weekly magazine of caricature,
light verse, puns, and satirical paragraphs."[7] Bengough used his unusual skills to educate and evangelize his readers and the audiences at
his numerous speaking engagements. In full accord with the Christian
reforming ideas of Henry George and of the English reforming novelist
Charles Dickens, Bengough worked for the salvation of his society and
the establishment of the Kingdom of God on earth, a kingdom of justice
and truth. However, like many of his fellow English-speaking Canadians of the turn of the twentieth century, this Protestant moralist would
have no truck with Canada's French and Catholic elements.

Agnes Machar was one of Canada's most gifted intellectual and
social critics at the turn of the century. Based in Kingston, Ontario,
Machar was a traditional Protestant who, like the prominent Presbyterian G.M. Grant, believed that individual conversion preceded the
conversion of society. Through her creative writing and scholarly readings she became convinced that the reform of society would be best
achieved through the intelligent application of the Christian faith in her
time. Machar believed in the efficacy of both prayer and Christian
social action. She was a liberal Protestant, convinced that the essence of
the Christian faith was its ethical teaching. During the last decades of
the nineteenth century, Agnes Machar became involved in the controversial issues of prohibition and of the place of women in society. She
was supportive of social reformers like the new Salvation Army, Christians who took the Sermon on the Mount as their primary charter. She
was another Christian reformer who laid the groundwork for the Social
Gospel.

Mennonites and Hutterites

Mennonites and Hutterites represent the Anabaptist wing of the Reformation of the sixteenth century. The name *Anabaptist* was used to
designate a collection of several reforming Christian communities in
early sixteenth-century continental Europe. The word means *rebaptizer*,
and designates those groups that claimed that the traditional baptism
of children in the Christian church was wrong; only believers, or adult
Christians who freely and deliberately confessed their faith, should be
eligible for baptism. This led to the rebaptism of the members of these
churches who had been baptized as children. Among the several
Anabaptist communities of the time, two eventually came to Canada, the
Mennonites and the Hutterites.[8]

Menno Simons (1496–1561) was a Catholic parish priest in Dutch Friesland until he joined the Anabaptists in 1536 when they were being persecuted because of the failed rebellion by a group of them in Münster where they had tried to found a theocratic Kingdom of the Saints. Simons spent the next twenty-five years organizing and caring for the scattered communities of Anabaptists throughout Holland and the surrounding territories. In time, his followers were known as Mennonites.

Menno Simons' teachings would become the distinctive creed of his followers to the present, namely the rejection of infant baptism, a strong suspicion or rejection of church organization, the autonomy of the local congregation, pacifism or the refusal of military service, the banning of oaths, and the refusal of public office. There are only two sacraments, namely the baptism of adults and a communion service which does not include the Catholic doctrine of transubstantiation. In Mennonite communities, both men and women may preach, and there is no standard common creed. This results in extensive doctrinal variety among Mennonite communities, some being openly Trinitarian while others are closer to Unitarians in their rejection of the Trinity. This eclectic doctrine has resulted in a large number of distinct Mennonite churches or denominations in Canada. The doctrinal divisions are further compounded by the divergent reactions of individual Mennonite communities to modernity and secularism. As is the case in many other religions and churches, a conservative wing desperately clings to the old ways, a liberal wing readily adapts to modern society, while a middle-of-the-road group accepts some acculturation.

Mennonites came to Canada in stages beginning in 1786. First were the 2,000 Mennonites who came to southern Ontario as part of the Loyalist migration from the United States in the wake of the American War of Independence. They settled in York and Waterloo counties and in the Niagara peninsula. Most of them came from Pennsylvania where their ancestors had settled in the late seventeenth century, fleeing the persecutions to which they had been subjected in German-speaking areas of Europe. Because of their German origins and dialects, they were known as Pennsylvania *Deutsch* (Germans). Then, between 1825 and 1870, there followed to Canada a stream of several hundred Amish Mennonites, the name originating from the seventeenth-century conservative Bishop Jacob Ammon. They settled in Waterloo County where their distinctive lifestyle may still be observed.

Beginning in 1870, because of persecutions in their Russian homeland where thousands of Dutch Mennonites had sought refuge from yet earlier persecutions in the Netherlands, a regular stream of Russian

Mennonites came to Canada. Most settled in southern Manitoba. Concerned with drawing new settlers into the rapidly developing Northwest, the government of Canada promised the Russian Mennonites free land, educational and cultural autonomy, as well as exemptions from military service. After 1890, other Mennonites from Prussia, Russia, and the United States also immigrated to Canada's Northwest, founding settlements throughout the southern prairies where their exceptional agricultural skills were soon paying dividends. The largest migration occurred after 1920 when some 20,000 Russian Mennonites fled the Bolshevik Revolution in their homeland, electing in turn to settle on the Canadian Prairies. Indeed, throughout the twentieth century, the migration of Mennonites, primarily to the Prairies resulted in a population of some 191,470 Mennonites in Canada by 2001. Small numbers of conservative Mennonites left Canada after World War I, in the perennial hope of securing the independence they sought in Mexico and Paraguay.

The Hutterites were a second sixteenth-century Anabaptist community that later found refuge in Canada, although in much more limited numbers. Originally centred in Moravia, a territory now part of Slovakia and the Czeck Republic, the group took its name from its first leader Jacob Hutter (d. 1536). Like the Mennonites, because of their beliefs and customs the Hutterites were frequently persecuted by both Catholic and Protestant authorities, persecutions which led to periodic dispersal of the communities; some of the latter ended up in the United States and Canada. There were only 26,300 Hutterites in Canada in 2001. The strong communal ties of Hutterites entailed the common ownership of property and a form of communal living. Their beliefs included pacifism, adult baptism, and the strict separation of church and state. Hutterites tend to be much more conservative than many Mennonites, preserving the ancient forms of dress, customs, and lifestyle of their ancestors.

Religious pluralism

Despite the growing common fronts built by the Catholic and Protestant evangelical crusaders in the latter nineteenth century, other religious options also were being defended in Canada. These included those of Judaism and of a number of newer religions or quasi-religions that included Spiritism, Theosophy, and Freemasonry. There were also a handful of Doukhobors in Canada, in addition to a number of individuals who seemed to fabricate their own religions, men such as Maurice

Fig. 12.   Hutterite settlers near Winnipeg.[9] National Archives of Canada,
c-036153.

Bucke, Colonel Robert Ingersoll, and T. Phillips Thompson. Ironically, at the time when the evangelical steamroller was gathering momentum, Canada seemed bent on becoming a religious mosaic.

Judaism

Upon the destruction of the one and only Jewish temple in Jerusalem by the Roman army in 70 C.E., teachers, or rabbis, took over the leadership of the defeated Jewish community. In the wake of the disappearance of the temple, the central and only place of worship of all Jews, rabbis developed a replacement teaching whereby they themselves became the pivotal leaders of Judaism. This was Rabbinic Judaism, the prevailing form of Judaism that has prevailed to the present. The strong authority of the rabbi in Jewish communities served them well during the thousand years of Muslim and Christian dominance in the Western world, from the seventh to the seventeenth centuries, a period when Jews were often oppressed and forced to live separately from others.

Although Jews have been in Canada since the 1760s when the first synagogue was founded in Montréal, for more than a century they were few in number. Initially they came as merchants in the wake of the British Conquest of Canada, seeking commercial opportunities in a new land; these first Jewish immigrants assimilated into the mainstream society centred in Montréal and Toronto, some of them moving on to the United States.

Given their distinct history and their long experience of persecution at the hands of religious adversaries, all too frequently Christian ones, it was not surprising that Canada's Jews proved at best reluctant to jump upon the evangelical bandwagons. Jewish faith and history made Jews a wary and cautious people. Evangelicalism, be it Protestant or Catholic, would not find fertile ground or any fervent converts among the Jews. In Canada, Judaism was a standing reminder that religious unanimity was not to be.

Spiritualism

The evangelical crusades that were launched in the mid-nineteenth century were important manifestations of a major religious revival, a spiritual and mystic resurgence that was sweeping the country. Another manifestation of the same phenomenon was the emergence of spiritualism after 1848. Spiritualists teach that one can communicate with the spirits of deceased people through means of a medium. By the mid-nineteenth century, many people were disposed to accept such a doctrine, influenced as they were by the work of the eighteenth-century Austrian physician F.A. Mesmer who had explored trances and clairvoyance; they were also aware of the writings of Emmanuel Swedenborg (1688–1772), the Swedish scientist and mystic who was conscious of direct contact with angels and the spiritual world through dreams and supernatural visions.

Spiritualism began in 1848 when Margaretta and Kate Fox of Hydesville, New York, communicated with a spirit by rapping, that is to say by tapping out messages on a table or board. Within two years, spiritualism had spread to Canada. Soon, its adepts could be found from coast to coast. All that was needed to start a spiritualist circle was a medium, that is to say a person with mediumistic abilities, and several of the latter were forthcoming. Given the resurgence of spiritualism, or neoshamanism in the late twentieth century, the beliefs and practices of the movement will be presented in Chapter 19.

Theosophy

In a broad sense, the word *theosophy* is used to designate any intuitive knowledge of the divine and can thus be applied to a variety of systems of thought akin to pantheism, natural mysticism, Buddhism, Gnosticism, or even the thought of Emmanuel Swedenborg. In a more specific sense, however, theosophy designates the movement begun in New York by the Russian immigrant woman H.P. Blavatsky (d. 1891), founder of the Theosophical Society (1875). Shortly after the movement had shifted its headquarters to Madras, India, Annie Besant (d. 1933) became its leader. A mixture of magic, pantheism, and rationalism, theosophy claims to borrow its teachings from Hindu sacred books such as the Upanishads and Sutras. It claims to combine the best in the religions of the world and insists on the immanence of God in the world. Theosophists teach the transmigration of souls, the brotherhood of man, and to deny a personal God, personal immortality, the divinity of Christ, and the validity of Christian Revelation.

One Canadian social critic and reformer who became a theosophist in the 1890s was T. Phillips Thompson. Thompson was a nonconformist, an atheist, and a poet who was primarily concerned with ethical questions and the relationship between religion and social values. Active in several secularist and free thought movements, he denounced the failure of Christians to live up to their own teachings. Much like his Social Gospel Protestant contemporaries, he believed that he could only serve God by serving humanity.[10] There were fewer than 800 theosophists in Canada in 1991.

Freemasonry

Freemasons were founded in England in the twelfth century by masons concerned with protecting the secrets of their craft. Established under the protection of St John the Baptist, the brotherhood's attitude towards religion has fluctuated over the centuries and varied according to the country in which it was found, particularly after the eighteenth century when the movement spread rapidly throughout Europe and North America. At times primarily concerned with the moral and religious education of its members, Freemasonry has always required belief in God. In the eighteenth century the brotherhood strongly endorsed Deism, or a rationalist Christian theology. Upon its spread to continental Europe, to France and Italy in particular, Freemasonry became a strong adversary of the Christian church and of religion in general. In German-speaking countries it favoured an undoctrinal form of Christianity wherein God, ethics, and the brotherhood of all men were stressed, while specific Christian doctrines were considered unimportant. Freemasonry seemed to be teaching that all religions were of equal value and equally of secondary importance. From the eighteenth century, this led the popes to condemn the movement repeatedly, particularly in the second half of the nineteenth century. In fact, membership in the Freemasons entailed automatic excommunication from the Catholic Church and from the Orthodox churches. In the United States and English Canada, Freemasonry demanded belief in God from its members but did not tend to be hostile to religion.

These cultural differences in the doctrines of Freemasonry resulted in divergent policies by the mainstream churches. In French Canada, in Montréal for example, Masonic lodges were considered strong and feared adversaries of the Catholic Church; Freemasonry, the subject of several encyclicals by Popes Pius IX and Leo XIII, was in turn condemned repeatedly by many of the bishops of French Canada in pastoral letters to their flocks. In English Canada, the issue of Freemasonry and

Christianity was hardly raised given the innocuous role that the lodges were perceived to be playing in matters of religion. There, the movement was largely ignored by Catholic bishops.

Amerindians

It was precisely after the mid-nineteenth century, the time when the evangelical crusades were building a strong head of steam, when a long dark night of neglect, abuse, and injustice descended on Canada's Amerindian people. By definition, crusading majorities are driven to relegate to the cultural sidelines, often to oppress, all minorities whose continued existence threatens the majority's dream of conquest and domination. All significant minorities were looked down upon by Canada's rampaging evangelical crusaders, including Chinese and Japanese Canadians, immigrants of different ethnic or racial origins such as Ukrainians or Africans, and Canadians of different religious beliefs, such as Jews.

Nevertheless, Canada's Amerindians suffered more than the others because of the gulf that separated their social, cultural, and economic existence from that of the Caucasian majority in Canada. Canadian society, like any other society, was built on shared social and cultural values, and the vast majority of Canada's people, immigrant or other, came from Europe or North America where a common linguistic, cultural, and religious foundation existed. The Englishman may not have understood the language of the German, or the Frenchman that of the Italian, but they and most other Canadians issued from a common Indo-European linguistic stock. It had not been too many centuries since the British, the Germans, the French, the Spanish, the Austrians, and others had all been part of the same Christian empire with shared royal blood lines; indeed, the shell of that empire lasted into the early nineteenth century. Protestants may have fought Catholics, not to mention other Protestants, in the nineteenth century, but less than four centuries earlier they had all been part of the same One, Holy, Catholic, and Apostolic church under the leadership of the pope. Protestants, Catholics, and Orthodox all prayed to the same God, and shared both the same Bible and a common first millennium of church history. Indeed, these Canadians had much in common, even if they did not always behave as though they did.

Amerindians had inhabited Canada for several millennia before the arrival of the Europeans. Albeit grudgingly, the latter learned to negotiate and cooperate with them because each needed the other if they were to achieve their goals. In fact, the fur trade would have been impossible without the Amerindian trappers and Canada could not have defeated American forces in battle without the strong support of Amerindian warriors. By the mid-nineteenth century, however, when the fur trade was on the wane and the wars with the United States had ended, Canadians considered that they no longer needed the assistance and cooperation of the Amerindians in order to fulfill their destiny. This feeling was reinforced by the floodtide of immigration from Europe and the United States that swamped the country, reducing year by year the proportional importance of Amerindians in Canada. It was reinforced again by the diseases that reduced Amerindian populations at a rate that allowed observers to predict the total disappearance of Canada's native people within a foreseeable future.

Some evangelicals began to see the will of God in these developments. Could it be that God's Providence was allowing the Amerindians to wither on the vine while the Canadian people grew by leaps and bounds in numbers, wealth, and influence? Such ethnocultural policies of self-promotion and oppression of Amerindians were implemented by the governments of Canada when they created reservations and residential schools during the nineteenth century. The evangelical Protestant and Catholic churches cooperated fully with the government in these enterprises. Missionaries helped to herd the Amerindians into small reserved plots of land, and founded and staffed residential schools that were all too often more akin to detention centres than to centres of learning.

Such efforts notwithstanding, Canadian Amerindian spiritualities and traditions survived, in spite of the serious harm that was done to the Amerindian people; in spite of the rampant alcoholism, broken marriages, dysfunctional families, idleness, and low self-esteem that all too often resulted from the joint policies of church and state; in spite of the rules that prohibited children from speaking in their native languages; in spite of the directives that banned Amerindian dress; in spite of the interdiction of major Amerindian festivals such as the Potlatch or the Sun Dance. The losses were nevertheless extensive. For example, of the three score Amerindian languages extant in Canada at the time of the arrival of the Europeans, only three have any chance of surviving today.

These tragedies notwithstanding, the persistence of Amerindian spiritualities, languages, and traditions stood as constant challenges to the evangelical crusaders. By their very existence, the Amerindians served as reminders that the crusades were not a total success, and that alternate spiritualities continued to exist. Although a strong majority of Amerindians converted to Christianity, some 85% by 1991, nevertheless most remained attached to the ways of their ancestors, despite the best efforts of many missionaries to eradicate all traces of 'Amerindianness.' This is confirmed by recent developments that show a strong resurgence of Amerindian traditions. Many of Canada's Amerindians may remain Christian, but will do so in their own Amerindian way. This translates into different liturgies, prayers, customs, and theologies.

Louis Riel

The Métis leader

While most of the alternate beliefs and religions noted above remained relatively discreet and seldom occupied the front pages of newspapers, the Métis leader Louis Riel (1844–1885) made headlines many times over. Riel challenged the power of the government of Canada, founded a new religion, set the terms for the creation of the Province of Manitoba, and led two armed insurrections that drew the Canadian army into Manitoba and Saskatchewan, which led to his arrest, trial, and execution on charges of treason. Not only would Riel have no truck with Protestant evangelicalism, he moved beyond Catholic ultramontanism by founding his own religion.

The Métis people of the Canadian Northwest were the descendants of the European and Canadian *coureurs de bois* and *voyageurs* on the one hand, and Amerindian women on the other, a mixed-race group whose lifestyle usually resembled that of their Amerindian ancestors with considerable borrowing from the ways of the Canadians. By the mid-nineteenth century, the majority of the Métis were French-speaking, while a strong minority was English-speaking, in addition to the Amerindian languages that they spoke. The Métis had developed their own group identity, seeing themselves as distinct from both the Canadians and the Amerindians. They lived in their own villages, usually around a Hudson's Bay Company (H.B.C.) trading post, because many of them earned their living working for the company; many manned the barges, carts, and trading posts that constituted the lifelines of the fur trade throughout the vast Northwest. They were the ideal middle-men and translators between the Canadians and the Amerindians.

Once modern Canada was formed at Confederation in 1867, the new country undertook to more than double its size by purchasing Rupert's Land from the Hudson's Bay Company. Rupert's Land was an immense domain that included all of western Canada with the exception of the British colony of British Columbia, in addition to all of northern Canada north of the height of land that bisected Ontario and Québec. Political considerations delayed royal assent to the official transfer of the land to Canada until 23 June 1870. However, several months before the transfer occurred, in October, 1869 surveyors working for the government of Canada descended on the Red River area intent upon drawing up survey plans of the region. The surveyors did not obtain the permission of the local Métis population which reacted by forcing them to cease and desist. Then, on 2 November 1869, William McDougall, the governor-elect of the forthcoming new Canadian territory, blundered in turn by presenting himself at the border intent on proclaiming his jurisdiction, when in fact Rupert's Land did not yet belong to Canada. When an armed Métis party blocked his access, he bided his time and then, on 1 December secretly slipped into Rupert's Land by night and read his proclamation to the empty prairie. The fat was in the fire for the Métis were determined not to join Canada unless it was on terms that they considered fair and acceptable. They were led by Louis Riel.

Much happened in Red River between October 1869 and 15 May 1870 when the *Province of Manitoba Act* received royal assent. Riel's Métis seized Fort Garry from the H.B.C. in November, formed a provisional government in December, called a convention of forty representatives of the settlement and prepared a list of rights in January, defeated an armed insurrection by some English Canadian rebels in February, and on 4 March executed Thomas Scott, the leading troublemaker in the English group. Then, a Métis delegation went to Ottawa and negotiated the terms of the *Manitoba Act*, 1870. The new Canadian régime would come into effect on 15 July 1870.

Upon the arrival of Canadian troops in Red River in the summer of 1870, Louis Riel was forced to flee the country, seeking refuge in the United States. The Métis leader spent most of the subsequent thirteen years as a fugitive or exile from his country, hounded as he was by the arrest warrant and the $5,000 price that had been put on his head in Ontario where most accused him of the "murder" of Thomas Scott. He was elected to Parliament three times over between 1872 and 1874, but could not occupy his seat for fear of being arrested in Ontario, and because the House of Commons voted to expel him. In 1875 the government of Canada granted him amnesty for his role in the insurrection in

Fig. 13.   Riel and his councillors during the Red River rebellion in 1869–70.[11]
National Archives of Canada, PA-012854.

Red River, but conditional upon his going into exile for five years. After one year in the United States, he spent two years (1876–1878) as an inmate in two psychiatric hospitals in the Province of Québec, and then returned to the United States where he married and taught elementary school at a Jesuit mission in Montana. Riel had become a U.S. citizen.

It was in this mission that a Métis delegation led by Gabriel Dumont found him in June 1884. They invited him to return with them to the Métis parish of St Laurent, near Fort Carlton on the South Saskatchewan River, in order to organize and lead the Métis in their land claims before the government of Canada. Beginning in July 1884, Riel took charge of the Métis case, expanding it to become a claim to aboriginal land title. In fact, the government of Canada granted most of the Métis demands including title to river lots and land grants. However, Louis Riel himself wanted more. He wanted the recognition of the independence and sovereignty of the Métis people.

Armed rebellion erupted on the Saskatchewan River on 18 March 1885, and was followed by the election of a provisional government on the morrow. Then a series of bloody clashes occurred: on 26 March the Métis fought and routed a column of one hundred Mounted Police at Duck Lake; on 2 April Big Bear's Cree massacred eight whites at Frog Lake, while Chief Poundmaker's Cree attacked Battleford.

Then, the Métis laid in wait at Batoche for the eight hundred soldiers of the Canadian army led by General Frederick Middleton. Gabriel Dumont's forces checked this advance at Fish Creek, but then succumbed after four days of fighting at Batoche, 9 to 12 May. In the latter engagement, Middleton lost half a dozen men to Dumont's dozen. The rebellion was over. There followed the arrest, imprisonment, trial, and execution of Louis Riel who was hanged at Regina on 16 November 1885.

Riel's religion[12]

Louis Riel was born and raised in a devout Catholic family in Red River; his father had spent a few months as a novice with the Oblates before leaving the order and marrying, and his mother had seriously considered becoming a nun. In 1858, Louis was sent to Montréal to further his education, thanks to the benevolent support of Bishop Alexandre Taché of Saint-Boniface; the latter was hoping to make a priest of the young Riel, but that was not to be. After seven years in the Catholic college of the Sulpician Fathers, and another year working in the city, Riel left Montréal in 1866, the same year that his sister Sara joined the Sisters of Charity in Saint-Boniface. After two years spent in St Paul and Minneapolis, he returned to Red River in 1868 on the eve of his engaging in the political activities outlined above.

After the six difficult and disappointing years of public life between 1869 and 1875, Riel the devout Catholic was ready to interpret events in a more promising way. While in Washington in 1874 and 1875 he led a devout and exemplary Catholic life. Chaste, modest, and virtuous, he didn't drink or smoke, ate sparingly, and attended Mass every morning in addition to frequently praying in churches. His painful experiences were God's punishment for his sins. Ultramontane Catholicism had taught him that God's Providence took care of things and that each person had a divine calling or vocation. Riel began to feel that he was discovering his calling, that he had been endowed with a special mission. This was confirmed by a letter written to him by Bishop Bourget on 14 July 1875. The bishop of Montréal wrote: "God, who has always led you and assisted you until the present hour, will not abandon you in the dark hours of your life, for He has given you a mission which you must fulfill in all respects."[13]

As Louis reflected on the words uttered by Canada's most powerful bishop, on 8 December 1875, while attending Mass at St Patrick's church in Washington, D.C., he underwent a conversion experience.

The date was significant because it was on 8 December 1869 that the provisional government in Manitoba had been proclaimed and that Pope Pius IX had opened the First Vatican Council, the one that would declare the pope to be infallible in matters of faith and doctrine and the supreme administrative authority in the Catholic Church. It was also on 8 December 1854 that the reigning pontiff Pius IX had proclaimed the dogma of the Immaculate Conception of Mary, and on 8 December 1864 that the same pope had issued his celebrated *Syllabus of Errors*, the foundational charter of ultramontane Catholicism.

About the event on 8 December during Mass at St. Patrick's church, Riel wrote: "I suddenly felt in my heart a joy which took ...possession of me ... I was immediately struck by an immense sadness of spirit ... But that great pain, as great as my joy, passed away in just as short a time."[14] He later claimed that this event was the commencement of his mission, that that was when God gave him divine gifts as "prophet of the New World." Only days afterwards, he noted that people began to treat him like a madman.

Thomas Flanagan tells of several subsequent mystical and visionary experiences by Riel, the spirit of God taking over his body and transporting his soul into heaven. Until the day he was hanged in Regina, Louis Riel saw himself as fulfilling the prophetic mission that had been given to him by the Spirit of God. Gradually, after the events of December 1875, Riel became more and more of a prophet and reformer, gradually distancing himself from the orthodox Catholicism that he had shared until then. During two of these years, from March 1876 to January 1878, he was interned in the asylums of Saint-Jean-de-Dieu at Longue Pointe near Montréal, and Beauport below Québec. His friends felt he was deranged; he thought he was God's prophet, continuing to have visions and to receive revelations.

After his release from the Beauport asylum in 1878, Riel spent most of his time in the United States, particularly in Minnesota and Montana. He dabbled unsuccessfully in a number of political and commercial activities before marrying and taking up school teaching in Montana. His outward behaviour was that of a Catholic, although he continued to hold his own peculiar beliefs regarding, among other things, his prophetic mission and the transfer of the papacy from Rome to Montréal. His was a form of millenarian Christianity, believing that the Kingdom of God was about to be established on earth. Thereupon, justice would finally prevail.

When Riel arrived in the Saskatchewan River valley in 1884, he undertook to realize his vision of establishing the Kingdom of God, although all the Métis people were really interested in was land rights. But given Riel's influence as a leader, the Métis accepted the peculiar religious doctrines and structures that he unveiled while they fought for their very survival. While Gabriel Dumont led the troops in battle, Louis Riel was in prayer, seeking and receiving new revelations. He considered himself the new prophet, with the Métis as God's new chosen people. Together they would triumph through God's intervention. In other words, a miracle was needed to prove the legitimacy of Riel's new religion. In the process, Riel alienated the Catholic missionaries in the area; the latter came to see him as an insane heretic. Flanagan concludes: "The North-West Rebellion was a politico-religious movement with a political emphasis among the followers but a religious emphasis for the leader."[15]

During his several months of imprisonment and five days of trial, Louis Riel never deviated from his belief in the prophetic mission he had received from God. The proof was in his mystical and visionary experiences, as is the case for all prophets. His mission was to reform Christian doctrine and worship, as well as to launch the Kingdom of God on earth. Although he signed a recantation of his heresies on 5 August 1885, and again just before his execution, witnesses, including his spiritual adviser and confessor, thought that it was a mere outward gesture. In fact, Louis Riel saw no contradiction between his revelations and beliefs on the one hand and Catholic doctrine on the other.

Indeed, Louis Riel tried to found a religion of the oppressed, a millennial Christianity that would liberate both himself and his Métis people from the chains of social, political, and spiritual oppression. His was an alternative to the evangelical religion of the crusading Protestant and Catholic majorities, forms of religion that left little room for minorities, be they ethnic, cultural, or religious.

The reaction to Riel's crusade

The Riel-led insurrections in Manitoba and the Saskatchewan River valley provoked different reactions on the part of the Amerindians, the Métis, the government of Canada, the people of Ontario, and those of Québec. Louis Riel had no ties to the Amerindian people of Canada. Consequently, the two Cree uprisings in the Northwest in the spring of 1885 were coincidental and not coordinated. Indeed, some Cree leaders like Big Bear were merely taking advantage of favourable circumstances created by the Métis rebellion.

The opposite was true for the Métis for whom Louis Riel had proven a charismatic and able leader in 1869–1870, the man who was largely responsible for their obtaining most of what they wanted from the government of Canada, including land grants and the terms of the creation of the Province of Manitoba. It was with this in mind that Riel was invited back to Canada, to the Saskatchewan River this time. The Métis hoped that he could repeat his earlier performance in their favour. Because of his talents, proven record of accomplishment, and sincerity, the Métis were disposed to overlook the religious peculiarities of Louis Riel. In the end this would cost them dearly. Nevertheless, Louis Riel was their leader; they would stand by him.

The government of Canada, in fact, responded positively to most of the Métis demands in both 1870 and 1884. However, this is not to mean that they should win the prize for virtue. In fact, in 1869 and 1870, John A. Macdonald's government blundered and stumbled more than once in dealing with the developing crisis in Red River. The government did not readily consult the people of Red River; its surveyors proceeded without due consultation and permission from the legitimate owners of the land they were surveying; its appointed governor Mcdougall was sent in before he had any right to be in place; upon their arrival in Red River in 1870, the government troops were allowed to bully and terrorize the local Métis people; and after prolonged delays and harassment, the two Métis leaders Louis Riel and Ambroise Lépine were refused unconditional amnesty in 1875. The latter went to prison for two years and the former chose exile for five years. The government of Canada agreed to the Métis demands in 1870 because it had to. Indeed, it had no means of enforcing its wishes in Red River. In fact, the terms of the *Manitoba Act*, 1870, were largely the result of Métis demands. Louis Riel had won.

When the Saskatchewan rebellion occurred, the government crushed the insurgents with troops, then accused and tried Riel for treason, a charge for which a guilty verdict entailed a mandatory death penalty. Then, John A. Macdonald's government refused to hear an appeal of the death sentence imposed by the court. Nevertheless, it was noted above that most of the Métis land claims were in the process of being granted even before the rebellion broke out.

In fact, it was the reactions in central Canada that made Louis Riel into a national figure – a demon in Ontario, and a saintly hero in Québec. Ontario public opinion, whipped into frenzy by the Orange lodges, undertook to destroy Louis Riel and everything he stood for. It did so under the pretext of avenging the death of Thomas Scott who had been executed by Riel's provisional government on 4 March 1870. In fact, it did so for many other reasons, foremost among which was his perceived French and Catholic identity. Although the execution of Scott had been unwise on the part of Riel's government and not carried out under the best appearance of justice, it had been a legal act by the only legitimate government in place at Red River at the time. Ontario public opinion got so excited about the deed that a warrant was issued for Riel's arrest and a five thousand dollar price was put on his head. In fact, English-speaking Canada was outraged by this upstart rebel who had dared obstruct English central Canada's plans to settle the West and make it into a faithful replica of Ontario society. Macdonald's government would not dare work against the national ambitions of the English Ontario bastion. Riel was a symbol of all things French and Catholic; he and his Métis people were to be put in their place.

French Québec reacted in kind, transforming the Métis leader into a favourite son. The hanging of 16 November 1885 became a symbol of the persecuting injustice that was the trademark of English Canada. A revitalized version of French Canadian nationalism was born, its legitimacy soon confirmed by the successive legislative campaigns in Manitoba, the Northwest Territories, and Ontario after 1889, all aimed at banning French as an official language in the courts and legislatures and outlawing public confessional, that is to say Catholic, schools. In Québec, the hanging of Riel sparked the emergence and election of Honoré Mercier's nationalist government in 1886.

The crusading nationalisms of both English Ontario and French Québec would continually clash for the next three decades, their sole apparent common ground being the shared vision of Louis Riel as a French Canadian Catholic leader. Ironically, Riel had fought for the Métis, not the French Canadians, while developing his own religious stance, one that was at odds with the Catholic Church. These facts were lost sight of as the two crusading nationalisms, which were all too frequently identical to the crusading evangelicalisms, fed off the rich symbolism of Louis Riel. The hanging of Riel put a seal on the profound divisions between English Canada and French Canada.

Suggested readings

Clark, Lovell. Ed. *The Guibord Affair*. Toronto & Montréal: Holt, Rinehart and Winston, 1971.

Cook, Ramsay. *The Regenerators. Social Criticism in Late Victorian English Canada*. Toronto: University of Toronto Press, 1985.

Flanagan, Thomas. *Louis 'David' Riel 'Prophet of the New World.'* Revised edition. Toronto: University of Toronto Press, 1996.

Marks, Lynne. *Revivals and Roller Rinks: Religion and Identity in Late-Nineteenth Century Small-Town Ontario*. Toronto: University of Toronto Press, 1996.

Miller, James R. *Shingwauk's Vision. A History of Residential Schools in Canada*. Toronto: University of Toronto Press, 1996.

——. *Skyscrapers Hide the Heavens. A History of Amerindian-White Relations in Canada*. Revised edition. Toronto: University of Toronto Press, 1991.

Stanley, George F.G. *The Birth of Western Canada: A History of the Riel Rebellions*. Toronto: University of Toronto Press, 1936, 1963.

CHAPTER 14

Confessional Education

Until the 1960s, the education of young Canadians, both in and out of school, usually bore a strong confessional imprint. While some schools were designated as confessional, Catholic or Protestant for example, many were merely designated as *public*, masking the fact that they too usually promoted a specific creed. Given the pervasive presence of confessional schools, Canada's churches were very much involved in the schooling of the nation at all levels. They also became much involved in the schooling of Canada's native people as some of the latter's traditional forms of communal teaching, the Sun Dance and the Potlatch for example, were banned by the government of Canada.

Education in Canada before 1850

Schools in New France

During the French régime in Canada (1608–1760), schools were a form of church apostolate, as they had been for some seven centuries in Europe. No law required that anyone attend school; indeed, such general legal requirements would await the second half of the nineteenth century in Canada as elsewhere. Nevertheless, seventeenth- and eighteenth-century Canada was well provided with schools because of the energetic apostolate of Jesuits, Sulpicians, Sisters of Notre Dame, and Ursulines to name only the most prominent promoters of schools.

Beginning in 1639, the afore-named congregations of sisters founded a growing number of elementary schools in the colony, first in the leading towns of Québec, Montréal, and Trois-Rivières, and then in the rural areas. Meanwhile, the Jesuits had founded their *Collège de Québec* in 1635 to provide more advanced schooling to the young men of the colony. Those who were preparing for the priesthood then proceeded to the *Séminaire de Québec* (1663). The *Collège de Québec* never reopened after the fall of Québec to the English. From 1766, it was replaced by the *Séminaire de Québec* which added to its former theological curriculum the more junior collegiate and secondary-school grades required to complete the curriculum offered by the numerous elementary schools in the colony.

So it was that at the time of the British Conquest in 1760, a complete network of schools was well-entrenched in Canada under the direction of the Catholic clergy.

Schools between 1760 and 1840

The nineteenth century would bring sweeping changes to the world of schooling. They were caused by the profound transformation of Western society resulting from the industrial, the American, and the French revolutions. The invention of the steam engine in England led to the development of steam-driven locomotives that revolutionized the world of transportation and commerce, and steam-driven manufacturing machines that led to the establishment of large factories that employed hundreds or thousands of employees. This translated into the growth of large manufacturing towns, with all the social, economic, political, and religious consequences that this entailed: uprooted families, large markets, increased trade, public health issues, political instability, etc. People came to realize that schooling was no longer a luxury that could be left to the offspring of the social elite. More and more people needed to be able to read, write, and perform arithmetic calculations in their rapidly changing world in order to survive and function effectively within it. Simultaneously, governments came to realize that if schools were becoming a necessity for all, they would need to become involved in regulating and funding them. Indeed, in the nineteenth century, schooling would become a major issue of public policy. Churches would no longer be left alone to provide schools as they saw fit.

The first serious effort to provide public schools was a law of 1801 creating in Lower Canada the Royal Society for the Advancement of Learning, a body entrusted with the supervision of subsidized elementary schools that would be open to all, French and English, Protestant and Catholic. Indeed, the British governing elite hoped thereby to succeed in Anglicizing and Protestantizing the French Canadian children of Lower Canada. Their efforts were doomed, however, since the law permitted the existence of private schools, a loophole of which Catholic leaders took advantage by opening a series of private parochial schools that pre-empted the founding of schools by the Royal Society.

In 1820, much remained to be done in Lower Canada. Only 4,000 out of an estimated 70,000 eligible school-age children attended school, half of them in some 100 church-run schools, the other half divided between twenty-five private schools and thirty-seven Royal Society schools. Then, in 1824, new legislation allowed parish priests to run elementary schools. By 1830, sixty-eight of them were founded, thereby reinforcing the presence of the church in education. By then, however, new lay initiatives in the legislative assembly of Lower Canada had led to the adoption of the *Assembly Schools Act* in 1829, a measure intended to thwart church control over education by authorizing the creation of elementary schools under the authority of the legislative assembly and the direct supervision of trustees elected in each parish. Despite the resistance of Catholic leaders, the new law led to the creation of hundreds of new schools, a total of 1,200 by 1836 when the law expired and was not renewed, much to the relief of the bishops. Indeed, during the 1830s, the number of schools was growing by leaps and bounds, the number of pupils enrolled multiplying tenfold. In Lower Canada, the Catholic Church was determined to continue to play a major role in schooling and to restrict as much as possible the influence of its lay rivals.

The immigration of Euro-Canadians to Upper Canada was of much more recent vintage, the vast majority of settlers having arrived after the founding of the colony in 1791. Their numbers were growing rapidly, however, to the point of surpassing the population of Lower Canada by 1851 when the new colony on the Great Lakes had 952,004 inhabitants compared to 890,261 in the downriver colony.

Although in 1797 the first lieutenant-governor of Upper Canada, John Graves Simcoe had foreseen the founding of major school facilities in his infant colony, it was not until 1807 that the first significant school legislation was passed by the legislature of Upper Canada. Consistent with the class consciousness of the governing elite of the time, the purpose of this first school law was to facilitate the founding of grammar schools in each of the districts of Upper Canada. Grammar schools were a kind of secondary school that charged tuition fees and were open to boys only. They were founded in the leading towns of the colony, and were intended to provide schooling to the children of the colony's governing political, commercial, military, and social elite. Registered pupils varied in age between five and seventeen years; the school year lasted ten months, and the teacher was usually a minister of the Church of England. Although eight such schools were founded in 1807, grammar schools never became popular. In fact, by 1829 when the population of Upper Canada had surpassed 200,000, only eleven grammar schools were in existence with a total enrollment of 280 pupils, most of who were still engaged in the elementary tasks of learning to read and write, or learning grammar and arithmetic. By 1838, grammar school enrollment increased slightly to 311 pupils.

In Upper Canada, government support for a general system of elementary schools began with legislation in 1816, creating common schools. By 1830, some 400 common schools were in existence, and by 1838 they enrolled 20,000 pupils, some 50% of the school-age children of Upper Canada. These numbers notwithstanding, the government of Upper Canada continued to discriminate in favour of the social elite's grammar schools by funding the latter at a rate of $18 per pupil, while granting a mere $2 per pupil to common schools.

Until 1840, in the colonies that would become Canada, no child was required to attend school at any time, and schools were at best available to less than half of school-age children. Whatever schools existed did so in inequitably varied forms, levels, and quality. Private unregulated and unsubsidized schools existed alongside government-subsidized ones. There were no controls over the qualifications of teachers. In fact, just about anyone could open and run a school in Canada, providing the aspiring teacher succeeded in convincing parents to enroll their children and to pay the fees. A school could open or close at any time, depending on the whim, availability, or health of the teacher. It was in such a context that a number of churches, the Catholic and the Anglican in particular, provided a measure of institutional stability, reliability, and responsible teaching to the developing school systems of the colonies. Indeed, while the governments exercised practically no control over schools, the Catholic and Anglican churches did. Therefore, it was not surprising that by 1840 the Catholic Church and the Church of England occupied positions of leadership in the schools of Canada.

The revolution in schools during the 1840s

Rebellions in Lower and Upper Canada in 1837 and 1838 led to the appointment of John George Lambton, first Count of Durham as governor-general. After less than six months in Canada (27 May to 1 November 1838), he returned to England armed with the reports of several commissions of inquiry into Canadian affairs. The inquiry into education was conducted by Arthur Buller, the brother of Lambton's personal secretary. In his report issued in January-February 1839, in addition to favouring the granting of responsible government to Canada, Lambton recommended the union of the Canadas in order to obtain, among other things, the Anglicization of the French Canadians. It was also with this in mind that he recommended the establishment of a system of English-language public schools. While favouring religious teaching in the schools, Lambton's report did not allow clergy to hold any powers of inspection or supervision of schools. He recommended compulsory taxation for the support of schools and the appointment of a general superintendent of schools.

Upon the union of the Canadas in 1841, the legislature of the Province of Canada adopted a school bill during its first session; it was given royal assent by Governor Sydenham on 18 September 1841. The new *Education Act* created the position of superintendent of education for the united country, supported by two assistant-superintendents, one each for Canada East and Canada West. During the committee debate on the bill, spokesmen for the Protestant minority of Lower Canada had obtained an amendment that allowed the confessional minority (Catholic or Protestant) of any school district to elect its own school trustees and to establish its own school that would be distinct from the school of the majority in that district. The added clause protected the Protestant minority in Canada East from the feared domination by the Catholic majority. However, given the new constitutional unity of the country, the same law applied to Upper Canada, thereby allowing their Catholic minority to establish minority confessional schools. All of these schools, whether of the majority or of the minority in a given school district, were common schools which were subsidized by public funds.

So it was that the *Education Act* of 1841 established in both sections of the Province of Canada a dual stream of government-funded schools: one stream was made up of the schools of the majority of the people in a school district, while the other stream consisted of the schools of the confessional minority in school districts where this same minority wanted a distinct school. Both were common schools. The irony was that this legal permission to establish a minority confessional school alongside the school of the majority in a given district, obtained by the Protestants of Lower Canada, was primarily invoked by the Catholics of Upper Canada, while the Protestants of Lower Canada felt no need to avail themselves of it. Indeed, this minority-school clause of the *Education Act,* 1841 would prove to be the cornerstone of the Catholic separate school system in Ontario.

During the first years of implementation of the new legislation, it soon became apparent that the school systems of Canada East and Canada West would evolve in different directions. While the chief superintendent of education for the Province of Canada became a mere figurehead, the deputy-superintendent for Canada East became the head of a system that was openly confessional. Indeed, all agreed that the schools of Canada East should be either Catholic or Protestant. A dual confessional system was soon enshrined in law, a system that stood until the end of the twentieth century. In 1996 the Province of Québec made school boards nonconfessional. Five years later, the same was done to the schools themselves.

In Canada West, it was the school system described in the law of 1841 that was established. Its leading artisan was the Reverend Egerton Ryerson (1803–1882), a Methodist minister who had distinguished himself for twenty years as a polemicist and pamphleteer in various public debates in Upper Canada. Appointed by Governor Metcalfe as deputy-superintendent (1844) and then superintendent (1846) of education for Canada West, Ryerson designed a system of schools founded on the premise that they should be accessible to all the school-age children in the colony. The system would be directed from Toronto. It was understood that these common schools would be Christian.

Public and confessional schools in Canada after 1850

Public schools

The term *public school* designates a school subsidized by public funds, and regulated by government, while a *private school* is not subsidized or regulated by government, other than being required to satisfy some basic educational requirements of provincial law. Before 1871, what we call a public school was known as a *common* school. Public schools can be either nonconfessional or confessional. As noted above, in the past Canada's public schools have usually been confessional and Christian, although several claimed to be nonconfessional. Today, most public schools make every effort to remain neutral in matters of religion. Among Canada's

Fig. 14.   The Reverend Egerton Ryerson.[1] National Archives of Canada, c-014235.

officially confessional public schools, the vast majority have been Roman Catholic, most Protestants being satisfied with the public schools that were open to all, but were in fact largely Christian-Protestant in orientation and spirit. However, in the provinces of Québec and Newfoundland, as was the case in Manitoba between 1870 and 1891, all public schools were confessional, either Catholic or Protestant, until 2001. Thereafter they were defined by language. In Ontario, in the spirit of the law of 1841, there exists a dual public school system, one *general* (the public school) and one *particular* (the separate school); with few exceptions, the latter is Roman Catholic.

    Between 1850 and 1960, the vast majority of schools in Canada, whether public, separate, private, elementary, secondary, or post-secondary, were confessional schools. Given the small numbers of Canadians of religions other than Christian, this meant that schools were usually Christian.

The main reason for this religious homogeneity was primarily the homogeneous nature of the population of the various provinces of Canada from the mid-nineteenth to the mid-twentieth centuries. Although a handful of Canadians belonged to religions other than Christianity, Jews and Chinese for example, Canadians were overwhelmingly either Protestant or Catholic and expected their subsidized schools to reflect their religious faith. This is why public schools were either Catholic or Protestant, or claimed to be non-denominational or non-sectarian while holding opening exercises or Bible readings drawn from the Christian tradition. Religious minorities simply had to make do either by enrolling in these schools and avoiding their explicitly religious teaching, or by establishing private schools at their own expense.

A second reason for the general Christian homogeneity of the schools was the ongoing militant evangelizing by the Christian churches, Catholic and Protestant, from the mid-nineteenth to the mid-twentieth centuries. With their growing institutional and clerical strength, the churches were gathering a growing percentage of Canadians into their pews, and making Christian understanding more and more pervasive. By the turn of the twentieth century, Canada's Catholic and Protestant churches had made significant gains in their distinct but similar campaigns to transform the Dominion of Canada into the Dominion of the Lord, and schools were key instruments in this enterprise. As the churches flexed their new-found muscle in a wide range of social areas (see Chapter 16), Canadians seldom thought of challenging them. The Christian view of reality appeared fully satisfactory and true. After all, what were the alternatives?

A third reason for the pervasive Christianity in Canada's schools was the heritage of confessional education in Canada and Europe. By the turn of the twentieth century, Christian educators could point to a millennium of confessional education in the Western world. As noted earlier, monks, friars, and clergy had founded schools and universities in the Middle Ages, while nuns, sisters, priests, and ministers had been the leading agents of schooling in Canada from the seventeenth to the nineteenth centuries. Such deep historical roots made for a strong sense of purpose and dedication in Canadian schools built on the foundation of Christian evangelism.

A fourth reason for the pervasive Christianity of Canada's schools was the diverse forms of confessionalism that they stood for. Indeed, some of Canada's public schools practised a hard-edged confessionalism in that they were officially Roman Catholic, Anglican, or other, and always endeavoured to be true to their denominational identity. These schools usually accepted pupils who did not belong to their denomination, but schooled them like all the others, in the hope of gaining their adhesion to their church. Examples of such explicitly confessional school systems were the separate schools of Ontario, the Protestant and Catholic public schools of Québec, or the various denominational schools of Newfoundland.

Many of Canada's public schools practised a much softer form of confessionalism. This was generally true of the general public school systems of most of Canada's provinces other than Québec and Newfoundland. Modelled on the Ontario public school system that had been built by Egerton Ryerson, these public systems were intended not so much to be nonconfessional, but rather to be non-denominational. The pervasive Christian ethos of their communities and pupils was obvious and taken for granted, just as it had been by Ryerson, and the government-led school system did not question it. Instead, it strove not to alienate or offend any particular Christian, regardless of the denomination to which he or she belonged. So it was that in many of these schools Bible readings, opening exercises, or the teaching of moral values reflected Christian teachings, but teachers would be at pains not to be identified with any particular denominational tradition. While the curriculum of these public schools did not include religious instruction, provincial legislation allowed ministers of various churches and religions to visit the schools after school hours and to teach such classes to pupils whose parents requested it.

During the twentieth century, most Canadians had a choice in the religious orientation of the public schools available to their children. In Québec and Newfoundland,[2] they could avail themselves of explicitly Catholic or Protestant public schools.[3] In Ontario, Saskatchewan, and Alberta, albeit in varying degrees, Catholics could enroll their children in Catholic schools, while all residents had a general public school system at their disposal. In Manitoba, Nova Scotia, New Brunswick, and Prince Edward Island, the public school systems were officially neutral, but each government negotiated compromise solutions with Catholics whereby Catholic schools were funded unofficially. In fact, the only province that maintained an exclusively secular public school system from the outset was British Columbia. Even there, however, provincial authorities agreed in 1977 to fund religious as well as secular or neutral private schools.

Indeed, it was a well-established tradition in Canada to have the state and the church cooperate in matters of education. Although the arrangements varied from province to province, some kind of compromise arrangement usually prevailed between provincial education officials and their province's leading religious groups, a compromise that made it possible to have both secular and religious public schools available. In addition, during the last quarter of the twentieth century, provincial governments showed more and more willingness to fund private schools partially, religious or otherwise. This resulted from the realization that Canadian parents attributed considerable importance to religious values in the education of their children.

Separate schools

The term *separate school* first appeared in the legislation of the Province of Canada in 1843; it designated those common (public) schools that were *separate* from those of the majority because of religious considerations. These separate schools developed in subsequent years in Canada West, the former Upper Canada and the future Ontario, as well as in Manitoba, Alberta, and Saskatchewan.

In 1849 there were more Anglican than Catholic separate schools in Canada West, but during the 1850s the number of Catholic separate schools grew rapidly primarily because of the growing polarization between Catholics and Protestants in the province. Then, in 1855, legislation restricted the right to found a separate school to Catholics only, most Protestants being content to support the public school of their community, and foregoing their right to a public denominational school. Although successive governments of Ontario repeatedly tried to thwart the development of their province's separate school system, the latter enjoyed the legal protection of the *British North America Act, 1867*, which had established Confederation. In recent years, as a result of changing mentalities and a growing percentage of Catholics in the population of Ontario (35.5% in 1991), the government of Ontario has begun to treat the Ontario separate school system, its *particular* public schools, in the same manner as the province's *general* public school system. Indeed, beginning in 1985, the government of Ontario extended full funding (up to the end of secondary school) to separate schools, changed its funding policies to make them more equitable to both separate and public schools, and has generally endeavoured to treat both systems fairly. At the turn of the twenty-first century, Ontario has, in both fact and theory, a dual public school system whose two streams are treated equitably by the provincial government.

The separate schools that were founded by the new provinces of Alberta and Saskatchewan in 1905 resulted from both the regional history of the Territories from which the provinces had been carved and from the Ontario model. Although the legislation regulating Alberta and Saskatchewan separate schools varies in some respects from that of Ontario, in effect all three provinces offer their Catholic residents the opportunity to have their children educated in Catholic schools that exist alongside *general* public schools.

In the three provinces where they exist, separate schools are distinct from *general* public schools in the Catholic religious instruction that is part of their curriculum and in the policies and spirit of the Catholic school boards that manage them, policies that conform to the teachings of the Catholic Church. Nevertheless, separate schools come under the jurisdiction of their respective provincial ministries of education and must abide by their ministries' educational, financial, administrative, and other requirements and directives, just as any *general* public school does. Separate schools in Ontario, Alberta, and Saskatchewan are public schools that have the distinction of being Catholic rather than neutral in their teaching and spirit.

Recent developments in public and separate schools

In recent years, public opinion and the courts have forced Canada's public education systems to clarify or change their confessional status. Invoking the Canadian Charter of Rights and Freedoms (1982), in 1990 the Ontario Court of Appeal ruled that no Ontario public school, as distinct from a separate school, could favour any religion or indulge in any proselytism or religious indoctrination, either in its teaching or in its opening exercises. This led the Ontario ministry of education to change its policies on both opening exercises and education about religion in schools. The Ontario curriculum at both the elementary and secondary levels may now include courses of education about religions, but no proselytism or indoctrination. For the first time, nearly 150 years after its founding, the Ontario public school system is required to be religiously neutral in its curriculum and activities. It was noted above that both the governments of Newfoundland and Québec have now transformed their confessional public school systems into religiously-neutral ones, with optional confessional education for those parents who want it.

At the beginning of this twenty-first century, the renewed attention given to the confessional status of schools is also forcing many confessional schools, separate schools for example, to reexamine their curriculum, practices, and policies with a view to better defining their educational purpose. How does a *particular* public school like a Catholic separate school distinguish itself from a *general* public school? Does it suffice to offer Catholic religious instruction in the school? If not, what else? Are Catholic teachers adequately trained? To what extent should the Catholic school reflect the teaching of the Catholic Church, Canada's bishops, the Catholic community? These and other questions are forcing many to reflect long and hard on the nature and quality of an institution that many have long taken for granted.

Members of other faith communities are also challenging the education policies of several provincial governments in matters of religion. As *general* public schools become in fact neutral, and as Catholics fine-tune the religious education in separate schools, members of other faith communities are establishing numbers of private confessional schools that are specific to their religion or denomination. Protestants of various persuasions – Jews, Muslims, Hindus, and many others – are benefitting from more favourable financial support for private schools from many provincial governments. Many question the fairness of the historical and constitutional status quo in Canada whereby Catholics frequently enjoy publicly-funded schools, while other faith communities do not. Some provinces such as Ontario have adopted a voucher system that allows residents to deduct from their school taxes a portion of the cost of supporting a confessional school. Others such as Alberta have authorized charter schools, schools that are governed by their own board of directors in conformity with a provincial charter particular to that individual school. Such schools are more autonomous than regular public schools, and may include religious education in their curriculum.

The education of women

Girls' access and opportunities in schools, confessional or not, reflected the status of women in society at large. As long as women were considered wards of their husbands and inferior to men in society, they suffered various forms of discrimination such as the inability to vote, the lack of access to universities, the legal inability when married to hold property in their own name, etc. At the turn of the twentieth century, Canada was changing from a primarily agricultural and rural society into an industrial and urban one. This resulted in a series of economic and social changes in Canadian society that had a direct impact on the status of women. Factors such as industrial production, large urban populations, increased trade and communications, wars, smaller families, and a developing feminist movement led a growing number of women to question their all-too-frequent second-class status in society. This led, during the second half of the twentieth century, to major changes in the place of women in Canadian society, a revolution that has already had a profound impact on our way of life, including the life of our faith communities.

Generally speaking, Christian churches and other faith communities reflected this changing status of women in society at large, as did the schools. Girls had always had access to schools in Canada; the schools of the Ursulines and Sisters of Notre Dame in early Canada provide a fine example. However, since the role of women in society was understood to be primarily that of wives, mothers, and homemakers, the curriculum in girls' schools, once the basic reading, writing, arithmetic, and religious instruction had been assured, revolved around the skills required by the wife, mother, and homemaker. Girls were taught to sew, to knit, to care for children, etc. Once they had learned these skills, they were expected to marry and raise a family. They were not offered the more advanced courses that were required for further study or for professional careers in commerce, industry, and the sciences. Women were not expected to pursue careers in business or the professions; they were not admitted to universities, at least not until the late nineteenth century. The same social discrimination was endemic in the churches where women frequently engaged in important supportive roles, as the sisters did, for example, but were barred from all positions of leadership, positions that usually required ordination, which was forbidden to women.

During the second half of the twentieth century, as women achieved equality in society at large, they also achieved equality of opportunity in education. As the full range of social occupations opened to them, women also had access to all the available school programs. Again, the various faith communities reflected these changes, most of them promoting women to various positions of leadership, including ordination to the ministry. In this latter case, notable exceptions are the Catholic

Church, Canada's largest church, and the Orthodox Church. Both still refuse to ordain women to the ministry.

Finally, it must be noted that as the status of women changed in Canadian society and Canadian schools during the twentieth century, people's attitudes and stereotypes about women also changed. The earlier restricted and second-class place of women in society had been reinforced and rationalized by value-judgements and stereotypes to the effect that women were physically, emotionally, and intellectually weaker than men. Such stereotypes were demonstrated to be patently false and unfounded as women assumed their full and equal place in society. Such changes in social values were also reflected in the schools of Canada.

Colleges and universities

Until the major social and cultural revolution in Canada during the 1960s, Canada's colleges and universities were more often than not founded by churches and churchmen. They were confessional, that is to say owned and operated by specific Christian churches, and dedicated to the advancement of the interests of the particular church which sponsored them. It was only during the last third of the twentieth century that the confessional ties of most of Canada's colleges and universities were severed.

True to the tradition of their medieval predecessors, it was clergy who founded Canada's first colleges and universities. One year before the founding of the U.S.A.'s first post-secondary institution, Harvard College (1636), the Jesuits opened the *Collège de Québec* (1635) which offered secondary school and collegiate training until its closure in the late 1750s during the Seven Years' War. The *Collège de Québec* was soon accompanied by the *Séminaire de Québec* (1663) established by Bishop Laval for the theological training of candidates for the priesthood. The *Séminaire* is still in operation today; as noted earlier, in 1766 it extended its program of studies to include the curriculum formerly offered by the defunct *Collège de Québec*. After nearly 200 years in existence, the venerable *Séminaire* was chartered as Laval University in 1852, the first French-language university in Canada.

Although the town of Windsor, Nova Scotia, was the site of Canada's first English-language college, King's College (1789), the founding of all other post-secondary institutions followed the War of 1812–1814.

Table 14.1   Leading Colleges and Universities of Canada (1635–1960)

Name	Location	Founded	Original religious affiliation
Collège de Québec	Québec, QC	1635	Catholic
Séminaire de Québec	Québec, QC	1663	Catholic
King's College	Windsor, NS	1789	Anglican
Dalhousie University	Halifax, NS	1818	Nondenominational/ Presbyterian
McGill University	Montréal, QC	1821	Nondenominational/ Anglican
King's/Trinity College	Toronto, ON	1827/1851	Anglican
King's College/University of New Brunswick	Fredericton, NB	1828, 1859	Anglican/Non-denominational
Acadia University	Wolfville, NS	1838	Baptist
Mount Allison University	Sackville, NB	1839	Methodist
Victoria College	Cobourg, ON	1841	Methodist
Queen's University	Kingston, ON	1841	Presbyterian
Bishop's University	Lennoxville, QC	1843	Anglican
University of Ottawa	Ottawa, ON	1848	Catholic
University of Toronto	Toronto, ON	1850	Secular
Saint Michael's College	Toronto, ON	1852	Catholic
Assumption College/ University of Windsor	Windsor, ON	1857, 1962	Catholic
Huron College/University of Western Ontario	London, ON	1863/1878	Anglican
Saint Francis Xavier University	Antigonish, NS	1866	Catholic
Université de Montréal	Montréal, QC	1876, 1920	Catholic
University of Manitoba	Winnipeg, MB	1877	Nondenominational
McMaster University	Hamilton, ON	1887, 1930	Baptist
University of Alberta	Edmonton, AB	1906	Secular
University of Saskatchewan	Saskatoon, SK	1907	Secular
University of British Columbia	Vancouver, BC	1908	Secular
Memorial University of Newfoundland	St John's, NF	1925, 1949	Secular
Université de Sherbrooke	Sherbrooke, QC	1954	Catholic
Laurentian University	Sudbury, ON	1960	Secular

The strong Christian denominational ties of Canada's colleges and universities are apparent in the above table which does not include a number of smaller denominational colleges in all regions of the country. Indeed, of the seventeen degree-granting institutions in Canada at the time of Confederation (1867), only four (Dalhousie University, the University of New Brunswick, McGill University, and the University of Toronto) had an official non-denominational basis, albeit a rather weak one given the strong and pervasive presence of various churches in these institutions. Moreover, several of the secular universities were in fact made up of a number of federated church colleges. This was the case for the University of Toronto which included then as now several federated denominational institutions such as Trinity University (Anglican), the University of Saint Michael's College (Catholic), Victoria University (United Church), Knox College (Presbyterian), etc. It was also the case for the University of Manitoba which in its early years encompassed the *Collège de Saint-Boniface* (Catholic), St John's College (Anglican), Manitoba College (Presbyterian), and Wesley College (Methodist). Subsequently other colleges were added. Other secular universities such as the University of Alberta and the University of British Columbia did likewise, resulting in a post-secondary network of institutions that had very close ties with the Christian churches.

It was only in the 1960s that these strong Christian denominational ties of Canada's universities would weaken or be severed. The rapid expansion of university education and its associated costs after World War II drove most Christian denominations to seek government subsidies for their post-secondary institutions. However, in the 1960s, most provincial governments would only agree to subsidize post-secondary institutions that were free of any control by religions or churches. As a result, many of Canada's Christian colleges and universities were compelled either to close their doors because of their inability to finance their growing institutions, or to abandon their denominational connection to become eligible for government funding. One example of the latter case is the Catholic University of Ottawa, which was secularized in 1965, its Catholic faculties becoming Saint Paul University, a distinct and autonomous university. The latter remained ineligible for equal provincial funding until 1997. Another example is Laurentian University founded in 1960 as a federation of the Catholic Université de Sudbury (1913, 1957), the United Church's Huntington University (1960), and the Anglican Thorneloe University (1963).

By the late twentieth century, many of Canada's denominational post-secondary institutions limited their academic programs to professional training for workers in their particular churches, or to programs that were specific to their church interests, such as theology, canon law, pastoral counseling, or spirituality. The wide range of other academic programs in the humanities, social sciences, pure and applied sciences, and professions were left to the government-funded universities of the country. Canada's churches which played a dominant role in establishing and developing post-secondary education in Canada were now content or compelled to devote their diminishing resources to much more limited objectives.

The education of Canada's Amerindians

The education of Amerindian children in Canada, the process whereby they learned the values, knowledge, and skills necessary in their adult life, had always taken place by a process of observation and practice, by listening to the counsel and teaching of parents and elders, and by participating in traditional feasts, ceremonies, and rituals.

Since the early seventeenth century, this oral and communal form of education had been supplemented by schools organized by Canadians of European origin. Canada's Amerindian children always had considerable difficulty in adjusting to the schools established by the latter, not only because the organization, curriculum, pedagogy, spirit, and discipline of these schools were foreign to them, but also because these schools usually had as a primary objective the thorough-going assimilation of the Amerindians to white Canadian Christian civilization. Indeed, with few exceptions, the schools that were made available to Canada's Amerindians usually had as an explicit objective to 'civilize' and 'Christianize' the Amerindian pupils, both terms being understood as interchangeable.

Over the four centuries of the white presence in Canada, Amerindian children received instruction in two basic types of schools, namely day schools and residential schools. Day schools were located near the place of residence of the children, who lived at home and only attended the school during designated hours. Residential schools were farther removed from the children's place of residence, and were of two basic types: the boarding school and the industrial school. The latter, the industrial school, is one specific type of residential school, one that existed from 1883 to the late 1960s and was subsidized by the government of Canada while being run by various churches, particularly the Catholic Church, the Anglican Church of Canada, the United Church of Canada, and the Presbyterian Church of Canada. All residential schools that were not designated by the government of Canada as industrial schools were known as boarding schools. Residential schools for Amerindian children came to an end in the 1960s, at a time when curricula in federally-run schools were being modelled on those of provincially-run schools; this was also the eve of the Amerindian people's taking over control of the schools of their children.

During the French régime, it was residential schools that were occasionally provided by the various missionary congregations such as the *Récollets*, the Ursulines, and the Capuchins. Usually, these schools only lasted a few years before disappearing for lack of Amerindian pupils. In response to government pressures to do more to assimilate Amerindian children, Sister Marie de l'Incarnation, the superior of the Ursuline Sisters in Québec wrote in 1668 that they had barely succeeded in 'civilizing' one Amerindian girl out of one hundred in their school at Québec in spite of a quarter-century of sustained effort.[4] In fact, the very limited number of Europeans in Canada during the 150 years of the French régime allowed Amerindians to persevere in their traditional lifestyle largely unobstructed. Only a handful of Amerindian children were exposed to schools.

During the seventy years that followed the cession of Canada to Great Britain (1760–1830), little was done by anyone to establish schools for Amerindian children. It was only after the British Crown's responsibility for Canada's Amerindians was transferred from the armed forces to civilian officials in 1830, a time when growing numbers of new immigrants were arriving in Canada, that colonial authorities showed a renewed interest in providing schooling for Amerindian children. This was also the time when Christian churches, Catholic and Protestant, were exercising new missionary zeal; Catholic, Anglican, Methodist, and Presbyterian missionaries, lay and ordained, began to appear in growing numbers in Canada, fanning out to evangelize the most distant reaches of Upper Canada and the immense Hudson's Bay Company lands in the North and West. Once the missionary had built his cabin and his chapel, his next priority was usually to establish a school.

Beginning in 1830, it was again the residential school that was preferred by the churches. In cooperation with the government, by 1900 no less than sixty-four church-run residential schools were established, including twenty-two industrial schools and forty-two boarding schools. This was in addition to 226 day schools funded by the federal government. During these years, the schooling of Amerindian pupils was further complicated by the new constitution of Canada (*The British North America Act*) that came into force in 1867. Thereafter, Canada's Amerindian people were divided into two categories with very different rights. While the government of Canada inherited the British Crown's responsibility for the Amerindians who had negotiated or would in the

Fig. 15.   Boarding school at the Catholic mission at Fort Resolution in the Northwest Territories in 1936.[5] Canada. Department of the Interior. National Archives of Canada, PA-042122.

Fig. 16.   Boys' class in carpentry at Sir Wilfred Grenfell's mission school at St Anthony on the northern tip of Newfoundland in 1906.[6] National Archives of Canada, c-023561.

future negotiate treaties with the Crown (status Amerindians), education rights included, the provinces of Canada became responsible for the education of all people within their boundaries, including the Amerindians who had never negotiated treaties (non-status Amerindians), the Inuit, and the Métis. Given that none of the latter had special treaty rights, their education came under the same jurisdiction as all other Canadians, namely their particular provincial government.

By the latter part of the nineteenth century, the schools that were available to Canada's Amerindian children were either private schools run by the churches, particularly the Catholic and the Anglican, or public schools run by either the provincial/territorial governments as part of their public schools network, or by the federal government. After 1830, a series of treaties were negotiated by various Amerindian nations and bands and the federal government. While the earlier treaties covered tribes and lands in Upper Canada, beginning in the 1870s most treaties covered Amerindian people and lands in today's Prairie provinces, Yukon, and Northwest Territories including today's Nunavut. A number of these treaties committed the federal government to provide schools for Amerindian children.

Pressed to provide more and better schools for Amerindian children, the government of Canada chose to subsidize and regulate established church-run schools, rather than establish new ones. This was not only cheaper, but it allowed the government to take advantage of the experienced teaching staff already in place in the church-run school network. Although this government subsidizing of church-run schools for Amerindians had been taking place since the 1830s, it was accelerated after 1880 because of the growing number of treaties that committed the government to provide schools in the Northwest. This was when the type of residential school known as an *industrial school* was founded, a school built and maintained at government expense, but staffed and run by the various churches.

The government-subsidized schools followed a curriculum set by the government; most of the residential schools, whether industrial schools or mere boarding schools, required their pupils to study for only half-days; they were required to work to support the school during the other half of the day. This meant that the Amerindian child enrolled in a residential school devoted only half his or her time to studying and learning. The rest of the time the boys worked in the fields or in the barn, cut firewood, or assisted in the maintenance of the establishment; the girls cooked, sewed, cleaned, etc. Over a period of years, the pupil in a residential school was only offered half the learning that a pupil received in a regular public school. The half-day system rested on the presupposition that Amerindian children would be returning to their communities and would need the practical skills of farming, woodworking, etc. It also resulted from the fact that these schools were perennially under-funded by governments; therefore, the schools needed the labour of the children to make ends meet.

In all the schools for Amerindian children that were staffed and run by the churches, religious instruction and proselytism were an important part of the program. Pupils were required to attend the religious exercises that were offered, were given religious instruction, and were expected to abide by the moral code of the particular church that ran the establishment. In retrospect, the most reprehensible aspect of the residential school experience for Amerindian children was the unabashed assimilationist purpose of these schools. From the mid-nineteenth century, Amerindian parents, much like their Canadian peers, realized that schooling was necessary for their children in the developing industrial society around them. This was why they obtained school commitments by the federal government in the treaties.

They had not bargained, however, for the assimilationist program of Canadian society. Rather than help the Amerindians establish and run their own schools, as is done currently, the government of Canada and the Christian churches conspired to establish schools whose purpose was to assimilate the Amerindian child, to take the Amerindian out of the child, and to transform him or her into an ersatz Canadian Christian. This was a primary reason why both churches and governments preferred to build residential schools, rather than day schools. Indeed, the residential schools were far removed from the Amerindians' place of residence, thereby forcing the child to be cut off from family and community influences for most of the year. Moreover, in some schools, the Amerindian child was forbidden to use his native language or to wear native dress, while all too many Canadian staff denigrated the child's culture and heritage. English was the only permissible idiom in the school. In fact, all of the familial, communal, and social supports of the Amerindian child's identity were removed from him or her during stay in residential schools. Is it any wonder that residential schools frequently left a bitter harvest of frustration, anger, self-depreciation, and despondency?

During these hundred years from the mid-nineteenth to the mid-twentieth centuries, Canadian society sincerely felt that theirs was *the best* civilization and the leading culture in the world, while the cultures of aboriginal people were perceived as backward, inferior, and destined for extinction. Euro-Canadians also truly believed that Christianity was the best, and only, true religion; Amerindian spiritualities were therefore to be eradicated wherever they were found. This was the arrogance of Canada's evangelical crusaders, both Catholic and Protestant. In pursuing their assimilationist program, most government and church agents felt that they were working in the best interests of the Amerindian people themselves. Like many assimilationists the world over, they had convinced themselves that they could best serve the Amerindians by removing their 'Amerindianness.' These benevolent crusaders rarely distinguished between Amerindian cultures and Amerindian spiritualities, dimensions of reality that are in fact difficult to distinguish from one another.

By the late nineteenth century, many of Canada's Amerindian people had been driven into reservations established by the treaties. This opened up most of the land of the North and West to white settlement. This was also the time when the government of Canada, aided and abetted by the churches, undertook to restrict or ban certain Amerindian rituals and ceremonies that were perceived as incompatible with Canadian ways. In 1884, the Potlatch, a 'give-away' feast of the Northwest Coast Amerindians was banned. As noted earlier, gift-giving was central in Amerindian cultures because that was the way Amerindian people expressed their intentions, sealed their alliances, redistributed their goods, and established their importance in the community. Among Northwest Coast Amerindians, the Potlatch was such a feast where the convener and host would give away everything he had, gaining in return prestige and status in his tribe. However, in the eyes of missionaries and government agents, these feasts were occasions for drunkenness, diverse moral abuses, and the impoverishment of the host who thereafter became an indigent. A feast of similar importance for Plains Amerindians, the Sun Dance, was effectively banned in 1895 when certain ceremonial endurance feats that were part of these summer festivals were prohibited. Then in 1906, this ban was extended to include several other Amerindian dances; in 1914, further government regulations banned all dances in Amerindian costumes. In the meantime, some had been endeavouring to have a ban imposed on totem poles.

Although such government directives were not always abided by and many Amerindians continued to dance and celebrate in secret, it is nevertheless clear that through the agency of the government of Canada,

Canadian society was trying to stop the songs, dances, and celebrations that were central to sustaining the cooperation and reciprocity that were the foundations of the sense of community in Amerindian villages. One culture was trying to crush the other.

So it was that while the Christian churches were major players in the schooling of Amerindian children in Canada, their Christian apostolic mission was frequently obscured by the veil of cultural assimilationist policies which the churches shared with the governments. Amerindian people are therefore divided and torn in their assessments of the role of the Christian churches in their history. While they acknowledged that the churches frequently provided them with much-needed schools and devoted teachers and missionaries, and this at times when no one else did, they profoundly regretted that this religious and cultural outreach was poisoned by a cultural and ideological agenda that in its arrogance brooked no variations or dissent.

Conclusion

During most of their four hundred years of history, Canada's schools have been confessional, that is to say either run or strongly influenced by specific Christian churches. These confessional schools have always been found in both the private and public school networks. Public schools in Canada have been and are confessional, semi-confessional, or nonconfessional. The latter category, the nonconfessional or religiously neutral school, has been rare in the past, given the homogeneous Christian character of Canadian society. The nonconfessional school has become much more widespread in the last third of the twentieth century as the Canadian Charter of Rights and Freedoms has been interpreted as not permitting religious proselytism or indoctrination in any public school that is not officially confessional.

Canada's universities, most of which had been founded by the Christian churches, began to evolve towards religious neutrality much sooner. Although some secular universities were founded in the nineteenth century, they usually existed in fact in their confessional affiliated colleges. In the late twentieth century, however, most universities became secular, having abandoned any confessional ties. Contrary to what was normative in the past, it is now the confessional colleges and universities in Canada that are in the minority.

Confessional schooling at all levels made a major contribution to the education of Canadians from the beginning of Canadian settlement. Although much controversy is still associated with the role of the churches in the schooling of Amerindian children, few would deny the foundational importance of the Christian churches in the schooling of successive generations of Canadians during the past four hundred years.

Suggested readings

Barman, Jean et al. Eds. *Amerindian Education in Canada*. 2 vols. Vancouver: University of British Columbia Press, 1986, 1987.

Choquette, Robert. *Language and Religion. A History of English-French Conflict in Ontario*. Ottawa: University of Ottawa Press, 1975.

Crunican, Paul. *Priests and Politicians: Manitoba Schools and the Election of 1896*. Toronto: University of Toronto Press, 1974.

Dumont, Micheline and Nadia Fahmy-Eid. *Les couventines. L'éducation des filles au Québec dans les congrégations religieuses enseignantes, 1840–1960*. Montréal: Boréal, 1986.

Galarneau, Claude. *Les collèges classiques au Canada français*. Montréal: Fides, 1978.

Gauvreau, Michael. *The Evangelical Century: College and Creed in English Canada from the Great Revival to the Great Depression*. Montréal & Kingston: McGill-Queen's University Press, 1991.

Lupul, Manoly. *The Roman Catholic Church and the North-West School Question: A Study in Church-State Relations in Western Canada*. Toronto: University of Toronto Press, 1974.

Magnuson, Roger. *Education in New France*. Montréal & Kingston: McGill-Queen's University Press, 1992.

Masters, D.C. *Protestant Church Colleges in Canada: A History*. Toronto: University of Toronto Press, 1966.

Shook, Laurence K. *Catholic Post-secondary Education in English-speaking Canada. A History*. Toronto: University of Toronto Press, 1971.

Sissons, C.B. *Church and State in Canadian Education: An Historical Study*. Toronto: Ryerson Press, 1959.

——. *Egerton Ryerson: His Life and Letters*. 2 vols. Toronto: Clarke Irwin, 1937–1947.

Stamp, Robert M. *The Schools of Ontario 1876–1976*. Toronto: University of Toronto Press, 1982.

Walker, Franklin A. *Catholic Education & Politics in Upper Canada*. Toronto: Federation of Catholic Education Associations of Ontario, 1955, 1976.

——. *Catholic Education and Politics in Ontario*. Toronto: Federation of Catholic Education Associations of Ontario, 1976.

Wilson J. Donald, Robert M. Stamp, and Louis-Philippe Audet. Eds. *Canadian Education: A History*. Scarborough: Prentice-Hall of Canada, 1970.

CHAPTER 15

Modernity versus Conservatism

Since the sixteenth century, modernity slowly developed as a cultural mindset in the West, to the point that it became the dominant one by the year 1900.

In the Christianity of the late nineteenth and early twentieth centuries, the primary current of evangelicalism had come to dominate the churches both Protestant and Catholic. However, Christian evangelicalism was simultaneously subdivided and buffeted by the numerous crosscurrents of holiness, millennialism, Pentecostalism, fundamentalism, and ultramontanism to name only the better known. Inevitably this crusading evangelicalism of the Christian churches clashed with modernity, because the former's primary criterion of truth was the Word of God and tradition, while the latter's was contemporary attitudes. In their fight against modernity, Christian evangelicals were driven to emphasize the traditional, the foundational, and the fundamental doctrines of their faith. I will designate this group as conservatives. At the same time, other religious believers, Jews and Amerindians for example, were also driven to react to the challenge of modernity.

The meaning of modernity

The word *modernity* can be understood in a number of ways. Basically, the word *modern* designates that which pertains to present and recent time as opposed to ancient or remote time. However, the word also pertains to the historical period that followed the Middle Ages, that is the period that began in the 1450s, the beginning of modern history. In addition, the word *modern* is used to describe attitudes and styles that are current, recent, and up-to-date, as opposed to those which are antiquated and outdated. In sum, *modernity* is simultaneously a time period and a cultural and ideological attitude that values the recent and present while denigrating the ancient, the traditional, and the customary. In the West at the turn of the twentieth century, a time of strong belief in progress, evolution, and similar values, all things modern were considered particularly good while all things traditional tended to be suspect of backwardness.

Modernity was the main challenge to conservative religion in the West at the turn of the twentieth century. All the religions of the world eventually faced the challenge of modernity, but in early twentieth-century Canada, the Christians and the Jews stood at the forefront of the battle within their own faith traditions. Indeed, a growing number of Protestants, Catholics, and Jews valued the new, the recent, and the novel in their cultures and societies, while questioning the traditional doctrines and practices of their religions. The challenge led to a polarization within each faith community, each party feeling compelled to harden its theological stance. This translated into the formation of doctrinal and theological parties within the religions, parties that frequently became new denominations or distinct associations that flew the standards of their particular belief. The conservatism that developed in reaction to modernity is sometimes designated as fundamentalism. However, the latter term usually designates the harder-edged traditionalists among the conservatives.

Modernity is the reverse side of the coin of conservatism or fundamentalism in religion. It was a cultural and ideological mindset that had grown from the sixteenth century through a series of major, indeed revolutionary, cultural, social, economic, scientific, intellectual, and political changes that had transformed Western society. From the fall of the Christian Byzantine city of Constantinople to the Muslim Turks in 1453, the customary dividing point between the medieval and modern periods, the fifteenth-century West had witnessed Gutenberg's inventions in print technology, the scandalous nadir in the morality of popes during the rule of Alexander VI (d. 1503), and the growing unrest within the Christian church that led to the Reformations of the sixteenth century. While the Protestant and Catholic Reformations transformed Christianity in the sixteenth century, world exploration led to the discovery of America by European navigators, the founding of new colonies there, and a revolution in trade and commerce that eventually transformed European society. There followed during the seventeenth century not only the growing strength of the American colonies, but the blossoming scientific and philosophical revolutions led by a brigade of intellectual giants such as René Descartes (d. 1650), Blaise Pascal (d. 1662), John Locke (d. 1679), and Isaac Newton (d. 1727). Then, during the European Enlightenment of the eighteenth century, another group of scholars and authors focused the new rationalist and empirical spotlights on the study of human beings and society. Denis Diderot (d. 1784), Voltaire (d. 1778), and Jean-Jacques Rousseau (d. 1778) led the intellectual charge against Christianity before the American Revolution (1775) and the French Revolution (1789) sounded the death knell of the traditional Christian church domination of Western society.

As the pace of change further accelerated during the nineteenth century, the modern mindset grew in strength. Ideologically, the American and French Revolutions marked the emergence of liberalism, a philosophical outlook that was grounded on the freedom of the individual person in society. Simultaneously, the industrial revolution that began in eighteenth-century England was growing into a major social phenomenon during the nineteenth century. Coupled with liberalism and the *laissez-faire* capitalism that accompanied it, the sweeping changes in industrial production and commerce led to massive social disruptions and personal misery for thousands.

This provoked a reaction among those who sought a philosophical alternative to the individualism that accompanied the liberal mindset. There emerged a variety of new philosophical doctrines founded on the acknowledgment of social responsibility for all members of society, and the recognition of minimal rights for all people, whether children, pregnant women, uneducated workers, or immigrants. Socialism, Marxism, communism, and various versions thereof all grew in importance as the nineteenth century wore on.

While the new social doctrines constituted a challenge to the Christian churches, the latter were not overly concerned given their long-standing and ongoing commitment to social work (see Chapter 16). Another face of the rampaging modernity of the nineteenth century that was of greater concern was the one that challenged Christianity's basic doctrines. Critical history, biblical criticism, evolutionary theory, and atheistic humanism all attacked some of the foundational teachings of the Christian church. So it was that the modernity that was perceived as the primary threat to the Christian churches at the turn of the twentieth century was an amalgam of many different factors that had together contributed to the progressively greater value attached to the recent, the current, the present, the new.

The meaning of Christian conservatism

While the word *conservatism* designates those evangelicals that resist modernity, the word *fundamentalism* has been understood in different ways. It was first applied to Christianity after 1910 when a group of American businessmen financed the publication of a series of twelve tracts entitled *The Fundamentals* (1909–1915), written by several leading evangelical Protestant theologians in the United States. The widely distributed booklets took issue with the liberal and modernistic tendencies in several Protestant churches, and led to the founding of the World's Christian Fundamentals Association (1919) and the eventual division of many Protestant churches into *modernist* and *fundamentalist* wings. Although they did not constitute a denomination as such, these fundamentalist Protestants created many distinct associations and parties, to the point of having many of the characteristics of a Protestant denomination. This was fundamentalism in its most specific incarnation.

Chronologically, this semi-denominational form of fundamentalism had been preceded by the development of fundamentalist doctrine during the last decades of the nineteenth century, in reaction to the growing importance of evolutionary theories and biblical criticism. This conservative Protestant reaction initially took the form of a series of Bible conferences across North America, culminating in that of Niagara-on-the-Lake in 1895 which issued a statement of belief. The latter contained what would later be referred to as the 'five points of fundamentalism.' These were: the verbal inerrancy of Scripture, the divinity of Jesus Christ, the birth of Jesus from a virgin, the physical resurrection and bodily return of Christ, and a substitutional theory of the Atonement. The latter meant that Christ had substituted himself for all other human beings in dying for their sins and recovering for them the grace of God.

These five points of doctrine became the badge of distinction of fundamentalist Protestants. Given that conservative Catholics also abided by them, although Protestants and Catholics differed on other grounds, fundamentalism in this doctrinal form was common to both. It is in this doctrinal sense that fundamentalism will be discussed in this chapter. In other words, in this book fundamentalism designates conservative Christianity with a doctrinal focus. In the latter decades of the twentieth century, a third and more sweeping meaning has been given to the word *fundamentalism*; the word was now sometimes used to describe all conservative or reactionary movements in religions, be they Islam, Buddhism, Christianity, Judaism, or others.

Compared to evangelicalism, which is a broader current of conservative Christianity, Christian conservatism or doctrinal fundamentalism is more focused, more restrictive, more conservative, more centred on doctrinal orthodoxy. In other words evangelicalism is usually understood as synonymous with conservative Protestantism, but not as sectarian as fundamentalism is. In this book, the meanings of evangelicalism, conservatism, and fundamentalism are extended to encompass both Catholicism and Protestantism. Indeed, a characteristic trait of fundamentalist Christians is their sectarianism, their belief that other Christians are traitors to the true faith. While evangelical Christians are not necessarily intolerant of other Christians, fundamentalists are. Their sectarianism is a reflection of their disenchantment with their society and their culture which they consider fundamentally corrupt and deserving of destruction. In their either/or mentality, there can be no middle ground. Whoever is not for them is necessarily against them and deserving of their full wrath. Also, fundamentalist Protestants harbour a special hatred towards Catholics, while fundamentalist Catholics, or integrists, are just as indisposed towards hard-line Protestants.

Religions divide over the issue of modernity

Protestants, Catholics, Jews, and even Amerindians divided over the issue of modernity versus tradition, because all had to come to terms with the new questions that were being put to traditional religions during the nineteenth and twentieth centuries. However, not all were to be affected in similar manner, or to the same degree.

While churches in the United States were more profoundly divided than the Canadian ones by the fight between the moderns and the conservatives in their ranks, in Canada the Baptist community experienced a protracted conflict over the issue. Canada's Catholics did likewise, but mainly from the sidelines as they observed with rapt attention an intensive doctrinal bloodletting between Pope Pius X and the Catholic Modernists in the years preceding World War I.

The story of Canada's Jews is different still. A small number of Reform Jews bent on adapting to Canadian society settled in Montréal but were outnumbered by coreligionists of Orthodox persuasion.

At the same time, Canada's Amerindians were also caught up in an internal debate between the conservatives and the modernists among them. As had been the case since the invasion of their land by the

Europeans, the Amerindians had to decide the extent of the acculturation and/or assimilation they would accept. The choice was never an easy one, considering the growing number of Euro-Canadians, the marginalization of the Amerindians by the advancing juggernaut of Canadian culture, and the real attraction that Canadian technology held for Amerindians. This led to a perpetuating and vicious cycle; the more that Amerindians acculturated, the more they lost their cultures and spiritualities. In the end, the revitalization of traditional Amerindian cultures and spiritualities would await the late twentieth century.

The Protestant reaction to modernity

The emerging conservative movement

The prevailing evangelicalism within the Protestant and Catholic churches at the turn of the twentieth century has been noted above. Within the Protestant churches of the English-speaking world, the main current of evangelicalism divided into the crosscurrents of revivalism, millennialism, holiness, Pentecostalism, and fundamentalism. In spite of their different emphases, these movements all favoured a heightened consciousness of the spiritual dimension of Christianity, the pervasive presence of the Holy Spirit, and a visceral opposition to modernity and its accompanying liberalism and secularism. In other words, each of the varied forms of evangelicalism reacted to modernity with a conservative emphasis. This translated into the emergence of a conservative evangelical common front within the Protestantism of the early twentieth century.

The story of the growing conservative evangelical Protestant movement was highlighted by key events in North American Protestantism. The first was one of a series of annual Bible study meetings and prophecy conferences held at Niagara-on-the-Lake between 1882 and 1897. The meeting of 1895 produced a statement of belief which contained what would later be known as the 'five points of fundamentalism.' They were noted above. Although lists of five points of doctrine only became characteristic of fundamentalist Protestants after the 1950s, in the half-century preceding that time several fundamentalist Protestant groups defined their beliefs by referring to similar clusters of doctrines.

The second turning point in the development of conservatism and doctrinal fundamentalism was the above-noted publication in the United

States of a series of twelve tracts entitled *The Fundamentals* (1909–1915). The booklets were distributed free of charge to pastors and church workers in the United States and Canada. They immediately became a reference point in debates on Christian doctrine, providing as they did a coherent defense of conservative Protestantism.

A third stage in the development of doctrinal fundamentalism began with the founding in 1919 of the World's Christian Fundamentals Association by the American Baptist William B. Riley. This marked the beginning of fundamentalism as a quasi-denomination. Indeed, much like the earlier evangelical movement of the nineteenth century which had developed in distinct associations such as the lay-led YM/YWCA or particular missionary societies, fundamentalism would follow a similar path in twentieth-century Protestantism. Fundamentalist Protestants remained members of their denominations, the Baptists or the Presbyterians for example, while also joining fundamentalist associations.

Another reference point in the development of twentieth-century fundamentalism was the celebrated trial of John T. Scopes held in 1925. The young high school teacher was accused and convicted of violating the state law of Tennessee by teaching the doctrine of biological evolution. This doctrine of evolution, or Darwinism, was in the eyes of fundamentalists the chief doctrine of modernity, theological modernism included. They argued that it was an unproven hypothesis and by 1925 they had obtained legislation in a number of states of the U.S.A. which banned the teaching of Darwinism in public schools.

Bible schools

A leading avenue for the promotion of conservatism in twentieth-century Canada was the Bible school, Bible institute, or Bible college. Although exact numbers are hard to come by, more than one hundred Bible schools were founded in Canada during the twentieth century; it is estimated that fully eighty-five were founded in Western Canada alone before 1952. More than 200,000 Canadians are said to have spent at least one academic term enrolled in a Bible school, enrolment standing at about 7,000 students in the early 1990s, of whom 5,000 were in the West, 1,300 in Ontario, and the balance of 700 spread out between Québec and the Atlantic provinces.

Bible schools had the dual objective of teaching the Bible as revealed truth and teaching Christian practical living. Contrary to the seminaries and theology schools of the leading Protestant churches who were more and more prone to teach the Bible as an academic subject using the scholarly methodologies of history and literary criticism for example, Bible schools aimed at making their students familiar with the Scriptures as living truth and moral code. While some of the Bible schools were denominational, others were non-denominational, serving the needs of several denominations. One of the better-known and most influential was the non-denominational Prairie Bible Institute (P.B.I.) in Alberta, an institution which trained thousands of missionaries and lay workers for Protestant churches in Western Canada and in various missionary lands.

In addition to the appeal of their conservatism, other factors explained the popularity of the Bible schools among conservative evangelical Protestants. Bible schools tended to admit categories of students who were excluded from mainstream Protestant seminaries, such as students who lacked a high school diploma, lay students who did not intend to join the ranks of the clergy, and women who were long forbidden access to the ranks of the clergy. Indeed, Bible schools were the first theological institutions in Canada to give women access to the specialized training that enabled them to engage in Christian ministry. In addition, Bible schools were economical to operate and attend, given their usual location in small rural towns, and their tendency to cut costs by operating their own farms assisted by the labour of the students. They also reduced costs by paying the lowest stipends to their staffs, many of whom supplemented their income by engaging in preaching and pastoral work during summers and weekends.

Throughout the twentieth century, Bible schools never had any truck with modernity and its associated liberalism and secularism. They stood as bastions of conservative, evangelical, Protestant Christianity.

Neo-orthodox theology

The theological expression of the conservative evangelicalism described above was varied. Some conservative voices would sing from the hymn book of the Swiss theologian Karl Barth (1886–1968) who led the charge against liberalism in Protestant theology. After several years in parish ministry, at the end of World War I, Karl Barth was serving as professor of theology in a series of German universities when the publication of his book *Commentary on Romans* (1919) propelled him into the limelight of German and international theology. Because of his strong resistance to Nazism, in 1935 he was expelled from Germany and continued his

Fig. 17.   The Calgary Prophetic Bible Institute in the 1930s.[1] National Archives of Canada, c-009444.

Fig. 18.   Mission study class of the Methodist Church at the turn of the twentieth century.[2] National Archives of Canada, PA-122656.

teaching career at the University of Basle in Switzerland. His influence was more apparent in international and American theological circles than in Canadian ones, although in time all of contemporary Christian theology would display some Barthian colouring.

Reacting against Protestant liberalism, Karl Barth urged a return to the principles of the Protestant Reformation of the sixteenth century, a return to the prophetic teachings of the Bible, a reliance on God's revealed truth, and a rejection of modern ideas that seemed to make social progress synonymous with the onset of the Kingdom of God. Above all, Karl Barth stressed the transcendence and supremacy of God, before whom all things human paled into insignificance. For Barth, human reason remained permanently perverted by original sin. Our only salvation was to be found in the grace of God through Jesus the Christ and his divine Word.

Barth's theology was most influential during the 1930s, the time when large numbers of Bible schools were founded in Canada. His scholarly neo-orthodox theology, centred on the sovereignty of the Word of God, provided conservative evangelical Christians with a refreshing alternative to the overly simplistic and literal reading of the Bible that all too frequently prevailed in fundamentalist circles. His remained a strong theological voice in international Christianity, both Protestant and Catholic.

Fundamentalism divides denominations

The fight between modernists and fundamentalists tore a number of Protestant churches apart, particularly in the United States where large denominations such as the Baptists and Presbyterians divided over the issue. In Canada, the Protestant churches were less affected, perhaps because of their traditionally closer relationship to their culture. However, one notable exception to this accommodation of modernity was the Baptist denomination.

The Reverend Thomas Todhunter Shields, pastor of Toronto's Jarvis Street Baptist Church (1910–1955), led the charge of the fundamentalists within the Baptist communion and Canadian Protestantism. A powerful preacher and controversialist and a virulent enemy of Catholics, Shields was much involved in the fundamentalist campaigns in the United States during the 1920s. In 1925, he attacked McMaster University, the leading institution of learning in the Baptist denomination. This led to the expulsion of both Shields and his congregation from the Baptist Convention of Ontario and Québec. Along with thirty other

Fig. 19. Jarvis Street Baptist Church in Toronto around 1885–1890.[3] Josiah Bruce. National Archives of Canada, c-087238.

parishes, Shields then founded a new denomination known as the Union of Regular Baptists. However, by 1933 the majority of his new disciples broke away from him to form a new Fellowship of Independent Baptist Churches. Dissension erupted again in 1949 when the Reverend Shields was expelled from his denomination; the fiery and controversial pastor thereupon established the new Conservative Baptist Association of Canada.

The stormy history of Shields and his colleagues during these three decades illustrates the perennially impossible task of building a stable Christian church on doctrine alone. In fact, as noted above, most conservative Protestants in Canada did not leave their original denominations, whether Presbyterian, Baptist, or other. Instead, they worked to shape and mold their particular congregations to better reflect their new understanding of the Christian faith. As a quasi-denomination, Protestant conservatism in Canada will be anchored in local congregations of diverse denominations and in several Bible colleges that will emerge in Canada after World War I.

The Catholic reaction to modernity

Faced with the same challenge of the growing modernity of their nineteenth-century society, many Catholics reacted as did the Protestants, by leaning more and more towards a conservative interpretation of their Christian faith. The difference was that the Catholics had a strong, centralized, and hierarchical international church structure, a powerful instrument at the service of whichever theological party controlled the church. Just as Christian evangelicalism was labeled ultramontanism in the Catholic church in that it stood for the same basic Christian doctrine, by the same token the form of conservative evangelicalism that was fundamentalism, was known as integrism in the Catholic church. An integrist Catholic was one who stood for Catholicism in its integrity. The major difference between Protestant fundamentalists and Catholic fundamentalists (integrists) was their attitude towards the pope. The former damned him while the latter celebrated him.

Reinforcing Catholic traditionalism

The powerful conservative thrust that had been building in Catholicism throughout the papacy of Pius IX continued unabated until the mid-twentieth century. In 1878, the year that Pius IX was succeeded by Pope Leo XIII, the Vatican issued a new directive requiring that all Catholic colleges, universities, and seminaries teach only the philosophy and theology of Thomas Aquinas, a thirteenth-century theologian whose *thomistic* system had come to dominate Catholic teaching since the sixteenth century.

Just as the invention of seminaries in the sixteenth century had served to remove the young candidate for the priesthood from the society of his time, so the directive of 1878 constituted another major step in the process of removing Catholic thought from the mainstream of modern society. Thereafter, all graduates of Catholic post-secondary institutions of learning were taught to view the sundry philosophies and theologies developed since the sixteenth century as of secondary importance when compared to the 'perennial' philosophy of Aquinas and of the Middle Ages. So it was that educated Catholics were further removed from the influential thought of the likes of René Descartes, Isaac Newton, Thomas Hobbes, Voltaire, Jean-Jacques Rousseau, Immanuel Kant, Friedrich Hegel, Karl Marx, Charles Darwin, and a host of other thinkers who had tried to make sense of modern society. More often than not, these major thinkers were presented to Catholics in footnotes in fine print at the bottom of the pages of textbooks that extolled the pre-eminent truth and value of the philosophy and theology of Aquinas.

While the imposition of thomism was being effected during the 1880s and 1890s, Pope Leo XIII further reinforced the authority of the Catholic Church by issuing a series of encyclicals and directives aimed at strengthening the ritual piety and devotion of Catholics. The Sacred Heart and especially Mary were the central pieces in this campaign to revitalize Catholic piety.

Mary was celebrated repeatedly under a variety of titles both old and new, be it as Virgin, Mother of God, Co-Redemptress, Immaculate Conception, Mediatrix of All Graces, or patronness and protector of diverse activities, professions, and places. Catholics continued reciting the centuries-old Hail Mary, the Rosary, and the Angelus, while holding special May and October Marian devotions, and going on pilgrimages to growing numbers of Marian shrines such as Lourdes in France, or Cap-de-la-Madeleine near Trois-Rivières, Québec. Old and new Marian feast days dotted the liturgical calendar, including the Assumption (15 August), the Nativity (8 September), the Purification or Presentation (2 February), the Annunciation (25 March), and the Visitation (31 May). A series of major Marian congresses would follow in the first half of the twentieth century, one of which was held in Ottawa in 1947 on the occasion of the centennial of the founding of that diocese.

Although the Catholic church would downplay its devotion to Mary after the Second Vatican Council, the Virgin and Mother of God stood very high in the devotions of ultramontane Catholics from the mid-nineteenth to the mid-twentieth centuries. It was arguably the central devotion promoted by the Catholic Church. In all of their prayers, Catholics were urged to appeal to Jesus through Mary. A measure of the importance of the devotion to her was found in the repeated presence of her name as the patronness of hundreds of parishes that were founded in Canada during those hundred years. From the Atlantic to the Pacific to the Arctic, the Canadian landscape was dotted with parishes such as Our Lady of the Snows, of the Sea, of Sorrows, of Mercy, of the Immaculate Conception, of the Assumption, of the Visitation. The list goes on. Many of the new religious orders and institutes that were founded at that time were dedicated to Mary, institutes such as the Oblates of Mary Immaculate (1826), the Sisters of the Assumption of the Virgin (1853), and others.

Modernism

This major revitalization of Catholicism during the latter decades of the nineteenth century was driven by the fear of modernity, a mindset whose main proponent within the Catholic Church of the turn of the twentieth century was the French priest and biblical scholar Alfred Loisy (1857–1940). The movement which he came to lead and represent in Catholicism is called *modernism*.

Loisy was to the turn-of-the-century Catholic Church what Félicité de Lamennais had been to the church of the 1830s, that is to say a brilliant, scholarly, and passionately committed critic of the church he loved, but that he held to be hidebound in its refusal to appreciate the merits of modern society. Ordained a priest in 1879, Loisy learned the historical-critical study of Christianity at the feet of the outstanding historian of early Christianity Father Louis Duchesne. Having special-ized in the study of biblical literature, Loisy came to feel that a profound renewal of Catholic teaching was needed. Upon his appointment as professor of Sacred Scripture at the *Institut Catholique de Paris* in 1890, Loisy began publishing a series of critical studies that led to his dismissal from his post three years later. For the next seven years, while holding a minor ministerial posting as a school chaplain, Father Loisy developed a new apologetic for Catholicism. In 1900 he returned to full-time scholarship by accepting a position at Paris' *École Pratique des Hautes Études*.

It was from that platform that he published his celebrated *L'Évangile et l'Église* (1902), a reply to the just as famous *Wesen des Christentums* (*The Essence of Christianity*, 1900) of the leading Patristic and liberal Protestant scholar of the day Adolf Harnack (1851–1930). Both scholars mastered the new historical-critical methods, but arrived at very different conclusions about the nature of Christianity. Harnack argued that the essence of Christianity was to be found in a few basic moral values embedded in the Bible, values such as the fatherhood of God, the brotherhood of man, and the eternity of the soul; he was skeptical before all the metaphysical accretions which allegedly weighted down the Christian faith. Loisy countered by arguing that the essence of Christianity was to be found in the faith of the church supported by the Spirit. Although church and sacraments were not founded by Jesus directly, nevertheless they stood as central in Christian life.

The controversy that followed the publication of Loisy's book became much more heated the following year when he published *Autour d'un petit livre*, a commentary on the controversy, and *Le quatrième évangile*, a commentary on the Gospel of John. Pope Pius X who had just succeeded Leo XIII, placed both books on the Index of forbidden books, the Vatican's catalogue of publications that Catholics were forbidden to read. Thereafter, Loisy and Catholic Church authorities would move progressively further apart. Loisy resigned his professorship at the *École Pratique des Hautes Études* in 1904, left the Catholic priesthood in 1906, and was excommunicated by Rome in 1908 after he published a telling criticism of the encyclical *Pascendi* and the papal decree *Lamentabili*, two documents published in 1907 that condemned Catholic modernism. For the next twenty-one years of his life (1909–1930), Loisy held a professorship in the history of religions at the prestigious *Collège de France*, where he continued his work as a biblical critic.

Modernism, the movement which Loisy purportedly led, was not in fact an organized movement. The word merely designated a motley group of Catholic scholars, scattered in different countries, who shared a certain number of ideas and tendencies in matters of interpretation of Christian origins and history. The movement was strongest in France, but also included scholars in Italy, Germany, Great Britain, and elsewhere. In France, in addition to Loisy, the group included Maurice Blondel, E.I. Mignot, Lucien Laberthonnière, and Édouard Le Roy. In Great Britain, the best known modernists were Friedrich von Hügel and George Tyrrell.

The ideas common to the modernists included the critical view of the Bible whereby the Bible was understood as the record of the gradual development of divine truth in history. This meant that modernists readily accepted the fact of inconsistencies between the books of the Bible and did not try to gloss over them or deny them, as most Christian interpreters had traditionally done. Modernists also tended to reject the prevailing thomistic theology in their church, preferring a theology that favoured practice, action, and pragmatism. Modernists were thus drawn to the writings of Maurice Blondel (activism), William James (pragmatism), and Henri Bergson (vitalism). Modernists were also inclined to adopt a view of history that focused on its outcome rather than its origin. Like Loisy, they felt that the essence of the Gospel lay in its full expression in their time rather than in its earliest kernel.

Pope Pius X reacted strongly to the modernists by issuing the decree *Lamentabili* in July 1907 followed by the encyclical *Pascendi* in September. Pius X argued that the modernists tended to support agnosticism by denying the value of rational demonstration in religious matters and that they seemed to claim that religious truth arose from man's vital needs rather than from God's revelation. Modernists were suspect of severing the link between history and faith. In addition, the pope feared that modernists tended to deny the presence of the supernatural in history.

The sweeping condemnations of 1907 were followed during the next five years by a series of Roman decrees condemning various modernist publications and their authors. Leading Catholic scholars such as Henri Brémond (1865–1933), Louis Duchesne (1843–1922) and Lucien Laberthonnière (1860–1932) had some or all of their work condemned, while others such as George Tyrrell and Loisy were excommunicated. The Vatican ordered a witch hunt to cleanse Catholic seminaries and universities of staff with suspect ideas; beginning in 1910, all teaching personnel in these institutions were required to swear an anti-modernist oath at the beginning of each academic year.

In fact, Rome's reaction to modernism was so swift and sweeping that, as a result, historical and biblical scholarship in the Catholic Church would be set back for nearly half a century. It was only after World War II that Catholic scholars were authorized by the Vatican to revisit the world of critical historical and biblical scholarship. Indeed, the dynamic evangelicalism of Catholic conservatism carried in its shadow the narrow witch hunting spirit of the integrist crusader. While thousands of missionaries, clergy, and Catholic lay apostles worked tirelessly for the promotion of the Gospel, some of their coreligionists and peers busied themselves with denunciations, accusations, and calumnies against some of their brothers and sisters in the faith.

Canada's Catholic leaders were in full accord with the Roman policies and directives against modernism. Nary a dissenting voice was allowed in the Catholic seminaries and universities of the country, institutions that had never distinguished themselves as leaders in creative theology. The result was a homogeneous but colourful and popular Catholicism. It was only after World War II that some Canadian Catholics began to question the rigid and uniform doctrines and practices of their church.

The Jewish reaction to modernity

Like Christians, Jews had to adjust their religious faith and understanding to the new reality of the development of modernity and secularism in the industrializing and revolutionary West after the fifteenth century. In Europe, the late eighteenth and early nineteenth centuries proved to be pivotal in the internal evolution of Judaism. After centuries of being relegated to the fringes of European society, Jews produced a major figure in the Enlightenment of the eighteenth century. Germany's Moses Mendelssohn (1729–1786) urged his Jewish coreligionists to change and adapt to their society, marking the beginning of a major movement of secularization among European Jewry. This meant that a growing number of Jewish communities gradually shed their distinctive communal traits, traits such as living in separate neighbourhoods (ghettos), attending Jewish schools, rabbinic control of various parts of their community life, and the controlled choice of marriage partners.

While some of these changed and secularized European Jews immigrated to Canada, most of Canada's Jews came from eastern Europe and were of orthodox Ashkenazi tradition. Although Canada had had organized communities of Jews since the 1760s, they were few and small in number, Montreal's synagogue being the first. Indeed, the major influx of Canada's Jews occurred between the 1880s and the 1920s. Canadian Jews would accommodate to their new society, acknowledging that they needed to acculturate if they were to enjoy the economic and social advantages of Canadian life. The result would be a Canadian Judaism that was highly secularized. The impact of modernity was profound on Canada's Jews.

The Amerindian reaction to modernity

Of all the social groups that were affected by modernity, Canada's Amerindians were probably the most vulnerable given their extensive social, economic, and technological weaknesses in the face of Canadian society. By the mid-nineteenth century the Amerindians had lost their social and political importance because the fur trade was on the wane and the wars with the United States had ceased. In addition, Amerindians stood in the way of the Canadian occupation of the land. Therefore, Canada's governments invented policies aimed at removing Amerindians from the land (reserves), and assimilating them into Canadian culture (residential schools). This threat to the very survival of Canada's Amerindians was compounded by their diminishing numbers because of the diseases, sometimes of epidemic proportions, that swept through Amerindian communities. The effects of the chronic poverty among Amerindians were reinforced by the twin blights of alcoholism and prostitution.

As was the case in other communities, the reactions of Canada's Amerindian people to the challenges of Canadian culture and its modernity covered the spectrum between complete acceptance and absolute denial. Some Amerindians simply accepted total assimilation, thereby rapidly losing their distinct Amerindian identity which rested on distinctive languages, customs, education, way of life, and spirituality. So it was, for example, that the more than three-score Amerindian languages of a century ago are now reduced to as few as three. A few wanted to turn back the clock, to refuse any accommodation to Canadian culture; they had to acknowledge that such a course of action was impossible to implement given the overwhelming number of Canadians.

The majority of Amerindians wisely sought to preserve as much as they could of their culture, while accepting the necessity of partial acculturation to the ways of the Canadians. For many years this proved very difficult, given that most Canadians, informed of their declining numbers, thought that Amerindians would become extinct. However, the situation changed after the population of Canada's Amerindians began a steady rise during the twentieth century, the result of improved health care. By the 1960s, Aboriginal leaders began to gain support for their policies of cultural preservation and development. Residential schools were abolished, Amerindian languages were taught to Amerindian children, the government of Canada invested more money in social services for Amerindians, and there was a revitalization of

Amerindian spirituality. Canada's Amerindians began showing some success in resisting the imperative of modernity.

Conclusion

Beginning in the sixteenth century, modernity was a major and profound challenge to all religions, in that the authority of tradition was not only questioned but frequently denied. Those Christians and Jews who accepted the new mindset without reservation soon realized that they had abandoned their traditional community of belief; they were no longer Catholics, Protestants, or Jews. Many of them replaced their traditional faith with a strong commitment to social action while denying the value of religious doctrine.

The believer's instinctive reaction to the challenge of modernity was a form of conservatism which underlined the importance of the foundations of one's traditional way of life. This conservatism developed among Protestants, Catholics and Jews, and Amerindians.

For those Christians and Jews who sought a middle road, the compromises between modernity and traditional Christianity or Judaism were rarely easy to make. Indeed, modernity and religious belief stood in constant tension with one another, given their diverging appreciation of the importance of the transcendent and of tradition. By the late nineteenth century, this uneasy relationship pushed many believers into heightened social 'engagement,' a kind of commitment which was in clear conformity with the Bible, while not raising too many embarrassing theological questions.

Suggested readings

Choquette, Robert. L'Église catholique dans l'Ontario français du dix-neuvième siècle. Ottawa: University of Ottawa Press, 1984.

Grant, John Webster. The Church in the Canadian Era. Updated and expanded. Burlington: Welch Publishing Co., 1988.

Marsden, George M. Fundamentalism and American Culture. The Shaping of Twentieth-Century Evangelicalism 1870–1925. New York: Oxford University Press, 1980.

——. Understanding Fundamentalism and Evangelicalism. Grand Rapids: William B. Eerdmans, 1991.

Marshall, David B. *Secularizing the Faith: Canadian Protestant Clergy and the Crisis of Belief, 1850–1940*. Toronto: University of Toronto Press, 1992.

Perin, Roberto. *Rome in Canada. The Vatican and Canadian Affairs In the Late Victorian Age*. Toronto: University of Toronto Press, 1990.

Rynne, Xavier. *Vatican Council II*. New York: Orbis, 1999.

Sandeen, Ernest R. *The Roots of Fundamentalism: British and American Millenarianism 1800–1930*. Chicago: University of Chicago Press, 1970.

Simard, Jean et al. *Un patrimoine méprisé: La religion populaire des Québécois*. Montréal: Hurtubise HMH. 1979.

Stackhouse, John G. *Canadian Evangelicalism in the Twentieth Century: An Introduction to its Character*. Toronto: University of Toronto Press, 1993.

Van Die, Marguerite. *An Evangelical Mind: Nathanael Burwash and the Methodist Tradition in Canada, 1839–1918*. Montréal & Kingston: McGill-Queen's University Press, 1989.

CHAPTER 16

Social Christianity

Introduction

If the Christian faith was not social, it was nothing. While this has been the case from the beginning of the history of Christianity, the profound and dramatic social questions that were raised at the turn of the twentieth century served to underline the fact anew. How would Protestants and Catholics respond to the troubling new social realities created by the industrial, economic, political, social, and ideological revolutions of the nineteenth century, the revolutions that had spawned communism, socialism, robber barons, international migrations of people, and urban misery on a scale rarely seen before?

The Bible is shot through with statements highlighting the centrality of the love of God and neighbour in the Christian economy of salvation. Faith and love go hand-in-hand, are indeed inseparable in Christian teaching. If a Christian does not love his or her neighbour, he or she is not a true Christian. Saint Paul writes to the Galatians: "The only thing that counts is faith working through love" (5:6). The whole law is summed up in a single commandment: "You shall love your neighbour as yourself" (5:14). And to the Corinthians: "Faith, hope, and love abide, these three; and the greatest of these is love" (1 Cor. 13:13). The Epistle of James is even more explicit: "What good is it, my brothers and sisters, if you say you have faith but do not have works? Can faith save you? If a brother or sister is naked and lacks daily food, and one of you says to them, 'Go in peace; keep warm and eat your fill,' and yet you do not supply their bodily needs, what is the good of that? So faith by itself, if it has no works, is dead" (2:14).

Although Protestants and Catholics would argue over the precise theological relationship between faith and works, neither would deny the central importance of the love of neighbour in Christian life. In fact, during their two millennia of history, Christians usually distinguished themselves in caring for their fellow men and women because their faith compelled them to do so.

The sweeping social problems that emerged in the wake of the industrial revolution provoked special concern among Christians in nineteenth-century France and Great Britain. In Catholic France, the agencies of choice for taking on new apostolic responsibilities were the religious orders and various lay charitable societies such as the Society of Saint Vincent de Paul which was founded in 1833. In Protestant Great Britain, similar responses to new social challenges were given by new groups dedicated to what some called social Christianity.

In Canada, the history of Christian social action was similar to that in Europe in that Catholic and Protestant churches or associations were usually responsible for social care in health, education, and poor relief. As was the case overseas, the intensified social problems of the second half of the nineteenth century caused the founding of new teachings and new associations. The revitalized social action by the Protestants was known as the Social Gospel, while that of the Catholics was highlighted by the Catholic Action movement.

The Social Gospel

The advocates of modernity within turn-of-the-century Protestantism shared a liberal and individualistic philosophical and theological outlook. Their modernist liberal Protestantism tended to fuse the secular and the sacred, to focus more on this world than on the next. Critics of the liberal Protestants felt that the latter did not give Christian Revelation and doctrine their due. Protestant conservatives reacted to modernism by advocating a return to past attitudes that centred on Revelation, God, and the transcendent. However, whether of modernist-liberal or conservative persuasion, most Protestants reflected the values of their time in focusing on the individual. While the liberal Protestant spoke of the rights and duties of the individual Christian in a free secular, modern society, the conservative Protestant also spoke of the conversion of the individual or the saving of the individual soul.

What is the Social Gospel?

Social Gospel reformers sought a change of perspective, one that moved away from individualism and closer to communalism in Protestant theology. While acknowledging the full importance of modern secular society, Social Gospel reformers wanted to find God in and through it. They were struck by the extent of misery and injustice in society; they wanted to extend the meaning of sin and justice not only to include the social, but to be primarily centred in society. For Social Gospel reformers, social justice became the way to sanctification rather than the result of it. The purpose of the Christian Gospel was first and foremost to establish the Kingdom of God on earth; the conversion and sanctification of the individual would be gained along the road to the establishment of that Kingdom.

Social Gospel reformers rejected the individualistic and voluntaristic thrusts of traditional Protestant theology because they seemed of little use in solving the major social problems of the time. They stressed the social rootedness of sin and the consequent priority that must be given to the conversion of society, to social justice. The theme of the Kingdom of God had to become the centre of the Gospel, and could not be limited to a personal spiritual possession. It was society that needed to be saved and the salvation of the individual would automatically follow. Social Gospel activists believed that personal spiritual renewal would result from a reformed social environment. Sin was primarily selfishness, while sanctification was service to others. In order to achieve these objectives, Social Gospel reformers sought to build a society where cooperation replaced competition, where big business and corporations worked hand in hand with workers and consumers in a cooperative effort aimed at the common good.

The Social Gospel was not an organization, but a complex movement that is difficult to define. It was simultaneously a theology and an active social reform movement within English-speaking Protestant churches. It began late in the nineteenth century, peaked around the time of World War I, and then declined in the late 1920s. Its theological ideas were imported into Canada from Europe and the United States, and were anchored in a handful of theological institutions such as the Presbyterian Queen's University in Kingston, the Methodist Wesley College in Winnipeg, and the Baptist McMaster University in Toronto (before it moved to Hamilton).

The leaders of the Social Gospel

The leadership of the Social Gospel movement was a loosely-knit conglomerate of theologians and church activists from Great Britain, the United States, and Canada. The foremost theologian of the movement was the American Walter Rauschenbush (1861–1918), while leaders of the movement in Canada included the Presbyterian William Irvine, and the Methodists J.S. Woodsworth (1874–1942), William Ivens, and Salem Bland.

Salem Bland was initially a Methodist pastor in Kingston, Ontario, before accepting an appointment as professor of church history on the theological faculty of Winnipeg's Wesley College in 1903. From this base of operations, the charismatic preacher and teacher propagated his social reform ideas before diverse agencies that welcomed him as a guest speaker, agencies such as the YMCA and the Lord's Day Alliance. After fourteen years of stinging social criticism, Bland was dismissed from his teaching position in 1917, the directors of Wesley College alleging that financial constraints compelled them to do so.

J. S. Woodsworth had been brought to Manitoba from Toronto as a child in the 1880s. This son of a Methodist pastor became in turn a Methodist preacher, his studies leading him first to Victoria University in Toronto, then to Oxford University in England (1899–1900) where he was able to observe big-city slums first-hand. After his return to Canada, he worked as a Methodist minister in Winnipeg, a time when that city was experiencing explosive population growth as a result of large-scale immigration.[1] The Reverend Woodsworth was pastor of one of the wealthiest parishes in a city where slums were a growing stain on the social fabric. He vigorously denounced the greed and callous disregard of too many of his parishioners to the plight of the poor among them. Woodsworth had found his calling. With each passing year, the Reverend Woodsworth found himself more and more concerned with the plight of the poor and more and more critical of government policies on education, immigration, and social welfare. Despite his own growing doubts about the quality of his Methodist faith, in 1907 he became superintendent of All People's Mission in Winnipeg, while becoming progressively more active as a public speaker in both Canada and the United States. He published two of the best-known books on the Canadian Social Gospel, *Strangers Within Our Gates* (1909) and *My Neighbour* (1911). In addition to denouncing the less-than-Christian behaviour of many of his contemporaries, Woodsworth accused the government of

Canada of admitting the wrong people into Canada and spoke out strongly against government support of both Catholic and bilingual schools. The disgruntled cleric was also critical of many Christian churches. He accused them of often being dominated by the wealthy, of being scandalously fragmented, and of being torn apart by sectarianism.

Woodsworth's disenchantment with his own church and society led to his resignation from All People's Mission (1913) and from the Methodist ministry (1918). Indeed, by the end of World War I, Woodsworth denounced his church as a reactionary instrument of the wealthy. He later became an active socialist and founder of the Cooperative Commonwealth Federation (CCF), the ancestor of Canada's New Democratic Party. Always siding with the poor and the downtrodden, Woodsworth remained a convinced pacifist throughout the two world wars.

The reaction of Protestant churches to the Social Gospel

Generally speaking, the principles of the Social Gospel received broad acceptance in the Protestant churches of Canada. Over the years, there were numerous declarations by various church spokespersons reflecting this support, statements on the systemic injustices of the economic order, on the need to rebuild the economy for the good of all, on the merits of an eight-hour workday, on the desirability of old-age pensions, on the rights of heads of families to a living wage, on the necessity of greater justice towards workers, etc. In fact, Social Gospel reformers were not fighting against an entrenched church establishment that sought to thwart their program of reform. Indeed, under the influence of the Social Gospel, a number of Protestant agencies changed their policies to better reflect the program of the reformers. So it was that the YMCA and YWCA changed their traditional discourse of evangelical personal conversion into one that took into account the wellbeing of the entire person in his or her mental, physical, social, and spiritual dimensions. Influenced by the Social Gospel, many Protestant associations and agencies became inter-denominational, cooperating rather than competing. Indeed, the Social Gospel was a major factor in the social reform of Canada from the late nineteenth to the mid-twentieth centuries.

The Protestant reform of Canada

Albeit of central importance, the Social Gospel was not the only plank in the broad Protestant reform program aimed at changing Canadian society between Confederation and World War II. Social Gospel reformers worked in conjunction with other reform-minded Protestants with objectives as diverse as banning alcoholic beverages, eliminating government funding for Catholic and bilingual schools, banning industrial and commercial activities on Sunday, and eliminating prostitution and child labour. All of these social reform movements were the reflection of a profound religio-cultural conviction among Canada's English-speaking Protestants that the Dominion of Canada was destined by God to become the Dominion of the Lord, a task which it was their duty to implement. The late historian N. Keith Clifford was cited in Chapter 12 to the effect that "the inner dynamic of Protestantism in Canada during the first two-thirds of the century following Confederation was provided by a vision of the nation as 'His Dominion.'" Clifford argued that this "Canadian version of the Kingdom of God had significant nationalistic and millennial overtones, and sufficient symbolic power to provide the basis for the formation of a broad Protestant consensus and coalition." Protestant denominations and many "Protestant-oriented organizations such as temperance societies, missionary societies, Bible societies, the Lord's Day Alliance, the YMCAs and YWCAs utilized this vision as a framework for defining their task within the nation, for shaping their conceptions of the ideal society, and for determining those elements which posed a threat to the realization of their purposes."[2]

This general Protestant conviction and common front underlay all the specific social reform programs launched between Confederation and World War II. This messianic millennialism was the bedrock upon which rested the emerging English-Canadian nationalism of the turn of the century.

One of the major Protestant campaigns of that era was noted earlier – the temperance campaign. Through agencies such as the Dominion Alliance and the Women's Christian Temperance Union (WCTU), reformers worked to control and ban the bottle. Beginning in 1900, but especially during World War I, they were spectacularly successful. In the wake of a series of provincial laws that imposed prohibition in all provinces by 1918, save Québec, by order-in-council the government of Canada banned inter-provincial trade in liquor. However, the victory was short-lived because during the 1920s all provinces save Prince Edward Island repealed their prohibitionist legislation. A century-long Protestant evangelical campaign thereby came to naught.

From its founding in 1888, the Lord's Day Alliance directed another reform campaign of the turn of the century aimed at making Sunday into a required day of rest. The movement was victorious by 1906 when the *Lord's Day Act* was adopted by Parliament with the support of some of Canada's leading labour unions. The *Act* regulated commercial and public events on Sundays; it would stand until the late twentieth century as another monument to the Christian public character of Canada.

The Protestant reform of Canada included a wide range of other issues taken up by diverse reformers bent upon implementing the Kingdom of God in the northern half of North America. While many individual Protestants fought local battles aimed at improving public health, public housing, public parks, and public ownership of utilities, the Methodist J.J. Kelso founded the Children's Aid Society in 1891. Upon the outbreak of World War I, just about all Protestant churches presented the war as a struggle for Christian civilization; indeed, Protestant pulpits were among the strongest defenders of the war effort, including conscription.

Downtown missions became important components in the evangelizing program of several Protestant churches. They provided meals and housing for the homeless, clinics with nurses, educational programs for children, manual training for workers, the teaching of English, reading rooms, libraries, and various recreational activities for all.

On the sensitive question of immigration, the work of the Protestant reformers proved divisive. At the turn of the twentieth century, Canada was opening its doors to foreign immigration to an extent rarely seen in the past. Hundreds of thousands of immigrants, more than 200,000 yearly after 1906, arrived on Canada's shores, usually taking up residence in the country's leading cities which grew by leaps and bounds. Immigrants competed for jobs while taking up residence in downtown neighbourhoods that soon reflected the sights, sounds, and tensions of various ethno-cultural groups. Some 25% of the immigrants were not English-speaking, many coming from southern and eastern Europe, areas of predominantly Catholic or Orthodox Christianity.

The presence of immigrants in Canada served to fuel the fear of a foreign peril among several Protestant spokespersons who perceived them as bearers of second-rate cultures and of religions of superstition. When Protestant leaders spoke of evangelizing the immigrant, they meant civilizing and 'Canadianizing' him and her. This assimilationist objective underlay many of the social reform endeavours and urban mission campaigns which the Protestant reformers directed. Indeed, in the eyes of the Protestant reformers, civilizing the immigrant was just as important as evangelizing him or her; one did not go without the other.

The social reform program of Canada's Protestant churches was wide-ranging and extensive from the late nineteenth century to the 1920s. The extensive social problems of the late nineteenth century had provoked the new theology of the Social Gospel, a theology and mindset that in turn transformed many of the Protestant churches and agencies. Protestants were made progressively more aware of the social matrix of sin and salvation. The result would be not only changed Protestant churches, but also a changed Canadian society. Indeed, the social safety net of which Canadians of later generations would be so proud was in many respects the result of the work of Canadian Protestant social reformers.

Catholic social doctrine

The social problems of the late nineteenth century would also move Catholics to modify their teaching and activities. Indeed, it may be argued that during the one hundred years between 1891 and 1991, the primary focus of Catholic doctrine became a social one. Seven of the nine popes that span that century distinguished themselves in issuing encyclicals that were not only centred on the social question, but that represent considerable innovation in renewing Catholic social teaching. This new focus on social doctrine was implemented in two phases. The first phase included the seventy years between the encyclicals *Rerum Novarum* (1891) and *Mater et Magistra* (1961). The second phase began with the opening of the Second Vatican Council in 1962 and continued until the 1990s. Over the years this doctrine was implemented by an extensive network of apostolic workers and agencies. The result was that by the 1970s, prompted by Latin American bishops, the Catholic Church had adopted as policy a 'preferential option for the poor,' and had become the leading agency of social reform in many countries.

The encyclical Rerum Novarum

Pope Leo XIII's response to the new social situation of his time was the encyclical *Rerum Novarum* issued on 15 May 1891, a document whose publication marked the beginning of a century-long development of Catholic social doctrine. *Rerum Novarum* maintained the traditional doctrine that society originated in the family, defended the importance of private property as a natural right of human beings, and condemned socialism as a violation of that right. Pope Leo defended the legitimacy of associations of workers (unions) or employers, at a time when Catholics still debated the merits of unions. Leo supported wage settlements by means of free agreement between parties. He preached the ideal of a just wage, which he defined as that capable of sustaining a wage-earner and his family in reasonable if modest comfort.

The publication of *Rerum Novarum* constituted the acknowledgment by the Catholic Church of the existence of a new order of rights and duties in society, namely the social order. It would no longer suffice to acknowledge a working man or woman as an individual with rights and responsibilities; they must also be perceived as workers with the rights and responsibilities commensurate with that status. The encyclical stood against the prevailing liberal philosophy with its radical individualism that insisted on treating all people as equal individuals and that refused to take into account one's place in society. Contrary to this, *Rerum Novarum* taught that in addition to his or her rights as an individual person, a male worker had rights as the head of a household and family, a female worker as a mother or mother-to-be, a child worker as a growing person, etc. In other words, each man, woman, and child is more than one individual among others; they are also defined by their place in their community and should enjoy corresponding rights and responsibilities.

In the wake of the publication of *Rerum Novarum*, the Catholic Church worked to propagate the new social conscience defended in the encyclical. Although Leo's two immediate successors Pius X (1903–1914) and Benedict XV (1914–1922) were not primarily concerned with social issues, his third successor Pius XI (1922–1939) revisited the question.

Quadragesimo Anno

Published on 15 May 1931, the fortieth anniversary of *Rerum Novarum*, Pius XI's *Quadragesimo Anno* confirmed and developed the teachings of the earlier encyclical. Pius stressed the evil results of unbridled free competition and administrative centralization, while strongly condemning socialism of any kind.

Given the year of its publication, less than fifteen years after the Bolshevik revolution in Russia (1917) and only two years after the onset of the Great Depression precipitated by the stockmarket crash of 1929, *Quadragesimo Anno* is best remembered as the charter of the anti-communist crusade in the Western world, a vigorously engaged crusade in Canada and the United States from the 1930s to the 1950s. Pope Pius XI flatly condemned socialism of any kind on the grounds that it was a doctrine contrary to that of the church. Not only did socialism deny the human being's natural right to private property, but it also stood for atheism, materialism, and class conflict, all grounds that the Catholic Church could not accept.

Some Catholics felt that the encyclical was a blunt instrument, useful in countering the worst excesses of communism, but lacking in insight in bundling all forms of socialism together in order to condemn them all. This transformed such relatively mild forms of socialism as that of Canada's CCF into condemned doctrines that Canadian Catholics were not authorized to support, whereas all who were familiar with that party knew that it did not stand for the sweeping atheism, materialism, and class conflict condemned by *Quadragesimo Anno*. In fact, Catholics would need to await the renewed Catholicism of popes John XXIII and Paul VI in the 1960s before receiving more nuanced directives on socialism. In the meantime, some interpreters feel that the anti-socialism of *Quadragesimo Anno* is largely to blame for the long-standing failure of any socialist party to gain a footing in traditionally Catholic French Canada.

Renewed social doctrine after 1960

Beginning in the 1960s, a major wave of reform and renewal swept through the Catholic Church. The movement was launched by the election of Pope John XXIII in 1958. During his short five years in office, the unorthodox elderly pontiff called the meeting of Vatican Council II (1962–1965) which launched the Catholic Church onto a path of renewal on a scale rarely seen in the course of its two-thousand-year history. A central focus of Catholic renewal was social doctrine and *engagement*. A new chapter in Catholic social doctrine was being written.

Dated 15 May 1961, the encyclical *Mater et Magistra* commemorated the seventieth anniversary of the publication of *Rerum Novarum*. Bearing on the recent developments of the social question in the light of Christian teaching, the papal letter urged all nations to overcome social disparities between groups and individuals in order to establish social justice on earth. One year later, John XXIII issued the encyclical *Pacem in Terris* (1962) urging all men and women of good will to work towards the establishment of peace among nations founded on truth, justice,

Fig. 20.   Soup kitchen in Montréal in 1931.[3] National Archives of Canada, PA-168131.

charity, and liberty. The pope distinguished between ideological systems which were intolerant by definition and human beings of whatever ideological persuasion who always retained the best of themselves in their inalienable human personal dignity, a dignity that must always be respected. God would always be present to assist all people.

Pope Paul VI

Elected on 21 June 1963, John's successor Paul VI (1963–1978) had a special predisposition in favour of working men and women, for social justice, and for cooperation and unity among Christians. Intent on building bridges between the church and the contemporary world, he reopened the ecumenical council and urged the Catholic Church to base its renewal on its sources in Christ and the apostles. Paul began an unprecedented series of papal visits to various parts of the world including the Holy Land where no reigning pontiff had ever set foot, and Bombay, India where he met leaders of other religions and pressed for

Fig. 21.   Cardinal Paul-Émile Léger with African child in Yaoundé, Cameroon, in the early 1970s.[4] Photograph Ken Bell. National Archives of Canada, PA-203443.

major efforts to fight Third World poverty. On 4 October 1965, Paul addressed the General Assembly of the United Nations in New York urging his audience to put an end to war. Two years later he visited Patriarch Athenagoras of the Orthodox Church in Istanbul, having already lifted (1965) the excommunication of the patriarch of Constantinople uttered in 1054. In 1970, on a similar visit to the headquarters of the World Council of Churches in Geneva, Switzerland, Paul urged his fellow Christians to greater cooperation in the Christian faith. In the course of other journeys to Colombia, Africa, Australia, and Samoa, the globe-trotting pontiff preached a message of sharing and fellowship among all.

The encyclical *Populorum Progressio* (1967) was Paul's key statement of social doctrine, expressing both anguish and hope about world prospects. There, he wrote that the social question was no longer limited to the industrializing nations of the West but had become a global problem; Paul also declared that social development was the new name for peace. Social concern had taken centre stage in the thought of Pope Paul VI. Some of Paul's policies were controversial, provoking sustained opposition among large numbers of Catholics. These included his reiteration of the long-standing Catholic disciplinary rulings limiting priestly ordination to unmarried men and prohibiting the ordination of women. Even more controversial was the encyclical *Humanae Vitae* (1968) on human sexuality and reproduction. The celebrated document condemned as grievously sinful the use of contraceptives on the grounds that their use constituted artificial interference with God's natural law. The teaching was not only disregarded by large numbers of Catholics, in North America in particular, but also opposed by those who felt that contraceptives were a necessary instrument of birth control for the control of overpopulation in the Third World.

Nevertheless, a number of other measures reinforced Paul's policy of openness and social justice for all. He created Vatican secretariats and commissions to coordinate church work in the areas of Christian unity, non-Christian religions and unbelievers, social justice and peace, and the apostolate of the laity. Paul fought racism and discrimination at every opportunity, welcomed visitors of all ideological persuasions, religions, and nations, read theology that reflected various Christian horizons, and internationalized the administrative structures and personnel of the Catholic Church. He commemorated the eightieth anniversary of *Rerum Novarum* with the encyclical *Octogesima Adveniens* (1971) wherein he stated anew his determination to make the Catholic Church responsive to the needs of the contemporary world. The death of Pope Paul VI on 6 August 1978 deprived the Catholic church of one of the strongest leaders it had had, a man who led the world's largest Christian church through fifteen years of profound change and renewal.

Pope John Paul II

After the brief thirty-three-day pontificate of John Paul I, Karol Wojtyla, the son of a Polish soldier, was elected on 16 October 1978. He took the name of John Paul II. The first non-Italian to hold the papal office since the early sixteenth century, Wojtyla had earned a reputation as a strong adversary of communism in his homeland. Upon acceding to the papal throne, John Paul II made clear his commitment to continue supporting the reforms of Vatican II, to continue the fight in favour of human rights, and to continue building bridges to contemporary cultures, always reminding any and all that it was Christ who gave meaning and fulfillment to men and women. The rights of men and women and the rights of God were the twin pillars of his teaching.

Just as his predecessor had done, he took up his pilgrim's staff and visited numerous countries. Within three years of his taking office, John Paul II had visited Mexico, Poland, Ireland, the United States, Turkey, and more than half a dozen African countries. Since then, he has visited an astonishing number of countries, on all the inhabited continents; Canada was graced with his presence in 1984 and in July 2002, to celebrate World Youth Day.

His first three years in office witnessed the publication of three encyclicals that called for the reordering of social and economic structures in our time. *Redemptor Hominis* (1979), *Dives in Misericordia* (1980), and *Laborem Exercens* (1981) all spoke of the church's responsibility before men and women who were created in the image of God. *Laborem Exercens* commemorated the ninetieth anniversary of *Rerum Novarum*. John Paul reminded his readers that the power of Christ's love was greater than that of hatred and violence, that they were created to live in justice and peace, and that they were called to work together in a Christian church grounded in the Gospel and open to the world. Christ was at the centre of the world and of history, the pontiff taught, while the church's task was to ensure the priority of ethics over technology, of persons over objects, and of spirit over matter.

John Paul's social doctrine was the continuation and reinforcement of the revitalized Catholic doctrine forged at Vatican II. The pope urged his listeners to respect all men and women because they were created in the image of God; he taught that it was the will of God that all private property be socially mortgaged. For John Paul, the future of men and women depended on culture, because it was only through culture that we became fully human. Indeed, the peace of the world depended on the primacy of the spirit, which could only be obtained through love.

Catholic social doctrine underwent profound change between 1960 and the beginning of the third millennium. Popes John XXIII, Paul VI, and John Paul II, mandated by the seminal Second Vatican Council, presided over a Catholic church that made social policy and action an overriding concern.

Implementing Catholic social doctrine

While the popes steered Catholic teaching towards a new emphasis on social action, numerous associations and individuals within the church endeavoured to implement the new teaching. During the first half of the twentieth century, three leading agencies for the teaching and marketing of Catholic social doctrine in Canada were the *Association catholique de la jeunesse canadienne (ACJC)*, a French Canadian nationalist society founded under Jesuit auspices in 1903; the *École sociale populaire* founded by Jesuit Father Joseph-Papin Archambeault in 1911; and the *Semaines sociales*, a kind of travelling college of Catholic social doctrine that gathered teachers and social activists on a yearly basis for one week of intensive instruction in Catholic social doctrine.

Perennial social engagement by the Catholic Church

Social action was not by any means a new discovery of the Catholic church of the twentieth century. For centuries many churchmen, missionaries, religious men, and women, and lay activists had devoted much time and effort to a variety of social endeavours ranging from the founding of schools, colleges and universities, to the establishment of hospitals, infirmaries, shelters, and emergency relief centres for the sick and the poor. The same was true in Canada from the time of the arrival of the first European settlers in the seventeenth century. It was only in the mid-nineteenth century that the first secular educational institutions were established in Canada, the vast majority of Canada's schools, universities and hospitals being founded by the churches, both Catholic and Protestant.

Intensified social action

The new social priorities and doctrine that emerged after the mid-nineteenth century caused a flurry of new social foundations in Catholic Canada. Beginning in 1848, French Canada's Catholic bishops had added colonization societies to their church's list of social accomplishments, endeavouring thereby to reduce the numbers of Canadians who were leaving Québec for the factories of New England.

These colonization societies consisted of organized recruitment, information, and financing networks in the dioceses and parishes of Québec, coupled with parallel organizations in areas of proposed settlement such as the valleys of the Ottawa River, the Gatineau River, or Lake Temiskaming in the Diocese of Ottawa. The faithful were urged to join their diocese's colonization society, attend a weekly meeting, pay a small weekly contribution, and pray for the success of the work. In return they received spiritual gifts such as a pious image and promises of indulgences. A priest was entrusted with the promotion of the colonization work, charged with touring parishes, and preaching to the assembled faithful at Sunday Mass. The collected funds were then deposited in a central colonization fund which was used to build chapels in new areas of colonization.

Beginning in the 1880s, these colonization societies were revitalized and others were founded to draw settlers into the Laurentians north of Montréal near Saint-Jovite and Sainte-Adèle, into northeastern Ontario near Temagami, or later into Québec's Abitibi region (1930s) and Alberta's Peace River district (1950s). The purpose of these colonization campaigns by the Catholic Church was to keep Canadian settlers in Canada and prevent them leaving for the United States. However, by the mid-twentieth century, public interest in colonization schemes diminished to the point that the church finally abandoned its promotion of them.

The men who led the colonization forces in the areas of settlement included a handful of colourful priests, some of whom were designated as colonization missionaries. One of the latter was Father J.-A.-M. Paradis. He worked in the Temagami region of northeastern Ontario. In the course of his unorthodox career, Paradis selected tracts of land where he wanted to establish settlers, chose the site, and built a chapel there; travelled to the United States and other parts of Canada to recruit settlers; and became a paid agent of immigration of the government of Canada. Paradis even staked claims to mining sites and devised a scheme to dam the Ottawa River in order to facilitate navigation. No doubt the most famous priest involved in colonization was Québec's Father X.-A. Labelle, the 300-pound giant and pastor of Saint-Jérôme who promoted colonization in the Laurentians, helped build a railway from there into Montréal, and then became a deputy minister in the government of Québec, entrusted with the work of colonization.

It was also at the turn of the twentieth century that agricultural clubs were founded among Catholics and that some priests were designated by the bishops of Québec as agricultural missionaries, charged with assisting settlers with everything from choosing a lot, obtaining government grants in aid of clearing the land or sowing crops, or serving as middlemen between the settlers and the government in order to obtain the construction of bridges and new roads.

Colonization societies and sundry Catholic religious orders also engaged in a variety of other social activities aimed at assisting settlers or minority groups in their hour of need. So it was that during the 1880s, in addition to building and operating two steamships to navigate Lake Temiskaming, the society for the colonization of the Lake Temiskaming region, chaired by an Oblate father, founded and built its own railway lines to bypass a set of Ottawa River rapids and to lead from Mattawa on the Ottawa River into colonization areas further inland. The railway spurs were later sold to the Canadian Pacific Railway. While these same Oblates had built a sawmill to help settlers in the Maniwaki region of Québec and built other steamships to supply their numerous missions on the Athabaska, Slave, and Mackenzie Rivers in the Northwest Territories of the late nineteenth century, other religious orders such as the Company of Mary or Montfortain Fathers and the Jesuits established orphanages and agricultural schools in the Laurentians.

The turn of the century was also a time of intensifying interest in labour unions, the majority of which were international unions with no confessional religious ties. Given that a growing number of Catholics belonged to these unions, the Catholic bishops of Québec sought to counter this rival ideology by favouring the establishment of Catholic unions. The effort that began in the first decade of the century would last until 1960 and was destined to remain Québec-based, few workers outside of Québec choosing to join or establish confessional unions.

The turn of the twentieth century was also the time when Catholic Church congregations in Canada, the Oblate Fathers for example, founded a number of newspapers and radio stations that served a number of ethnic groups or linguistic minorities such as the Ukrainian, German, or French Catholic communities in Ontario and western Canada. Oblate, Dominican, and Jesuit Fathers also lent the services of some of their men and the use of their facilities to various linguistic minority associations, particularly the French Canadian ones. So it was that the Oblate Fathers established the daily newspaper *Le Droit* (1913) for the benefit of the Franco-Ontarian community that was engaged in a prolonged and bitter dispute with the government of Ontario over the rights of French schools. Similar gestures were made in the West with the establishment of the newspapers *La Liberté* and *Le Patriote*. The same Oblate Fathers also provided staff and services to the Franco-Ontarians'

main defensive community association, the ACFÉO, in addition to founding radio station CKCH for the same purpose.[5] After 1960, the Oblate
Fathers sold their interests or walked away from such socio-cultural and
political involvement, as did most other Catholic agencies.

Catholic Action

The name *Catholic Action* designates a movement of organized apostolate
by lay men and women. It began in Brussels, Belgium, in 1924 where
Father Joseph Cardijn and a lay friend announced the founding of a
movement to evangelize young working men. The movement was
distinctive in that it called upon lay people, as opposed to clergy, to
evangelize their unbelieving colleagues in the workplace. Catholic Action
was founded on the assumption that in order to achieve successful
evangelization, the workers' environment needed to be changed. Cardijn
named his movement *Jeunesse ouvrière chrétienne* (JOC), with a sister
association for young women (JOCF). The priest published a textbook for
JOC workers in 1925.

Soon after its founding, the movement spread to France, to the rest
of Europe, and to Canada where it took root in Québec in the late 1920s.
In fact, the movement rode the crest of a wave of support for such an
endeavour at the highest echelons of the Catholic Church. Indeed, Pope
Pius XI (1922–1939) had urged lay apostolic action in his encyclical *Ubi
Arcano* (1922). Then in his more celebrated encyclical *Quadragesimo
Anno* (1931), the pope urged workers to evangelize workers, students to
evangelize students, etc. Clearly, in the eyes of Catholic leaders, the
time for Catholic Action had come.

The Catholic Action movement expanded first to agricultural workers (JAC & JACF), students (JÉC & JÉCF), and then to a number of other
occupational groups. Each movement was independent of the others,
and grew rapidly, frequently replacing other youth movements. In the
1930s, the youth movement spread to adult workers, families, and others.
These were the 'specialized' Catholic Action movements that were
supplemented after World War II by a new 'general' Catholic Action
movement sponsored by Catholic bishops who hoped to revitalize the
Christian apostolate in the parishes of their dioceses.

The JOC and its sister associations adopted a method of careful
inquiry and research, often based on questionnaires, in order to better
understand the workplace they sought to evangelize. Their findings
were then compared with church social doctrine which they were re-

quired to learn. A plan of action and vigorous apostolate followed. The motto of Catholic Action was "Observe, judge, and act."

The European Catholic Action movement was imported into Canada after 1927. A leading promoter of the movement was Georges Gauthier, coadjutor-archbishop of Montréal; one of the earliest advocates was Oblate Father Henri Roy. It was his religious congregation of Oblates that would prove to be the leading apostles of the JOC. Roy, the founder of the movement in Canada, was sent to Belgium in 1931 by Gauthier to study the methods of Catholic Action first-hand. Upon his return to Canada, while winning young working men and women back to the church, Roy made the JOC into a primary bulwark against communism. As Canadian bishops endorsed the movement, local chapters of the JOC appeared throughout French Canada, with some chapters in English Canada under the name of Young Christian Workers (YCW). The JOC issued monthly publications which were sent to its thousands of members.

For more than thirty years, the JOC, the JÉC, as well as several other Catholic Action movements served to revitalize the Catholic Church in French Canada. By the time of the movement's demise in the 1960s, Catholic Action in Canada included two general movements, and seven specialized ones. The general movements, those fully integrated into Catholic parish and diocesan structures, were the *Ligue du Sacré-Coeur* for men and the *Dames de Sainte-Anne* for women; both societies changed their names in 1962 to *Chrétiens d'aujourd'hui*, and *Chrétiennes d'aujourd'hui*, before disappearing in the wake of the reforms of Vatican II after 1965.

The seven specialized Catholic Action movements in Canada were: *Jeunesse ouvrière chrétienne* (JOC), *Jeunesse étudiante catholique* (JÉC), *Jeunesse indépendante catholique* (JIC), *Jeunesse rurale catholique* (JRC), *L'Action catholique rurale* (ACR), *Mouvement des travailleurs chrétiens* (MTC), and *Renouveau chrétien* (RC). Some of these movements had a much more modest existence in English-speaking parishes. Some, the JOC in particular, also spawned other specialized Catholic Action movements. For example, a very successful Marriage Preparation Service was created by the JOC and its Oblate mentors in 1941, a service that would help tens of thousands of couples to prepare for successful marriage.

From the 1930s to the 1960s, the Catholic Action movement had a major impact on Catholicism and society, especially in French Canada. In fact, it was the most important social action movement of the Catholic Church in Canada. The movement educated and trained a number of the country's leaders in public life, men and women such as Gérard Pelletier, Jean Marchand, Jeanne Sauvé, Simone Chartrand, and Claude Ryan. The movement taught them to observe a situation dispassionately, to research an issue thoroughly, to accept responsibility for effecting change in society, and to work tirelessly to achieve their objectives in full confidence that the Lord helped those who helped others. Catholic Action also taught its members that they had a right and duty to stand up for their fully responsible adult status as lay people in the Catholic Church. This message was learned through a number of conflicts with some Catholic bishops who considered the specialized Catholic Action movements overly independent of the church hierarchy; the bishops sought to exert greater control over the agencies.

Conclusion

Throughout the twentieth century, Canada's Catholic and Protestant churches have devoted a growing proportion of their time and energy to social questions. In itself, this social *engagement* was not particularly revolutionary in that Christian churches have been the primary agencies of social rescue and service for many centuries. What is new is the growing importance of social questions in the priorities and agendas of the churches. Before 1900, Christian churches viewed social misery and suffering as an unfortunate but necessary part of life in this world, in this valley of tears that had been created by the sins of men and women. Increasingly, as the twentieth century wore on, because of changing theologies and the emergence of social sciences, the churches came to understand social misery and suffering as systemic injustice, as an evil that could be alleviated if not totally removed. The injustice resulted from unjust social, economic, and political structures, forms of social organization that reflected the selfish dispositions of sinful men and women. Increasingly, the churches undertook to work for social change, not merely for the alleviation of suffering. This made the churches more radical in their social discourse; they issued increasingly stronger challenges and denunciations of the exploitation of the poor by the rich, of minorities by majorities, of the Third World by the First World. The social preoccupations that had been marginal in former times became more and more central to the policies and discourse of the churches.

Both the Protestant and Catholic churches distinguished themselves in this new social concern, the former through the Social Gospel and the numerous social service agencies it spawned during the first half of the twentieth century, the latter through its Catholic Action movement in French Canada, and more recently through the almost revolutionary social doctrine that issued forth from Catholic leaders since Vatican II. The latter has given birth to a variety of new theological interpretations, including the liberation theology that emerged from Latin America after 1968, the same region that promoted the policy of the 'preferential option for the poor' that has since been adopted by international Catholic leaders.

During the one hundred years that have followed the publication of *Rerum Novarum* and the emergence of the Social Gospel movement, Catholic and Protestant churches in Canada have taken a decided turn in favour of the underprivileged and the oppressed in society. Whereas it was relatively easy a century ago to find churchmen and churches who clearly sided with the economic establishment and exploiters, by the beginning of the twenty-first century it has become more and more difficult to do so. Today, the cries of the oppressed are more often than not voiced by Christians. Social Christianity had indeed come of age.

Suggested readings

Allen, Richard. Ed. *The Social Gospel in Canada*. Ottawa: National Museum of Man, 1975.

——. *The Social Passion: Religion and Social Reform in Canada 1914–28*. Toronto: University of Toronto Press, 1973.

Baum, Gregory. *Catholics and Canadian Socialism. Political Thought in the Thirties and Forties*. Toronto: James Lorimer & Company, 1980.

Choquette, Robert. *La foi gardienne de la langue en Ontario, 1900–1950*. Montréal: Bellarmin, 1987.

——. *Language and Religion. A History of English-French Conflict in Ontario*. Ottawa: University of Ottawa Press, 1975.

Christie, Nancy and Michael Gauvreau. *A Full-Orbed Christianity. The Protestant Churches and Social Welfare in Canada 1900–1940*. Montréal & Kingston: McGill-Queen's University Press, 1996.

Clément, Gabriel. *Histoire de l'Action catholique au Canada français*. Montréal: Fides, 1972.

Cornwell, John. *Hitler's Pope. The Secret History of Pius XII*. New York: Penguin Books, 1999.

Crerar, Duff. *Padres in No Man's Land : Canadian Chaplains and the Great War.* Montreal & Kingston: McGill-Queen's University Press, 1995.

Dussault, Gabriel. *Le curé Labelle. Messianisme, utopie et colonisation au Québec, 1850–1900.* Montréal: Hurtubise HMH, 1983.

Ferretti, Lucia. *Entre voisins. La société paroissiale en milieu urbain: Saint-Pierre-Apôtre de Montréal, 1848–1930.* Montréal: Boréal, 1992.

Fraser, Brian. *The Social Uplifters: Presbyterian Progressives and the Social Gospel in Canada, 1875–1915.* Waterloo: Wilfrid Laurier University Press, 1988.

Grant, John Webster. *The Church in the Canadian Era.* Updated and expanded. Burlington: Welch Publishing Co., 1988.

Hebblethwaite, Peter. *John XXIII: Pope of the Council.* London: Chapman, 1984.

——. *Paul VI: The First Modern Pope.* London: Harper Collins, 1993.

Horn, Michiel. *The League for Social Reconstruction: Intellectual Origins of the Democratic Left in Canada, 1930–1942.* Toronto: University of Toronto Press, 1980.

Kertzer, David I. *The Popes Against the Jews. The Vatican's Role in the Rise of Modern Anti-Semitism.* New York: Vintage Books, 2001.

McNaught, Kenneth. *A Prophet in Politics. A Biography of J.S. Woodsworth.* Toronto: University of Toronto Press, 1959, 1971.

Ryan, William. *The Clergy and Economic Growth in Québec, 1896–1914.* Québec: Presses de l'Université Laval, 1966.

Sheridan, E. F. Ed. *Love Kindness! The Social Teaching of the Canadian Catholic Bishops 1958–1989.* Sherbrooke: Éditions Paulines, 1991.

——. *Do Justice! The Social Teaching of the Canadian Catholic Bishops 1945–1986.* Sherbrooke: Éditions Paulines, 1987.

Utz, Arthur. Ed. *La doctrine sociale de l'Église à travers les siècles.* 3 vols., Paris: Beauchesne, 1970.

Vidler, Alexander R. *A Century of Social Catholicism, 1820–1930.* London: SPCK, 1964.

Weigel, George. *Witness to Hope. The Biography of Pope John Paul II.* New York: Harper Collins Publishers, 1999.

CHAPTER 17

Secularization and Church Reform

World War II stands as a watershed between the traditional Canadian, Western, and Christian worlds and a new age ushered in by vast migrations of people, the arrival of television, the onset of the nuclear age, and spreading Western consumerist societies that challenged all traditions whether social, political, or religious. A major social and ideological reflection of these rapidly changing times was secularization. As Canadian, Western and then Third World societies became progressively more secularized during the second half of the twentieth century, the Christian churches were driven to adjust to the new realities, to reform themselves from the ground up. The most sweeping of these renewal movements was the Catholic Church's Second Vatican Council.

Secularization

A phenomenon of modern times in the West, secularization was usually understood as the gradual emancipation of this world from the *other* world, the transcendent world, the world of God. Secularization was a process whereby segments of society and culture were withdrawn from the authority of religious institutions and symbols. The more secularization progressed, the more the secularized persons, objects, institutions, or places were perceived as autonomous, separate from the transcendent. For many interpreters, secularization designated a sweeping social process of progressive removal of our world from the world of God. The sociologist Bryan Wilson wrote: "Sociologists have used this word to indicate a variety of processes in which control of social space, time, facilities, resources, and personnel was lost by religious authorities, and in which empirical procedures and worldly goals and purposes displaced ritual and symbolic patterns of action directed toward otherworldly, or supernatural, ends... Briefly defined, secularization is the process in which religious consciousness, activities, and institutions lose social significance. It indicates that religion becomes marginal to the operation of the social system, and that the essential functions for the operation of society become rationalized, passing out of the control of agencies devoted to the supernatural."[1]

As the various components of our society affirm their autonomy, the transcendent presupposition that underlaid our traditional understanding of the world slipped away. We then reach the point where people think less and less of the transcendent. It seems natural to them to explain everything without invoking it. God has been removed from his leading position. Most social institutions then become deaf and dumb about the supernatural, an area that is left to specifically religious institutions, agencies that specialize in religious things. God has been marginalized along with all of the sacred and all of the transcendent.

According to this common understanding, as secularization increases, religiosity decreases in the same proportion. While secularization is tied to the growth of industry, science, and reason, religiosity is tied to faith, miracles, myth, emotion, and credulity. Some interpreters challenge such an understanding, arguing that rather than being on the wane in our time, religiosity is merely more diversified than heretofore. This would explain contemporary phenomena such as the rise of fundamentalisms, the multiplication of sects, and the emergence of numerous new religious movements. According to these critics, contemporary society would be better explained if the traditional concept of secularization were shelved, in favour of the alternative concept of the *displacement of the sacred*. For them, far from being on the wane, religiosity is on the increase in our time, but under various guises and names rather than within the confines of traditional religions.

As a leading member of Western society, Canada is a prime example of secularization. Overwhelmingly Christian in the late nineteenth century, during the twentieth century the country's people and institutions gradually severed their numerous ties with the Catholic and Protestant churches. Indeed, the extended Christian presence in Canadian society that was described above gradually gave way to thoroughly secularized hospitals and social service agencies, schools, and universities. Although

English Protestant and French Catholic Canada secularized at different times and in different ways, the end result is almost identical, that is to say a contemporary Canada whose institutions, symbols, leaders, and discourse make little reference to God or the supernatural. Some would argue that even the consciences and value systems of Canadians are largely secularized.

It was this emerging and threatening phenomenon of sweeping secularization that prompted Canada's Christian churches to launch major reform movements during the 1960s. The most important of these movements was the Catholic Church's Second Vatican Council.

Vatican II: the reform of Catholicism

In January 1959, only three months after being elected pope, the septuagenarian Angelo Roncalli announced to the world his intention to call the meeting of an ecumenical council. John XXIII surprised most people, and shocked some, with this bold gesture. Indeed, with the exception of the truncated First Vatican Council in 1869–1870, there had not been an ecumenical council in the Catholic Church since the sixteenth-century's Council of Trent which had been called in response to the challenge of the Protestant Reformation. After two years of preparatory work, the Second Vatican Council was officially convened on Christmas day 1961 to meet for the first time in October 1962. By the time it ended in December 1965, it had met in four sessions, each in the latter months of the years 1962, 1963, 1964, and 1965. Among its voting members – the bishops, who were more than two thousand strong – the council brought together hundreds of heads of religious orders, theologians, historians, and expert advisers in a variety of fields.

In addition to endless meetings, reams of working papers, draft documents, and policy papers, Vatican II produced sixteen official documents that were endorsed by the Council fathers and promulgated by the pope. The most important of these were the four *Constitutions* or foundational texts bearing on the liturgy, the Church, Christian Revelation, and the Church in the modern world. Next in order of importance were nine decrees which dealt with the more specific questions of the means of communication, ecumenism, eastern rite Catholic churches, the mandate of bishops, seminaries, the renewal of religious life, the apostolate of laypeople, the ministry and life of priests, and the missionary activity of the church. Finally, the Council issued three declarations bearing in turn upon religious freedom, Christian education, and the relations between the church and non-Christian religions.

The central objectives of Vatican II

Vatican II sought to revitalize the Catholic Church, to bring it up to date in a rapidly changing world, and to adjust its teaching and policies to the new realities of the late twentieth century. Its official documents were a vivid testimonial to that. Perhaps more important than the specific decisions and changes, however, was the *event* of Vatican II, including the very fact that it was held at all, the dialogue and changes of heart that it occasioned among many participants, and the new priorities that it fostered throughout Catholicism. A church that had become all too rationalistic, juridical, judgemental, and self-sufficient in its ways, found itself invited to trust, to dialogue, and to respect others be they Catholic, Protestant, Jewish, Hindu, Muslim, or other. Catholics were reminded that all men and women were children of God and thus deserving of respect and love. In the process, many Catholic clergy and faithful rediscovered the Gospel and felt a breath of fresh air, a new springtime in their community of faith.

Pope John sought the *agiornamento* or renewal of the Catholic Church by reforming it in head and members. He sought renewal in all aspects of Catholic life, including theology, liturgy, government, organization, moral teaching, spirituality, and evangelization. He wanted to rebuild bridges between the church and its host societies, entities that had all too often become estranged during modern times. Pope John wanted to foster brotherhood among all people, including friendly relations with non-Christian religions and closer ties with other Christian churches, with a view to reuniting all Christians. In the eyes of the pope, these objectives were all part of better preaching the Gospel in our time, in order to hasten the liberation or salvation of humankind.

Means to achieve these objectives

The means of achieving these objectives of renewal of Christian life and of relations between the church and society were to revisit the sources of Christian life, to renew Catholic teaching, and to reform Catholic attitudes towards themselves and others.

Revisiting the sources of Christian life meant looking anew at the sources of God's Revelation in the history of the church. Here, the primary emphasis was on the Bible, but a fresh look at the teachings of the Fathers of the Church and at the vast tapestry of church history were also on the agenda. Indeed, in the wake of the Protestant reformation of the sixteenth century and its strong focus on the Bible, the Catholic Church had at times played down the importance of the Bible while emphasizing the role of the church in God's Revelation. In an effort to rectify the situation, Vatican II not only couched most of its teachings in thoroughly biblical language, but also issued a dogmatic constitution on divine Revelation, the constitution *Dei verbum*, in November 1965.

Revisiting the sources of Christian life included rethinking, redefining, and reformulating Catholic theology. Given that theology is a discourse about the Christian faith, any recasting of that faith entails the renewal of the discourse about it. From the 1930s at least, European theologians, especially from France and Germany, had been putting new questions to the Christian church in an effort to come to grips with the rapidly changing industrializing, urbanizing, and secularizing societies of the twentieth century. By the time of Vatican II, Catholic theologians such as Yves Congar, René de Lubac, Edward Schillebeeckx, Karl Rahner, and Jean Daniélou were deeply engaged in a process of putting new questions to the Christian faith and producing refreshing and different answers that resulted from both their inquiring minds and their profound knowledge of both Scripture and history, not to mention contemporary systems of philosophy. The reforming churchmen of the council steeped themselves in their teaching, set aside the traditionalist proposals of other churchmen, and undertook to build a renewed Catholic theology. The result was a dramatically transformed Catholic discourse.

Underlying the new theology that issued forth from Vatican II was a new appreciation of the goodness of all created things, because God had created in a gesture of giving and loving. The children of God, whom he loved more than everything else, stood foremost in this created order of men and women. This new appreciation of human beings coloured all aspects of the teaching of the council. If all people were the beloved children of God, it followed that they deserved respect, that they had basic human rights, and that they were endowed with a personal dignity that nobody was entitled to trample underfoot. It meant that it was every Christian's duty to establish and sustain dialogue with other Christians, with other believers, and with unbelievers.

According to the council, these children of God, endowed with rights and personal dignity, also had the law of God inscribed in their hearts from the moment of creation. The voice of that divine law in each of us was called conscience. Therefore, the council taught that none may disobey their enlightened conscience; each one of us must obey our right conscience, whatever our circumstances, whatever our religion. Such an emphasis was refreshing, indeed news, for most Catholics. The consequences of this teaching were far-reaching in terms of the moral behaviour of the faithful, be it in matters of personal morality such as the use of contraceptives, or in matters of public morality such as legislation on the death penalty.

Favouring the opening and sustaining of dialogue with other Christians was also a significant change in policy for a Catholic Church which had usually refused any dialogue with other churches considered as equals. Until Vatican II, the Catholic Church considered that it had the truth and that it was up to others to acknowledge that; it was willing to instruct others, but not dialogue with them in matters of religious belief. The new respect accorded to others included the recognition that the Eastern Orthodox were true Christians that became separated from communion with Rome in 1054 C.E. because of regrettable events. It included the recognition that Protestants could not be labeled as *heretics* and simply set aside or condemned as they had been in the past. Vatican II chose to refer to them as *separated brethren*, acknowledged that portions of their teaching had been misunderstood, confessed the many sins of the Catholic Church that had been instrumental in fostering the Protestant Reformation, invited Protestants to dialogue, and prayed that the unity of Christians may be restored, God willing.

Indeed, the council's decree on ecumenism, *Unitatis redintegratio* (1964), turned the page on many long years of contempt for Protestants in the Catholic Church. The Catholic Church's transformation into an ecumenical church was strongly reinforced by the Secretariat for Christian Unity, a Vatican agency established by Pope John XXIII shortly after his election and headed by Cardinal Augustin Bea, a Jesuit biblical scholar. In addition, the council made it clear that anti-Semitism was inadmissible in the Catholic Church. Some of the traditional stereotypes used to attack Jews were explicitly rejected. Not all Jews and certainly not those of subsequent generations were guilty of having put Jesus to death. Instead, Christians were reminded not only that Jesus and the founders of the Church were Jews, but also that in many respects Christian theology was grounded in the religion of Israel.

Another foundational means of achieving the objectives of the council was to acknowledge the importance of cultural realities and identities in the process of evangelization. Indeed, in spite of periodic reminders by some pontiffs that all human beings were children of God, that their cultures were to be respected, and that young men and women of all cultures were to be welcomed into the ranks of the Catholic clergy, in actual fact, over the course of several centuries the Catholic Church had more often than not become identified with Western and European civilization. The Roman Catholic liturgy, official prayers, official language, governing structures, and legislation were uniformly Roman. The philosophy and the theology taught in Catholic institutions throughout the world were uniform and had to be approved by the Vatican. Indeed, on the eve of Vatican II, the Roman Catholic Church wore the full dress uniform of Western and European civilization. This promotion of Western and Roman ways had the effect of discrediting other languages and cultures; indeed, why waste one's time and energy on other cultures and languages when they did not matter in the church?

Given that one of the primary objectives of Pope John XXIII in calling a council was to rebuild the bridges between the church and the world, it came as no surprise that one of the key documents produced by Vatican II was the pastoral constitution on the Church in the modern world. When *Gaudium et spes* was adopted by the council fathers on 7 December 1965, it was the culmination of several years of debate, discussion, and speculation by many Catholic leaders and faithful. In *Gaudium et spes*, the assembled prelates addressed themselves to all men and women, declared their church's solidarity with them, and invited them to dialogue in order to achieve the renewal of humankind while fostering a new sense of brotherhood among all. The document was divided into two parts, the first being a reminder of some basic teachings while the second addressed some specific issues such as marriage and the family, the relationship of cultures with the church, war and peace, and some of the economic and political challenges of the present.

After describing the situation of contemporary men and women and noting the ongoing promptings of the Holy Spirit in our world, the council fathers reminded their readers of the fundamental doctrine of men and women being created in the image of God. Because of this divine image in all of us, the basic dignity of the human person was established, both the physical and spiritual dimensions of the human person were founded, and the dignity of the intellect, of truth, and of wisdom were posited. This divine image was etched within every man and woman: "Deep within his conscience man discovers a law which he has not laid upon himself but which he must obey. Its voice, ever calling him to love and to do what is good and to avoid evil, tells him inwardly at the right moment: do this, shun that. For man has in his heart a law inscribed by God. His dignity lies in observing this law, and by it he will be judged. His conscience is man's most secret core, and his sanctuary. There he is alone with God whose voice echoes in his depths. By conscience, in a wonderful way, that law is made known which is fulfilled in the love of God and of one's neighbor. Through loyalty to conscience Christians are joined to other men in the search for truth and for the right solution to so many moral problems which arise both in the life of individuals and from social relationships."[2]

Gaudium et spes went on to speak of the excellence of freedom, because "man's dignity... requires him to act out of conscious and free choice ... by freely choosing what is good."[3] The document denounced atheism, noted the communitarian nature of men and women, speaking of the interdependence of men and women, of the common good of all, and of the essential equality of all people which demanded social justice for all. While earthly affairs were autonomous, human activity was infected by sin and consequently needed divine redemption through Christ.

In striking contrast to most other ecumenical councils, Vatican II spoke with the acknowledgment that it was part and parcel of the world it was discussing; the fathers did not address their audience from a pedestal of their own making, propounding doctrines from another world. Rather they were reaching out to fellow men and women, urging them to engage in dialogue with the church with a view to achieve a better understanding of themselves and their world through the Gospel. The tone and style of the documents of Vatican II were as revealing as their contents.

Another means of achieving the central objectives of the council was the renewal of the liturgy, the forms of piety, and the devotions of the Catholic Church. It was these manifest parts of the reform program that were most visible to many of the faithful and to outside observers. Several languages had enjoyed pride of place in the history of the Catholic Church. From the outset, the Semitic languages of the Jews and others of Palestine and the Middle East had been enriched by Greek and then Latin, the successive common languages of the surrounding empires and civilizations. So it was that the Christian Bible was originally written in Hebrew, Aramaic, and Greek. Latin gradually supplanted Greek in the churches of the West after the fourth century C.E., in the wake of the fall of the Roman Empire and the gradual separation of the civilizations of the East and West. As medieval civilization gathered strength after the year 1000 C.E, Latin became its official language as a result of the Christian church directing and coordinating the rebirth of civilization in the West. However, just as medieval civilization reached its apogee in the twelfth and thirteenth centuries, the birth of a variety of nationalisms and their respective languages were forces pulling the world of Christendom apart. Thereafter, Rome was gradually pushed to the periphery of Western civilization as national capitals like Paris, Vienna, Madrid, and London took centre stage in Western history. An important part of the emerging nationalisms was the distinctive language of the nation-state. So it was that French, English, German, and Spanish came to dominate Western civilization, just as Russian and Chinese did farther to the East.

By the time of the Reformations of the sixteenth century, Latin had become a dead language, except for its continued role as the official language of the Roman Catholic Church. Given the latter's strong policies of centralization after the sixteenth century, Rome found it convenient and useful to maintain Latin as the language of the church. The price it paid, however, was a sustained and widening gap between the official church with its Latin liturgy, Latin prayers, Latin missals, and Latin Gregorian chant on the one hand, and the faithful with their diverse languages and cultures on the other hand. From the sixteenth to the mid-twentieth centuries, religious services in a Catholic Church were usually not only colourful and dramatic, but mysterious and apparently magical given that few understood what was being said or sung. The clergy performed their official rituals while the flock indulged in their own discrete forms of worship that were not always related to the ritual celebration they were attending.

The reformers that promoted Vatican II wanted to transform the Catholic Church into a church of the people, a people of God to use the words of the dogmatic constitution on the church *Lumen Gentium* (1964). This meant that Latin had to be replaced in the liturgy by various living languages, languages that people actually spoke, read, and understood. Although in 1962 Pope John XXIII attempted to reinforce the use of Latin and the council considered that it should continue to be used in the liturgy, in fact its use in the church rapidly diminished after 1962 to the point that it is on the verge of extinction in Catholic worship. Vernacular languages are now the standard in the Catholic Church, except in some official Roman documents and among a handful of conservative clergy who have wrested special permission from their bishops to continue to use Latin in liturgical services.

The rapid abandonment of Latin after 1962 entailed a number of consequences, including the disappearance of Gregorian chant from Catholic worship and its necessary replacement by newly composed hymns and music. Since the latter could not readily match the time-tested beauty and resonance of the centuries-old Gregorian chant, many Catholics felt that their worship services had been impoverished. The introduction of vernacular languages also meant that the faithful could better appreciate, or understand for the first time, the meaning of the words used in the liturgy. This led to renewed questioning of doc-trine by many Catholics along with a lessening of their sense of awe and mystery which had been sustained by the hoary and inspiring sounds of Latin verse and song. In the eyes of many, Catholic worship became a more mundane exercise and therefore easier to set aside. Somehow, God seemed more distant from a more readily understand-able liturgy. Attendance at Sunday worship became irregular for a growing number.

In spite of the drawbacks noted above, however, most Catholics rejoiced at the now understandable words used in the liturgy. Many felt that their church was moving closer to them, an ideological, theologi-cal, and spiritual *rapprochement* that most longed for. Despite the fact that there was a price to pay for this change in Catholic policy, they knew that it was nevertheless necessary. These were the faithful who responded positively to their leaders' invitation to assume full respon-sibility for their Christian life while acknowledging that their clergy were no longer the rulers but the servants of the community, of the people of God. The abandonment of Latin marked a turning point in the history of the Catholic Church.

In addition to dropping Latin in favour of vernacular languages, the Catholic liturgy changed in a number of other ways. The position of the main altar in churches reflected this. During the centuries of Latin and Roman liturgy, the altar stood against the front wall of the sanctuary at the front of the church where the priest celebrated Mass with his back to the congregation. This positioning reflected the prevailing theology which underlined the sacrificial and mysterious dimension of the Mass along with the exclusive powers of the priest who consecrated the bread and wine thereby transforming them into the body and blood of Christ; the Mass became a spectacle where the congregation was reduced to the role of spectator. Vatican II changed this theology by emphasizing that the Mass was also a celebration by the assembled congregation led by the priest. So that the presider would face the congregation with whom he was celebrating the Eucharist, the altar was moved closer to the congregation from the front extremity of the church; in some churches the altar was positioned in the midst of the congregation.

The new emphasis on congregational celebration and on the priest's role as presider also resulted in the effective disappearance of side altars in Catholic churches. Indeed, since the Middle Ages, Catholic churches were usually equipped with a number of side altars so that several priests could individually but simultaneously celebrate Mass. This was considered legitimate because the Mass was understood as primarily the priest's doing. When Vatican II changed this latter understanding, the use of side altars was doomed.

Vatican II's reform of theology, piety, and forms of devotion led to many other changes in Catholic life. Statues, those perennial signs of Catholic devotion that decorated churches and dotted the landscape of Catholic countries, were demoted in the order of priorities of the Catholic Church. This resulted from the renewed theology that prevailed in Catholicism after Vatican II, a theology that focused on Holy Scripture, on the redemptive role of Christ, and on the living of an authentic evangelical Christian life. This meant a return to basics in Christian living. Also, in its concern with establishing fruitful dialogue with other Christians, Vatican II was sensitive to the oft-repeated criticism that Catholic devotions to saints and to the Virgin sometimes smacked of idolatry, or at least of misplaced or exaggerated cults centred on the creature rather than on the creator. Catholics were reminded that God as Father, Son, and Spirit and Christ's birth, death, and resurrection were at the centre of Catholic doctrine, worship, and devotions and needed to remain there.

Any devotions that appeared to subtract from that God-centredness or Christ-centredness were to be reconsidered. This included the cult of Mary, a devotion that had been important in the Christian church since the early centuries, but that had sometimes been abused. It also included the numerous and varied devotions associated with pilgrimages, shrines, and popular piety in general. Mary and the saints remained important in the church of Vatican II, but not as alternatives or equals to God and Christ which they were never supposed to have become.

The renewal of Catholic piety also implied changes in Catholic rules for fasting and abstaining from specific foods and beverages. From the origins of the Christian church, self-denial through abstinence and fasting had been a normal requirement of Christian living. It was justified on the basis that the denial of bodily cravings served to remind Christians of their spiritual origin and calling and of the superiority of the latter over one's physical needs. The forms and rules of self-denial had varied over the years. Beginning in the 1950s, while maintaining the value of self-denial, the Catholic Church had softened its rules for abstinence and fasting, a reflection of the more humane, consumerist, permissive Western society after World War II. The church of Vatican II confirmed this tendency. It moved away from requiring Catholics to observe detailed rules in this regard, be it in relation to fasting before receiving the Eucharist, during Lent, or at certain times of the year. The Vatican II church was content to remind the faithful that self-denial was still important, but that it was up to the individual faithful to decide on the forms and modalities that such self-denial would take for them.

One of the more significant reforms of the Vatican II church was the modification of the church's philosophy of government and its governing structures. As was noted above, the new theology that prevailed at Vatican II defined the Catholic Church as the people of God, a concept that entailed a changed role for both clergy and laity. While seeking to empower the laity, the Vatican II church spoke of a hierarchy of service rather than of domination in the church. Bishops were invited to exchange their previous role of rulers for that of shepherds of their flock and priests likewise. Although bishops, in their capacity as successors of the apostles, retained their role as the first officers of their respective dioceses, they were strongly urged to share much of their authority with other clergy and laity.

This changed outlook resulted in sweeping consequences. Among the structural changes were the creation of a host of new committees, boards of directors, advisory councils, task forces, and synods at all levels of government of the Catholic Church. Specifically, these included an international synod of bishops charged with advising the pope, diocesan synods of priests entrusted with advising the local bishop on matters of interest to their members, diocesan and parish administrative advisory boards responsible for the financial and property management of the diocese, diocesan and parish pastoral committees that counseled the bishop on pastoral policy, and numerous committees created to deal with issues as diverse as media relations, the education of the faith, ecumenical dialogue, social service, the renewal of religious life, etc. Indeed, some Catholic laypeople and clergy of Vatican II vintage seemed to spend the better part of their months and years in meetings, a phenomenon that eventually led many to question the value of seemingly endless meetings producing few results. In fact, in many instances during the 1960s, the 1970s, and beyond, governance of the Catholic Church continued unchanged while a series of new advisory committees met, debated, resolved, and adjourned without obtaining any significant changes in the ongoing administration of their parish, diocese, religious order, or region.

Another result of the changed theology and governing structure of the Catholic Church was a crisis in the identity of the priest who no longer understood his role in the church. The same was true for men and women in religious orders. Many priests failed to understand how they were to transform themselves overnight from directors to servants of their flock. Men who were used to ruling were now supposed to become mere facilitators. Confusion over their uncertain identity was undoubtedly a key factor in the decision of many Catholic priests and religious to cast off their frocks and leave the ministry after 1965.

The Vatican II church also redefined the roles of clergy and laity by deciding to shift major areas of social responsibility from the former to the latter. This meant that dioceses and religious congregations of brothers and sisters were urged to withdraw their services from many social service institutions such as hospitals, schools, and colleges in order to concentrate their efforts in areas of greater perceived need such as poor relief, missions, and community activism. Overnight, Canada's provincial governments replaced the sisters and brothers, purchasing the erstwhile Catholic hospitals, colleges, and schools and transforming them into new provincially-funded and chartered institutions that were staffed by lay employees. This rapid change of private into public institutions meant the simultaneous instant disappearance of thousands of men and women in clerical garb from the public square. The result was that any visible religious presence practically disappeared from Canada's schools and hospitals. In renewing itself by showing greater respect for laypeople and Canada's new secular society, the Vatican II church had in effect made itself invisible to many.

There were many other changes that Vatican II brought about in contemporary Catholicism. Although only time will tell the real importance of Vatican II, it will probably stand alongside the Council of Nicaea (325) and the Council of Trent as one of the handful of pivotal councils in the history of the church. The importance of Vatican II resulted not so much from any of its individual decisions or documents but rather from the event of the council itself. It was the experience of the council that changed the understanding of many of its participants and observers. It served as a catalyst for a renewed understanding and appreciation of the Gospel and of the importance of evangelizing contemporary society. Catholics would never be the same afterwards.

Protestantism in question

While the response of Catholics to secularization culminated in Vatican II, that of Canada's Protestants also generated some decisive changes during the second half of the twentieth century.

The fifteen years following World War II were a period of rapid growth in the numbers of buildings, clergy, and faithful of Canada's Protestant churches which seemed to be expanding in step with the country's suburbia, yet the proportion of church members in Canada's total population was slipping. In fact, Canada's growing secular and consumerist mindset seemed to be sapping the foundations of the faith of Canada's Protestant Christians. The proportion of Canada's Protestants that attended church regularly once a week was dropping at a rapid rate. Indeed 60% of Protestants had attended church weekly in 1946, but only one third did so twenty years later. Critics raised some serious questions about the state of Protestantism in Canada.

One such critic was Pierre Berton. A lapsed member of the Anglican Church of Canada, Berton was invited by it to reflect the views of Canada's disaffected Anglicans in order to provide that church's faithful with a valid instrument for renewal. The book *The Comfortable Pew* (1965) was the popular historian's answer. Without asking for any radical changes in the church, Berton invited his erstwhile Anglican brothers and sisters to live up to their own principles in the areas of worship, evangelism, preaching, social concern, and fellowship. As things were, he found them sadly wanting. *The Comfortable Pew* proved to be a bestseller, provoking extensive debate and controversy. While some took it to be a new gospel, others judged it superficial, just another blurb in the period's quest for relevance.

Shortly before the publication of the Berton book, the Anglican Church of Canada had issued a revision of the *Book of Common Prayer* (1959); in 1983 it would approve a book of alternative services. In 1962 the Presbyterians issued a new *Book of Common Order*. Always at the forefront of innovation and change, The United Church of Canada also disturbed many of its flock in 1968 when it adopted a new creed to serve as an alternative to the Apostle's Creed in its services. It came on the heels of the new curriculum adopted for church teachers in 1962 and preceded by fifteen years the adoption of a *Book of Alternative service* (1983). Some members of that church judged that the new texts were centred more on humanity than on God. The debate would prove protracted.

In addition, it became commonplace in Canada's churches after 1960 to replace the traditional sermons, music, hymns, and musical instruments of worship with popular counterparts such as social commentaries or discussions from the pulpit, the guitar, folk music, and multi-media presentations. All of these measures were supposed to make the churches more relevant to contemporary society, to move them closer to contemporary Canadians. Many were disturbed at seeing their beloved music and liturgical customs jettisoned in favour of some perceived less-than-tasteful contemporary compositions. When the venerated King James English translation of the Bible was given some less-than-felicitous competition, some were outraged. Some were shocked when the government of Canada changed provisions in the country's Criminal Code that dealt with issues such as abortion, divorce, homosexuality, and contraception. Important elements of the traditional Christian moral code were being set aside in the laws of the land.

In the area of theological education, profound change was also occurring after 1960. In the majority of Canada's public universities, departments and programs of religious studies were being created, frequently replacing the traditional study of divinity and its associated theological orientation with a secular humanistic study of religions, an allegedly more scientific and objective approach. The study of theology with its foundation in Christian faith would continue in professional schools that were usually attached to confessional institutions. Theology programs would also be reorganized after 1969 when the Toronto School of Theology was founded, a cooperative venture by various churches, both Protestant and Catholic, whereby joint programs of study were established. Similar joint enterprises were founded in Halifax, Vancouver, and elsewhere.

While Canadians have innovated in the organizing of theological education, they have not usually been in the forefront of theological research and writing. Despite some exceptions such as Bernard Lonergan, more often than not it is European, British, and American theologians who are studied and read in Canadian schools and churches. So it was in Canadian Protestantism after 1960. Much debate centred on the Englishman J.A.T. Robinson's *Honest to God* (1963), on the American Episcopalian's James Pike's questions on the existence of God, and on Harvard Professor Harvey Cox's *The Secular City* that seemed to celebrate the disappearance of the sacred from our public squares. Many studied the work of European theologians like Karl Barth, Dietrich Bonhoeffer, Rudolf Bultmann, and Paul Tillich; the latter in fact worked in the United States. And much of this intellectual endeavour was done in a climate marked by the popularity of existentialist philosophy as reflected by European scholars such as Jean-Paul Sartre and Martin Heidegger. The social climate was also one of renewed commitment to social justice as reflected in the influence of the American social rights leader Martin Luther King and Prime Minister Pierre Elliott Trudeau.

Despite a continuing decline in membership after 1970, Canada's mainline Protestant churches continued to innovate and to provoke much debate among their members. Their efforts at church union will be considered below. Other areas of change included the publication of a joint hymnbook in 1971 by the Anglican and United Churches, the more frequent ordination of women in most churches, and the approval of the ordination to the ministry of active homosexuals in the United Church of Canada in 1988. This decision led to the secession of some United Church congregations, while several remaining members of the church continued to question the decision. The same debate was ongoing in the Anglican Church of Canada, a number of whose ministers had also seceded in the late 1970s over the question of the ordination of women.

After 1970, it was evangelical or traditionalist Protestants who were at the forefront. While continuing to insist on common basic points of doctrine such as the Bible, evangelism, and personal piety, they added a renewed social outreach to their program. They developed a network of joint or trans-denominational alliances primarily in areas of social concern, but also in missions, theological activities, and evangelism. By the beginning of the twenty-first century, Canadian Protestantism was not only organized into several denominations, but an important number of these same Protestants belonged to a growing coalition of like-minded conservative or evangelical Protestants that crossed denominational lines.

Cooperative Christianity

While Vatican II represents the crystallization of reform in twentieth-century Catholicism, a more diversified but equally important phenomenon developed in most Christian, but primarily Protestant churches over the course of the same century. I have designated the movement *cooperative Christianity* because it brought together both the ecumenical movement and a growing movement of social cooperation between many Protestant and Catholic churches. This cooperative Christianity rested on a theology very similar to that of Vatican II and was driven by several new ecclesiastical organizations that were established specifically to foster ecumenism and cooperation. Among the better-known cooperative sponsoring organizations were the World Council of Churches, the Canadian Council of Churches, the Canadian Council of Catholic Bishops, and the Evangelical Fellowship of Canada. Singly or in combination, these organizations established a number of joint agencies dedicated to a variety of social issues such as the rights of Aboriginal people in Canada, peace and disarmament, economic rights, the plight of the poor, Third World issues, etc. For the first time in more than four hundred years, Christian denominations and churches managed to set aside their differences in order to cooperate in areas of common social concern.

Cooperative Christianity had begun earlier, however, among Canada's Protestants. In fact from the last quarter of the nineteenth century, some of Canada's leading churches began a process of *rapprochement* that led first to mergers of Presbyterian denominations (1875), then of Methodist denominations (1884), and later of many individual traditionalists, Adventists, and millenarians under the umbrella of the growing conservative movement that was described earlier. The process of progressive fragmentation that had formerly characterized many Canadian Protestant churches was thus reversed. The crowning achievement was the formation of the United Church of Canada in 1925, a merger of the Methodists, Congregationalists, and some two-thirds of Presbyterians in Canada. Canada's largest Protestant church was thus born. As a result, many of Canada's Protestants became well-versed in the art of negotiation and in the forbearance required in creating common religious fronts.

Indeed, the protracted negotiations that had eventually led to the formation of the United Church of Canada in 1925 were fraught with unforeseen surprises and disappointments. The negotiations that be-gan in an earlier era of consensus, ended in the twenties, a very frac-tious decade. Protestants, particularly in the West, had longed for union to resolve the quandary that was often their lot: two, three, or more small Protestant churches all competing for a very limited pool of potential members in numerous scattered communities across Canada's prairies. Many wondered why the churches remained apart. Local church unions were an obvious way out of this box; a number of such unions preceded the union of 1925. However, this union of a majority of Canadian Protestants also reinforced the continuation of a distinct Presbyterian Church of Canada. The union of 1925 was at best a weak beginning for those who dreamed of a united Christian church. But a beginning it was.

The World Council of Churches (WCC)

Although differences and divisions always existed among Christians, efforts to reunite the divided flock had also been with us from the beginning. Nevertheless, the twentieth century witnessed the strongest and most sustained campaign to re-establish unity among Christians. The ecumenical movement nourished and sustained several attempts at effecting reconciliation among Christians. The World Council of Churches represents one of the most important of these, the institutional embodiment of the ecumenical movement.

The World Council of Churches whose beginning is usually dated from the Edinburgh Missionary Conference of 1910, was itself the product of earlier efforts to reunite Christians. From this movement would eventually issue the Universal Christian Conference on Life and Work founded in Stockholm in 1925; it was principally concerned with the application of Christianity to social, political, and economic issues. Two years later in Lausanne, Switzerland, the first world conference on Faith and Order took place; it was concerned with the theological basis of Christian unity. Both Life and Work and Faith and Order became movements that fostered unity discussions in many countries, several of which established their own national councils of churches during the 1930s and 1940s. So it was that the Canadian Council of Churches was founded in 1944. Then, upon the end of World War II, the World Council of Churches was founded at a meeting in Amsterdam in 1948 to bring together the Life and Work and Faith and Order movements, as well as the several national councils of churches.

The initiative for establishing this confederation of churches came primarily from Protestant leaders, the Church of England included, although both the Eastern Orthodox and Oriental Orthodox churches had been members of the World Council from the outset. When the Russian Orthodox Church overcame initial reservations and joined in 1961, the vast majority of Christian churches were members, with the glaring exception of the Roman Catholic Church. However, this soon changed as it was also in 1961 that for the first time, the Vatican delegated official observers to the Third Assembly of the World Council of

Churches in New Delhi. The gesture had been preceded by the official visit of Anglican Archbishop G.F. Fisher of Canterbury, the leader of the worldwide Anglican Communion, to Pope John XXIII in 1960. It was followed by Pope John's invitation to non-Catholic Christian churches to send observers to Vatican II. When the Council issued its decree on ecumenism in 1964, Protestant and Orthodox leaders were pleased to observe that they were no longer described as being outside the Church; rather, they were designated as separated brethren. Another step had been taken towards Christian unity.

Although the Catholic Church has not become a full-fledged member of the World Council of Churches, since the 1950s it fully participated in discussions and worked towards Christian unity alongside the World Council. In its constitution, the World Council of Churches defines itself as "a fellowship of churches which confess the Lord Jesus as God and Savior according to the Scriptures and therefore seek to fulfill together their common calling to the glory of the one God, Father, Son, and Holy Spirit."[4]

With headquarters and a secretariat in Geneva, Switzerland, the World Council of Churches is governed by a representative assembly that meets every six to eight years. The assembly elects a 150-member Central Committee which meets annually; a number of advisory committees are established by the Central Committee to assist the Council's permanent staff. General assemblies of the World Council have been held at Amsterdam (1948), Evanston, Illinois (1954), New Delhi (1961), Uppsala (1968), Nairobi (1975), Vancouver (1983), and Canberra (1991).

The Canadian Council of Churches (CCC)

From its founding in 1944, the Canadian Council of Churches fulfilled much the same function in Canada as the World Council does on a broader stage. It was a confederation of autonomous churches that chose to consult and cooperate in planning and action in a variety of endeavours such as social action, evangelization, missions, and faith education. It included many, but not all Christian churches in Canada. As was the case with the World Council, the Roman Catholic Church cooperated with the Canadian Council but was not a full-fledged member of it. It became an associate member in 1985.

With headquarters in Toronto, the Canadian Council of Churches was directed and supported by its member churches, being governed by a triennial Assembly and a semi-annual General Board. Its work was coordinated by three commissions dealing respectively with Justice and Peace, Ecumenical Education and Communication, and Faith and Witness.

The Evangelical Fellowship of Canada (EFC)

Founded in 1964 with headquarters in Markham, Ontario, the Evangelical Fellowship of Canada gathered together some twenty-four Protestant denominations and a number of individual Protestants from other denominations that do not belong to it. With the Pentecostal Assemblies of Canada as its largest constituent member, this gathering of mainly conservative Protestants also included a number of smaller denominations such as the Salvation Army, the Mennonite Brethren Church, the Christian Reformed Church, and the Christian and Missionary Alliance churches. All Protestant denominations that were members were represented on its general council.

Directed by a full-time executive director, a commission on social action, and two task forces on the family and evangelism, the association tried to foster cooperation, interaction, and renewal among its members. This may have contributed to the merger of two Lutheran churches into the Evangelical Lutheran Church in Canada in 1986. The EFC claimed to represent over one million evangelical Protestants in Canada.

The Canadian Conference of Catholic Bishops (CCCB)

Although Canada's Catholic bishops have always had some kind of regional cooperative agency, usually in the form of meetings of bishops of ecclesiastical provinces, before World War II such meetings were not held on a regular basis. Moreover, national meetings were rare, one reason being that the Vatican did not encourage the development of regional autonomy within the Catholic Church. This changed in 1943, as Canada's bishops established the Canadian Catholic Conference, an association whose name was later changed to the Canadian Conference of Catholic Bishops. During the second half of the twentieth century and particularly after Vatican II, the CCCB grew in importance, becoming the leading agency for cooperation and coordination among Canada's Catholic bishops. Through biannual general assemblies, an elected national executive committee, various commissions, and anglophone and francophone general secretaries, the CCCB coordinated consultations, policy development, external relations, and public interventions by the bishops of Canada. While each bishop continued to bear primary responsibility for his diocese under Roman guidance, the CCCB allowed Canada's bishops to keep abreast of the news in other dioceses and to coordinate their activities.

With headquarters in Ottawa, at the beginning of the twenty-first century the CCCB gathers together 135 Canadian bishops, seventy-six of whom are entrusted with the management of Canada's Catholic dioceses. The others include eighteen auxiliary or assistant bishops and forty-three *emeriti* or retired bishops. They are the leaders of Canada's 12.9 million Catholics, 43% of the population. The emergence of the CCCB as a leading voice of Canada's Catholics reflects the changed governance of the Catholic Church since Vatican II, a church where national consensus is now encouraged. It is noteworthy that Canada's bishops have also established lively regional groupings of bishops in Atlantic Canada, Québec, Ontario, and western Canada.

Ecumenical social action

The sweeping changes of the 1960s included not only Catholic and Protestant renewal but also a general commitment to reform among Canada's Christians. A rejuvenated sense of justice emerged which led to ecumenical social action among Canada's Protestants and Catholics beginning in the late 1960s. They wanted to work together to fight poverty, to assist victims of the Bangladesh and Biafran crises, to narrow the gap between rich and poor nations, and to coordinate relief and development activities in Latin America and the Third World.

Grounded in a common conviction that it was justice rather than charity that was required, Protestants and Catholics joined in collective endeavours to assist their fellow men, women, and children. They created the GATT-Fly project to generate effective constructive criticism of Canada's role in the rich man's club known as the General Agreement on Tariffs and Trade. They created Project North on aboriginal rights and northern development, the Inter-Church Committee on Human Rights in Latin America, the Church Council on Justice and Corrections, Project Ploughshares on defense policy and disarmament, and the Interchurch Committee for Refugees. They also established PLURA, an organization named after its Presbyterian, Lutheran, United, Roman Catholic and Anglican sponsors; it assists local anti-poverty organizations.

All of the above agencies, as well as a number of others, worked on the assumption that evangelization required that unjust social structures be changed. The fact that Catholic and Protestant Canadians were able to come together and work together for these objectives of social justice stood as eloquent testimony to the significant changes that swept through the Christian churches of Canada during the 1960s and 1970s. Christianity in Canada would never be the same thereafter.

Recent developments in Canadian Christianity

During the 1990s, the situation of Canada's Christian churches changed again. The dynamic traditional mainstream churches that had contributed so much to Canada before 1960, desperately engaged in soul-searching and radical change between 1960 and 1990. They were driven by the concern that they were losing touch with the people. Between 1960 and 1990, mainstream churches were in turmoil as they contended with the disenchantment and falling away of many of their members and the consequent difficulties such as reduced clerical recruitment, diminishing revenues and budgets, fading credibility, competing values, and the confusion and silence of many of their leaders. Simultaneously fundamentalism seemed resurgent, within and without Christianity, as people seemed to seek out simple, clear, and unequivocal answers to the perennial questions that mainstream churchmen were wont to avoid or to fudge. Also, the promising ecumenical movement of yesterday seemed to have stalled, while a host of new sects and religions appeared whose leaders promised their audience everything from spiritual interplanetary travel, to healing through crystal-gazing, or salvation by rolling on the floor, or groaning, or speaking in indecipherable tongues, or swearing absolute obedience to a leader; the latter was at times an angel, a self-declared prophet, or God himself.

These same churches, the Anglican and Roman Catholic in particular, were also faced with costly lawsuits by some Canadian Aboriginals who were once pupils in the residential schools run by the churches and the government of Canada. The plaintiffs contended that they were abused in the schools and claimed financial damages that amounted to huge sums for the accused churches; indeed the latter struggled to pay the legal fees occasioned by the charges. Some Amerindian plaintiffs went so far as to accuse the churches of cultural genocide; they too sought financial damages.

During the one hundred and ten years between 1891 and 2001, significant changes appeared in the numbers and proportion of believers in Canada. The proportion of Catholics grew slightly from 42%–43% of the population; that of Protestants dropped from 56%–29% and those who declared 'no' religion grew to 16% of the population. During the same time period, religions other than Christian grew from 2%–6% of the population of Canada, a percentage that includes the Jews who represent 1.1% of the population in 2001.

During the four decades between 1960 and 2000, the Census of Canada shows that the proportion of Canadians identifying with Canada's four mainline Protestant denominations shrank significantly: the United Church, from 20%–9.6%, the Anglican Church from 13%–6.9%, the Presbyterians from 4%–1.4%, and the Lutherans from 4%–2%.[5] These were also the years when the weekly church attendance by Catholics was also in freefall, in Québec in particular. Sociologist Reginald Bibby reports that in the year 2000 a much higher proportion of conservative Protestants (58%) attended church on a weekly basis than did mainline Protestants (15%); Roman Catholic weekly attendance averaged out at 26%, the mean between the 20% rate in Québec and the 32% rate among other Canadian Catholics. That of other religions stood at 7%. The rate of weekly church attendance appears to have stabilized since 1990, even to have increased in some of the churches.[6]

Bibby also underlines the fact that the proportion of Canadians that identify with the conservative family of Protestant churches has remained stable for more than a century, since the census of 1871, at an unchanging 8% of the population. While this stability translates into significant numerical growth given the growth in the population, it also means that, given their minority status, Canada's conservative Protestants have had to work hard to maintain their share of the religious market. Bibby explains that this growth in numbers is primarily attributable to the conservative Protestant retention of both their children and their geographically mobile members. Little in this growth in numbers would be attributable to proselytism or conversions from other faith groups.

At the beginning of the twenty-first century, as religious benchmarks rapidly disappeared from Canadian society, no individual church was capable any longer to claim hegemony or normative status. Although 75% of Canadians declared themselves to be Christian (2001), people were faced with a kaleidoscope of religious choices at a time when many were perhaps least able to choose intelligently among the offerings, given the almost total absence of any education about religion in most Canadian schools. While many Christian churches earnestly endeavoured to renew themselves, they were faced with the daunting prospect of having to evangelize Canadians who lacked the most basic elements of a religious culture.

They were also faced with a host of new religions, large and small, most of which only appeared in Canada since 1960.

Suggested readings

Alberigo, Giuseppe. *History of Vatican II*. Vols. I & II. Maryknoll: Orbis, 1995, 1997.

Bibby, Reginald W. *Fragmented Gods*. Toronto: Irwin Publishing, 1987.

——. *Restless Gods. The Renaissance of Religion in Canada*. Toronto: Stoddart, 2002.

——. *Unknown Gods*. Toronto: Stoddart, 1993.

Clifford, N. Keith. *The Resistance to Church Union in Canada*. Vancouver: University of British Columbia Press, 1985.

Flannery, Austin. Ed. *Vatican Council II, The Conciliar and Post-conciliar Documents*. 2 vols. Revised edition. N.p.: n. publisher, 1996.

Grant, John Webster. *The Canadian Experience of Church Union*. London: Lutterworth Press, 1967.

——. *The Church in the Canadian Era*. Updated and expanded. Burlington: Welch Publishing Co., 1988.

Hebblethwaite, Peter. *John XXIII: Pope of the Council*. London: Geoffrey Chapman, 1985.

Muir, Elizabeth Gillan and Marilyn F. Whiteley. Eds. *Changing Roles of Women Within the Christian Church in Canada*. Toronto: University of Toronto Press, 1995.

CHAPTER 18

Immigration and Religions

Diverse religions of the world

Until World War II, Canada was a visibly Christian country in just about every respect, the only exceptions being handfuls of members of other faith communities, Jews, Amerindians, and Muslims for example. In the aftermath of the war, the floodgates of immigration to Canada were opened wide. Large numbers of new Canadians arrived from many countries of Europe, Asia, Africa, and Latin America. The complexion of Canadian religion changed dramatically, not only as tens of thousands of Italian and Latin American Catholics settled in Ontario, the heartland of traditional Anglo-Canadian Protestantism, but also as thousands of Muslims and Hindus took up residence and citizenship in cities like Montréal, Ottawa, Toronto, Edmonton, and Vancouver. They were accompanied by Sikhs, Buddhists, and devotees of a wide range of smaller religious movements. Indeed, well before new religious movements and new religions (see Chapter 19) came into their own after the 1960s, religious diversity was already well-established and growing in Canada.

The definition and classification of religions is an enterprise fraught with many pitfalls. Numerous categories and terms are used by various authors to designate religions – terms both geographical and descriptive such as world religions, great religions, primitive religions, primal religions, native religions, new religious movements, New Age, etc. In addition, some prefer to designate religions according to the ethnic or national identity of their adherents, the Jews, the Japanese, the Indonesians, or the people of India for example.

In this book, a simplified combination of these approaches will be used. First, all the religions of the world will be classified under three general headings, those of world religions including aboriginal religions, new religious movements, and new religions. In this chapter a number of the more prominent religious groups belonging to the world religions that have emerged in Canada during the second half of the twentieth century will be examined. New religious movements and new religions will be the subject of the next chapter.

Among world religions, three are of Mediterranean origin (Judaism, Christianity, and Islam) and three are of Asian origin (Hinduism, Buddhism, and Confucianism); each group of three religions has close affinities with each other. Of the religions of Mediterranean origin, we know that Christianity has been present in Canada since the arrival of the first European settlers at the turn of the seventeenth century, while Judaism's arrival is dated from the morrow of the British Conquest of Canada in the 1760s. Only Islam is a relative latecomer on the Canadian scene, a fact no doubt explained by the largely Christian countries of origin of almost all Canadian immigrants before World War II. Islam's solid establishment in today's Canada corresponds in time to that of the world religions of Asiatic origin, Hinduism, and Buddhism, to which must be added Sikhism, which is a religion based upon both Islam and Hinduism. The founding and growth of all Eastern religions in Canada is a direct result of the removal of discriminatory immigration regulations after World War II.

Given that the categories of the census changed over the years in question, the numbers in Table 18.1 should not be taken as rigorously exact. For example, there are no distinct listings for Hindus, Sikhs, and Muslims in the census reports of 1941 and 1971; they are packaged into the 'other' category. By the same token, the census of 1991 lists Protestants as one general category, while those of 1941 and 1971 do not.

During the sixty years covered by Table 18.1, the total population of Canada nearly tripled, growing from 11,506,655 (1941), through 21,568,310 (1971) to 29,639,030 (2001). Meanwhile, the relative importance of the various religions changed as a result of the changing numbers of faithful within each religious tradition.

The transformation of Canada from a Christian monochrome to a religious kaleidoscope during the second half of the twentieth century meant that a growing number of diverse world views and theologies appeared. These different and varied explanations of our world reflected not only the radically different world views of East and West, but also the growing diversity within Catholic, Protestant, and Orthodox

Table 18.1   Membership of leading religions in Canada, 1941–2001

Religions	1941	1971	1991	2001
Catholic	4,986,552	10,202,625	12,335,255	12,793,125
Protestant	6,003,918	9,456,078	9,780,710	8,944,055
Eastern Orthodox	139,629	316,605	387,395	433,835
Total Christian	11,132,040	19,977,279	22,505,351	22,171,015
Jewish	168,375	276,025	318,070	329,995
Muslim	–	–	253,260	579,640
Buddhist	37,868	16,175	163,415	300,645
Hindu	–	–	157,015	297,200
Sikh	–	–	147,440	278,410
Aboriginal	–	–	10,840	29,820
No religious affiliation	133,500	929,575	3,386,365	4,796,325

Source: Statistics Canada, Census years 1941, 1971, 1991, 2001.

Christianity, the resurgence of aboriginal religions, and the changing relationships between religious believers on the one hand and proponents of scientific world views on the other.

Nevertheless, religious believers represented some 84% of Canada's people (2001), and the fundamentally different world views put forward by the religions of the East constituted a radically new element in Canadian society. Although new Canadians belonging to Eastern religions like Hinduism, Buddhism, or Sikkhism represented a mere 2.9% of Canada's population (2001), their radically different beliefs, their forms of worship, their sacred architecture, their customs and cultures of origin had an impact on Canadian society that went beyond what their numbers suggested. When the 2% of Muslims were added, the proportion of Canadians with new religious faces grew to a more impressive 4.9%.

One fundamental difference in the world views of the religions of the East and the West was their conception of time. Over the centuries, the Jewish and Christian West came to understand the world in historical terms, a world that began at a given point in time, developed through a sequence of other moments in time, and was destined to end at another point of time in the future. In the West, time could be represented on a horizontal line that began in the distant past, ran through the present, and will end at some point in the future. Western science grew upon such an understanding. Judaism and Christianity, not to mention Islam, adopted the same understanding in their teachings about the creation of the world, the sins of our forefathers, the emergence of the Jewish people, the history of the prophets, the coming of Jesus the Christ, the origins and development of the Christian church, and the death and life everlasting of all. That was why Judaism, Christianity, and Islam were historical religions, meaning that specific moments in time mattered a great deal to them.

The religions of the East proposed a fundamentally different explanation of reality because of their different conception of time. In the East, time was best represented as a circle upon whose circumference was to be found all living creatures along with the pain and sorrow of reality. The ultimate goal of human striving was one's escape from this circle of time, of pain, of sorrow, of suffering, of death. The believer strove to escape into another world beyond time and the limitations of life on earth.

There was some commonality in the basic thrust of the religions of the East and of the West. For example, there had always been some Christians who emphasized their pilgrim status on this earth, their belief that this world was but a vale of tears from which they sought to escape into another world, God's Kingdom. However, these Christians were usually a minority. The majority of Christians believed that the Kingdom of God was already among us, albeit not fully realized. Therefore, they judged this world much more favourably than did the faithful of Eastern religions. They believed that their accomplishments on this earth contributed to the building of that Kingdom.

Such profound differences in perspective made for very basic differences in political, social, and cultural life, indeed in one's entire world view. So it was that basic differences in the fundamental religious outlook of the faithful of the religions of the East and of the West, led the latter, on the one hand, to give more importance to this world and its science, culture, society, government, and environment. Religions of the East, on the other hand, tended to emphasize the methods and techniques that served to better detach the faithful from worldly ties – yoga, meditation, and self-discipline for example; political and social engagement become of secondary importance.

The growing presence of the religions of the East in Canada during the second half of the twentieth century contributed to the relativization of the formerly dominant Christian perspective. Although such believers were not very numerous, nevertheless their presence made Canadians become aware that there were other world views competing with their traditional Christian one. When added to the growing secularism of Canadian society during the same time period, the result was the transformation of Canada from a Christian bastion to a secular society where all religions became private.

World religions in contemporary Canada

Amerindian religions

Nearly 30,000 of the half-million Canadians of acknowledged aboriginal origin claimed to hold to Aboriginal spirituality (2001). Nevertheless, although precise numbers were unknown, many other Amerindian and Inuit Canadians, while belonging to Christian churches, also believed in and practised aboriginal spiritualities and rites. These showed resurgence during the late twentieth century because of the resurgence of Amerindian identities in North America coupled with the new openness of the Roman Catholic, Anglican, and United Churches towards Amerindian cultures and religions.

This new popularity of Amerindian religions included the revival of a number of traditional rites and festivities such as the Sun Dance, sweat lodges, feasts of the dead, spiritual advising, and shamanism. It seemed that many Amerindian Canadians believed and practised a dimorphic religion, that is to say one that was simultaneously Aboriginal and Christian.

Orthodox Christianity

Previously absent from the Canadian story, the Orthodox family of Christians appeared on the scene late in the nineteenth century upon the arrival of growing numbers of immigrants from eastern Europe. Sometimes designated as the Greek, Eastern, or Greco-Russian Church, these churches all shared the same faith and acknowledged the honorary primacy of the Patriarch of Constantinople. The Orthodox Church consisted of several self-governing churches centred in the eastern Mediterranean, Russia, Greece, and eastern Europe, and included a number of autonomous but not fully independent churches in regions such as Finland, China, and North America. Not included in the same communion were the Oriental Orthodox churches (i.e. the Armenian, Coptic, Syrian, and Ethiopian) who differed in their understanding of the nature of Christ; they were previously known as monophysite and Nestorian churches. Both Eastern and Oriental Orthodox Christians have been present in Canada for the past hundred years.

The Orthodox Church was originally the Christian Church of the eastern Roman or Byzantine Empire that was centred in Constantinople where Greek culture predominated. After having suffered the secession

Fig. 22.   Galician immigrants in Québec in 1911.[1] William James Topley. National Archives of Canada, PA-010401.

of an important portion of their churches in the fifth and sixth centuries, that of the Nestorian and monophysite churches, now known as the Oriental Orthodox Church, the homelands of the Orthodox Christians were conquered by Muslim forces in the seventh century. This was followed in 1054 by a major split between the Christian churches of the East and West following a centuries-long growing estrangement between the two portions of Christ's flock. The schism was the result of a number of cultural, political, and theological differences that had been festering for a very long time. Thereafter and until our day, the sees of Rome and Constantinople, the centres of Latin and Orthodox Christianity would remain apart. On the eve of its split with Rome, beginning in the ninth century, the Orthodox Church expanded northwards into the lands of the Slavs. Bulgaria, Serbia, and Russia among other countries were converted to Orthodox Christianity. When the Muslim Turks conquered Constantinople in 1453, the Russian Orthodox Church, the largest and most influential church, became the replacement driving force in Orthodoxy, although the Ecumenical Patriarch of Constantinople

Fig. 23. St Nicholas Greek Catholic Church, Winnipeg, Manitoba, ca. 1890–1910.[2] L.B. Foote. National Archives of Canada, PA-122667.

continued his primacy of honour. Nevertheless, during the five centuries between 1453 and the downfall of the Soviet Union in 1989, the hostility of both Muslim and then Communist rulers in the eastern Mediterranean, eastern Europe, and Russia usually translated into oppression and persecution of Orthodox Christians. Canadian Orthodox Christians were usually refugees from these lands. The Orthodox Church that they imported into Canada was modelled on that of their countries of origin, which were highly Balkanized, each parish displaying strong ethnic allegiances.

In matters of doctrine, the Orthodox Church was very close to the Roman Catholic, although some differences remained. The doctrine of the Orthodox Church claimed to be that of the seven first ecumenical councils of the Christian Church, the series ending with the Second Council of Nicaea in 787. A few subsequent regional councils elaborated on this doctrinal foundation. Nevertheless, much of Orthodox doctrine is found in the liturgical texts that are used in worship. While willing to acknowledge the pope as the honorary head and first bishop of the

Christian Church, Orthodox Christians differed from Catholics in refusing the administrative jurisdiction of the pope over all churches; lay people had considerable prominence in their tradition. While acknowledging seven key sacraments as did the Catholics, the Orthodox shared a broader and more diversified understanding of the sacraments. Monasteries were as important in the Orthodox tradition as they were in the Catholic. While priests were usually married in Orthodoxy, bishops were chosen from the ranks of the celibate clergy exclusively. These were only some of the points that would need to be harmonized should the Orthodox and Roman Catholic Churches manage reconciliation after a thousand years of separation. The matter of reconciliation was one of the fondest hopes of recent popes from John XXIII to John Paul II.

Canada's Orthodox Christians are divided into several distinct groups. The largest denomination is that of the Greek Orthodox who represent nearly one half of all of Canada's Orthodox Christians (215,175 out of 433,815). Other groups include the Ukrainian Orthodox (32,720), the Serbian Orthodox (20,520), the Russian Orthodox (15,600), and several others. The bulk of Canada's Orthodox Christians are found in Ontario and Québec, central Canada sheltering some three-quarters of them. Each Orthodox parish worshiped in the language of its faithful, a policy which served to reinforce the great ethnic and cultural diversity that characterized the Orthodox Church worldwide.

Judaism

The central belief of Judaism has always been the reality of one God, a faith summarized in the *Shema* which was recited in all public and private devotions. The *Shema* began with "Hear, O Israel: the Lord our God, the Lord is one." Until 70 C.E., Judaism was a religion centred on a temple in Jerusalem where prayers and sacrifices were offered to the God of Israel. After the destruction of the temple in 70 C.E. by the Roman legions which were engaged in crushing a rebellion in Palestine, rabbinic Judaism developed, a form of Judaism where rabbis (teachers) played a central role. Rabbinic Judaism became the dominant form of Judaism in the world and in Canada.

Rabbinic Judaism taught that the God of Israel, the creator of heaven and earth, made a covenant with the ancestors of the Jews, his chosen people, a covenant which was then entrusted to Moses on Mount Sinai in the form of a dual revelation or Torah. One revelation was in written form: it was the Pentateuch, the first five books of the Hebrew Bible.

The other revelation was given orally to Israel's religious leaders who handed it down to their successors, the rabbis. Jewish rabbis claimed that they possessed religious authority because of their knowledge of the entire Torah, both written and oral. This authority resided in their persons and in their pronouncements. Over the centuries, rabbis also expressed this authority in written form: the Mishnah, the Palestinian and Babylonian Talmuds, and various codes and commentaries.

During the 2,000 years of our era, the widely scattered Jewish communities that developed in the Mediterranean countries came to be known as the Sephardim, while those that developed in northern, central, and eastern Europe were known as the Ashkenazim. There, they often lived in ghettos. During the European Enlightenment of the eighteenth century, just as pressures were building in favour of the emancipation of the Jews and the end of anti-Judaism, some Jewish leaders were also urging their coreligionists to knock down the walls of the ghettos and to become full-fledged members of society. One of their demands was to allow the language of the country to be used in the synagogue. The foremost leader of this party was the Berlin philosopher Moses Mendelssohn (1729–86). The proponents of this revolution in rabbinic Judaism who sought to reconcile Judaism with contemporary Europe were known as Reform Jews.

Two groups of Jews opposed reform. Those who sought a rejection of secular culture and a return to the old ways based on the Torah were known as Orthodox Jews. Simultaneously, Hasidism, a mystical movement that stressed the importance of a personal spiritual life, condemned reform as it did all forms of modernity. Finally, between the two poles of reform and Orthodoxy, arose an intermediate way, that of Conservative Judaism which sought to reconcile Jewish tradition with modern knowledge. The latter party was destined to develop primarily in the United States.

The Jews who immigrated to Canada after 1760 were under the authority of rabbis who controlled God's law that had been entrusted to Moses. This control included not only religious matters such as prayer, worship, feasts, and festivals, but also law, business, and family affairs. The rabbis were the acknowledged leaders of the Jewish community. However, some of Canada's Jewish immigrants were of Reform tradition. Also, the Canadian community remained diverse with francophone Jews of Sephardic tradition alongside the anglophone Jewish community in Montréal.

As was the case in every country to which they migrated, Jews in

Fig. 24.   Holy Blossom Synagogue, Bond Street, Toronto, in 1923. John Boyd.
National Archives of Canada, PA-086052.

Canada were soon compelled to adapt to their new society and surrounding culture. As a result of their minority status and the dominant position of French-Canadian or English-Canadian Christian cultures, like many of their co-religionists elsewhere, Canada's Jews sometimes had to contend with religious discrimination. One instance of this occurred at the beginning of the nineteenth century in Trois-Rivières. Ezekiel Hart, a prominent local merchant and businessman, was elected in an 1807 by-election to the legislature of Lower Canada by the majority Catholic and francophone constituents of his riding. However, the election having taken place on the Sabbath, that is on Saturday, 11 April 1807, Hart refused to take his oath of allegiance at that time. He would await the opening of the session of the legislature in Québec the following January. But Hart was perceived as a partisan of the bureaucratic party of the gtovernor and his British clique in the political quarrels of the day. The majority francophone and Catholic members of the assembly who were at odds with this party voted to exclude Hart from the legislature, invoking his religion as their grounds. They argued that since Hart had not sworn the required oath, with its phrase *in the year of Our Lord*, he was not qualified to sit. So it was that a citizen duly elected by a majority francophone and Catholic constituency was excluded by an equally francophone and Catholic assembly. In the general election of 1809, Hart was re-elected by his constituents and he swore an oath of office identical to that of his Christian colleagues. Nevertheless, after a protracted debate, Hart was again excluded from the assembly because of his religion. Faced with contradictory legal advice, Governor Craig thereupon queried government officers in London. His answer came on 7 September 1809 when Lord Castlereagh, Secretary of State for the Colonies, confirmed that a Jew was not entitled to sit in the legislature of Lower Canada. This remained the law until legislative changes in 1831–32 acknowledged full civil rights of Jews in Canada.

Over the centuries, Rabbinic Judaism developed two primary forms of religious expression, the Sephardic (Spanish) and the Ashkenazi (German). The former is a cultural inheritance of customs and mores that developed under Muslim Arab influence in North Africa and the Iberian Peninsula during the seven centuries of Muslim dominance in the region (700 to 1500 C.E.). This Sephardic Judaism was then carried to France, Britain, and beyond after the expulsion of the Jews from Spain in the late fifteenth century. The Ashkenazi tradition of religious expression grew in central and eastern Europe and then divided into Orthodox, Reform, and Conservative parties during the nineteenth century.

It was only after 1870 that larger numbers of Jewish immigrants arrived in Canada, mainly from eastern Europe. By 1921, their numbers had grown to 125,000, originating mostly from regions and countries such as Russia, the Ukraine, Poland, Lithuania, Prussia, Austria, Hungary, and Romania. Many had fled pogroms and persecutions that fed on the anti-Semitism that prevailed in Europe at the time. Despite the ravages of the Holocaust in Nazi-controlled Europe, Canada did not open its doors to Jews in any significant numbers during the 1930s and 1940s. After 1950, more Jews were allowed into Canada; they originated in Russia, Hungary, Morocco, Tunisia, and Algeria. Some also came from Middle Eastern countries after the establishment of the state of Israel in 1948. Most of these Jews were refugees fleeing various forms of oppression in their homelands.

Canada's Jews were well aware of the discrimination against them. When anti-Semitism reared its ugly head in the Western world in the late nineteenth and early twentieth centuries, many would cringe before the racist rhetoric that too often soiled the pages of some of Canada's leading newspapers and religious journals. Jews were presented therein, not only as a different religion responsible for the killing of Christ (a centuries-old Christian accusation), but as a race apart, one that was guilty of the basest passions. They were at times identified with communists, traitors, murderers, and persecutors of Christians. Although Canada and its churches never indulged in the extreme anti-Semitism manifest in the Holocaust, there were numerous cases of bigotry, culpable indifference, and inaction.

Canadian Jews ended up practising a very selective rabbinic Judaism. By the end of the twentieth century, most Canadian Jews disregarded their religion's ban on labour on the Sabbath and on key Jewish festivals such as New Year, the Day of Atonement, and Passover; dietary laws were usually set aside, as were directives for daily prayer, distinctive dress, the study of the Torah, and laws regarding business and the courts. They frequently forgot to attend synagogue on a regular basis. Nevertheless, some Jewish customs persisted, such as the reciting of special prayers on certain days such as New Year (Rosh Hashanah) or the Day of Atonement (Yom Kippur). Many Jewish families still had a Friday evening meal to mark the beginning of the Sabbath; few, however, honoured the Sabbath itself. Although God and the Torah are not always apparent in Canadian Judaism, the family and the Jewish people are held in very high esteem.

A number of private Jewish schools existed in Canada, schools where the pupils learned the Hebrew language and studied Jewish Scriptures, history, and religious traditions. In 1982, 112 synagogues existed in Canada, fifty-seven of which were in the three cities of Montréal, Toronto and Winnipeg. Of these synagogues, fifty-two belonged to Orthodox Judaism, forty-five to Conservative Judaism, and fifteen to Reform Judaism. In Canada, the differences between these Jewish denominations is more of degree than of kind; all were in communion with one another, all competed with one another for members, and the synagogue was the primary vehicle for Jewish traditions. In fact, most Canadian Jews are secularists, thereby forcing Jewish denominations to play down their theological differences and cooperate.

Today, Canada's 329,995 Jews are primarily based in Montréal and Toronto. They strongly support certain key national voluntary organizations such as the Canadian Jewish Congress and B'nai B'rith, in addition to a number of local associations. Most support Zionism, the movement that was founded in the late nineteenth century in order to promote the establishment of a separate homeland for Jews. The founding of the State of Israel in 1948 fulfilled that dream. It stands as a guarantee of the survival of their people. The central values of the Jews seem to have become their people and their families, with God frequently remaining in the shadows.

Islam

The youngest of the three 'Western' religions, Islam was founded in Arabia six hundred years after the death of Jesus. Today it is the religion of 1 billion faithful worldwide, second in size only to Christianity (2 billion). Although Muslims are mainly found in south and west Asia, in southeast Asia, especially in Malaysia and Indonesia, and north and east Africa, increasing numbers are to be found in Europe and North America as a result of the extensive migrations of people since World War II.

The word *Islam* was derived from Arabic and meant *submission*: surrender, obedience, and peace. The submission was to God (Allah) whose revealed will was found in the Qur'an, Islam's sacred Scripture. Written in Arabic, the contents of the Qur'an were revealed to the Prophet Muhammad between the years 610 and 632 C.E, the year of Muhammad's death.

The Qur'an teaches belief in God, his prophets or messengers, his books, angels, and the Day of Judgment. God reveals himself in nature

and history. He guides human beings through his prophets and messengers who began with Adam and ended with Muhammad. God entrusted
each prophet with a book; for example Moses was entrusted with the
Torah and Jesus with the Gospels. However, the followers of each of these
messengers would have falsified their teachings until Muhammad came
along and preserved God's Revelation without any falsification. So it is
that the Qur'an and Muhammad are the ultimate and perfect Holy
Scripture and Prophet of the one true God.

The religion of Islam has no clergy or sacraments. However, it does
have a number of ritual practices performed in obedience to the commandments of God. Specifically, there are five ritual acts of worship
that are required of all believers. These five acts are frequently referred
to as the *Pillars of Islam.*

The first pillar, the *shahadah*, the foundation stone of everything else
in the Islamic religion, is bearing witness in public that "there is no god
but God and Muhammad is the Messenger of God." This confession
shows the foundational monotheism of Islam, as well as the central
importance of the prophet Muhammad in it. These are the first words
that both the newborn and the dying faithful hear; they remind them of
the contract that binds each Muslim to God.

The second pillar, *salat* or ritual prayer, consists in praying five
times a day, that is to say at dawn, noon, afternoon, dusk, and evening.
Although Muslims are urged to pray together at the mosque on Friday
noon, their prayers are usually performed elsewhere and privately, in
their residences, places of work, or wherever they happen to be. The
ritual prayers serve to remind the faithful of their ongoing devotion to
God. They are preceded by ablutions that serve to cleanse the hands,
face, mouth, nostrils, arms, head, neck, ears, and feet. The praying
Muslim removes his shoes, a man needing to be covered from the navel
to the knees, while a woman must cover her whole body with the
exception of her face and hands. The prayers are said in various positions, including standing, bowing, kneeling, and prostrate.

The third pillar, *zakat*, the tithe or alms-giving, goes hand-in-hand
with prayer; it is an act of purification, the expression through the
community of the faithful's commitment to God. The latter are called
upon to give as much as 2.5% of their total assets for the benefit of the poor
and others in need.

The fourth pillar, *sawm*, consists in fasting during the lunar month
of Ramadan, a period of some thirty days. Fasting involves abstaining
from food, drink, and sex from dawn until dusk. As is the case in

Judaism and Christianity, fasting is a time of repentance which serves to foster self-discipline in addition to strengthening the bonds of the community of believers

The fifth pillar, *Hajj*, is going on a pilgrimage to Mecca in Arabia at least once in one's lifetime, if one can afford it. The pilgrimage symbolizes the faithful's obedience to God, and is marked among other things by abstaining from worldly pleasures and walking around the Kaaba, the main building of the mosque at Mecca.

Like other great religions, over the centuries Islam has experienced internal divisions. Some 90% of the 1 billion Muslims throughout the world belong to the Sunni tradition. The name Sunni derives from *Sunna* (path or way) which is made up of the life and example of Muhammad, reflected in the sayings (*hadith*) of the prophet in addition to his deeds and silent approval. Sunni Muslims are those who claim to follow the *Sunna* of the prophet. Over time, they have also given themselves a group of interpreters or doctors of Islamic law called the *Ulema*. The Sunni code of life or *shari'a* or Revelation of God to the community is based on four roots, namely the Qur'an, the Sunna, the consensus of the Ulema, and reasoning based upon accepted interpretations of the Qur'an and Sunna.

Ten per cent of Muslims are Shii's or Shiites, most of whom are found in Iran and Iraq. Some are found in Canada. The division between Shii's and Sunnis dates back to political differences several centuries ago. One aspect of their differing views is that contrary to the Sunnis, the Shii accept Imams as divinely ordained leaders of their communities and as continuing sources of doctrine, although most Shiis believe that the line of Imams ended in the ninth century.

Because of dramatically higher numbers of immigrants during recent years, Canada's Muslim community now numbers 579,640 (2001), double the number of 253,300 of a decade earlier. Muslims now represent 2% of Canadians. It is a much diversified community however, because of the numerous countries of origin represented among the faithful. Indeed, Canada's Muslims come from India, Pakistan, Indonesia, Malaysia, Jordan, Lebanon, Morocco, Syria, numerous African nations and elsewhere. They are faced with the usual challenges of immigrants, particularly that of adapting their religion to the customs of a host country of Christian heritage that has been largely secularized. Like Muslim immigrants to Europe or the United States, they must learn to say their daily ritual prayers in a society that is not organized to accommodate them; they are challenged by the free and easy relations between men and women in Canada because Islam teaches the segregation of the sexes and

Fig. 25.   The Ottawa Mosque, 1993. Pat McGrath. The Ottawa Citizen Archives.

forbids women to marry non-Muslims. As is to be expected, some Muslim Canadians constructively adapt their religion to the customs of their host society, a minority tries to segregate itself in order to avoid compromising its faith, while others drift away from their Islamic religious moorings and assimilate into the mainstream of a secularized Canadian society.

Hinduism

Of the five hundred million Hindus in the world, 297,200 were in Canada in 2001. The religion of the people of India, *Hinduism* embraces a great diversity of cults, gods, devotions, theologies, and spiritualities. Originating in India some four thousand years ago, Hinduism in itself, or in its offshoots such as Buddhism, is at the root of the religious beliefs of many of the people of Asia.

For the Hindu, all human, animal, or material life is founded in God, the universal Spirit towards whom all strive. Although the world has no beginning for it has always been, there are cycles of the universe in existence; we are presently in one such cycle, which was preceded by another and which will be followed by another. Hinduism teaches that each individual is locked into a cycle of birth and rebirth until he or she manages to escape life on earth into the company of God. In other words, life on earth is a burden characterized by suffering because of our separation from God; we must therefore strive to escape this life in order to live in the company of God the universal Spirit. Each individual's life or lives is determined by one's karma or moral law which is set according to one's behaviour during one's previous life. So it is that on the one hand, if I die after leading a morally reprehensible life, I will be reborn on a lower level of society, perhaps even as an animal. If on the other hand, I die after having led a good moral life, I may be reborn higher up on the quality-of-life scale.

This doctrine of reincarnation is manifested in the caste system, which holds that one may be reborn at one of four levels in descending order: those of priest or teacher, warrior or politician, merchant or professional, or servant or labourer. In time, another class appeared in India, that of the untouchables who were the pariahs of society.

In order to achieve release from this endless cycle of rebirth and of suffering, Hinduism teaches that there are three paths or ways (yogas). They are the yogas of knowledge, of action, and of devotion. In the yoga of knowledge, a series of psychological techniques serve to remove the karmic obstructions of previous lives, allowing the individual to achieve his or her true self, that of union with God. In the yoga of action, through the consistent performance of their duty, the faithful achieve an inner purification which results in their union with God. Similarly, in the yoga of devotion, that chosen by most of the faithful, through intense and prolonged devotions, worship, and prayers, the faithful manage to remove karmic obstructions dating from former lives and achieve union with God.

Hinduism is perhaps the most open and 'ecumenical' of all religions. It acknowledges that people can represent and communicate with God in a wide range of ways and each of these diverse representations in image or doctrine is valid and true. This has led to a very close association between the religion of Hinduism and cultural customs in India, to the point that it is not always clear where the religion ends and the culture begins. It has also led Hinduism to be most receptive to other forms of religious beliefs, leading in time to their absorption into the diverse cultures of India.

Although some Hindus have been present in Canada since the early twentieth century, most have arrived since 1960. Canadian Hindus frequently divide along ethnic, cultural, and linguistic lines. In the leading Canadian Hindu centres of Toronto and Vancouver for example, one finds Hindu temples serving specific ethnocultural communities such as the West Indian, the Indian, or the African. In cities with only one temple, out of the variety of Hindu traditions and forms of belief and worship that are reflected among Canada's faithful the *Sanatanist* religious tradition tends to dominate.

Canada's Hindus have also adapted to the cultural and social customs of their host country. So it is that they tend to gather and worship in their temples on Sundays, much like Christians do in their churches. Although Canada's Hindus tend to marry along the same caste lines as they do in India, the custom is weakened by the egalitarianism of Canadian society. Despite the constraints of small numbers and wide dispersal, Canada's Hindus endeavour to maintain their religious traditions by gathering together the faithful that share a similar spiritual way, by engaging in traditional devotions in their homes, and by receiving guest gurus (teachers or guides) and swamis (monks) from India and elsewhere.

Sikhism

Numbering only some eighteen million faithful worldwide and centred primarily in the Punjab in northern India, Sikhism does not compare in size with the other great world religions. Nevertheless Canada's 278,410 Sikhs (2001), a number equivalent to that of the Hindus and Buddhists, have had considerable impact on Canadian society partly because of the political events associated with their coreligionists in the Punjab and partly because of their distinctive dress and code of behaviour.

Founded by Guru Nanak (1469–1538) in the Punjab, Sikhs (disciples) accepted teachings drawn in part from Hinduism and from Islam, two major religious traditions that Guru Nanak sought to reconcile. He only succeeded in founding another religion. Nanak taught that there was only one God, rejected the numerous idols of Hinduism, as well as the caste system, bodily mortification, and asceticism. He taught that anyone could be saved through devotion to God and the leading of a responsible, moral, and selfless life. Nine gurus, who in turn succeeded Nanak as heads of his movement during the sixteenth and seventeenth centuries, reinforced his religion by condemning practices such as the seclusion of women and widow burning in India, by founding Amritsar, Punjab, as headquarters of the Sikh religion, and by collecting Sikh scriptures into one book entitled the *Adi Granth* which became the written base of Sikhism.

Sikhs engage in Sunday prayer services, the temples being open to all who abide by the rules of entering shoeless and with covered head. Many Sikhs practise daily personal devotional routines which include rising early for a bath and prayers, reading an inspirational passage from the *Guru Granth Sahib*, the reading of a hymn at sunset, and the recitation of a hymn and prayer at night. Sikhs are required to abstain from tobacco and alcohol; theft, gambling, and adultery are condemned.

In a context of increasing ethnic tension, consciousness, and militancy in the Punjab, the tenth and last Guru, Gobind Singh (1666–1708), promoted a further development in Sikh theology by creating within Sikhism a community of believers known as the *Khalsa* (the pure). These men and women received ritual baptism at which the men were given the name *Singh* (lion) and the women *Kaur* (princess). Khalsa men were instructed to observe the five 'Ks,' that is to say not to cut their hair and beard (*kes*), to wear a comb (*kangha*), to wear a steel bracelet (*kara*), to wear soldier's breeches (*kach*) and a dagger (*kirpan*). Most Sikhs accepted these new requirements which became characteristic of Canadian Sikhism in the twentieth century. In fact, they would lead to some controversy when Sikh officers in the Royal Canadian Mounted Police insisted on wearing their turban instead of the usual

RCMP stetson. They would be authorized to do so. It was likewise when Sikh students wanted to carry their symbolic daggers on their person into schools when such weapons were banned.

During the eighteenth, nineteenth, and twentieth centuries, despite constant turmoil and upheaval in the Punjab, Sikhism grew by making numerous converts. During the British domination of India (1846–1949), Sikhs became important members of the British army, thereby migrating to various parts of the British Empire. So it was that the first Sikhs entered Canada in the early twentieh century, settling in British Columbia in particular. Despite discrimination by Canadian authorities, their community grew around the temples (*gurdwaras*) that they built in several towns and cities of British Columbia after 1908.

The relaxing of Canadian immigration restrictions beginning in the 1950s led to a strong increase in Sikh immigration to Canada. The new arrivals were frequently highly educated and less committed to traditional ways. Many of them settled in several Canadian cities throughout western and central Canada, leading to the founding of temples in most of the main cities of Canada's West and Centre. A growing number of these temples are more diversified than their predecessors in the Sikh customs and traditions that they reflect. Nevertheless, they continue to serve as places of worship and community centres engaged in community organization, receiving guest theologians and gurus from India, celebrating marriages and funerals, teaching language classes such as the *gurmukhi* script of their Scriptures, and coordinating Sikh social activities and political representation.

Many Sikh Canadians undertake pilgrimages to Sikh shrines in India, especially the central shrine known as the Golden Temple, in Amritsar, Punjab. This is the temple that was taken over in 1984 by a Sikh sect that wanted the political secession of the Punjab from India. The Indian army's retaliatory assault on the shrine resulted in the killing of the sect's leader and one thousand of his followers. In retaliation, Prime Minister Indira Gandhi of India would later be assassinated by two of her Sikh bodyguards, on 31 October 1984, a crime which in turn led to 2,500 Sikh rioters being killed in the following social turmoil. Now as numerous as Hindus and Buddhists, Canadian Sikhs will no doubt achieve greater visibility in Canada.

Buddhism

Of the world's three hundred million Buddhists, 300,345 resided in Canada in 2001. Buddhism was founded in northeastern India, in today's

Nepal, around 500 B.C.E. by Siddhartha Gautama (563–480 B.C.E.), an Indian prince who, at age twenty-nine, renounced his kingdom, his wife, and his child to become an ascetic and the leader of a new religion-philosophy. Gautama was reacting to the sacrificial religion of the ortho-dox Hinduism of the Brahmins, Hinduism's priestly caste, a religion that he considered overly ritualistic, formal, and class conscious. Gautama sought enlightenment or spiritual awakening as an ascetic. After six years of engaging in the most extreme forms of self-denial, poverty, and itinerancy, Gautama emerged as Buddha, a word based on the Sanskrit language's *bodhi*, meaning enlightened.

During his spiritual quest, Buddha had come to recognize that all phenomena are interdependent and therefore temporary and relative; that everything will sooner or later be dissatisfying; that nothing has an exclusive nature; and that ultimate happiness results from detachment from all beings and values. He therefore taught his growing number of disciples to acknowledge that nothing, their soul included, had an eternal essence. One became a Buddha by accepting that insight or *dharma*, that of the finitude and relativity of everything. Gautama Bud-dha elaborated on this insight by teaching the *four noble truths*: all existence is suffering; suffering is caused by desire; freedom from suf-fering is *nirvana*; and the means of achieving *nirvana* is the eight-fold path. This path to *nirvana* is made up of a combination of ethical conduct, mental discipline, and wisdom, including as an important element the practice of meditation. Gautama Buddha taught for forty-five years; the monks who followed him became the first Buddhist congregation or *sangha*. Buddhism is founded on three pillars, or jewels: the Buddha, the *dharma* or insight, and the *sangha* or congregation.

Over time, three distinct ways of being Buddhist emerged, that of those who focused on the Buddha's way to enlightenment, that of those who stressed the experience of enlightenment itself, and that emphasiz-ing meditation. The first was named the Theravada system (also called *Hinayana*) and developed in Burma, Sri Lanka, Cambodia, Thailand, and other parts of outheast Asia. The second way was named the Mahayana (including the *Vajrayana*) and developed in Korea, Vietnam, Japan, China, Tibet, and other East-Asian countries. The third, which centred on meditation, developed in China during the sixth century C.E. and was exported to Japan shortly afterwards; it is known as Zen Buddhism. In each of these countries, Buddhism adapted to the native customs and languages, leading in time to diversified forms of Bud-dhism throughout the world including that of Pure Land which is very influential in East-Asian Buddhism.

While some consider Buddhism to have no God, within the Mahayana tradition there developed the doctrine of *Bodhisattva* which holds that the historical Buddha was but a brief manifestation in time of an eternal absolute Buddha. Other *Bodhisattvas* exist; they are saints who have qualified for *nirvana*, but who choose to remain in the world in order to assist others who are striving for enlightenment and release from suffering. Devotees can pray to them. For Buddhists of this school, all humans can now become Buddhas. For them, the spiritual world is very real in addition to the material world.

In Canada Buddhists incorporate under the *Societies Act*. As elsewhere, some Buddhists understand Buddha to be a celestial being, while others consider him a terrestrial being. For some, *dharma* is law, for others a guiding principle. For some the *sangha* is a community of ordained monks, for others an inclusive community of all Buddhists, monastic and lay. So it is that some consider Buddhism to be a religion, while others prefer to consider it a philosophy.

The functions of each Canadian Buddhist society also vary. The names of the leaders of the societies may include titles such as monk, sensei, teacher, spiritual director, minister, or reverend. Their functions range from the more secular, such as teaching languages or counselling, to the more religious functions of spiritual directors or advisers, depending upon the individual society and its understanding of Buddhism. Canadian Buddhists meet on Sunday, not because that day has any particular significance in their religious tradition, but because is is more convenient to do so in Canada. Like other religions, Buddhism has a series of annual feast days such as Nirvana Day, New Year's Day, and Bodhi Day; Buddhists also have rites of passage to celebrate key moments in an individual's or family's life such as birth, confirmation, marriage, and death.

As is the case with other world religions, the doctrinal and ethnic diversity within Buddhism has led its Canadian congregations to show a wide range of beliefs and practices.

Religions of China and Japan

Canadians of Chinese and Japanese origin are further removed than are the faithful of other religions from the religious traditions of their forebears in China and Japan. This is due in part to the fact that the religious

Table 18.2   Religious affiliation of Chinese Canadians (1991)[3]

Catholic	78,145
Protestant	91,215
Eastern Orthodox	85
Jewish	100
Eastern non-Christian	72,095
No religious affiliation	344,595
Total Chinese population	586,235

Source: Statistics Canada, Census 1991.

traditions of these countries are more diffuse, more enmeshed in cultural customs, less distinct as specific religions.

Chinese people first came to Canada during the Fraser River gold rush of 1858. Others followed during the 1870s and 1880s in order to work on the construction of the Canadian Pacific Railway. Young Chinese men, seeking to earn some money to assist their families in China, continued coming to Canada until the government of Canada closed the country's doors to them between 1923 and 1947. Thereafter, restrictions were gradually lifted, allowing more immigrants into the country. In 1991, nearly 600,000 Canadians were of Chinese ethnic origin.

Table 18.2 shows that more than half of Chinese Canadians declare no religious affiliation. Of the remaining 250,000, most are Christians, almost equally divided between the Catholic and Protestant Churches. A small and diminishing number of 72,000 claimed to belong to Eastern non-Christian religions such as Buddhism or Confucianism.

However these statistics are misleading, given that the religious traditions of China were so closely enmeshed and intertwined with cultural, social, and family customs that they could easily be mistaken for the latter and not identified as specific religions. In other words, the 344,595 Chinese Canadians who declared that they had no religious affiliation, nevertheless may well have believed and behaved religiously. Despite the fact that mainland China has been under communist rule since 1948 and therefore officially atheist, China was always religious during its previous three millenia of history. Buddhism, which had begun in India, flourished in China as it would in Japan, beside other native religions, Confucianism and Taoism in particular. They were founded in China before they influenced Japan. In China, the Tao was the path or way of the universe, manifested in nature and believed to reflect the eternal Tao which was hidden from view. The Tao or way of all things was the product of two forces that worked in dynamic tension, namely the Yang principle and the Yin principle. Yang is the male side of the Tao and dominates in the dry, hot, bright, and active parts of nature. Yin is the female side of the Tao and prevails in cool, dark, moist, and passive parts of reality. Both principles are considered equal and must exist in balance; both are found everywhere and in everything. For the Chinese, heaven is distinct from earth, while both exist in balance. Earth is Yin and heaven is Yang; their dynamic tension seeks harmony in the world. The eternal Tao contains the flow of all these dynamic realities in balance, harmony, and peace. This is the way of the universe in traditional Chinese thought-religion.

Although practically invisible in Canada, Confucianism was the most influential philosophy in China for more than two millennia. The followers of Kung Fu Tzu (551–479 B.C.E.), or Confucius, sought to live by the ideals of their great teacher who worked to develop good government in China by forming responsible leaders and people through sound ethical principles and education. He taught that the world is a good place; he believed that people were naturally good, and that they learned best through example. Therefore, Confucius sought to lead a model life and to train others to do likewise. He taught that harmony should prevail in the home and in society. Customs and rules of propriety, righteousness, humaneness, and compassion were required to achieve such harmony. Confucius was a sage whose principles transcended material and worldly things and pointed to heaven. He supported the traditional ancestor-worship of the Chinese people. He did not have a personal God who was worshiped through hymns and prayers. However, he offered sacrifices to heaven where his ancestors served as deities.

Commentators have long debated whether the teachings of Confucius were to be designated a philosophy or a religion. Although a diminishing number of Chinese Canadians claim to be adepts of traditional Chinese religions or philosophies, there is no doubt that such religio-philosophical ideas and views influence many, perhaps most Chinese Canadians, whatever religion or non-religion they claim as their own.

Most Canadians of Japanese origin immigrated to Canada at the beginning of the twentieth century; by the beginning of World War I in 1914 some ten thousand Canadians claimed Japanese origin. Most settled in British Columbia. Immigration dwindled to a trickle thereafter because of the restrictions imposed by the government of Canada, as a result of the anti-Asian sentiment prevalent in British Columbia. A handful of new Japanese immigrants came to Canada after 1967 when Parliament finally removed the last discriminatory barriers to their immigration. Today most Canadians of Japanese origin are fully assimilated into the mainstream English-speaking society. Very few maintain conscious ties with the traditional religions of the homeland of their ancestors whether Zen Buddhism or Shinto, just as few speak Japanese and most marry outside their ethnic group. If their religious heritage from Japan still has some influence on them, it is a minimal one.

Ethnicity and religions

Canada is a nation of immigrants. Since the beginning of European settlement in the early seventeenth century, ethnic groups have been in constant contact and relation with each other, sometimes in a constructive way, frequently in destructive ways. All of these groups, including the Amerindians, the French, the British, the Irish, the Chinese, the Jews, and the more recent Italians, Africans, and Asiatics have found that their chosen religions served simultaneously to reinforce their real or perceived minority ethnic identities and to facilitate their acculturation and assimilation into the mainstream society of Canada. In other words, the religions and churches of Canada served both as the bulwarks of the country's ethnic groups and as the doorways to their entry into the host society.

In spite of what many faithful believe, all religions take on a cultural colouring. Indeed, the fact of expressing itself through a given language, in a given country, in a specific century, and through particular institutions and individuals makes any religion unique and distinctive. In addition, the fact that religions address fundamental questions of birth, life, happiness, suffering, and death in both time and eternity make them part and parcel of culture, civilization, and its varied social issues.

So it was that Catholic Christianity in Canada was strongly French Canadian, then Irish Canadian in the nineteenth century, before becoming progressively more multicultural in the latter half of the twentieth century. Protestant Christianity was militantly British when it arrived on the ships of the British army in 1760. It then became a kaleidoscope of English-speaking diversity in step with the growing number of immigrants from the United States and Great Britain, people who were simultaneously English-speaking and Irish, English, Scots, American, not to mention republican, democratic, voluntarist, or royalist. The varied ethnic origins of Canada's Jews were noted above. Likewise for Canada's Amerindians who include a multitude of nations and tribes. While contemporary Pentecostalism is a mosaic of ethnic congregations, today's Canadian Muslim and Orthodox Christian communities are also.

Indeed, immigration has markedly affected the religions of Canada, just as the latter have strongly conditioned and continue to mold the stories of our country's ethnic groups. And all Canadians are part of ethnic groups. When trying to understand the religions of Canadians, one should never lose sight of their particular ethnic conditioning and affiliation, both past and present.

Canada's reactions to the newcomers

Generally speaking, human beings welcome strangers into their societies providing these strangers do not threaten them, either individually or collectively. However, when they are perceived as a threat, hostility usually comes to the fore. Canadians were and are no different from others in this respect.

In New France, Amerindians welcomed the European newcomers, until they discovered that the latter constituted a real threat to their way of life, their livelihood, their cultures, and their lives. Amerindians then became much less generous to the Europeans; self-interest and cunning replaced hospitality as the badge of distinction of Amerindian relations with the white man. The French, the missionaries in particular, worked tirelessly to Christianize and 'civilize' diverse Amerindian nations, until they realized that their efforts to assimilate the latter were futile. Thereafter, the missionary thrust became much less energetic, while the French traders and settlers proved just as self-interested as the Amerindians.

In Canada between 1760 and 1867, the ruling British government initially feared two adversaries, the Catholic Church of the French Canadians and the emerging United States. Then they neglected and dismissed the Amerindians, whose usefulness to British interests was waning after the War of 1812 and the decline of the fur trade in Canada. Although it was the British and not the Catholics who were the newcomers in 1760, the conquerors felt that their new subjects needed to accept the new religion imported from England. After a half century of conflict and failed attempts to discourage Catholicism and promote Anglicanism, the British government settled its differences with the Catholics and harmony prevailed thereafter between the state and the Catholic Church. The conflictual relations with the new American republic to the south were settled on the battlefields during two wars won by the British forces. The upshot of the peace treaties of 1783 and 1814 would be increased immigration from the United States into Canada of people whose varied religious views would serve to undermine the hoped-for establishment of the Church of England in Canada. Great Britain may have won the battles, but in time would lose the war to preserve the British way of life in Canada. In other words, despite their control of the government, the ruling British in Canada would be changed as much as the defeated Americans and Canadian Catholics. In the case of the Amerindians, the neglect and abuse that began to prevail after 1815 would prove more long-lasting.

During the first century of Confederation (1867–1967), Canada was determined to have its English Canadian and French Canadian majorities prevail in all parts of the vast country. The former was largely Protestant and the latter almost exclusively Catholic. There resulted a Canadian linguistic and cultural duality wherein third parties, whether linguistic, cultural, ethnic, or religious were tolerated in direct relation to their cultural, religious, and linguistic proximity to the two ruling majority groups. In fact, the latter were also rivals, some of their leaders hoping to somehow conquer and dominate the other.

These cultural and linguistic rivalries and conflicts were simultaneously religious jousts, given the different religious identities of the parties. So it was that Ontario's perfervid opposition to Louis Riel between 1870 and 1885 was simultaneously linguistic and religious, as was Québec's reaction to Ontario's perceived bigotry. By the same token, Dalton McCarthy's intervention in the Manitoba Schools debate after 1889 was both linguistic and religious, anti-French-Canadian feeling galloping alongside anti-Catholicism. Canadians reacted with similar Janus-faced discrimination to the arrival in Canada of several groups of immigrants such as African Americans, Russian Doukhobors, Russian

Fig. 26. Sikh immigrants aboard the ship Komagata Maru in the Port of Vancouver in 1914.[4] National Archives of Canada, c-75260.

Mennonites, the Chinese, the Japanese, the Ukrainians, and various peoples from eastern Europe.

Several other ethnic and religious minorities bore the brunt of Canada's discriminatory laws and attitudes during the first century of Confederation. These included the Jehovah's Witnesses in Québec during the 1930s, not to mention the Communists who had been outlawed by Parliament. Canadians of the period shared the views prevalent in the Western world, views whereby Western Christian civilization was considered superior to any other. In English-speaking Canada, a white anglo-saxon Protestant (WASP) was considered superior; Jews, Catholics, Muslims, or Asiatics among others were held to be inferior.

Canada's new immigration legislation of 1967 put an end to a century of racism and white supremacy. The law was confirmed and enshrined by the Canadian Charter of Rights and Freedoms which was made part of the constitutional law of the land in 1982. Thereafter,

Canadians of all ethnic, national, and religious origins would be equal before the law.

The churches' reactions to the newcomers

In some respects, Canada's churches were in a dilemma when faced with the arrival in Canada of people of other religions and other nationalities. On the one hand, Christians had to abide by the Christian doctrine upheld by all the churches, that a stranger was to be welcomed into one's home, and made into one's neighbour, for as the Bible stated: "When an alien resides with you in your land, you shall not oppress the alien. The alien who resides with you shall be to you as the citizen among you; you shall love the alien as yourself, for you were aliens in the land of Egypt: I am the Lord your God" (Lev. 19, 33–34).

On the other hand, by the turn of the twentieth century, Canada's churches represented the vast majority of Canadians and thereby reflected not only the strengths, but also the weaknesses of their fellow-citizens. Racism and white supremacist ideas were part of these weaknesses. So it was that while holding a discourse of welcome to the newcomers, most Canadian churches simultaneously worked to assimilate and convert them. Churchmen generally felt that the immigrants could only become truly Canadian, and Christian, by abandoning their foreign language, culture, and religion and donning the cloak of English-speaking Canadian culture.

While several churches evangelized the newcomers, some churches made greater efforts and proved more successful than others. Before the major social and religious changes of the 1960s, Christian churches usually sought simultaneously to evangelize and civilize and civilization meant that of the mother country of the missionary, be it France, England, French or English Canada, or the United States. During the more than three centuries of Christian evangelization of Canada's Amerindian people, the leading missionary churches were first the Catholic Church and second the Church of England. Most other Christian churches only came on the Amerindian scene after the late nineteenth century. That is why 85% of Canada's Amerindian people are Christian today, most of them within the ranks of the Catholic and Anglican Churches.

As was the case with the Amerindians, some churches invested much more than others in missions to specific groups of immigrants. Many of the new Canadians who belonged to religions other than Christianity, Islam or Hinduism for example, chose to remain within their traditions; they did not welcome Christian proselytism.

Since the 1960s, a sea of change occurred among Christian churches with regard to their attitudes towards other religions. With the exception of some more conservative groups, most Christian churches now acknowledge openly the legitimacy and value of other religious faiths, including Judaism, Islam, Hinduism, and Amerindian spiritualities. Rather than condemn and repel them as they usually did in the past, they now seek to understand better and to cooperate with other faiths. The churches seem less concerned with seeking the conversion of others to their own faith and more inclined to work with them on social and community projects of joint concern. This new attitude has led to a new openness among all religious parties, a new mutual interest and respect, a new willingness to work with and learn from each other.

Canada's new immigrants have given the country not only a much more diverse religious face, but also contributed to the development of a society much more open to change and difference.

Suggested readings

Abella, Irving. *A Coat of Many Colours. Two Centuries of Jewish Life in Canada.* Toronto: Lester & Orpen Dennys, 1990.

Abella, Irving M. and H. Roper. *None is Too Many: Canada and the Jews of Europe, 1933–1948.* Toronto: Lester and Orpen Dennys, 1983.

Brym Robert J., William Shaffir, and Morton Weinfeld. Eds. *The Jews in Canada.* Toronto: Oxford, 1993.

Hinnels, John R. Ed. *A New Handbook of Living Religions.* London: Penguin Books, 1998.

Hopfe, Lewis M. *Religions of the World.* Sixth edition. New York: Macmillan College Publishing Company, 1994.

Langlais, Jacques and David Rome. *Jews and French Québecers: Two Hundred Years of Shared History.* Waterloo: Wilfrid Laurier University Press, 1991.

Nigosian, S. A. *World Religions. A Historical Approach.* Third edition. Boston and New York: Bedford-St. Martin's, 2000.

Sharma, Arvind. Ed. *Our Religions.* San Francisco: Harper Collins, 1993.

Tulchinsky, Gerald. *Branching Out. The Transformation of the Canadian Jewish Community.* Toronto: Stoddart, 1998.

——. *Taking Root. The Origins of the Canadian Jewish Community*. Toronto: Lester Publishing, 1992.

United Church of Canada. *Faith in My Neighbour. World Religions in Canada: An Introduction*. Toronto: The United Church Publishing House, 1994.

Vigod, Bernard L. *The Jews in Canada*. Ottawa: Canadian Historical Association, 1984.

CHAPTER 19

Alternative Religions

Introduction

Given the number of old and new churches, religions, denominations, sects, cults, spiritualities, movements, etc. and the varying definitions thereof by various authors, it is necessary to begin any discussion of the subject by defining my terminology.

In the literature of the twentieth century, the vocabulary used to designate religious communities has varied. Initially, the word *church* was reserved for those communities that were the established religion of a given Christian country, for example the Church of England in England, or the Roman Catholic Church in Spain or in pre-revolutionary France. Other Christians in these countries were known as dissenters or heretics, members of deviant *sects*, that is to say groups that had broken away from the mother Church. When the growing number of dissenting groups of Christians in the United States were taken into account, a country where there was no established church, the term *denomination* emerged to designate each of the different communities of Christians, the latter representing a strong majority of the population. The words *sect* and *cult*, particularly the latter, developed derogatory connotations. They implied not only small size, but projected the image of small, petty, unreasonable, and unenlightened religion.

Since the 1960s, however, the situation of religions in Western society has changed dramatically. The long-established Christian churches of Europe and North America have lost their dominant and exclusive position. Simultaneously, while growing numbers of immigrants from all parts of the world brought other great religions with them, the mainstream religions have fragmented to the point that no one religion or church is now dominant or normative. Pluralism in religion has accompanied social and cultural pluralism. The hundreds, indeed thousands of religious communities must now be designated in more neutral terms. This is why the expression 'alternative religions' is used here with its two components of *new religions* and *new religious movements*.

Today's new religious movements also differ from the typical sects of the past in that they are frequently larger, international, and administered by a bureaucracy similar to that of the mainstream churches. They tend to be less 'sectarian,' although there still are 'cults' in the traditional meaning of the word, that is to say preachers and adepts of marginal and strange doctrines that fly in the face of reason, science, and common sense. These latter 'cults,' such as those of Jonestown or the Solar Temple, usually recruit only a handful of members.

In this book, all religious movements other than Aboriginal and mainstream religions are designated alternative religions. They will be classified into two categories. First, I will designate as new religious movements (NRMs) those which are rooted in one of the traditional mainstream religions, aboriginal spiritualities included, and that continue to teach some fundamental doctrines of that religion. Examples include shamanism, which is based on Aboriginal religion, Hare Krishna and Yoga which are based on Hinduism, the Baha'i religion which emerged from Islam, Adventism, Jehovah's Witnesses, and the Pentecostal movement in both its Protestant and Catholic forms, all of which came out of Christianity. In the past, these NRMs were frequently designated as 'sects'. I will avoid this term because for many people it has a derogatory connotation, as does the word 'cult.' NRMs are the subject of the first part of this chapter.

Second, I will designate as new religions those that seem concerned with creating something new: a new doctrine, a new culture, a new revelation, a new truth frequently combined with elements drawn from a variety of traditions and cultures. New religions frequently seek to spiritualize science or scientize the occult. They include some Amerindian religions, Scientology, and New Age with its variety of movements such as astrology, channelling, and psychic healing among others. New religions will be the subject of the second part of this chapter.

Following is a review of some new religious movements and new religions that have had significant impact in the West and in Canada in particular. Other such movements are not dealt with here, because of space limitations and the small number of members in many of them.

New religious movements

Primal North-American religion

The revitalization of aboriginal cultures in twentieth-century North America has been discussed earlier. A fundamental dimension of this revitalization was the resurgence of Amerindian spiritualities, the soul of aboriginal cultures so to speak. A key part of these Amerindian religions was the shaman.

Shamans existed in many aboriginal cultures, in Siberia, Japan, and North America for example. They were the individuals that the tribe recognized as particularly gifted to communicate with the supernatural, with the spirits, and the gods.

In the late twentieth century, the waning of Christian domination in Western society and new research in Aboriginal religions led to a new understanding of shamanism. Shamanism is based on ecstasy, or standing outside oneself, or trances. In a spontaneous or self-induced trance, the shaman has direct experience of the supernatural. In a trance, the shaman claims to have visions and revelations of truths communicated to him by the spirits. The shaman can serve as a channel of communication between the natural and supernatural worlds. Shamans, both male and female, make 'out of body' journeys. Their function is to incorporate and control the spirits which may be good or evil. Potentially evil spirits are neutralized by the shaman who incorporates them into his or her own body. The means that the shaman uses to induce trances include bodily exercises, chanting, dancing, drumming, the use of tobacco, alcohol or hallucinogens, and meditation.

This rediscovery of aboriginal religion and shamanism has led some non-aboriginal North-Americans to practise neo-shamanism. This practice is particularly associated with the New Age movement discussed below.

Yoga

Many Canadians and Americans learned to practise yoga during the second half of the twentieth century. Originating in a Sanskrit word meaning 'yoke' or 'union,' the term *yoga* comes from Hinduism and refers to the different paths leading to spiritual liberation. Yoga is a form of activity designed to harness its practitioner to knowledge of the divine. It is one of the six orthodox systems of Hindu philosophy. It is aimed at the spiritual purification of its practitioner through a series of eight stages and under the guidance of a teacher and guide. The first four of these eight stages teach restraint, religious observance, physical preparations, and exercises; these prepare for the subsequent stages which involve withdrawal of the senses, concentration of the mind and meditation. The final stage is union with the divine. In North America, the first four stages have frequently been adopted as forms of exercise and relaxation, while fitness courses borrow the yogic control of breathing and postures.

Hare Krishna (ISKCON)

The International Society for Krishna Consciousness (ISKCON) is the official name of a Hindu sect brought to the West in the 1960s. Based on the teachings of Guru Chaitanya (d. 1534), some of its members dedicate themselves to an austere monastic life of service to Krishna. In Hinduism, Krishna (or Krsna) is the eighth and most famous incarnation of the god Vishnu and is the object of much devotion by Hindu faithful.

ISKCON forbids its faithful to drink alcohol or eat meat. It teaches the spiritual benefits of dancing, ecstatic trances and chanting. Followers frequently repeat the mantra, "Hare Krishna, Hare Rama," as a means to concentrate their mind in devotion to Lord Krishna and Vishnu. Devotees are encouraged to chant and proselytize in the streets.

Baha'i faith

This is a monotheistic religion founded in Persia (Iran) in the 1860s by Baha u'llah (d. 1892); his first successor was his eldest son Abdu'l-Baha who was leader from 1892 to 1921, followed by the founder's great-grandson Shoghi Effendi from 1922 to 1957. From 1963, the religion has been led by an elected body called the Universal House of Justice.

Originating in Baha u'llah's Islamic Shi'ism, the founder preached a message of global social and religious reform and claimed to be proclaiming the promised *one* religion that gathered the best elements from all religions. Converts were attracted from throughout the Middle East and, by the turn of the century, from Europe and North America; after 1950, the Baha'i faith spread into the Third World. Islamic authorities regard Baha'is as heretics and have frequently persecuted them.

Followers of Baha u'llah believe in one God who is completely transcendent and unknowable. Therefore, the religious doctrine centres on a series of 'Manifestations of God,' individuals who reveal the divine purpose for humankind. Among these Manifestations of God are Abraham, Moses, Zoroaster, Gautama Buddha, Jesus, Muhammad, The Bab, and Baha u'llah. Additional Manifestations will appear in time until the end of humanity. [1] Spiritual progress is potentially unlimited for the faithful; it requires recognition of the Manifestations of God, obedience to their directives, and good deeds. Baha'i faithful seek the unity of all peoples and religions of the earth. This implies the establishment of one-world government, one-world language, world peace, the abolition of all prejudice, slavery, economic inequality, and gender inequality. Baha'i faithful proclaim the harmony of true science and true religion.

Baha'i faithful practise daily personal devotions, annual fasts, regular communal gatherings, missionary activity, and celebrate annual feast days. They value monogamous marriage and stable families and frown on divorce. They condemn extramarital sexual relations, homosexuality, gambling, partisan politics, and the consumption of alcohol and drugs. The Baha'i faith has no priesthood; administration of the religion depends on a series of elected councils, with supreme authority resting with the Universal House of Justice headquartered in Haifa, Israel. Canada's governing council is the Spiritual Assembly of the Baha'i of Canada. There were 18,020 Baha'i faithful in Canada in 2001.

Mormons

The Church of Jesus Christ of Latter-day Saints (Mormons) was founded in the United States by Joseph Smith (1805–1844). Smith claimed to have been instructed by the angel Moroni as to the whereabouts of some buried gold tablets on which were inscribed the words of God. Smith published a translation of the tablets in 1830. This *Book of Mormon* tells of two lost tribes of Israel that would have come to America; all members eventually perished except for the faithful Mormon, who wrote the text of the tablets and his son Moroni who buried the latter near Palmyra, New York, in the year 438 C.E. In addition to the *Book of Mormon*, the sacred scriptures of the Mormons include their own edition of the Bible and two books that contain the writings of Smith: *The Pearl of Great Price*, and *Doctrine and Covenants*.

After Joseph Smith was killed by a mob in Carthage, Illinois, in 1844, Brigham Young (1801–1877) succeeded him as leader of the movement. This skilled administrator led his flock to Salt Lake Valley in Utah which became the Church's headquarters, their Zion or holy city in the wilderness.

Mormons have several unique and controversial beliefs. Contrary to mainstream traditional Christianity, their doctrine of the Trinity holds that the Father, Son, and Holy Spirit are three separate Gods who have in common only their purpose and perfection. They believe that God is self-made and that only matter is eternal. They believe that Christ visited America after his resurrection. An adventist movement, Mormons hold that at the Second Coming of Christ, the people of Israel will be reunited, the ten tribes restored, and that Christ will reign over a new earth centred in the Western hemisphere. They believe that Christian churches have denied the true faith, but that the latter has been restored by Joseph Smith.

The most controversial part of Latter-day Saints' teaching and prac-tice was that instituting polygamy. Smith claimed to have received a revelation in 1843 sanctioning plural marriage, a practice that became part of Mormon customs. However, they set this teaching aside in 1890 because of their long dispute and confrontation with the U.S. govern-ment which insisted that U.S. civil law prevail in this matter. Neverthe-less, some Mormon sectarians still practise plural marriage and it is official doctrine of that Church that the custom will be restored upon the Second Coming of Christ.

Another distinctive Mormon custom is that of baptizing the dead in order that the latter may share in the promised millenium. It is with that in mind that the Church has gone to great lengths to collect birth and baptismal records of deceased people belonging to a wide range of faiths. This has served as an unintentional boon to many archival centres in several countries, Canada included; they have been given microfilm copies of these extensive collections of baptismal records, a precious tool for researchers in history and genealogy.

Mormons build and run both local churches (wards) and temples. Ceremonies of marriage and baptisms of the dead can only be per-formed in these. The faithful are required to donate one-tenth of their gross income to the church, thus ensuring the latter's healthy financial situation. The Latter-day Saints practise baptism by total immersion, an unusual custom among twentieth-century Christians. The Church also stresses the importance of missionary activity, so much so that all male faithful are required to devote two years of their life to such mission work and to do so at their own expense. Many women do likewise.

At the end of the twentieth century, the Church of Jesus Christ of

Fig. 27.   Mormon temple in Cardston, AB, in 1922. R. Fletcher. National Archives of Canada, PA-018956.

Latter-day Saints is deeply rooted in the United States, in Utah in particular. It has a total membership of eight million faithful, one half of whom are in the United States. In Canada, Mormons number 101,805 (2001); the vast majority, more than 93,000, belongs to the main denomination, while the others belong to the breakaway Reorganized Church of Latter-day Saints.

Jehovah's Witnesses

This is the name given by most people, since 1931, to the Watch Tower Bible and Tract Society, founded in the 1870s by the adventist preacher Charles Taze Russell (1852–1916). Russell claimed that Jesus Christ was a perfect man, but not God, who had returned to earth in 1878 to prepare the Kingdom of God which would begin in 1914 after the battle of Armageddon. Believers were urged to study the Bible and to warn as many people as possible of the coming 'end time' so that they could survive on earth, in turn, the First Judgment, Christ's thousand-year reign, and a Second Judgment. Russell taught that only a small flock of 144,000 saints drawn from all of human history would obtain eternal life in heaven.

Despite the outbreak of World War I, Armageddon did not happen in

1914. In a context of numerous schisms, defections, and reinterpretations, the leaders of the society ended up by not imposing any specific date for Armageddon, but by teaching that the Kingdom of God began, albeit invisibly in 1914. Russell's successors transformed the society into a highly centralized theocracy, an institution with headquarters in New York which demanded from its members total and exclusive commitment and obedience. Because the Watch Tower Bible and Tract Society categorically condemns the world and its cultures, including governments, religions, and churches, it frequently engaged, at least until World War II, in confrontations with governments, churches, and individuals.

In Canada, these confrontations resulted from Witnesses' refusal to salute the flag, to accept blood transfusions, or to serve under arms, and their militant, aggressive, and abusive rhetoric condemning Christian churches, the Catholic Church in Québec in particular. There, during the 1930s and 1940s, numerous arrests and charges were brought by crown attorneys against many Witnesses who refused to abide by laws and bylaws that restricted or banned their kind of proselytism.

Jehovah's Witnesses engage in door-to-door proselytizing, worship in Kingdom Halls, and sell their magazines *Awake* and *The Watchtower* to the public. They often hold large assemblies in stadiums or arenas, practise total immersion baptism, and have their own translations of the Bible. They are perhaps best-known today for their refusal to accept blood transfusions, even when their lives or those of their children are at stake.

There are some four million Witnesses worldwide, with 154,750 in Canada (2001).

Christian Science

The Church of Christ (Scientist) was founded in the United States by Mary Baker Eddy (1821–1910). Having suffered from various ailments for most of her life, in 1862 Eddy learned from Phineas Quimby the possibility of cures without medicine. In 1866, the year of Quimby's death, Eddy claimed to have experienced a cure from a severe injury that occurred when she fell on the ice. This cure was obtained without medicine, but rather after meditating on the story of the healing of the paralyzed man in Matthew 9. Eddy thereupon set out to recover the healing emphasis that was present in early Christianity.

In 1875, Eddy completed the first edition of the manual *Science and*

Health, a book revised with *Key to the Scriptures* in 1883; in 1879, the Church of Christ (Scientist) was founded and incorporated in Boston. It is an organization based on largely autonomous local congregations and structured according to Eddy's instructions in her *Church Manual* (1895). The church is run by a board of five directors who appoint their successors.

Sunday worship services in the Church of Christ (Scientist) are based on readings from the Bible and Eddy's *Science and Health.* They also include hymns, the recitation of the Lord's Prayer, and silent prayer. During mid-week meetings, members give accounts of healings. Since the Bible and Eddy's writings constitute the only basic teachings in the movement, the Church establishes reading rooms as a means of proselytism. This was also the motivation for the foundation of its daily newspaper *The Christian Science Monitor,* the instrument by which this small church is best known.

Christian Science believes that "all reality is in God and his creation, harmonious and eternal. That which he creates is good, and he makes all that is made. Therefore the only reality of sin, sickness or death is the awful fact that unrealities seem real to human, erring belief, until God strips off their disguise."[2] Therefore, health, happiness, and holiness are found by applying to one's life practices and attitudes consonant with divine harmony and not by consulting physicians or psychologists. Sin and illness are errors that are overcome by Truth.

The Church of Christ (Scientist) is established in the United States and in other English-speaking countries. It is present in Canada, although its members are few.

The Pentecostal movement

The word *pentecost* is based on the Greek word meaning 'fiftieth day'. It was the Greek name given to the Jewish Feast of Weeks which occurred on the fiftieth day after the central Jewish feast of Passover. The Feast of Weeks was when the first fruits of the corn harvest were presented and the giving of the Law by Moses was commemorated. Since the Holy Spirit is believed to have descended on the Apostles on this day (Acts 2:1), the name Pentecost was given to this feast day in the Christian liturgical calendar. Another name was Whitsunday, a name said to come from the custom of wearing white robes for the baptisms that usually took place on that occasion in medieval times. So it is that the feast of Pentecost occurs fifty days after the feast of Easter in the Christian liturgical calendar; which it follows as the second most important feast day of the year. In the Eastern Church, it is celebrated as the feast of the Holy Trinity.

As a distinctive movement, Pentecostalism began at the turn of the twentieth century in the United States. Participants believe that they can receive the same spiritual gifts and live the same experience as the early Christians did on the day of Pentecost (Acts 2:1–4). Pentecostals stress the practice of the gifts recorded in the book of Acts: speaking in tongues, prophecy, spiritual healing, and exorcism. All true Christians allegedly possess these gifts, but Pentecostals claim that the power to exercise them is obtained from God in an experience designated as 'Baptism in the Holy Spirit,' or 'Spirit Baptism,' which is distinct from both regular sacramental baptism and conversion. They claim that this 'Spirit Baptism' is signified by the recipient breaking into tongues, spiritual tongues that is, or *glossolalia*.

These distinctive beliefs first appeared in 1900 among a variety of Holiness groups, the latter being a reformist Methodist tradition in nineteenth-century U.S. Protestantism. Members of Holiness groups believed that sanctification of the whole person takes place instantaneously in a crisis experience, rather than gradually during the normal course of living, aided by the nurturing of the Church. In fact, Holiness was closely associated with revivalism and revivalist techniques of instantaneous decisions for the Lord and visible evidence of conversion. It was promoted by preachers such as Phoebe Palmer (d. 1874), and Charles G. Finney (d. 1875), and led to distinctive camp meetings and associations in the late century. Holiness influenced a significant number of Protestants of several denominations. Some distinct Holiness congregations emerged, one being the Church of the Nazarene, founded in 1908. By 1900, physical healings were claimed to occur in Holiness meetings and experiences of sanctification were called baptisms of the Holy Spirit. The emergence of distinct Pentecostal congregations after 1906 was a split in the Holiness movement.

The movement of Pentecostalism was launched in Los Angeles in 1906 when Spirit Baptisms occurred during the prayer services of a group of Adventist believers. A growing number of Pentecostal Churches would then appear throughout the United States with names such as The Church of God, The Church of God in Christ, the Assemblies of God, etc. Indeed, because of the central role of the Spirit in Pentecostal theology and the necessary freedom of the Spirit, great diversity, or fragmentation, characterizes Pentecostalism, a movement that remains divided along ethnic, linguistic, theological, class, or other lines. It is more a cluster of various movements than a unified movement.

The Canadian Robert McAlister of Cobden, Ontario, was present at the manifestation of the Spirit in Los Angeles in 1906. He is considered the founder of Pentecostalism in Canada. Although the census of Canada of 1911 lists only 515 Pentecostals, more than two dozen assemblies soon appeared in the country. During World War I they came together in two organizations, namely the Pentecostal Assemblies of Canada (PAOC) and the Western Canada District Council of the Assemblies of God, U.S.A. Pentecostals were soon known as an aggressively evangelical branch of Canadian Protestantism, believing as they did in the imminence of the millenium and the urgency of salvation. One of their early leaders was James Eustace Purdie who, between 1920 and 1950, founded several Bible schools including the first Canadian Pentecostal Bible School in 1925. With a curriculum centred on the Word of God and prayer, these schools emphasized practical training in preaching and evangelism. Their graduates were the missionaries and field workers that would lead the Pentecostal assemblies after World War II.

Pentecostals would be on the leading edge of the rapid growth of evangelicalism in Canadian Protestantism after World War II. While only 58,000 (0.5%) Canadians declared themselves to be Pentecostals in 1941, 144,000 (0.8%) did so in 1961, and 341,000 (1.4%) in 1981. However, the denomination itself only reported 125,000 (0.5%) in 1981, a little more than one-third of the self-identified members. In 1991, 436,000 Canadians declared themselves Pentecostal, a number that dropped to 369,475 in the census of 2001. Some Pentecostals became prominent in Canadian society. For example, Pentecostal pastor David Mainse leads the popular television program *100 Huntley Street*, while another pastor, Brian C. Stiller directed the Evangelical Fellowship of Canada.

By the late twentieth century, Canada's Pentecostals, while remaining diversified, moved much closer, indeed, became part of the mainstream of evangelical Protestantism in Canada. Until the late 1960s, Pentecostalism remained a fragmented denomination within Protestantism, in the U.S. in particular. Then, some of the key Pentecostal, or charismatic ideas, made inroads into several Christian churches, the Roman Catholic Church included. In addition, Pentecostalism has spread worldwide. This has meant an even more diversified Pentecostal movement that can no longer be as closely identified with fundamentalist Protestantism as it was earlier. Also, this greater diversity among Pentecostals has moved them closer to other Christians.

New religions

Other than the new religious movements, the second category of alternative religions is that of the new religions which are very diverse. Although there is rapid turnover in their membership, many Canadians have been influenced by them to some extent.

New religions are distinguished by their endeavour to create something entirely new, in many cases a new culture. While incorporating insights from other cultures, they often seek to spiritualize science and make the occult appear scientific, all the while insisting on the importance of personal religious experience as the means of validating and establishing truth. Reason and Scripture have little importance in new religions as sources of truth. They seek God within the self; indeed, rather than seeking to know God, each individual is urged to become God. They share a monistic or unified world view where there is little distinction between the sacred and the profane.

The following are some of the new religions that have appeared in North America since the eighteenth century. The stage is continental rather than exclusively Canadian because most of these religions know no national boundaries, although most originated in the United States.

New religions among the Amerindians

The traditional religions or spiritualities of North America's Amerindian people were closely tied to, indeed a fundamental part of, a given tribe's culture, customs, and lifestyle. Whenever new religions have emerged among them, it has usually been in an attempt to come to terms with the culture-shock of the encounter with Canadian or American civilization. While some of these new religions sought a peaceful accommodation with Canadians and Americans, others preached war and the eradication of their alien presence.

The religion of Handsome Lake among the Iroquois was explained earlier. It was one instance of a religion of accommodation. In contrast, the religion of Tenskwatawa, or the Shawnee Prophet, taught active opposition to the evil represented by the Europeans. In the years preceding the War of 1812, the Shawnee people were dispossessed of their land by the invading British and American forces. They were demoralized, as was Tenskwatawa, an alcoholic shaman of dubious repute. However, after falling into a coma and appearing to be dead, Tenskwatawa revived and told of revelations that he had received while in a trance. He saw heaven which he described as a perfect hunting and agricultural ground where unworthy Shawnees were punished. Having reformed his own life, Tenskwatawa entered other trances where he had visions of a completely reformed Amerindian society. This reform entailed the abandonment of the borrowed ways of the European and the return to the traditional Amerindian lifestyle. His message spread to other Amerindian tribes like the Miami, Winnebago, and Kickapoo; new rituals were adopted to accompany the message. However, when the Amerindians were defeated by the British army at the battle of Tippecanoe on 7 November 1811, Tenskwatawa lost his credibility in favour of his brother Tecumseh who stood for a traditional military response to the invasion by the Europeans.

Another new religion to develop among the Amerindians was the Ghost Dance of 1890, and this only twenty years after another short-lived movement of the same name. It began among the Paiute of northern Nevada before spreading widely to other tribes of the Plains and further East. The prophet of the Ghost Dance of 1890 was Wovoka, a healer and shaman whose first revelation occurred when he had apparently fallen dead during a solar eclipse. Like Handsome Lake and Tenskwatawa, Wovoka taught a strong ethical message. He also announced the coming of a millennium when the world would be renewed, the spirits of the dead would return, and all suffering would end. This millennium would be preceded by cataclysmic events that would destroy the Europeans' culture and all unworthy Amerindians; the righteous ones would be temporarily removed while the earth was reborn. All this would be the work of God. Meanwhile, Wovoka taught his followers to await these events in peace, while performing the Ghost Dance periodically.

Many tribes took up the Ghost Dance which was performed by men and women who had painted their bodies to illustrate the content of their revelations. They danced in concentric circles, with their arms resting on the shoulders of their neighbours, and did so for five days without interruption. This resulted in collective exaltation and trances, some receiving revelations from spirits or deceased relatives. Wovoka taught that the more the Dance was performed, the sooner the new world would arrive. However, the Ghost Dance suffered a major setback with the massacre at Wounded Knee on 29 December 1890. There, the U.S. army slaughtered a group of innocent Sioux Ghost Dancers, in the belief that they were preparing a rebellion. Nevertheless, the Ghost Dance would continue to be performed by some for many years afterwards.

The Native American Church is another new religion to emerge among the Amerindians. It is a fusion of various tribal religions with Christianity. It is distinctive for its use of the drug peyote in worship, a custom that had long prevailed in Mexico. In the twentieth century, this peyote religion has spread in step with a growing Amerindian desire to preserve their ancestral lifestyle and customs. By consuming peyote, devotees achieve a state of altered consciousness which they consider a religious experience; they consider the drug itself to be sacred medicine.

The Church of Scientology[3]

This originated in the writings of L. Ron Hubbard (1911–1986) who created the world view and organization of Scientology. Hubbard's foundational book was entitled *Dianetics: the Modern Science of Mental Health* (1950). Hubbard coined a new vocabulary that became part of Scientology; some of his new concepts are *engram, reactive mind, analytical mind, auditing,* and *clear.* He taught that his was a "science of mind" that was built on natural laws like those of the natural sciences. His science of mind claimed to be "a therapeutic technique with which can be treated all inorganic mental ills and all organic psychosomatic ills, with assurances of complete cure."[4]

Hubbard blended concepts drawn from science, psychology, and religion with his own vocabulary.

Scientology has been much criticized, and has faced a number of lawsuits, in Canada and elsewhere. Points of contention have included its doctrines and its tax-free status; the group has also tried to obtain censorship of some books written on them. It claims that its adepts can simultaneously be members of other religions. There were only 1,525 members of the Church of Scientology enumerated in Canada in 2001.

New Age

The New Age began in the United States in the 1970s, peaked in the 1980s, and seems on the wane early in the twenty-first century. However, although the movement itself may be in decline, its influence on contemporary culture has been profound and will likely prove enduring in many respects. This is why it is important to understand it.

Far from being an organized movement, New Age is diffuse and disorganized. It is a conglomeration of various movements, cults, associations, publishing houses, practices, and beliefs that have in common an enthusiasm for the creation of a new age of harmony and enlightenment in the world. Many consider that the Bible of the New Age is a book by Marilyn Ferguson entitled *The Aquarian Conspiracy* (1980); it gives a clear and comprehensive presentation of New Age goals.

The expression *New Age* refers to the Age of Aquarius, which in astrology is the era of 2,150 years when the celestial constellation of Aquarius and the zodiacal sign of Aquarius will coincide. Indeed, astrologers believe that every 2,000 years we enter a new zodiac sign and a new age begins. The Age of Aquarius follows the Age of Pisces where a similar coincidence prevails. While some New Agers believe that the Age of Aquarius has already begun, others believe that it will do so shortly; this is because astrologers disagree as to the exact date of the change. Along with astrologers, New Agers attribute real meaning to these astrological symbols (Pisces, Zodiac, etc.). They believe that the world's ending Age of Pisces was primarily structural, institutional, and industrial, one where Christianity prevailed and occult knowledge was not given its due. In contrast, the new Age of Aquarius will evolve primarily in a psychological, social, and spiritual direction. Science, religion, and art will merge, resulting in a new era of peace and progress. In turn, this will lead to the development of a new mind and a new consciousness in the world, a new stage in the evolution of human beings in psychological, social and spiritual terms. Moreover, New Agers celebrate change; their movement is thus constantly in flux.

New Age followers recognize a wide range of movements, customs, objects, and beliefs. They include crystals, channelling, neo-shamanism, holistic health practices, belief in reincarnation, self-improvement psychology, occult books, hypnotherapy, and astrology. In its natural humanism, the priority it gives to the individual, its belief in the radical goodness of human beings and its relativism, the New Age reflects its time. However, in addition to being a product of its time, that of late twentieth-century North America, New Age reflects long-standing trends in the Western world.

When set in the context of the history of philosophy and religion, New Age stands apart from Judaism and Christianity, religions that teach that God is wholly distinct from the world which he created, that men and women were created in God's image and likeness to dominate the natural world which stands as a third level of being intended to sustain human needs and development. Although Christianity has some influence on New Age teachings, these fit more naturally into the philosophical and religious tradition of monism which teaches that there is only one unified reality, that human beings have a divine essence, and that that there is no distinction between man and nature. In this monistic tradition, personal growth comes through the expansion of one's consciousness. Dualism, a third long-standing world view, has also influenced New Age. In dualism, two eternal realities, spirit and matter, one good, the other evil, contend for domination of the world.

In its monistic tradition, New Age is in the company of the occult sciences, spiritualism, and Eastern religions, all having a direct influence on its growth, along with psychology. Other beliefs that also share in such monism are animism and pantheism. The occult refers to hidden wisdom and includes various forms of divination such as astrology, palmistry, and tarot. Spiritualism is the belief that the human person survives death and that there can be direct communication between the living and the dead through a human medium. Eastern religions like Hinduism and Buddhism are the original sources of the monistic world view. Twentieth-century psychology and para-psychology (telepathy, clairvoyance, psycho kinesis, precognition, psychic healing) have also had a major influence on New Age.

New Age evokes religious philosophies of the early Christian era, Neo-Platonism and Gnosticism in particular.[5] The ancient school of Gnosticism taught many of the doctrines prevalent in New Age. The material world is evil; spiritual individuals have sparks of divinity within them; salvation comes in the form of secret knowledge (*gnosis*) of one's self, one's origin, and destiny; at death the spiritual individuals escape from the prison of their bodies to be united with God; only spiritual elite will obtain the secret knowledge that saves them.

During the Middle Ages, the domination of Western society by the Christian church drove occultism underground. However, as Renaissance and Reformation swept Europe from the fourteenth to the seventeenth centuries, occultism flourished. Older movements such as alchemy, astrology, witchcraft, and Kabbalah[6] were revitalized, while the new Rosicrucianism appeared. Then they were driven underground again with the rationalism of the new science and the Enlightenment of the eighteenth century. The occultism associated with magic, alchemy, astrology, and witchcraft withered. But there followed a new occultism more concerned with metaphysical and spiritual realities Rosicrucianism,[7] Freemasonry, Swedenborgianism, and Mesmerism. It is these movements that are echoed in New Age.

Emmanuel Swedenborg (1688–1722) is considered by many to be the precursor of New Age. This Swedish intellectual and visionary claimed to have had a vision that carried him into the spiritual world where he learned eternal truths. Like the Spiritualists, Swedenborg taught that one could communicate with deceased persons; like the Gnostics and Kabbalists, he taught that one had spiritual life both before and after death; like the Gnostics he taught that some spiritual events could only be known through secret knowledge available only to a few; he had a monistic understanding of God; he claimed that the Second Coming of Christ occurred in the year 1757, the year which marked the beginning of the New Age; he claimed to have taken out of body journeys to both heaven and hell; he claimed to have direct revelations from the angels. Many New Age doctrines are found in Emmanuel Swedenborg who published voluminously 300 years ago.

During the nineteenth and twentieth centuries, a number of movements prepared the way for New Age teachings, among them Transcendentalism, Spiritualism, Theosophy, New Thought, and Christian Science. Since World War II, Eastern religions and psychology have played an important role in influencing occultism and thus New Age.

A basic component of New Age is Eastern religions with their monism and belief in reincarnation among other doctrines. For many years, Eastern religions were kept away from North America by laws in the United States and Canada that severely restricted the immigration of people from Asiatic countries. However, the lifting of this discriminatory legislation in both Canada and the United States in the 1950s and 1960s allowed a growing number of immigrants, religious leaders included, to establish Hindu, Buddhist, Zen, and other Eastern religions in ever-larger areas of the continent.

Another major factor influencing New Age was modern psychology whose focus on the inner self became one of New Age's foundational components. Both look inside the self for answers to life's basic questions. This search for the self is simultaneously a search for psychological wholeness and a search for divinity. Indeed, in the West of the twentieth century, psychology frequently became a surrogate religion, psychological wholeness replacing salvation as the objective sought. For New Age, it is self-awareness, self-realization, or awareness of one's divinity that replace conversion, while personal transformation replaces salvation. New Age dismisses religion as irrelevant and invites people to look inside themselves for wholeness and divinity.

HEALING

Belief in non-medical forms of healing is called alternative medicine, a part of the holistic health movement. It is a basic characteristic of New Age, whose alternative medicine includes acupuncture, crystal healing, herbal remedies, and psychic healing. In fact the holistic health movement and New Age have merged. New Agers believe that holistic or natural approaches to health work better than medicine or drugs, while some believe that crystals assist in healing. They reject medical orthodoxy's belief in organic and material factors in disease.

Some adepts of alternative medicine believe that the causes of illness are supernatural; they explain disease by invoking spiritual or metaphysical causes and promote healing of the same order. For this latter group, healing can be found in God or in the divine energy found in living beings. New Age medicine teaches that spiritual and mystical energy regulates good health, the latter being a condition where one's body, mind, and spirit are well-integrated and balanced.

The holistic health movement recalls the centuries-old tradition where shamans and faith-healers invoked supernatural causes and cures for disease. This belief was secularized in the nineteenth century when Mesmerism and Swedenborgianism proposed a 'harmonial' model of the universe wherein an inner harmony was said to exist between the spheres of the universe. Energy flowed from the upper to the lower levels, with God indwelling as a cosmic force.

This harmonial model allowed diverse therapies to develop including diet programs, homeopathy, and hydropathy. Grahamism, for example was a dietary practice based on the belief that healing was found in the energy contained in certain foods, wheat in particular. Homeopathy taught that like is cured by like. For example, a patient suffering from poisoning would be given a small dose of the same poison as a cure. Hydropathy taught that curative powers were found in water. This led to the development of many curative springs where the ill would flock to bathe. Other alternative medical practices followed in the nineteenth century, including Christian Science, chiropractic, osteopathy, and New Thought.

New Age medicine also includes acupuncture and psychic and spiritual healing. Acupuncture is a Chinese medical practice that developed from Taoist theory. It holds that energy (Ch'i) flows through pathways (meridians) in the body. If that circulation of energy is blocked, an imbalance occurs. Pain or disease follows. The remedy is to stimulate certain points of the body by the use of heat and needles (acupuncture), allowing the circulation of energy to increase, thereby decreasing or eliminating the blockage. Acupressure is a similar therapy, where the needles are replaced by pressure exerted by the therapist's fingers.

Psychic healing is sometimes called spiritual healing or faith healing. Psychic healers claim that the power that they draw on comes from an energy field that surrounds us. Faith healers claim that the power that they invoke is the power of God who intervenes directly to restore the patient's health. Obviously, such claims are beyond scientific validation. The psychic healer transfers to the patient the power, the energy to heal. This is done by various means such as the laying on of hands, therapeutic touch, or prayer. Psychic diagnosis also exists where the practitioner diagnoses the illness of the patient by using some supernatural or extraordinary means such as clairvoyance, spirit guides, and the like.

Alternative medicine and New Age medicine share the same monistic and holistic doctrine, namely that the universe is made up of one, undifferentiated, impersonal reality, variously called Universal Consciousness, the One, Life Energy, Bioenergy, God, or some other name. Given that everything is one, or God, humans become gods. Human beings are but one material manifestation of this universal, spiritual energy. Therefore, a divine energy force flows through each individual; disease is caused by a blockage of that energy and healing occurs when one learns to manipulate that energy force to overcome the blockage; the latter consists of an imbalance of energy or unenlightened conscience. Healing, whether physical, mental, or spiritual, can occur when one becomes aware of one's divinity and unity with the universe. The key to healing is found in the spiritual unity of everything.

RITUALS AND FADS OF THE NEW AGE

While serious New Age writers focus on issues such as personal and social transformation, ecology, peace, and holistic health, more trendy New Age rituals and fads that capture the popular imagination include some eastern religious practices, channelling, neo-shamanism, crystals, astrology, hypnotism, and reincarnation. While some Eastern religious practices seemed to be in the forefront of the New Age in the 1970s, Zen and yoga for example, channelling came to the fore in the 1980s, while neo-shamanism and Amerindian religions seemed to be in the limelight in the 1990s.

The channel is the conduit between the world we see and the one we don't. In the occult-metaphysical world view reality is one and undivided. There can be no separation between the natural and the supernatural realms. Spiritual beings are just as real as material ones and communication with them must be possible and normal. Channeling is that communication of information to a human being from an entity belonging to a supernatural world through the intermediary of another human being, the channel. Channeling is a form of spiritism. However, while spiritism is about communication with a dead relative, channelling deals with communication from a spiritual entity who need not be a dead relative.

Channelling was most popular in the 1980s, thanks to its promotion by Hollywood actors like Shirley MacLaine whose third autobiography entitled *Out on a Limb* (1983) spoke of various occult activities.[8] Indeed, channels are the new names for the traditional seer, shaman, oracle, or medium. Channels teach sacred information revealed to them by a spirit. Such activity was normal in traditional Christianity where mystics and prophets were the mouthpieces of God, but was discouraged during the modern period with its rationalist mindset. In the late nineteenth century, it reappeared in Madame Blavatsky's Theosophy. Channelling came into its own during the twentieth century when several allegedly sacred books were channeled, including the *Urantia Book* in the 1930s. The latter's full 2,100 pages would have been channeled by automatic writing to an anonymous source. It teaches new things about Jesus and the earth.

In the 1970s, several channeled books were published. Among the best known are books containing what the spiritual entity named Seth would have revealed to Jane Roberts (d. 1983) of Elmira, New York. In *The Seth Material* (1970), *Seth Speaks* (1973) and other publications, Roberts speaks of the messages she received while in a trance. Then *A Course in Miracles* (1975) appeared where psychologist Helen Cohn Shucman claimed that, beginning in 1965, she heard an inner voice, that of the biblical Christ. During the next several years she transcribed the messages she received through automatic or inspired writing. This led to the publication of a 1,200 page, three volume text. The work undertakes to explain that our daily existence is illusory, filled with obstacles to the presence of love. We must remove the obstacles. During these same 1970s, David Spangler published a number of books including *Revelation: The Birth of The New Age* (1976) in which he claims to have spent three years as the channel for a disembodied spirit named John.

Then channelling became a growth industry. In the United States, channels such as J.Z. Knight, Jack Pursel, and Kevin Ryerson became widely known in the 1980s. Knight dealt with the spirit Ramtha, who would have lived 35,000 years ago. Shirley MacLaine and others endorsed Knight's teaching which was disseminated in seminars, books, videos, and cassettes, making the channel wealthy in the process. Jack Pursel dealt with the spirit Lazaris who communicated with him while he was in a trance. Kevin Ryerson is distinct in that he communicates with more than one spiritual entity. He too became popular after Shirley MacLaine promoted his work.

Channels teach a common New Age message which includes strong critiques of modern civilization where governments, religions and science would have enslaved people. They teach the natural goodness and wisdom of the self, of each individual person. They invite all to achieve liberation from all these enslavements, including those to family, the economy, and all social institutions. They teach that the old age is breaking down, and a new age is dawning. They teach that God is within each of us, that we are responsible for creating our own reality and for realizing our own divinity.

Neo-shamanism became a leading fad in New Age, especially during the 1990s. It developed along with the new interest in Amerindian spirituality, a movement romanticized by New Agers. Indeed, the New Age includes a host of masters, magicians, magi, and mediums who claim to be the heirs of the shamans, medicine men, sorcerers, seers, and wizards of old. Both the traditional shamans and the neo-shamans of the New Age diagnose illness in the holistic way, and rely on non-medical forces to work their cures.

The best known symbol of the New Age is the crystal. It became popular in the 1980s, adorning houses, people, etc. In many traditional societies, crystals were considered to have occult and magical qualities. This led to crystal balls becoming the instrument of choice of fortune tellers. New Agers embraced crystals for similar reasons, considering them instruments of transformation and healing. In New Age teaching, each individual's higher self has the ability to perform healings and psychic feats. However, the mental obstacles that people have erected prevent the natural flow of cosmic energies from entering their minds and bodies. Crystals can allegedly alleviate this problem by helping to realign the individual's flow of energy. Crystals are believed to be a catalyst or conductor of this cosmic energy which they would receive and transmit in the form of vibrations, constituting an energy field around the crystal. The individual can then manipulate this energy by means of meditation or other techniques, thus facilitating the transformation of the individual. Crystals are used in New Age healing practices, because New Agers believe that illness is a disruption of energies in one's spiritual or etheric body, the source of spiritual energy. The crystal would help in healing by restoring the natural harmony between the physical and etheric or spiritual bodies.

Conclusion

Since the beginning of recorded history, there always have been dissident and sectarian groups that have become new religious movements or new religions. This is because there is never unanimity among adherents of a religion as to the right interpretation to give to the revelations and doctrines of their religion. Normal debate and discussion of these differences can easily turn into conflict and institutional splits.

What is new in modern times, particularly in the nineteenth and twentieth centuries, is the sheer number of new groups. Many reasons can be invoked to explain this recent phenomenon including the weakening hold of tradition on the minds and consciences of people, as well as the exaggerated importance of institutions and of theological orthodoxy in modern societies. More recently, the mixing and movement of people on a global scale has engendered much more diversity and pluralism in a growing number of societies. Indeed, Canada was a largely homogeneous society until the mid-twentieth century: a small number of Amerindians and Jews alongside two majorities of Christians, the one French-speaking, and the other English-speaking. This is no longer true at the beginning of the twenty-first century. Indeed, Canada's largely Christian heritage has been rapidly transformed into the multi-ethnic and pluralistic society of today. New religions and new religious movements have become very important in understanding the new Canada.

Suggested readings

Dawson, Lorne L. *Comprehending Cults. The Sociology of New Religious Movements*. Toronto: Oxford, 1998.

Hexham, Irving and Karla Poewe. *New Religions as Global Cultures*. Boulder, Colorado: Westview Press, 1997.

Kyle, Richard. *The New Age Movement in American Culture*. New York: University Press of America, 1995.

Melton, J. Gordon. *Encyclopedic Handbook of Cults in America*. New York: Garland Publishing, 1986.

Melton, J. Gordon. *The Encyclopedia of American Religions*. 4th edition. Detroit: Gale Research, 1993.

Miller, James R. *Equal Rights: The Jesuits Estates Act Controversy*. Montréal & Kingston: McGill-Queen's University Press, 1979.

Miller, Timothy. Ed. *America's Alternative Religions*. N. p: State University of New York Press, n.d.

Palmer, Susan J. *Moon Sisters, Krishna Mothers and Raneesh Lovers*. N.p: Syracuse University Press, 1994.

Penton, M. James. *Jehovah's Witnesses in Canada*. Toronto: Macmillan of Canada, n.d.

Robbins, Thomas and Susan Palmer. *Millennium, Messiahs and Mayhem. Contemporary Apocalyptic Movements*. New York/London: Routledge, 1997.

Saliba, John A. *Understanding New Religious Movements*. Grand Rapids: William B. Eerdmans Publishing Company, 1996.

Stark, Rodney and William Bainbridge. *A Theory of Religion*. New York: Peter Lang, 1987.

Wilson, Bryan R. *The Social Dimensions of Sectarianism. Sects and New Religious Movements in Contemporary Society*. Oxford: Clarendon Press, 1990.

CHAPTER 20

Epilogue: The Future of Religions in Canada

The history that was outlined in the preceding chapters has shown that, from the outset, religions have played a central role in the Canadian story. Canadians of whatever origin, be it Amerindian, French, British, American, Ukrainian, Italian, African, Arab, or Asiatic, have understood the world and their place in it in ways proposed by their religious faith community, be it Aboriginal, Christian, Muslim, Jewish, Hindu, or other. The faith of Canadians has provided them with their basic understanding of the origin of the world and of its people; the meaning of life, love, justice, suffering, and death; the fundamental nature and purpose of the family and society; the necessary rules of behaviour in life; and the destiny of each human being. With few exceptions, Canadians believe that our time on earth is but one phase in a living journey that began in the eye of God and that is rooted in a spiritual and transcendent world, that extends beyond the grave, and that is destined to end in eternal bliss in the company of God. Each religion explains these fundamental realities in its own way, each providing its faithful with the assurance of understanding in faith, and the necessary hope in the life to come.

Notwithstanding the above, the four centuries that have elapsed since the arrival of the Europeans in Canada have often been characterized by rivalry, acrimony, and conflict among the leading religions in place. European Christians worked to eradicate Amerindian spiritualities, Protestants fought Catholics and vice versa, Jews were frequently the victims of discrimination by Christians, and Asiatic Chinese and Japanese were the targets of repressive legislation. That has been because each religion considered that it had the monopoly of truth; all others were in error. Therefore, the religious group that was dominant usually made life difficult for all religious minorities.

This four-centuries-old story of conflict began to change after World War II, when global migrations and population mixing, coupled with a revolution in communications led to a radical reassessment of our perceptions of both ourselves and others. The growing number of immigrants to Canada from other-than-European and other-than-North-American countries of Asia, Africa, and elsewhere led Canadians to discover the rich diversity and richness of the religions of the world. These new Canadians also compelled us to ensure that our public institutions, such as schools, did not engage in religious proselytism and indoctrination. While learning to come to terms with the new pluralistic religious reality of today's Canada, Canadians reinterpreted and redefined their relationship with these new fellow citizens. The walls of the traditional imposed or self-imposed religious ghettoes, Catholic, Protestant, Jewish, and other, crumbled as Canadians learned to appreciate their new neighbours.

This was the context in the 1960s when social and cultural revolutions swept the Western world and Canada in particular. While the Catholic Church was experiencing its Second Vatican Council and the United States underwent a dramatic crisis manifest in its counter-culture and the Vietnam War social trauma, Canada's central cultural and economic engines, Québec and Ontario, underwent profound and rapid social change. In Québec it was called the Quiet Revolution, a sudden and dramatic turning away from the old ways symbolized by the *curé*, the *habitant*, the large family, and the Union Nationale governing party of Maurice Duplessis. Overnight, the Liberal Party of Jean Lesage was elected to serve as the new broom. The state took over education at all levels, as well as other social services, health care in particular. It stepped back from its long-standing partnership with the Catholic Church, a separation which suited the new Vatican II church. New religions and new religious movements soon appeared to take advantage of the new openness in Québec society.

In Ontario, the heart of English Canada, a similar social and cultural revolution occurred, albeit more quietly than in Québec. Among other innovations, new statutes instituted French-language schools in the public school system, the French language was recognized in the legislature, and the traditional Christian-Protestant emphasis of Ontario's secular public schools was set aside. In 1984, Ontario's Catholic public school system (separate schools) was extended to the end of high school studies. In addition, the same multiculturalism that had become federal government policy in 1971 was applied in Ontario government circles. The heartland of Canada's traditional white anglo-saxon Protestantism rapidly became a pluralist's utopia. The City of Toronto, long the bastion of straight-laced Anglo-Protestant conservatism, became a booming, colourful, and multicultural metropolis. Religions and churches that had long existed side by side in isolation were now engaged in dialogue and joint social projects. Canada and its religions would never be the same. The new mood was reflected in the Canadian Charter of Rights and Freedoms which was part of Canada's new Constitution adopted in 1982. Therein, discrimination of many kinds was made illegal and the equality of all Canadian citizens became a fundamental element in the basic law of the land.

While aborning, this brave new age of the heady 1960s and 1970s witnessed not only the counterculture, but also a new chapter in the development of Christian ecumenism and ecumenism in general. All hopes were permitted, not only to the revitalizing Catholics with Vatican II, but to all Christians who now launched ambitious projects that sought the unity of Catholics and Anglicans, Anglicans and the United Church of Canada, etc. Several churches agreed to pool their resources for the theological training of their clergy. While theologians reinterpreted long-standing doctrinal differences, church leaders multiplied gestures of reconciliation, clergy planned common endeavours, and faithful of different churches joined in fraternal discussions. Some dared to hope for the reunion of several Christian churches in their lifetime.

Nevertheless, this thrust towards unity coexisted with continuing diversity. As the twentieth century wound down, not only did the traditional religions and churches, without exception, continue their discrete existence, but new groups appeared on the religious horizon with disconcerting regularity. Increased dialogue and ecumenism had no doubt fostered greater understanding between the many religious groups, but few if any had seen fit to end their continued discrete existence. In fact, by the 1990s, the ecumenical movement seemed to have stalled. The enthusiasm and boundless hope of a generation ago seem to have faded.

What is the future of ecumenism, Christian and other? Will the work undertaken since the 1960s bear fruit in the future? The answer depends on the level of unity that is sought. If full institutional integration of various Christian churches is the objective, it may be long-awaited. For example, Roman Catholics and Anglicans have agreed on some points of doctrine and polity, but are far apart on others, the authority of the pope being only one example. The same is true for most other unions that have been contemplated. However, short of full institutional integration, the objective of ecumenical discussions may be simply a greater measure of agreement on some points of doctrine, better cooperation in social projects or in the use of physical resources, or better understanding between the churches or religions. If any of these is the measure of success in ecumenical discussions, then much hope is possible. Indeed, much has been achieved in the past generation and much can be achieved in the coming years.

A related question is that regarding the future of fundamentalism. If ecumenism stalls, does it mean that fundamentalism will intensify? For example, since assuming office in 1978, Pope John Paul II has steered the Roman Catholic Church in a decidedly conservative direction, one that some would label fundamentalist. During the 1980s and 1990s, as ecumenical dialogue stalled, the Catholic Church was moving further and further away from the insights and openness that had characterized Vatican II. In the church of John Paul II, liberal-minded bishops were shunted aside to make room for conservative-minded ones, these being the only ones selected for new appointments. Similarly, John Paul's church has not shown any new openness to the laity or to women, or any new flexibility in its teaching on sexual matters. Most observers are convinced that the Catholic Church of the twenty-first century has stepped back from the commitments and lost the spirit of Vatican II.

If indeed, in the year 2000 most religions in Canada showed a neo-conservative face, it corresponded to that of our society in general which seemed to have moved away from its strong social *engagement* of the 1960s and 1970s. Will such conservatism or fundamentalism tend to unite or divide people? The question remains open.

The history of Canada's religions shows how closely intertwined the latter have been with the people and the society of Canada. Until very recently, each major group in our society has had its very own faith community that served both to cement the unity and solidarity of the group and to facilitate the group's acculturation into Canadian society. But it must be remembered that if the churches and religions served such specific social functions, they were primarily gatherings of believers who understood the world in a particular way and who came together to worship and serve God as one. In the eyes of their members, the social functions of the churches were well and good, but secondary to their primary *raison d'être* which is the gathering of the people of God.

These churches were usually very close to their flocks and reflected that flock's particularity and either its sense of domination over others, or its sense of alienation from others. This made these religions part of the warp and woof of Canadian history. Their fate was that of their people. So it was that from the mid-nineteenth to the mid-twentieth centuries the Protestant churches were leading agents of white anglo-saxon Protestant promotion and defence; the Roman Catholic Church was the primary armature of both French-Canadian nationalism and Irish Canadian ethnoculturalism throughout Canada; the Orthodox church is fragmented into ethnocultural enclaves, as are the Muslims; and the same is true for many other ethnic groups such as the Aboriginals, the Asians, etc.

Yet, religions are also the junction point, the hyphen that joins a community to its God. Therefore, they not only reflect their human community but are simultaneously places where one finds the divine. And unity and universality are the goals of all faiths. This existence on the edge, on the boundary between the human and the divine, between the particular and the universal, makes religions places of tension. They are agents of unity that reflect diversity. This is their inheritance and the burden that they all carry.

A number of ambiguities and ironies result from the above. One is the uneasy alliance that always exists between a person's ethnocultural identity and religious identity. In Canada as elsewhere, religions have simultaneously reinforced ethnocultural identities of many groups and urged them to move beyond such limited identities towards a more catholic understanding. Oftentimes, the success of any given religion can be measured by the degree to which it manages to stay close to its flock's social, cultural, and political agendas while maintaining its authentic religious message of universal openness and salvation. If if fails on either of these two fronts, the religion is considered either unrepresentative or false. Indeed, in the end, all religions in Canada have preached liberation for all, but each has done so in its own way. Religions in Canada have proven to be simultaneously agents of ethno-cultural preservation and of acculturation. They speak of God in human language.

What does the future hold in store? The new openness of religions towards the world and each other that became manifest after the 1960s corresponded with a distancing of these same religions from their various ethno-cultural communities. This meant that these religions became further removed from these communities' particular interests. The result was a loosening of the ties that bound these communities to their religions of choice, be it French Canadians and the Catholic Church, or many English-speaking Canadians and the Protestant churches. Will the resurgence of fundamentalism in the late twentieth century herald conversely a renewed alliance between certain religions and their ethno-cultural groups of choice? Only time will tell.

Finally, the question of the identities of Canadians arises. We all have several identities, ethnic, cultural, political, economic, and religious to name only some. We wear our identities like different layers of clothing; some are more important than others. During most of Canada's history, religious identity was a key one in the composition of the overall identity of most Canadians. Almost without exception, we were Catholic, Protestant, Jewish, etc. This became less the case after 1960. Yet the census of Canada of 2001 still shows that 84% of Canadians declare a specific religious identity. In the coming years will the neo-conservative thrust of our society translate into a resurgence of religious awareness and association? If so, will this translate into a corresponding increase in the visibility, influence, and presence of religions in Canada? What is certain is that in the long run, Canadians will continue their dance with their religions that simultaneously bolster their flocks' social aspirations and remind them of God's presence and promise.

Notes

Chapter 2. The Religious World of Canada's Amerindians

1. R.G. Thwaites, Ed. *The Jesuit Relations and Allied Documents, 1610–1791*, 73 vols. (Cleveland: Burrows, 1896–1901, I, 1636), 109–110. Author's translation.
2. Sam D. Gill, *Native American Religions. An Introduction* (Belmont, California: Wadsworth Publishing Company, 1982), 20–22. Gill, in turn takes the story from A.F.C. Wallace, *The Death and Rebirth of the Seneca* (New York: Vantage, 1969), 86–91.
3. Sam D. Gill, *Native American Religions*, 27. Gill bases his story on Paul Radin, *The Trickster* (New York: Schocken, 1956), 19–20.
4. Ibid., 29–32.
5. After death, the Amerindian was believed to continue living in another world, for some as spirit, for others reincarnated. Feasting and celebrations were part of the rites of passage that varied from one Amerindian nation to another.
6. Tobacco was a staple in many Amerindian tribes. Elaborately decorated medicine pipes were often used in a variety of rituals including communicating with the spirits.
7. Medicine bags or bundles, such as these Piegan ones, contained the special sacred objects associated with the Amerindian's contacts with the spirits.

Chapter 3. European Religions on the Eve of Encounter

1. Cited in Jean Delumeau, *Le péché et la peur. La culpabilisation en Occident (xiiie–xviiie siècles)* (Paris: 1983), 334.

2. The above paragraph is based on Robert Choquette, "French Catholicism Comes to the Americas," in Charles H. Lippy et al., *Christianity Comes to the Americas 1492–1776* (New York: Paragon House, 1992), 135–136.
3. A monk and Catholic priest until his estrangement from Rome after 1517, Luther is considered the father of the Protestant Reformation. He led the challenge to the Catholic Church, taught that the Bible alone was the source of divine Revelation, and proposed different interpretations of several elements in Christian doctrine.
4. Belden C. Lane, *Landscapes of the Sacred: Geography and Narrative in American Spirituality*, 4–5, cited in Jennifer Reid, *Myth, Symbol and Colonial Encounter*, 23–26.
5. For a useful review of church doctrine see Michael Stogre, *That the World May Believe. The Development of Papal Social Thought on Aboriginal Rights* (Sherbrooke: Éditions Paulines, 1992).
6. Ibid., 59.
7. Leslie Green and Olive Dickason, *The Law of Nations and the New World*, noted in Stogre, *That the World May Believe*. 73–74.
8. See the Gospel of Matthew, 28:16–20.
9. *Sublimus Deus*, cited in Michael Stogre, *That the World May Believe*, 86–87.

Chapter 4. The Encounter between Amerindians and Europeans

1. *The Jesuits in North America in the Seventeenth Century* (Toronto: n.p., 1900), 131.
2. The Feast of the Dead occurred in Huron society every 12 to 15 years when the entire village moved from one location to another. It occurred at such intervals because that was the time it took to deplete a region of game and firewood. The Feast involved the disinterment of all those who had died since arriving in the area, the cleaning of their bones, and their reburial in a common grave. This was accompanied by elaborate ceremony and ritual.

Chapter 5. Missions of Many Kinds

1. Genesis 12:1–3.
2. The Septuagint edition was prepared in Alexandria, Egypt.
3. Acts 11:20.
4. See Paul's letter to the Galatians.
5. Galatians 3:6–16.
6. Ephesians 2:14.

7. 1 Timothy 2:5–6.
8. 1 Corinthians 9:16.
9. Matthew 28:19–20.
10. See Chapter 4.
11. The *Récollets* were reincorporated into the main Franciscan family, the Franciscan Observants, by papal decree in 1897.
12. They were Fathers Denis Jamet (superior), Jean Dolbeau, and Joseph Le Caron, and Brother Pacifique Duplessis.
13. Gabriel Sagard, *Le grand voyage au pays des Hurons*, 2 vols. (Paris: Tross, 1865).
14. Québec had twenty residents in 1620.
15. See Chapter 3.
16. The *Récollets* who had asked for help, rejoiced at the arrival of the Jesuits in Québec in 1625. They would later spurn the Jesuits, mistakenly believing that the latter plotted to deny the *Récollets* the right to return to Canada between 1632 and 1670.
17. For a more detailed presentation see Robert Choquette, "French Catholicism Comes to the Americas." 154–158 and *passim*.
18. The *Récollets* felt that their vow of poverty did not allow them to own any corporate property. Therefore, they lived off the proceeds of daily begging, a practice that did not sit well with most settlers in the colony.
19. See Chapter 4.
20. See Chapter 4.
21. Le Jeune himself wintered with the Montagnais in 1634–1635.
22. In the summer of 1634, Fathers Jean de Brébeuf, Ambroise Davost, and Antoine Daniel accompanied a party of trading Hurons on their return home.
23. The post opened in 1634.
24. This St Charles Mission is taken over from the *Récollets* in 1635.
25. It is noteworthy that this *Collège de Québec* was the first college founded in North America. Its full classical curriculum would only develop over the years.
26. See Chapter 7.
27. Fort Sainte-Marie was rebuilt by the government of Ontario at its original location near the town of Midland. Its staff wears period costumes to show visitors around.
28. These lay workers or *donnés* had been instituted by Father Lalemant. They were laymen who contracted with the Society of Jesus to work in their missions free of charge, in return for free lodging and food. *Donnés* included men of many trades, including bakers, carpenters, and black-

smiths. Contrary to religious brothers, they could bear arms when necessary.

29. Five largely autonomous nations made up the Iroquois confederacy. They were the Mohawk, the Oneida, the Onondaga, the Cayuga, and the Seneca. A sixth nation, the Tuscarora, would join them in the 1720s.

30. See a more detailed presentation in Robert Choquette, "French Catholicism Comes to the Americas," in Charles H. Lippy et al., *Christianity Comes to the Americas 1492–1776*, 204–213.

31. See ibid., 207–213.

32. These first Sulpicians in Canada were Fathers Gabriel de Queylus, Dominique Galinier, Gabriel Souart, and the deacon Antoine d'Allet.

33. See Chapter 6.

34. See Chapter 6.

35. These men were François de Salignac de La Mothe-Fénelon, Claude Trouvé, and Lascaris d'Urfé.

36. See Chapter 3.

37. 24 March 1620.

38. Until very recently, it was customary for women who chose the religious life as nuns or sisters to abandon their maiden names for a religious name.

39. They occupied this three-story stone convent in 1642.

40. The nurses belonged to the *Hospitalières de la Miséricorde* (Hospitalers of Mercy) of the *Hôtel-Dieu* of Dieppe.

41. Founded in 1639 by a handful of nursing sisters from France, the Hôtel-Dieu has continued to shelter and care for the sick to the present day. It was these same nursing sisters who founded the Québec General Hospital in 1694 by order of Bishop Saint-Vallier.

42. The *filles du roi*.

43. Some four thousand women now belong to the congregation.

44. See Chapter 6.

45. Cited in Jean Delanglez, *Frontenac and the Jesuits* (Chicago: Institute of Jesuit History, 1939), 46.

46. See above.

47. See Robert Choquette, "French Catholicism Comes to the Americas," 183–185.

48. René Latourelle, "Jean de Brébeuf," in Francess G. Halpenny, Ed. *Dictionary of Canadian Biography*, 14 vols. (Toronto and Québec: University of Toronto Press and Les Presses de l'Université Laval, 1966–present), Vol. I, 129.

49. See John Webster Grant, *Moon of Wintertime* (Toronto: University of Toronto Press, 1984).

Chapter 6. The Development of the Catholic Church

1. Cistercians are a twelfth-century offshoot of the Benedictines.
2. See Chapter 5.
3. The Order of Friars Minor (Franciscans) was founded by Francis of Assisi in 1209. It was characterized by St Francis' insistence on the practice of complete poverty, both individual and corporate. As the order expanded, the ideal proved unworkable and was abandoned. This led to a rift within the order, the idealists forming the party of the Spirituals, while the majority adopted a more moderate view. In subsequent centuries, continued debate over the place of poverty in the Franciscan order led to the formation of various reforming offshoots that included the Observants (1517), the Capuchins (1529), and the *Récollets* in the late sixteenth century. Most branches were reunited by Pope Leo XIII in 1897.
4. The Order of Preachers (Dominicans) was founded by St Dominic (1170–1221) shortly before his death. It was renowned for its dedication to preaching and study. As was the case with the Franciscans, the order's initial ban on corporate property was rescinded by papal authority. Dominicans came to Canada in the 1860s.
5. The Order of Our Lady of Mount Carmel (Carmelites) was founded in Palestine, in the region of Mount Carmel, in 1154. It adopted a rule of extreme asceticism. After the end of the crusades, members of the order migrated to Europe where their organization resembled that of the mendicant friars.
6. The Augustinian Hermits or Friars were a union of a variety of groups of hermits (solitary monks) ordered by the pope in 1256. Their organization was modelled on that of the Dominicans. It was to one of their reformed branches, the German Reformed Congregation, that Martin Luther belonged.
7. The Order of Servants of the Blessed Virgin Mary (Servites) was founded in 1240 in Florence, Italy, by seven wealthy men who wanted to devote their lives to the Virgin. They were organized according to the Rule of St Augustine, while borrowing some elements from the Dominicans.
8. For all practical purposes, a religious *congregation* is identical to a religious order such as the Dominicans, Benedictines, or Franciscans. The difference between an order and a congregation is a technical one in

church law. Members of religious orders make *solemn* vows, while members of religious congregations make *simple* vows.

9. Escriva died in 1975 and was declared a saint by Pope John Paul II on 6 October 2002. His successors at the head of Opus Dei have been Alvaro del Portillo (d. 1994), and Javier Echevarria.

10. The Acts of the Apostles in the New Testament bear witness to this.

11. Denominations such as those of the Presbyterians, Methodists, Lutherans, etc.

12. Ultramontanism will be explained in Chapter 10.

13. The bull *Unam Sanctam*, issued by Boniface VIII on 18 November 1302, claimed that outside the church there was "neither salvation nor remission of sins."

14. Paris was the capital, except during the years 1682 to 1789 when the capital was in Versailles, just outside Paris.

15. Saint-Vallier's *Rituel du diocèse de Québec* was published in 1702. See Chapter 7.

16. One example of this is the *Lettres provinciales* (1656–1657) of Blaise Pascal, a leading defender of the Jansenists.

17. The same was true in Acadia where a third order, the Capuchins, was active alongside Jesuits and *Récollets*.

18. King Louis XIV (1643–1715) was still a minor at this time. He would only assume his royal duties in 1661.

19. Having resigned his position of Bishop of Québec in 1684, Laval continued to reside in Canada and assist in the work of its church until his death.

20. From the founding of Port Royal to the definitive conquest of Acadia by the English, Capuchins were one of the groups of priests that worked in the region. Others were the Jesuits, the *Récollets*, the Sulpicians, the Québec Seminary priests, and individual secular priests.

21. See Chapter 5.

22. See Chapter 5.

23. Beginning in the 1830s, the Sisters of Charity of Montréal would send out sisters to places like Québec City, Saint-Hyacinthe, Ottawa, and Saint-Boniface to found hospitals among other activities. These foundations would in turn become the cradles for similar institutions in other parts of North America.

24. The successive bishops of Québec during the French régime were François de Laval (1658–1687), Jean-Baptiste de Saint-Vallier (1687–1727), Louis-François Mornay (1727–1733), Pierre-Herman Dosquet (1733–1739), François-Louis de Lauberivière (1739–1740), and Henri-Marie de Pontbri-

and (1741–1760). For a more detailed presentation see Robert Choquette, "French Catholicism Comes to the Americas," 215–216.

Chapter 7. Theology, Beliefs, Customs, and Piety

1. Arianism and Pelagianism were heresies condemned by the Christian church in the fourth and fifth centuries.
2. Cited in Terry Crowley, "The French Regime to 1760," in Terrence Murphy, et al., *A Concise History of Christianity in Canada*, 42.
3. In the region of Québec, there were eight confraternities dedicated to the Rosary (1656), the Scapular (1656), Saint Ann (1657), the Virgin (1657), the Holy Family (1664), Saint Francis, and the Sacred Heart (1716), in addition to one for young girls.
4. For example, it is at Lake St Anne, Alberta, that the Amerindians and Métis of Western Canada hold a major religious gathering every summer. They do so on the feast day of Saint Anne, on 26 July.
5. *Travels Into North America* (Barre, Mass: The Imprint Society, 1972), 397.
6. See Chapter 5.

Chapter 8. The Church, the British Conquest, and the *Québec Act*

1. When France later lost all of Acadia during the Seven Years' War, the Treaty of Paris (1763) allowed it to have the islands of Saint-Pierre and Miquelon off the south coast of Newfoundland.
2. The official declarations of war occurred in 1756, although fighting had been taking place since 1754.
3. See Chapter 7.
4. His full name was Jean-Baptiste de La Croix de Chevrières de Saint-Vallier. La Croix was his family name, but he is usually known as Saint-Vallier. This is the name used in this book.
5. Such crosses were found throughout French Canada from the seventeenth to the twentieth centuries. Many may still be found today.
6. His full name was Henri-Marie Dubreil de Pontbriand. Dubreil was his family name, but he is usually known as Pontbriand. This is the name used in this book.
7. His full name was Louis-François du Plessis Mornay.
8. His full name was François-Louis de Pourroy de Lauberivière. His family name was Pourroy, but he is usually known as Lauberivière. This is the name used in this book.

9. Two *Récollets* priests worked in English Nova Scotia after 1710, namely Félix Pain who was pastor in Grand Pré until 1725, and Justinien Durand who was pastor of Port Royal until 1726.

10. The Sulpician fathers included Jean-Pierre de Miniac, Claude-Jean-Baptiste Chauvreulx, Charles de La Goudalie, and Jean-Baptiste de Gay Desenclaves.

11. They included Jesuit Fathers Joseph Aubéry, Jean-Baptiste Loyard, Jean-Pierre Daniélou, and Charles Germain.

12. The most detailed study of the material damages resulting from the British Conquest is Marcel Trudel, *L'Église canadienne sous le régime militaire, 1759–1764*, 2 vols. (Montréal: Les études de l'Institut d'histoire de l'Amérique française, 1956).

13. More specifically, there were 40 Hospitalers from the Hôtel-Dieu, 38 from the General Hospital, and 35 Ursulines.

14. Adam Shortt and Arthur G. Doughty, *Documents relating to the Constitutional History of Canada, 1759–1791* (Ottawa: The Historical Documents Publication Board, 1918), I, 6.

15. Article 30, ibid., 31.

16. Article 27, ibid., 30.

17. Article 28, ibid., 31.

18. Article 32, ibid., 31.

19. Article 33, ibid., 31–32.

20. Article 34, ibid., 32.

21. Article 4, ibid., 115.

22. Ibid., 177.

23. John Moir, *Church and State in Canada 1627–1867* (Toronto: McClelland & Stewart, 1967), 77.

24. The Board of Trade "created by the king in 1696 and abolished by parliament in 1782, exercised a general supervision over the detailed administration of the colonies... It was an advisory body acting through the secretary of state or the privy council." A.L. Burt, *The Old Province of Québec* (New York: Russell and Russell, 1933, 1970), 76.

25. Adam Shortt and Arthur Doughty, I, 191–192.

26. Bishop Briand wrote in 1774 that during his first eight years in office he had ordained twenty-five priests but thirty-two had died.

27. The chapter was a council of twelve senior priests who were entrusted with the administration of the diocese while the see was vacant.

28. The concordat of Bologna of 1516 established new rules for the appointment of bishops in France.

29. A *mandement*.

30. John Moir, *Church and State in Canada 1627–1867* (Toronto: McClelland & Stewart, 1967), 74.
31. Father Briand was paid 20£ from 1762 and 200£ after he became a bishop.
32. Adam Shortt and Arthur Doughty, I, 71–72.
33. This was Louis-Philippe-François Mariaucheau d'Églis, who continued in his pastor's duties while co-adjutor bishop of Québec. Upon Briand's death in 1784, Églis became bishop of Québec (1784–1788), only to select immediately a co-adjutor who administered the diocese in his place.
34. John Moir, *Church and State in Canada 1627–1867*, (Toronto: McClelland & Stewart, 1967), 81–82.
35. The Board of Trade penned a report to that effect in 1769. They asked that the full range of powers given to the governor over the church be invoked, including the appointment of pastors, etc. Adam Shortt and Arthur Doughty, I, p. 389–390.
36. The opinions of both law officers are found ibid., 428, 482–483.
37. Ibid., 484.
38. Thomas Gage (1720–1787) was military commander of the Montréal district from 1760 to 1763 when he succeeded Amherst in New York as commander-in-chief of British forces in North America, a post he held until 1775.
39. Ralph Burton (d. 1768), was military commander of the district of Trois-Rivières (1760–1764) and Montréal (1764–1766), before returning to England.
40. Frederick Haldimand (1718–1791), a career soldier, was Governor of Canada from 1777 to 1786.
41. *The Québec Act, 1774*, in Adam Shortt and Arthur Doughty, I, p. 572.
42. Ibid., 570–576.
43. Carleton was back in Québec on 18 September 1774, and remained there until 30 July 1778, when his successor Frederick Haldimand arrived. In 1786, he returned to Canada as governor-in-chief of the three provinces of Québec, Nova Scotia, and New Brunswick, in addition to Newfoundland. He was also given the title of Baron Dorchester. After resigning his position, he left Canada in July 1796.
45. Cited in M. Brunet, G. Frégault, and M. Trudel, Eds., *Histoire du Canada par les textes* (Montréal: Fides, 1952), 124.

Chapter 9. Revivals in the Late Eighteenth and Early Nineteenth Centuries

1. Some of the best and most comprehensive studies of the religious history of Atlantic Canada are by Terrence Murphy. See his chapter entitled "The

English-Speaking Colonies to 1854," in Terrence Murphy and Roberto Perin, Eds, *A Concise History of Christianity in Canada* (Toronto: Oxford University Press, 1996), 108–189.

2. Ibid., 112.
3. Dissenters were those English Christians who "dissented" from the established churches of England, Scotland, and Ireland.
4. The total resident population of Newfoundland in the 1780s is estimated at above 10,000. Terrence Murphy, *A Concise History*, 111.
5. In Canada, the Church of England changed its name to the Anglican Church of Canada in 1955. In Québec, and the United States it is known as the Episcopal Church.
6. Nova Scotia included all the territory that later became the separate provinces of Prince Edward Island [St. John Island] (1769) and New Brunswick (1784). Cape Breton, independent from 1784, was annexed anew in 1820.
7. Cited in John Moir, *Church and State in Canada 1627–1867*, 33.
8. For example, a Nova Scotia statute of 1783 repealed the sections of the law that banned the exercise of priestly functions by Catholic priests.
9. J. Garner, "The Enfranchisement of Roman Catholics in the Maritimes," *Canadian Historical Review* 34, 3 (1953), 203–204. John Moir, ibid., John Moir, *The Church in the British Era* (Toronto: McGraw-Hill Ryerson, 1972). J.R. Miller, "Anti-Catholicism in Canada: From the British Conquest to the Great War," in Terrence Murphy and Gerald Stortz, *Creed and Culture* (Montréal: McGill-Queen's University Press, 1993), 25–48. Terrence Murphy, "The English-Speaking Colonies to 1854," 108–189.
10. A landholder paid rent to a lord who owned the *seigneurie*. In the British system, the landholder owned the land.
11. By "Protestant clergy," the British legislators meant the clergy of the Church of England.
12. Adam Shortt and Arthur Doughty, I, 1045.
13. The first Church of England bishop outside Great Britain was Charles Inglis (1734–1816), appointed to the see of Nova Scotia in 1787 with jurisdiction over all of British North America, including Newfoundland and Bermuda. In 1793, Jacob Mountain, first bishop of the new Church of England diocese of Québec, became the second Church of England bishop in Canada.
14. The industrial revolution of the West began in the second half of the eighteenth century in England when the steam engine was invented, leading to the invention of locomotives, steamships, and manufacturing machines for mass production.

15. Baptists trace their origin to John Smyth who in 1609, from his exile in Amsterdam, reinstituted the baptism of conscious believers, or adults, as the only legitimate rite of entry into the Christian church. Some of his followers founded a church in London, England, in 1612. The denomination later grew very rapidly in the southern United States.

16. Quakers, officially the Religious Society of Friends, were founded in England by George Fox (1624–1691) in the mid-seventeenth century. Rather than abiding by the Bible, they believe in the doctrine of the Inner Light as the source of Revelation for each Christian. They reject sacraments, ministry, and established forms of worship. Quakers refuse military service and oaths.

17. John Wesley (1703–1791), ordained in the Church of England, experienced a personal conversion on 24 May, 1738. Thereafter, he dedicated his life to evangelism and practical religion.

18. The Church of Scotland became Protestant in the Calvinist tradition after 1560. In the eighteenth century it was torn by various internal disputes that led to the forming of four distinct secession churches after 1733. Then occurred the disruption of 1843 that divided it even more by creating the 'Free' church. Most of these groups were presbyterian in polity and rejected bishops.

19. The Church of England in the United States was renamed the Episcopal Church after the War of Independence.

20. Congregationalism designates a form of Protestantism grounded in the belief in the full independence and autonomy of the local congregation. It began in late sixteenth-century England with groups of faithful who rejected the polity of the Church of England. Its theology is in the tradition of Calvin.

21. The Church of Scotland in its several divisions had a presbyterian polity, meaning that it was governed by a presbyterium, or committee of priests along with lay elders. The term *presbyterianism* is usually used to designate members of these denominations.

22. Mennonites were an Anabaptist group founded by Menno Simons in the sixteenth century. They came to Ontario as Loyalists from Pennsylvania during the American War of Independence and settled in the area of Kitchener and Waterloo. After 1870, other Mennonites came to Manitoba from Russia.

23. The Moravian Church is the common name for the *Unitas Fratrum* (Unity of Brethren), a communal group that goes back to the early fifteenth-century reformer Jan Hus. In 1727 they merged with a group of German pietists drawn from Lutheranism and launched important foreign mis-

sionary enterprises. These Moravians founded missions in Labrador in the 1770s, and came to Fairfield, Upper Canada, with a colony of Delaware Amerindians in 1792.

24. Unitarians trace their origins back to the Reformation of the sixteenth century. Unitarians have no formal creed and reject the doctrines of the Trinity and the divinity of Christ. They value reason and conscience as their sole criteria for belief and practice.

25. This denomination teaches that all intelligent beings will ultimately be saved.

26. The Disciples of Christ were founded in the U.S.A. in 1827 by the Presbyterian Alexander Campbell. Sometimes known as Campbellites, they teach that Scriptures are the sole basis of faith and reject all creeds. They practice believers' baptism.

27. The Catholic Apostolic Church promoted the teaching of E. Irving. Founded in the 1830s, they believed in the imminent Second Coming of Christ.

28. Until the death of their founder John Wesley in 1791, Methodists did not form a separate denomination, but were part of the Church of England.

29. Many authors set 1801 as the year of its beginning, but others argue for a date as early as the 1780s.

30. Redemption means "buying back" the Christian sinner who, without such intervention, would deserve eternal punishment. Atonement means "making one," or reuniting God and the Christian sinner.

31. Christian doctrine traditionally taught that Christ would return, the second coming, at the end of time to judge the living and the dead.

32. See Chapter 11.

33. F.L. Cross and E.A. Livingstone, Eds., *The Oxford Dictionary of the Christian Church*, Third edition (Oxford and New York: Oxford University Press, 1997), 1183.

34. Another revival occurred among the Methodists of Nova Scotia at this time. See Terrence Murphy and Roberto Perin, Eds., *A Concise History of Christianity in Canada*, 130.

35. Abel Stevens, *Life and Times of Nathan Bangs*, 76, cited in John W. Grant, *A Profusion of Spires* (Toronto: University of Toronto Press, 1988), 60.

36. Subsequent volumes appeared in 1820 and 1823.

37. Lartigue was appointed in 1820 and ordained bishop in 1821.

38. See Chapters 10 to 12.

39. Sally M. Weaver, "The Iroquois: The Consolidation of the Grand River Reserve in the Mid-Nineteenth Century, 1847–1875," and "The Iroquois: The Grand River Reserve in the Late Nineteenth and Early Twentieth

Centuries, 1875–1945," in Edward S. Rogers and Donald B. Smith, Eds., *Aboriginal Ontario. Historical Perspectives on the First Nations* (Toronto: Dundurn Press, 1994), 196.

40. Sally Weaver, "The Iroquois: The Grand River Reserve, 1875–1945," 214–217.
41. Charles Hamori-Torok, "The Iroquois of Akwesasne (St. Regis)," in Edward S. Rogers and Donald B. Smith, Eds., *Aboriginal Ontario*, 262.
42. Ibid. See also John Webster Grant, *Moon of Wintertime*.

Chapter 10. Missionary Agencies

1. The S.P.C.K. was distinct from a similarly-named society of the Church of Scotland, based in Edinburgh, namely the *Society for Propagating Christian Knowledge*.
2. Its name was later changed to *Commonwealth and Continental Church Society*.
3. The name Anglican Church of Canada was only adopted in 1955.
4. The term designates those Christians who believe that only adults may be baptized, and not children.
5. This was called *colportage*.
6. Chiniquy had married in 1863.
7. In the absence of firm statistics, this is the estimate of one contemporary scholar. See Roberto Perin, "French-Speaking Canada from 1840," in Terrence Murphy and Roberto Perin, Eds., *A Concise History of Christianity in Canada*, 193.
8. Guy Laperrière, *Les congrégations religieuses. De la France au Québec 1880–1914* (Sainte-Foy: Les Presses de l'Université Laval, 1996), 46–47. Much information is found here, the author summarizing the findings of Claude Langlois, *Le catholicisme au féminin* (Paris : Les Éditions du Cerf, 1984) and Bernard Denault and Benoît Lévesque, *Éléments pour une sociologie des comunautés religieuses au Québec* (Sherbrooke and Montréal: Université de Sherbrooke and Presses de l'Université de Montréal, 1975), among others.
9. Matthew 28:19–20.
10. *Missions O.M.I. 2*, 1863, p. 177. Cited in Robert Choquette, *The Oblate Assault on Canada's Northwest* (Ottawa: University of Ottawa Press, 1995), 194.
11. Roothaan entrusted the Canadian mission to the Jesuit province of France.
12. In France, the numbers grew from 55,000 in 1790 to 100,000 in 1861. In Québec, the numbers grew from 304 in 1800 to 650 in 1850. See Claude

Langlois, *Le catholicisme au féminin*, and Bernard Denault and Benoît Lévesque, *Éléments pour une sociologie des communautés religieuses au Québec*.

13. See Chapter 5.
14. This was the name of the congregation of Sisters of Charity based in Ottawa between the 1880s and the 1960s.
15. This was the name of the congregation that broke away from the Ottawa order in 1926. It is based in Pembroke, Ontario.
16. Shortly afterwards (1848) and for similar reasons, another widow Rosalie Jetté, née Cadron, founded the Sisters of Mercy dedicated to the service of unwed mothers.

Chapter 11. The Churches and the State

1. At this time, the Catholic Bishop of Québec received a government salary of £200. Milnes proposed to raise the salary in return for the bishop ceding to the governor the right to appoint pastors and the right to select candidates for the priesthood.
2. Alexander Macdonell and Angus Bernard MacEachern were ordained bishops in Québec by Bishop Plessis, the former on 31 December 1820 and the latter on 17 June 1821.
3. Jean-Jacques Lartigue and Joseph-Norbert Provencher were ordained bishops by Bishop Plessis, the former on 21 January 1821, the latter on 12 May 1822.
4. See Chapter 14.
5. Some of these branches were the Methodist New Connexion, the Primitive Methodist Church, the Bible Christians, the United Methodist Free Churches, the Methodist Episcopal Church, the African Methodist Episcopal Church, the Methodist Episcopal Church in Canada, the Canadian Wesleyan Methodist Church, the Free Methodists, the Methodist Church in Canada, and the Methodist Church of Canada.
6. See Chapter 9.
7. The year was 1819 in Upper Canada.
8. Other denominations that applied for such revenues after 1848 included the Lutherans, Moravians, Catholics, and Wesleyan Methodists.
9. In 1841, Upper and Lower Canada had been united to form the Province of Canada, Canada East corresponding to the former Lower province, while Canada West was the new name for the western section, the former Upper Canada. This constitutional framework was in place until Confederation in 1867 created the provinces of Québec and Ontario.

10. See Chapter 14.

Chapter 12. The Evangelical Crusade

1. "Proceedings of the Second Convention for Bible Missions, Held in Albany September Second and Third," 1846, 4–5, cited in Leonard I. Sweet, "Nineteenth-Century Evangelicalism," in Charles H. Lippy and Peter W. Williams, eds., *Encyclopedia of the American Religious Experience*, vol. II, 875.
2. Ibid., 876.
3. "His Dominion," SR 2, 4 (1973), 315.
4. See also Chapter 12.
5. The word 'apocalypse' means a revelation or unveiling.
6. Revelation 20. Author's emphasis.
7. See Chapter 19.
8. For a complete listing for the Province of Québec, see Guy Laperrière, *Les congrégations religieuses*, tables 5 and 6.
9. *Zouaves* were men who enlisted to serve as soldiers in the papal army.

Chapter 13. Alternatives to the Evangelical Crusade

1. See Chapter 16.
2. Francis Bacon (1561–1626) was an English philosopher and essayist who lent his name to a method of inquiry based on induction, that is to say that an observer arrived at truths by drawing conclusions based on observed phenomena.
3. The canon is the acknowledged list of inspired books that make up the Bible.
4. See Chapter 15.
5. See Ramsay Cook, *The Regenerators* (Toronto: University of Toronto Press, 1985).
6. See Chapter 15.
7. Ramsay Cook in *The Regenerators*, p. 123.
8. Anabaptists of the early sixteenth century included followers of Thomas Münzer (d. 1525) and the Zwickau Prophets who were in Martin Luther's Wittenberg in 1521; the Swiss Brethren who were in Zurich in 1525; the Hutterites who took their name from their founder Jacob Hutter (d. 1536); the followers of Melchior Hoffman (d. 1543); a group in Münster led by Jan Mattys (d. 1534); the Mennonites led by Menno Simons in Holland and Friesland.

9. Disciples of the sixteenth-century leader Jacob Hutter (d. 1536), Hutterites are Christians who refuse child baptism and believe in the baptism of adults only. Fleeing continuous persecution by European Protestants and Catholics, beginning in the nineteenth century they established settlements in Canada based on the common ownership of property, a practice that led to conflict with some provincial governments, particularly in Alberta.

10. For more on Thompson and many other religious nonconformists of the late nineteenth and early twentieth century in Canada see Ramsay Cook, ibid.

11. Front: Bob O'Lone and Paul Prue. Seated: Pierre Poitras, John Bruce, Louis Riel, W.B. O'Donoghue, François Dauphinais, and Thomas Spence. Standing : Le Roc, Pierre De Lorme, Thomas Bunn, Xavier Pagé, André Beauchemin, and Baptiste Tereaux.

12. The primary source for the following section is Thomas Flanagan, *Louis 'David' Riel 'Prophet of the New World,'* Revised edition (Toronto: University of Toronto Press, 1996).

13. Ibid., 52.

14. Ibid., 56.

15. Ibid., 165.

Chapter 14. Confessional Education

1. Raised in a strong Loyalist and Protestant evangelical tradition, Egerton Ryerson chose Methodism at age eighteen and never looked back. He became a minister in 1827 and distinguished himself as a spokesman for social reform in Upper Canada during the 1820s and 1830s, challenging establishment spokesmen such as John Strachan, and arguing in favour of a more democratic and egalitarian society. A lifelong student and a hard worker, he was appointed superintendent of schools for Canada West in 1844. He was primarily responsible for the building of Ontario's system of public education during its formative years. He retired at age seventy-three in 1876, upon the creation of a ministry of education in Ontario.

2. In 1997, the government of Newfoundland changed this confessional school system into a nonconfessional one, one year after the government of Québec changed its confessional school boards into language-based ones (French and English). In 2001, Québec also abolished its confessional public schools and made them into French or English schools.

3. In 1969, in Newfoundland, several Protestant denominations including the Anglicans, the Salvation Army, the United Church of Canada, and the Presbyterians agreed to forego their denominational particularities and

cooperate in the running of the province's Protestant schools. Pentecostals and Seventh-Day Adventists were denominations that did not join in this venture.

4. See Chapter 5.

5. Industrial schools served Amerindian children, were funded by the government of Canada, and directed and staffed by the Catholic, Anglican, United, and Presbyterian churches from the 1880s to the 1970s. Their curricula were partly academic and partly industrial including farming, woodworking, sewing, and cooking. In addition to the industrial schools that were funded by the government of Canada, the churches ran private boarding schools and day schools. Here Oblate Bishop Gabriel Breynat is seen with a group of Amerindian boys.

6. Sir Wilfred Grenfell was an Englishman who, inspired by the preaching of the American evangelist Dwight Moody, undertook the medical rescue of fishers and others in Labrador and the remote coasts of Newfoundland. While not representing any church, Grenfell was motivated by the Gospel. His work consisted primarily of founding hospitals, schools, and small industries that helped people help themselves. Having first set foot in Labrador in 1892, his group of professional and volunteer workers soon earned the respect and gratitude of all.

Chapter 15. Modernity versus Conservatism

1. William Aberhart (with the hat) and E. C. Manning are seen here in the company of two unidentified men. Bible colleges were important in the development of evangelical Protestantism in the twentieth century. Both Manning and Aberhart played a leading role in their promotion and in the political life of the country. William Aberhart, pastor of the Calgary Prophetic Bible Institute, had a weekly religious radio broadcast where he introduced in 1932 the Social Credit theories of C.H. Douglas. His Depression-era followers received his economic theories with the same reverence that they granted to his prophetic religious pronouncements. This led to Aberhart becoming Premier upon winning the 1935 general election in Alberta. He and his legislative colleagues promised to grant a monthly dividend of $25 to every man, woman, and child in the province, a sum drawn on the resources of the province. They failed to deliver, one reason being the disallowance of some legislation by the federal government. Upon his retirement in 1943, Aberhart designated E.C. Manning as his successor, the same Manning who had succeeded him as Pastor of the Calgary Prophetic Bible Institute. Their Social Credit party, later led by W.A.C. Bennett, focused on frugal and conservative government. For

many years, their political conventions opened with a hymn. They later won some seats in the Parliament of Canada, some of them from Québec.
2. The chart on the wall shows a religious census of the world. Both Protestant and Catholic Christians at the time felt that they had a God-given duty to evangelize the world in their lifetime.
3. This was the largest and wealthiest Baptist church in central Canada.

Chapter 16. Social Christianity

1. Between 1901 and 1908, the population of Winnipeg tripled in size, going from 42,000 to 140,000 residents.
2. "His Dominion," SR 2, 4 (1973), 315.
3. Canada's churches have always been involved in a broad range of social services. These include shelters, clothes distribution counters, soup kitchens, orphanages, hospitals, homes for the elderly, shelters for immigrants, etc. during the economic Depression of the 1930s, soup kitchens for the poor multiplied in Canada's cities.
4. Léger straddles the line of demarcation between the traditional triumphant Catholicism of French Canada that was in place until 1960 and the new church that resulted from Vatican II and Québec's Quiet Revolution of the 1960s. Léger was archbishop of Montréal, then Canada's largest diocese, from 1950 until his resignation in 1968. He then announced that he would spend the rest of his life serving the poor in Africa. Cardinal Léger was influential at Vatican II.
5. Association canadienne-française d'éducation d'Ontario.

Chapter 17. Secularization and Church Reform

1. Mircea Eliade, Ed. *The Encyclopedia of Religion*, vol. 13 (New York: Macmillan Publishing Company, 1987), 159–160.
2. "*Gaudium et spes*," paragraph 16, in Austin Flannery, Ed. *Vatican Council II*, Vol. 1, new revised edition (Northport, New York: Costello Publishing Company, 1996), 916.
3. Ibid., paragraph 17, 917.
4. *The Oxford Dictionary of the Christian Church*, third edition, 1765.
5. Statistics Canada, Selected Religions for Canada, http://www12.statcan.ca/census01.
6. Reginald Bibby. *Restless Gods. The Renaissance of Religion in Canada* (Toronto: Stoddart, 2002).

Chapter 18. Immigration and Religions

1. Galicia was a region within the defunct Austo-Hungarian Empire, a region that included portions of today's Poland, Ukraine, Hungary, and Slovakia. These territories were reapportioned after the empire was dismantled after World War I; the name Galician then fell into disuse, replaced by the newer national identities of Pole, Hungarian, Ukrainian, and Slovak.
2. The majority of Ukrainians (or Galicians) who came to Canada at the turn of the twentieth century belonged to a Christian church of an Eastern or non-Roman rite, but one that was in communion with the pope. Consequently they are members of the Catholic Church. One distinctive characteristic of these Catholics is that they have always had married priests among them. Several such Eastern rites exist within Christianity. However, unlike the majority of Ukrainians who came to Canada, the majority of Eastern Christians in the world are members of the Orthodox Church, which is not in communion with Rome. Instead, most Orthodox acknowledge as their honourary international leader the Patriarch of Constantinople.
3. Breakdown statistics from Census 2001 not released at the time of publication.
4. In a direct challenge to Canada's discriminatory immigration laws, Gurdit Singh, a Canadian Sikh businessman working with a Vancouver Punjabi society, chartered this ship to carry 376 Punjabis from India to Canada. Most were Sikh, but there were also some Hindus and Muslims on board. Coming from India, a member of the British Commonwealth, all were British citizens. Upon their arrival in Vancouver, because of the pressures exerted by British Columbians and others, Canadian authorities refused to authorize the immigrants to land, forcing the Punjabis to remain on the small ship for two months enduring very difficult conditions. After armed confrontation between some passengers and Canadian officials that included the Vancouver police, immigration officers and naval personnel, the ship was forced to leave Canadian waters on 23 July 1914.

Chapter 19. Alternative Religions

1. The Bab was Sayyid 'Ali Muhammad Shirazi (1819–50), a merchant from southern Iran, who claimed that he was the bearer of a new religion in

succession to Islam; he claimed that he was the *Bab* (the gate) to this new religion.

2. Cited in John Bowker, *The Oxford Dictionary of World Religions* (Oxford: Oxford University Press. 1997).

3. Mary Farrell Bednarowski, "The Church of Scientology," in Timothy Miller, Ed., *America's Alternative Religions* (n.p., State University of New York Press. n.d.), 381–391. See also L. Ron Hubbard, *Dianetics: the Modern Science of Mental Health.*, and *Basic Dictionary of Dianetics and Scientology* from the works of L. Ron Hubbard (Los Angeles: Bridge, 1973).

4. L. Ron Hubbard, *Dianetics: The Modern Science of Mental Health* (Los Angeles: Bridge, 1950, 1978), 6.

5. Neo-Platonism was taught by Plotinus (204–270 C.E.) who reinterpreted the philosophy of Plato (d. 347 BCE). Plotinus taught that the world emanated from the One and that the goal of humanity was to return there by a mystical experience whereby all physical limitations would be overcome.

6. *Kabbalah* means the 'esoteric teachings of Judaism.'

7. Rosencreuz was the supposed fifteenth-century founder of the Rosicrucian Order.

8. Actors Burt Reynolds, Clint Eastwood, and Richard Chamberlain were also associated with channelling.

Index of Proper Names